Psychological Testing in the Age
of Managed Behavioral Health Care

Psychological Testing in the Age of Managed Behavioral Health Care

Mark E. Maruish
United Behavioral Health

LAWRENCE ERLBAUM ASSOCIATES, PUBLISHERS
2002   MAHWAH, NEW JERSEY   LONDON

Lawrence Erlbaum Associates, Inc., Publishers
10 Industrial Avenue
Mahwah, NJ 07430

Cover design by Kathryn Houghtaling Lacey

Library of Congress Cataloging-in-Publication Data

Maruish, Mark E. (Mark Edward)
Psychological testing in the age of managed behavioral health care/ Mark E. Maruish
p. cm.
Includes bibliographical references and index.
ISBN 0-8058-3643-8 (cloth: alk. paper)
1. Psychodiagnostics. 2. Managed mental health care.
RC469.M367 2002
616.89′075—dc21

2001040511
CIP

Books published by Lawrence Erlbaum Associates are printed on acid-free paper, and their bindings are chosen for strength and durability.

Printed in the United States of America
10   9   8   7   6   5   4   3   2   1

To those friends and colleagues who have encouraged
and supported my work over the years.

Contents

Preface

The growth of managed care as the predominant form of general health care delivery has had an enormous impact not only on patients, but also on practitioners, insurers, employers and other parties that have a stake in the care and well-being of patients. Adapting to this system of health care has not been an easy one for mental health and substance abuse professionals, particularly psychologists. In addition to limitations placed on the other services they provide, psychologists have seen dramatic restrictions imposed by managed behavioral health care organizations (MBHOs) on their use of psychological testing. For some, these restrictions have resulted in a loss of not only income, but also the freedom to exercise professional judgment in the assessment and treatment of their patients.

Contrary to earlier predictions, managed care is not a fad and it will not be going away any time soon. In fact, continued growth is expected. Although some may view the continuation of managed care with a sense of fear and anxiety, there are indeed positive aspects of this system of health care. For example, stakeholders in the managed health care delivery system will continue to influence the operation of managed care organizations (MCOs) and the benefits they manage. There also will be a continued focus on the development of empirically based guidelines, the measurement and management of outcomes, and the quality of care in general. Psychologists who are willing to work within the constraints of the policies and procedures of MBHOs, to develop new approaches to psychological testing and treatment, and to diversify their practices to include nontraditional activities should find the practice of psychology professionally satisfying and rewarding. In short, the opportunities are and will be there for those who are willing to evolve as this country's health care system evolves. This fact has served as the impetus for this book.

To provide a context for the remainder of the book, chapter 1 presents a general overview of managed care in general and managed behavioral health care specifically. Among the topics discussed are the distinctions among the various types of MBHOs, the positive and negative effects of managed care, the status of psychological testing in MBHOs, and recommendations for how psychologists can survive in this new era of health care.

Chapter 2 presents a discussion of the many ways in which testing can help MBHOs meet some of the pressures that are placed on them by various external parties. In essence, these pressures represent potential opportunities for psychologists.

Chapter 3 offers a general description of the service delivery process in MBHO settings, including where psychological testing fits into that process. Also included here are common criteria used by MBHOs to determine whether testing should be authorized or not, along with recommendations for what psychologists can do to increase the likelihood that MBHOs will authorize their requests for psychological testing.

A discussion of the various types of psychological test instruments that can be useful in MBHO settings is presented in chapter 4. Also presented is a review of the criteria recommended for selecting instruments for general and specific uses. In addition, there is a discussion of some of the technological advances that have been applied to the administration, scoring, and interpretation of psychological tests.

Whereas the reader is likely familiar with the more popular commercial psychological test instruments (e.g., MMPI-2, SCL-90-R), there are a number of low- or no-cost psychological instruments that can be useful in MBHO settings. Several of these instruments are presented and discussed in detail in chapter 5.

The increasing pressures on managed care companies to gather and use outcomes data for care management and quality improvement purposes provides tremendous opportunities for psychologists. In recognition of this burgeoning area of testing, chapters 6 and 7 are devoted entirely to issues related to the development and implementation of outcomes assessment systems in MBHOs.

The growing number of psychologists who work in general health care settings support the belief that the increasing integration of behavioral health care services— including psychological testing—in primary care and other medical settings represents an improvement over the more traditional model of segregated service delivery. Integrated health care also offers opportunities for providers of mental health and substance abuse care services, particularly in the area of testing. Chapter 8 discusses various aspects and models of integrated health care and, as in chapter 5, presents a number of free or inexpensive instruments that can be particularly useful in medical settings.

Given the concerns that have been raised in the past, any discussion of psychological services offered in MBHO settings would be incomplete without addressing the ethical issues that have been reported either informally or in the literature. In chapter 9, the more commonly raised issues are identified. This final chapter also presents both general and specific approaches to the resolution of ethical dilemmas in managed behavioral health care systems.

Managed care has tightened the reigns on authorizations for reimbursable testing. Despite this barrier, psychological testing can continue to play an important part in psychological practice and behavioral health care service delivery. The push to demonstrate positive outcomes, the need to meet quality improvement standards, and the push toward integration of primary and behavioral health care are but a few of the pressures that MBHOs must contend with in order to stay in business. Consequently, even though MBHOs may view the use of psychological testing in the *traditional* way with some degree of skepticism and restrict its use, they also acknowledge that it can bring value to the organization in meeting external demands and surviving in a highly competitive market place.

M. E. Maruish

Acknowledgments

My appreciation goes out to my colleagues at United Behavioral Health who have mentored me in my position as Director of Quality Improvement for the Health Plan Division of UBH. The knowledge and experiences in the managed behavioral health care industry that they have shared, and which they continue to share, have been invaluable to me both on the job and in writing this book. Special thanks go to Ed Bonnie and Anne Nelson for their comments, ideas, and suggestions related to specific chapters contained herein. I would also like to express my gratitude to those friends who have provided the encouragement and support that was needed to complete this project.

Introduction

Probably in no other period in time has so much change in the field of health care taken place than during the past century. Breakthroughs and technological advances in the diagnosis, treatment, and prevention of diseases abounded during the 20th century. Never has so much progress occurred in such a relatively short period of time than what we have just witnessed. But at the same time, never have so much controversy, debate, and upheaval surrounding this country's health care delivery system taken place as have occurred during the past decade. Out-of-control costs and the delivery of inefficient and sometimes ineffective services have led to drastic changes in this country's health care delivery system. Few would disagree that the most drastic of these changes has been the introduction of what is referred to as "managed care." This system not only affects the way treatment for physical problems is delivered but also the way in which behavioral health care—mental health and substance abuse services—is provided. Indeed, managed care has become the dominant force in the delivery of mental health care services (Cushman & Gilford, 2000). Depending on one's point of view, the effects may be considered positive or negative. However, the general opinion that one is likely to uncover about managed care is a negative one.

All behavioral health care professions have been affected by managed care, not the least of which is psychology. The extent to which the effects of managed care on psychology are perceived as threatening to its practice and the people who seek its services can seen in the American Psychological Association's support of legislative and judicial efforts that seek to curb managed care policies and practices. One area of psychological practice that has been significantly affected by managed care is psychological testing—the one truly unique and (some would argue) defining aspect of psychology among the behavioral health care professions. Indeed, the importance of psychological testing to the field's identity and, more significantly, the contribution this activity can make to the ultimate well-being of those whom the profession serves through a system of managed health care is the impetus for the development of this book.

To fully appreciate how psychological testing can become an integral component in a managed system of health care, first it is important to have a good working knowledge and context of what we call "managed care": what it is, how it came into being, how it has impacted behavioral health care services and the profession of psychology, and how it is likely to change and impact behavioral health care in the future. This chapter is intended to provide that context and to set the stage for the chapters that follow.

A BRIEF INTRODUCTION TO THE BASICS OF MANAGED CARE

Managed behavioral health care is both a reflection and an outgrowth of the system of general managed health care that preceded it. Thus, to better understand managed behavioral health care and its impact on the psychologists' practices, it is important first to better understand managed care in general.

What Is Managed Care?

It is important to understand what is meant by "managed care." The term has come to mean different things to different people. The variability in perceived meaning of the term is great, with discrepancies being the greatest between groups of health care consumers and groups of health care providers and provider organizations.

There is no shortage of conceptualizations of the term in the professional literature. Some are very general, such as Benedict and Phelps' (1998) definition of managed care as "the collective term for the myriad cost-containment strategies and financing arrangements currently dominating this country's evolving health care system" (p. 29). United HealthCare (1994) defines it as "a system of health care delivery that influences utilization and cost of services and measures performance. The goal is a system that delivers value by giving people access to quality, cost-effective health care" (p. 45).

There are other conceptualizations that are slightly more detailed. Ford (2000), for example, describes managed care as

> a comprehensive approach to health care delivery that encompasses planning and coordination of care, monitoring of care quality, and cost control. Managed care uses systems to approve the delivery of service before they are provided (prior authorization and concurrent review). It also includes new systems of financing health care delivery, such as placing providers, rather than the insurer, financially at risk for the cost of service delivery. (p. 311)

With any more specificity and detail, the definition of managed care is likely to be descriptive of a particular *type* of managed care. The various types of managed care arrangements that are available to health care consumers will be discussed later in this chapter. However, for the general purpose of this chapter, Ford's (2000) conceptualization of managed care will serve as a good reference.

An Historical Perspective

Like many others, Miller (1996) views the impetus for the rise of today's system of managed care as the health care cost increases that were appearing under the traditional indemnity or fee-for-service insurance system that was prevalent in the United States during the 20th century. The increase of health care expenditures from 6% to 12% of the gross national product between the years 1965 and 1990 is cited as evidence of the failure of indemnity plans to control costs. This should not be surprising, given that indemnity plans reimburse care providers on the basis of the number and types of services they offer. This has the unintended effect of encouraging plan members to seek more services, and practitioners and facilities to provide more services (Edmunds, Frank, Hogan, McCarty, Robinson-Blake, & Weisner, 1997). Managed care came about as a solution to the skyrocketing health care costs that resulted from the widespread indemnity plans. How would this be accomplished? As Miller stated,

> The essential features of managed care do not restore cost consciousness to consumers; rather, these features attempt to correct the incentive problem by creating two additional alterations in the market economics. First, a new party, either a managed care company or a provider with a capitated contract, replaces the consumer in evaluating the cost versus the value in health care decisions. Second, this new party has the incentive, either directly or indirectly, of increased financial success when treatment costs are reduced. (pp. 350–351)

It is commonly thought that managed care is a relatively recent movement in health care delivery. The fact is that managed care has been around since the first prepaid group practices sought to improve the quality and coordination of care and increase efforts toward prevention in the 1930s (Edmunds et al., 1997). These might be considered the first health maintenance organizations, or HMOs (see later). Managed care began to thrive in the 1970s when federal legislation authorized HMOs and loosened previously imposed restrictions (Hoge, Thakur, & Jacobs, 2000). The Center for Substance Abuse and Treatment (CSAT; as noted in Edmunds et al., 1997) reported that since the mid-1980s, managed care has gone through three phases in its approach to health care delivery. The first phase focused on the implementation of procedures such as utilization review and preadmission certification to limit access to care. Utilization review, fee-for-service provider networks, selective contracting, treatment planning, and managed benefits characterized the second phase. During the third phase, the focus shifted to managing care through an emphasis on appropriateness of care. Edmunds et al. also identified yet another phase, one in which the outcomes of a full continuum of treatment are managed through an integrated system of services. In addition, Hoge et al. have identified an emerging fifth phase that is consistent with this author's observations. This is a focus on illness prevention and health promotion.

Types of Managed Care

As Edmunds et al. (1997) point out, there are many different types of managed care plans or arrangements. However, there are a few commonalities among them. They all employ explicit criteria for selecting practitioners and facilities to provide specific health care services to plan members under specific contractual arrangements, and members have financial incentives to use the plan's providers and procedures. They also have established formal programs utilization review, quality assurance, and quality improvement programs. It is the administrative and benefit features that distinguish the numerous types of managed care organizations and plans from another. The distinctions among the plans and organizations allow them to be grouped within a generally accepted typology. Following are some of the more common types of managed care organizations.

Health Maintenance Organizations (HMOs).   Managed care and health maintenance organizations (HMOs) were essentially synonymous until the 1980s when other forms of managed care began to appear (Harwood, Beutler, Fisher, Sandowicz, Albanese, & Baker, 1997). The HMO is still viewed as the most common type of managed care organization (Kent & Hersen, 2000). Broadly defined, it is "an entity that provides, offers or arranges for coverage of designated health services needed by plan members for a fixed, prepaid premium" (UHC, 1994, p. 38). Characterizing the various forms of HMOs are the provision of all health care services for a flat *capitation* fee, commonly paid to the service provider on a per member per month (PMPM) basis. For this fee, the provider agrees to go at risk of losing money to provide the contracted services. Utilization management and review are employed to monitor and control the utilization of member services.

There are four basic models of HMOs (Harwood et al., 1997; UHC, 1994). In the *staff model*, the providers of care are salaried employees of the HMO who may receive additional financial incentives for profitability or performance. HMOs employing a *group model* contract with a specific group of practitioners to provide services for a per-member capitated fee. The main difference between this model and the staff model is that the services may be offered at either a single location or at the practitioners' offices. In the model of *independent practice associations*, or IPAs, there is a contract with a large number of providers to deliver services from their own locations for a capitated or reduced fee. The IPA then contracts with the HMO to provide services to its members for a somewhat higher capitated fee. In a *network model*, the HMO contracts with individual practitioners and groups of practitioners to provide services to the plan members in their offices with little if any reliance on centralized clinics.

Preferred Provider Organizations (PPOs).   These organizations consist of a network of providers that agrees to treat participating plan members, sometimes at reduced fees. They may also see patients other than those in the contracted plan. Plan members may see practitioners other than these "preferred providers" but usually with a copayment, or one that is higher than that required for a preferred provider visit. According to Harwood et al. (1997), PPOs are particularly beneficial to psychologists because they provide a steady stream of referrals, are prompt in their payments, and afford the psychologist opportunities to sit on the board of directors for PPO policy and be both a broker and participant in the organization's profits.

Employee Assistance Programs (EAPs).   Although sometimes not considered managed care organizations, employee assistance programs (EAPs) often function like capitated programs in offering behavioral health crisis intervention, problem assessment, brief treatment, and referral services to a company's employees and their families (Harwood et al., 1997). Those staffing the EAP may be employees of the company or contracted professions from the community. Depending on the EAP, the services may be offered in offices housed at the work site, or they may be offered at the site of contracting service providers. The services offered by EAPs are limited, with the focus on brief interventions and referral to an outside provider in those cases requiring more extensive interventions.

Point-of-Service Plans (POSs). Edmunds et al. (1997) describe point-of-service plans (POSs) as having features of both HMOs and PPOs. These plans maintain a network of providers through a capitation or fee-for-service reimbursement arrangement. As with PPOs and certain HMO plans, plan members incur higher financial penalties for going to providers outside the network.

Administrative Services Only Programs (ASOs). Large, self-insured employers commonly use administrative services only programs (ASOs; Bobbitt, Marques, & Trout, 1998). Here, care for plan members is arranged for by the ASO. It provides the administrative services necessary for plan members to obtain needed care. A third party—the member's employer, for example—assumes financial responsibility for the care.

THE EMERGENCE OF MANAGED BEHAVIORAL HEALTH CARE ORGANIZATIONS

Managed behavioral health care organizations, or MBHOs, did not accompany managed care (in the more global sense of the term) as it began to exert its presence in and influence on the field of health care service delivery. It might be considered a relatively new development in the ever-evolving field of health care, but its impact has been nonetheless significant on the delivery of services to that segment of the population with mental health or substance abuse problems.

Behavioral Health Care: Managed Carve-Outs

The delivery of behavioral health care services through a system of managed care has gone through somewhat of an evolution. Initially, many managed care companies offered behavioral health services through their standard system of health care delivery (Kent & Hersen, 2000). As HMOs employed mental health professionals on their staffs, insurers developed PPOs consisting of panels of mental health professionals. Difficulties in controlling costs and managing services through these means eventually led to the development of behavioral health specialty companies, or "carve-outs," which provided behavioral health services independent of the insured's other health care services. Feldman (1998) defines a *behavioral health carve-out* as

> a body of specialized knowledge and practice with services provided by freestanding organizations that are neither subunits of, or financially dependent on, a general health-care organization. Independence, at least at the service delivery level, is not only structural but also suggests different sources of funding, specialized multidisciplinary practitioners often trained outside of traditional academic medical centers, and direct access to care. (p. SP59).

The 1990s saw the growth of the behavioral health carve-out. Kiesler (2000) reported that of the 170 million people enrolled in some form of managed mental health care, 150 million (88%) are served by a behavioral health care specialty plan. The emergence and acceptance of carve-outs reflect a number of factors. In addition to those mentioned by Kent and Hersen (2000), Hersch (1995) mentions three other factors: the continuing stigma of mental illness, the lack of validity or credibility of psychotherapy in the eyes of insurance purchasers (e.g., corporate leaders), and the lack of "easily quantifiable outcomes." Bobbitt et al. (1998) also talk about difficulties in "defining the process and outcome in behavioral health care" (p. 55). Feldman (1998), on the other hand, views carve-outs as being a reflection of the separation of mental health care and general health care that has existed in the United States for more than 200 years. He attributes this separation not only to the stigma of mental illness, but also to the influence of mental health advocates who view the delivery of behavioral health services separate from general health care as being a means of both obtaining greater visibility and resources and preventing such services from becoming underfunded and undervalued. Kiesler's (2000) perspective on the popularity of behavioral health carve-outs is a bit different:

> A lack of consensual agreement on appropriate treatment and particularly on the length of treatment, ambiguities about whether treatment of substance abuse and other mental health problems belonged in the same category, claims that savings on health treatment occur with the addition of mental health services (but no agreement on who should get those savings), and an unwillingness or inability to make firm demographic guesses all led to mental health professionals' reluctance to be involved in managed care. These ambiguities also reinforced the stereotypes that the health field had of mental health care, and full partnerships between health and mental health services were not urged. The combination has led to an almost universal tilt toward the carve-out. (pp. 482–483)

Characteristics of managed care, in general, were discussed earlier. In addition, Feldman (1998) identified characteristics of typical MBHO carve-outs. First, they have contracts with any of various types of customers, such as HMOs, insurers, self-insured employers, or public sector agencies (e.g., Medicare, Medicaid), to provide behavioral health care services to a defined consumer population. Second, payment for these services comes in the form of a monthly fee per member or employee for whom the customer is purchasing the services. For this fee, the MBHO assumes the risk of the costs for all clinical and administrative services that may be provided to the consumer of the services. Note that the employer, insurer, government agency, or whoever pays for the service is generally considered the MBHO's *customer*, whereas the patient is considered only as the *consumer* of the services offered by the MBHO (Miller, 1996; O'Brien, 2000). Cummings, Budman, and Thomas (1998) refer to the purchaser of the services as the *direct consumer* and the patient as the *end-consumer*. Regardless of how one labels these stakeholders in the patient's care, the important point to recognize is that "the key relationship is between the signators of the contract, decidedly not the patient" (O'Brien, 2000, p. 256)

The third characteristic of MBHO carve-outs identified by Feldman (1998) is that they maintain a network of clinicians and facilities that provide the behavioral health services for which the MBHO is responsible. Services are generally reimbursed either through discounted fees, a capitated payment, or a flat case-rate fee. The fourth characteristic is that they possess a technology that facilitates the collection and use of extensive information related to patients, providers, and rendered services. This includes information related to such things as cost, service utilization, provider credentials and specializations, patient outcomes and satisfaction information, and patient diagnostic and treatment information. Finally, rather than being free-standing, these MBHOs typically are owned by larger corporations. Bobbitt et al. (1998) identified other typical characteristics of MBHOs. At least to some extent, MBHOs are identified as business entities that offer a full range of services, employ utilization and care management processes, use systematic quality management and quality improvement processes, and assume financial risk.

Effects of Managed Behavioral Health Care

Managed behavioral health care, as a separate or carved-out entity, now has been around for nearly 2 decades. Any informal poll among providers and patients would likely yield some reports of problems and the occasional horror story related to their experiences with managed care. And indeed, as presented later, the results of formal surveys of practicing psychologists' views of managed care do suggest that the profession has a less than favorable opinion about managed care and its contribution to behavioral health care in the United States. But if one puts aside personal experiences, what has been the effect of managed behavioral health care for the people and institutions it is meant to serve? Careful consideration of the behavioral health care field since the introduction of managed care yields both expected and unexpected findings and conclusions.

Positive Aspects and Accomplishments. Cummings (1998a, 1998b, 2000) identified several accomplishments that have come about as the result of the introduction of managed behavioral health care. The first is *cost containment*. The rate of inflation for behavioral health care services dropped from the premanaged care rate of 16% to 4.4%. Cummings contends that its capping costs and going at-risk have saved the mental health and substance abuse benefits from erosion or elimination. In addition, services have expanded or been substituted for other services, and the number of both patients and practitioners have increased. The fact that 75% of the insured market is covered by managed behavioral care is offered as evidence of a clear societal need is being served. Behavioral health care has become more accountable to its customers through MBHOs' employment of treatment guidelines and outcomes programs. Through accreditation, outcomes programs and the implementation of standards of quality, the industry moved closer to self-regulation. Moreover, managed behavioral health care has provided a mechanism for coordinating care both within itself and with primary care, and it provides an opportunity to demonstrate value to customers through its resulting reduction in costs

Kent and Hersen (2000) also point out how managed care has made behavioral health practitioners more accountable for their treatment and their use of psychological testing. It has promoted the use of brief therapies and has permitted more people access to psychological services. This, in turn, has increased the patient base to which psychologists have access.

Another major accomplishment of managed behavioral health care is actual *cost savings*. Marsh and Cochran (2000), noting findings from the Substance Abuse and Mental Health Services Administration (SAMHSA), reported that behavioral health care spending rose from $44.2 billion in 1987 to $85.3 billion in 1997. At the same time, behavioral health care spending as a percentage of total health care spending declined from 8.8% to 7.8%, with health spending growing by 8.2% and behavioral health spending growing only 6.8%. In addition, Feldman (1998) notes that it is not unusual for payers to achieve a 30 to 40% cost savings in the first year under managed care, with stabilization of these savings being achieved in the third year. Also, behavioral health benefits in large companies now represent less than 10% of total health benefits costs as compared to 15 to 18% of the total cost in the mid-1980s. Feldman attributes these cost savings to several factors, including the shift away from inpatient treatment to more community-based approaches, flexibility in how patients can use their benefits, and the ability to negotiate low fees with clinician and facilities. More people are now seeking behavioral health care services, but cost savings still accrue because the treatment episodes are also shorter and goal-oriented.

Feldman (1998) identified two other aspects of managed behavioral health care that have achieved at least some progress from the introduction of managed behavioral health care. The first is in the area of quality and outcomes of care. In the past, the industry has relied more on measurements such as patient satisfaction and recidivism/readmission rates as indicators of quality and outcome. Although findings in these areas are generally positive, the methodological rigor with which these types of data have been gathered and other concerns suggest great room for improvement in these areas. The other aspect of health care for which there has been limited improvement is in the area of care coordination. The success experienced in this area has pretty much been limited to the coordination of mental health services with substance abuse services. The important goal of demonstrating the effects of the coordination of behavioral health and medical services has yet to be fully realized.

Finally, there is a very important, positive aspect of behavioral health care that is easy to overlook, that is, the quality of care that has come about as a result of its presence (E. A. Nelson, personal communication, December 7, 2000). Previously, individuals in seeking mental health or substance abuse services had been "flying blind" — not knowing what services they needed or who the best provider for those particular services were. Through adherence to the various systems of internal and external policies, procedures and regulations, MBHOs have improved in many ways the quality of behavioral health care a patient receives. Examples include ensuring that their patients receive the most appropriate treatment from providers who meet stringent credentialing standards, providing oversight of that treatment, and helping patients better understand behavioral health care and their rights and options therein. Patients generally did not have the benefit of this type of assistance in finding and receiving care, nor to similar types of benefits prior to the establishment managed care as the predominant model of health care delivery.

Disappointments and Failures.   Not everything about managed behavioral health care has turned out as one would have hoped. Cummings (1998a, 1998b, 2000), an early proponent of managed care, does not hesitate to point out some of the disappointments that have occurred. First, there has been a loss of clinical focus. He feels that efforts of containing costs through clinically effective care were lost to the cost-containment strategies of "bean counters." Next, the need to underbid for contracts with payers negatively impacted such things as access to care, the services that were offered, and the quality of those services. There is some evidence, however, that this is changing.

The "merger mania" that has been common in other industries also has taken place in the MBHO industry, supporting the public's idea that MBHOs are getting richer in the face of limited services to plan members (Cummings, 1998a, 1998b, 2000). Related to (and perhaps because of) this is the competitive nature of the industry that has bred distrust among the companies vying for contracts with perspective payers. In addition, the pressure that payers put on MBHOs to cut costs has been passed on to practitioners and facilities, encouraging them to join forces with patients in their protests against managed care. The result has been what Cummings feels is a public relations disaster. Finally, as alluded to earlier, managed behavioral health care has not been very successful in integrating with medical health care or more specifically, primary care.

Winners and Losers. Who came out ahead as the result of the implementation of managed behavioral health care? According to Cummings (2000), those who pay the bills — employers, insurers, and the government — are the winners in the "industrialization of health care." The losers are psychiatric hospitals and private practitioners. Utilization management and review, along with the expansion of the continuum of care, have limited the number of admissions and days per admission in private hospitals. Private practitioners have seen a reduction in their rates and an increased use of less expensive master's level practitioners in the delivery of therapeutic services. Perhaps more importantly, practitioners have lost the ability to decide what type of treatment their patients receive and for how long.

The Challenges of Managed Behavioral Health Care for Psychology

As was just shown, the delivery of behavioral health care has undergone significant adjustment under the managed care system. Consequently, behavioral health care providers have had to face new ways of thinking about the way their services are delivered and have had to adapt accordingly. This has not always been easy nor will it cease to be difficult in the future. It has brought about several challenges, not the least of which present themselves to psychologists who provide the majority of their services through a system of managed care.

Kent and Hersen (2000) have identified and grouped the challenges that psychologists must face under managed care into three general categories: clinical, administrative, and professional. Unsurprisingly, the greatest challenges posed by managed care in the clinical arena have to do with the bread-and-butter services that psychologists offer, that is, assessment and psychotherapy. In both areas, the psychologist's autonomy in deciding how best to assess and treat his patients has been curtailed. Previously, psychologists have had the freedom to choose when to conduct psychological assessment, which tests to use, and how many tests to administer. Now, managed care demands justification for administering psychological tests. Sometimes, decisions to authorize testing are based on a cost–benefit analysis; in other words, does the gain or value from the assessment warrant what it is going to cost the MBHO for the testing? The restrictions in the authorization of psychological testing have contributed to the negative feelings on the part of the psychological community toward managed care and indeed, they served as one reason for the development of this book.

As Kent and Hersen (2000) point out, changes in the way therapy is authorized and provided under managed care represents the greatest impact on and challenge for the profession. The primary clinical challenge here is the emphasis on brief therapy and group therapy. At least in previous years, psychologists have not received adequate (if any) training in either of these types of treatment. However, this author's experience suggests that psychologists (particularly those more recently licensed) have realized the current trends and are now obtaining training in brief therapeutic models and techniques. It would seem that a similar movement toward acquiring the skills necessary to conduct therapeutic groups will be necessary in order for the profession to remain an active competitor in the era of managed care.

The administrative challenges of managed care come from several directions (Kent & Hersen, 2000). These include the utilization review process and the accompanying demands that are placed on the psychologist. Completion of forms, calls to care managers to request authorization for additional treatment, and adherence to numerous policies and procedures related to such things as practitioner availability to patients are examples here. These types of demands add to the psychologist's cost of doing business with the MBHO. All of this, of course, is accompanied by a lowering of reimbursement rates.

From the perspective of the profession in general, Kent and Hersen (2000) see challenges to doctoral-level psychologists to demonstrate their value over that of less costly master's-prepared practitioners to MBHOs. This matter becomes even more troublesome as there is some question about whether there is a surplus of doctoral-level psychologists. However, Bobbitt et al. (1998) identify a much broader challenge that the profession faces. As they have put it,

> The field of professional psychology has become strongly identified with the provision of psychological services. The growth of the private practice community in professional psychology has been extraordinary. Unfortunately, it has not been clearly possible to differentiate psychologists from other providers based on the way in which psychologists provide the modal form of treatment that dominates the field—individual psychotherapy. As the system moves away from a focus on individual psychotherapy in a private practice environment, it will be important for psychology to refocus its efforts on aspects of the field that make it distinct—the application of scientific principles, the appropriate use of psychological testing, and especially the use of behavioral medicine techniques. It is in these areas that psychology clearly has an advantage over other nonmedical behavioral health providers. This issue relates to the identity of professional psychology. Unfortunately, psychology's intellectual and educational pluralism, which has been a major strength of the field, has also made it difficult to be clearly defined in the current health care climate. (pp. 62–63)

PSYCHOLOGISTS' VIEWS OF MANAGED BEHAVIORAL HEALTH CARE

The previous discussion has identified many challenges facing the field of psychology in this era of managed behavioral health care. Certainly, there are a number of indisputable positive results that have come about as a consequence of the introduction of a managed system of behavioral health care service delivery. Savings in behavioral health care costs are a prime example. At the same time, the principles and practices that characterize this cost-saving system of health care delivery frequently go contrary to what psychologists have been trained to do and their concept of what comprises good, ethical practice in their profession.

What do psychologists think about managed care? Anecdotal reports and general informal impressions elicited from members of the profession would probably suggest that psychology's view of and attitude toward managed care is less than positive. Fortunately, a few psychologists have applied their scientific training to empirical investigations of this topic, permitting a more accurate picture of psychologists' thoughts and perceptions. Although the findings of these surveys are not too surprising, they are interesting and informative from the standpoint of how and to what extent psychologists view problems in managed behavioral health care. Knowing this can provide a better sense of what those who wish to be employed by an MBHO or to serve in an MBHO provider network may have to contend with. It may also provide useful information to present to MBHOs in efforts to improve the relationship between the two parties.

The CAPP Survey

In a survey conducted in 1995 by the American Psychological Association's Committee for the Advancement of Professional Practice (CAPP; Phelps, Eisman, & Kohut, 1998), almost 16,000 psychological practitioners responded to a survey consisting of questions related to workplace settings, areas of practice concerns, and range of activities. Most of the respondents (55%) were practitioners whose primary work setting was group or solo independent practice. Other work settings—government, medical, academic, group practice—were fairly equally represented by the remainder of the sample, with 29% of those primarily working in one of these settings also indicating involvement in part-time private practice.

Even though there were not any real surprises, there were several interesting results, which were reported by primary work setting—independent practice, academic, government, and medical (Phelps et al., 1998). Combined work setting results also were presented. The principal professional activity reported by the sample respondents was psychotherapy, with 44% of the sample acknowledging involvement in this service. Assessment was the second most prevalent activity, with 16% reporting this activity. Among the more important findings were the following:

- 79% saw managed care's impact as negative, 10% saw its impact as positive, and 11% reported no effect.
- 58% reported that managed care changed clinical practice.
- 49% said utilization management and utilization review requirements were excessive.
- 48% reported decreased income as a result of managed care's fee structure.
- 42% reported ethical dilemmas created by managed care.
- 40% reported fewer clients due to managed care.

Phelps et al. (1998) interpreted the CAPP survey findings as confirming the "impressionistic and anecdotal reports that changes in the health care delivery system have significantly affected thousands of members of APA's practice community" (p. 35). At the same time, a significant percent of the respondents were spending three fourths of their time in psychotherapeutic and assessment activities in independent practice settings. Relatively little time was being spent in nontraditional activities involving consultation, teaching, and research—activities that psychologists are also

trained for. There were indications that when practitioners had a secondary work setting, this tended to be a medical setting. Phelps et al. saw this finding as possibly indicating some shift toward the profession's identity from that of a mental health provider to a health service provider. Ethical concerns were evident regardless of the
respondent's setting. In addition, despite possessing the necessary skills, psychologists were doing little in terms of outcomes research. Overall, the authors saw a need
for psychologists to capitalize on these and other skills to promote psychology's role
and standing in the health care delivery system.

The Division 42 Survey

The views of independent practitioners were fleshed out in more detail in Murphy,
DeBernardo, and Shoemaker's (1998) survey of 442 members of APA's Division of Independent Practice (Division 42). Although 84% of the respondents indicated that
they were members of either an HMO or PPO provider panel, 91% said that their
practices were affected by managed care. This suggests that even when not directly
tied to a managed care organization, one's practice may be affected by it. The proliferation of a managed care system of behavioral health care delivery was evident by
the fact that at the time of the survey (1996), half of the survey respondents' services
were provided under managed care plans. This compares to the 10 to 15% rate that
was estimated to have occurred 5 years earlier.

Among the findings related to the impact of managed care, Murphy et al. (1998)
noted the following:

- 81% of the respondents reported that managed care had no positive impact on
  their practice, 70% said it had a highly negative impact, and only 10% said it had
  no negative impact.
- 42% indicated that they had moved from a solo practice to a larger practice or an
  integrated network, and 23% anticipated that they would join a group or integrated network in the future. Only 13% indicated that they had left or would
  leave their practice.
- 85% reported deriving income from managed care sources, with this income
  representing a median of 34% of their income. Reported percentages obtained 5
  years earlier were 60% and 14%, respectively.
- 88% reported that managed care did not result in any positive impact on the
  quality of care whereas only 2% did report positive impact. At the same time,
  47% indicated that there had been at least some negative impact on quality of
  care.
- 84% indicated that managed care controlled aspects of treatment and patient
  care that should be controlled by clinicians.
- 79% indicated that managed care has resulted in inappropriate and/or insuffi-
  cient treatment; 71% reported that it has led to the use of inappropriate practitioners; and 65% said that it has led to the rejection of patients with certain diagnoses.
- 70% reported ethical dilemmas resulted from their involvement with managed
  care.
- 75% believed that patient confidentiality is compromised through their contact
  with managed care companies.

Overall, Murphy et al. (1998) concluded that most independent practitioners have accommodated the demands of managed care. And as in the Phelps et al. (1998) survey, the results indicated a move for practitioners to align themselves more with the medical side of the health care industry. Moreover, a reluctance to diversify their practices beyond the traditional activities was again noted.

The New Jersey Psychological Association Survey

Rothbaum, Berstein, Haller, Phelps, and Kohout (1998) reported the results of a 1996 survey of 812 members of the New Jersey Psychological Association (NJPA). The purpose of the survey was to assess the types of problems NJPA members had been experiencing with managed mental health care. Eighty-two percent of the respondents were working in independent practice settings. On average, 29% of the respondents' caseloads were managed care patients.

In general, the greater the percentage of managed care patients in a respondent's caseload, the more likely the psychologist was to report an increased number of patients in his caseload, increased paperwork, a decrease in the average number of sessions, and pressure to both change the quality of care and compromise ethics (Rothbaum et al., 1998). Percent of managed care patients was also positively associated with changes in morale, professional identity, and therapeutic approach. Perhaps more telling in the survey were the types of problems that the survey respondents reported in their encounters with specific MBHOs. Across the 10 MBHOs that respondents indicated familiarity with, the problems yielding the highest average problem-endorsement ranking had to do with the following: getting accepted on a provider panel, the length of precertification procedures, the length of screening requirements, being forced to discharge patients before their being clinically ready to be discharged, dealing with patient care decisions made by less well-trained MBHO personnel, the speed at which requests for approval for sessions were responded to, number of authorized treatment sessions, and the paperwork required by the MBHO. Each of these problem areas was endorsed by at least 30% of the sample.

Other Survey Findings

Miller (1996) summarized the results of three other surveys of psychologists' views of managed care. As reported by Miller, Tucker and Lubin's national survey of 718 APA Division of Psychoanalysis (Division 39) psychologists yielded results that are fairly consistent with those of the three surveys just discussed. Ninety percent of the respondents indicated utilization reviewers interfered with treatment plans; 79% said that they were dissatisfied with these reviewers' knowledge and expertise; 72% reported that the quality of the treatment they provided was negatively affected by their experience with managed care; and 49% indicated that treatment delays or denials adversely affected their patients. In Hipp, Atkinson, and Pelc's survey of 223 Colorado psychologists, 64% reported inappropriate discontinuation of treatment by managed care, and 59% reported misleading advertising directed to patients by managed care. Moreover, Denkers and Clifford's survey of 173 California psychologists found that denial of treatment based on rigid criteria was reported by 55% of the respondents, whereas 57% reported that managed care denials had adversely affected their patients' progress.

STATUS OF PSYCHOLOGICAL TESTING AND ASSESSMENT IN THE ERA OF MANAGED BEHAVIORAL HEALTH CARE

The purpose of this book is assist psychologists and other qualified practitioners in using and promoting psychological testing in a health care delivery system that heretofore has appeared to many to be less than "test friendly." A large portion of what is generally reported about the acceptance of psychological testing in MBHOs and how this has affected the practice of psychology in those systems of care is based on impressionistic and anecdotal information. There are, however, other sources of information that present a more accurate picture of the situation.

Survey Findings

Where does psychological assessment currently fit into the daily scope of activities for practicing psychologists? The newsletter *Psychotherapy Finances* ("Fee, Practice and Managed Care Survey," 1995) reported the results of a nationwide readership survey of 1,700 mental health providers. Sixty-seven percent of the psychologists participating in this survey reported that they provide psychological testing services. This represents about a 10% drop from the level indicated by a similar survey published in 1992 by the same newsletter. Also of interest in the more recent survey is the percent of professional counselors (39%), marriage and family counselors (16%), psychiatrists (21%), and social workers (13%) offering these same services.

Watkins, Campbell, Nieberding, and Hallmark (1995) surveyed 412 randomly selected APA members with a clinical specialty, all of whom were engaged in assessment services. This study essentially sought to replicate a study that was published 18 years earlier and to determine what, if any, changes in assessment practices had occurred over that period of time. Among the findings of this investigation was the fact that the most frequently used assessment procedures had changed little over almost 2 decades. Among the most frequently used tests were those which one might expect—MMPI, the Wechsler scales, Rorschach, TAT, Beck Depression Inventory, and so on. However, the most frequently used *procedure* was the clinical interview, being reported by 391 of the 412 survey respondents. The implication here is that regardless of whatever tests they may employ in their assessment, most clinical psychologists rely on the clinical interview as part of their standard assessment procedures. In one sense, this supports MBHOs' view that interviews are all that are really required for diagnosis and treatment planning. However, as Groth-Marnat (1999a) points out, this may be true for dealing with "routine difficulties" but not so in other instances, such as those where the possibility of liability issues (e.g., a patient with suicidal or homicidal potential) or complex diagnostic questions come into play.

Taking a closer look at the impact that managed care has had on assessment, Piotrowski, Belter, and Keller (1998) conducted a survey in the Fall of 1996 that included mailings to 500 psychologists randomly selected from that year's *National Register of Health Service Providers in Psychology*. The purpose of the survey was to determine how managed care has affected assessment practices. One hundred thirty-seven useable surveys (32%) were returned. Sixty-one percent of the respondents saw no positive impact from managed care; and consistent with the CAPP survey findings, 70% saw managed care as negatively impacting clinicians or patients. The testing practices of 72% of the respondents were affected by managed care, as reflected in their performing less testing, using fewer instruments when they did test patients, and having lower reimbursement rates. Overall, they reported less reliance on those tests requiring much clinician time—such as the Wechsler scales, Rorschach, and TAT—along with a move to briefer, problem-focused tests. The results of their study led the Piotrowski et al. (1998) to speculate many possible scenarios for the future of assessment. These included such things as providers relying on briefer tests or briefer test batteries, changing the focus of their practice to more lucrative types of assessment activities (e,g., forensic assessment), using computer-based testing, or, in some cases, referring testing out to another psychologist.

Another large-scale, testing-specific survey was conducted by Camara, Nathan, and Puente (1998; also published in 2000) to investigate which tests were most frequently used by 933 clinical psychologists and 567 neuropsychologists; the time required to administer, score and interpret these tests; and other aspects of test use in the era of managed care. Although the neuropsychologists were selected from the membership of the National Academy of Neuropsychology, the clinical psychologists included APA, doctoral-level independent practitioners whose primary or secondary employment involved the provision of mental health services. Because this book is intended for clinical psychologists involved in general testing activities, only the findings for the clinical psychologist sample will be reported here. Readers interested in the findings from the neuropsychologist subsample are encouraged to see Camara et al. (2000).

Perhaps one of the most telling of Camara et al.'s (2000) findings was the fact that 755 (81%) of the 933 clinical psychologists spent less than 5 hours in testing activities (administration, scoring, interpretation) in a typical week. However, using only the results of the 179 clinical psychologists who spent 5 or more hours per week in these activities, Camara et al. found the following:

- 97% of the psychologists performed testing for personality–psychopathology assessment, 88% for intellectual-achievement assessment; and 47% for neuropsychological assessment.
- The annual mean and median full-battery assessments conducted in each of these three areas were 80.4 and 50.0, respectively, for personality–psychopathology assessment; 87.3 and 50.0, respectively, for intellectual-achievement assessment; and 63.6 and 30.0, respectively, for neuropsychological assessment.
- Across these three assessment areas and five other assessment areas (e.g., developmental), test battery administration accounted for 45% of the total assessment, scoring accounted for 36% of the assessment time, and interpretation accounted for 19% of the assessment time.
- The mean number of minutes to administer, score, and interpret the tests in a full-battery assessment in each of the same three areas was 241.7 minutes for a personality–psychopathology assessment, 211.3 minutes for an intellectual-achievement assessment, and 366.5 minutes for a neuropsychological assessment. Mean and median administration, scoring, and interpretation times for the 50 most frequently used tests also were reported and are presented in chapter 2.
- The 10 most frequently used tests were, in descending order, the WAIS-R, original MMPI/MMPI-2, WISC-III, Rorschach, Bender Visual–Motor Gestalt Test, TAT, WRAT-R/WRAT-III, House–Tree–Person, Wechsler Memory Scale-Revised, and Beck Depression Inventory and MCMI (tie).

- Computer services were infrequently used for assessment purposes, with only 3.6% of tests having been reported to be administered by computers, 10.4% being scored by computers, and only 3.9% being interpreted by computer services.

Stout and Cook (1999) conducted a survey of 40 managed care companies regarding their viewpoints on the reimbursement for psychological assessment. The good news is that the majority (70%) of these companies reported that they did reimburse for these services. At the same time, the authors pointed to the possible negative implications for the covered lives of those other 12 or so companies who do not reimburse for psychological assessment. That is, these people may not be receiving the services they need because of missing information that might have been revealed through the psychological assessment.

Although not specific to testing issues, the surveys discussed earlier in this chapter revealed a number of interesting points related to managed care's impact on psychological testing and assessment. In the CAPP study, Phelps et al. (1998) found that assessment was the second most prevalent activity, occupying an average of 16% of the professional time of the nearly 16,000 respondents. Much variability in percent of time spent in assessment activities was reported by setting, ranging from 5% in academic settings, to 15% in independent practices, to 19% in government settings, to 23% in medical settings. Phelps et al. also found that 29% of the respondents were involved in outcomes assessment, with those with least number of years of postlicensure experience being more likely to report the use of outcomes measures than those with more postlicensure experience. The highest rate of use of outcomes measures (40%) was found for psychologists in medical settings. A 10% random sample of all the returned questionnaires revealed no consistency in the types of measures or criteria used for outcomes measurement.

Seventy-one percent of Murphy et al.'s (1998) Division 42 respondents indicated that they provided psychological testing services, with 64% of these providers also reporting problems in getting reimbursed for these services. For neuropsychological testing, these figures were 18% and 29%, respectively. In addition, 70% of these respondents felt that managed care led to inadequate or inappropriate assessment. The study's authors saw this as an indication of the need for "continued study and concerted action." Somewhat surprisingly, Rothbaum et al. (1998) did not find "request for psychological testing denied" among the common complaints endorsed by their sample of New Jersey psychologists. Minimization of this as a problem area held up across 10 specific MBHOs.

Other Considerations

Numerous articles (e.g., Ficken, 1995; Piotrowski, 1999) have commented on how the advent of managed care has limited the reimbursement for (and therefore the use of) psychological assessment. Certainly, no one would disagree with Ficken, who sees the primary reason for this as being a financial one. In an era of capitated behavioral health care coverage, the amount of money available for behavioral health care treatment is limited. MBHOs therefore require a demonstration that the amount of money spent for testing will result in a greater amount of treatment cost savings. As of this writing, this author is unaware of any published or unpublished research to date that can provide this demonstration. In addition, Ficken notes that much of the informa-

tion obtained from psychological assessment is not relevant to the treatment of patients within a managed care environment. And understandably, MBHOs are reluctant to pay for gathering such information.

Werthman (1995) provides similar insights into this issue, noting that

> Managed care . . . has caused [psychologists] to revisit the medical necessity and efficacy
> of their testing practices. Currently, the emphasis is on the use of highly targeted and fo-
> cused psychological and neuropsychological testing to sharply define the "problems" to
> be treated, the degree of impairment, the level of care to be provided and the treatment
> plan to be implemented.
>
>   The high specificity and "problem-solving" approach of such testing reflects MCOs'
> commitment to effecting therapeutic change, as opposed to obtaining a descriptive nar-
> rative with scores. In this context, testing is perceived as a strong tool for assisting the
> primary provider in more accurately determining patient "impairments" and how to
> "repair" them. (p. 15)

In general, Werthman (1995) views psychological assessment as being no different
from other forms of patient care, thus making it subject to the same scrutiny, the same
demands for demonstrating medical necessity and/or utility, and the same consequent limitations imposed by MBHOs on other covered services.

Piotrowski (1999) best summed up the current state of psychological assessment
by stating

> Admittedly, the emphasis on the standard personality battery over the past decade has
> declined due to the impact of brief therapeutic approaches with a focus on diagnostics,
> symptomatology, and treatment outcome. That is, the clinical emphasis has been on ad-
> dressing referral questions and not psychodynamic defenses, character structure, and
> object relations. Perhaps the managed care environment has brought this issue to the
> forefront. Either way, the role of clinical assessment has, for the most part, changed. To
> the dismay of proponents of clinical methods, the future is likely to focus more on spe-
> cific domain-based rather than comprehensive assessment. (p. 793)

The foregoing representations of the current state of psychological assessment in
behavioral health care delivery could be viewed as an omen of worse things to come.
In this author's opinion, they are not. Rather, the limitations that are being imposed
on psychological assessment and the demand for justification of its use in clinical
practice represent part of health care customers' dissatisfaction with the way that
things were done in the past. In general, the tightening of the purse strings is a positive move for both behavioral health care and the profession of psychology. It is a
wake-up call to those who have contributed to the health care crisis by either uncriti-
cally performing costly psychological assessments, being unaccountable to the payers and recipients of those services, and generally not performing psychological assessment services in the most responsible, cost-effective way possible. Providers
need to evaluate how they have used psychological assessment in the past and then
determine the best way to use them in the future. As such, it is an opportunity for
providers to re-establish the value of the contributions they can make to improve the
quality of care delivery through their knowledge and skills in the area of psychological assessment. As will be shown throughout this book, there are many ways in
which the value of psychological assessment can be demonstrated.

THE FUTURE OF MANAGED BEHAVIORAL HEALTH CARE

The impact that managed care in general, and managed behavioral health care in particular, has had on the quality of care provided has been dramatic. A lot has changed over the past couple of decades—some for the better and some for the worse, depending on one's perspective. The fact is that managed care is not going away, at least not in the foreseeable future. And as Shueman (1997) has pointed out, it will continue to evolve as a result of social and economic forces as well as other important considerations, such as health policy issues. How will it be impacted? There have been many predictions about what will happen to managed care in the future by several knowledgeable parties. Following is an overview of what this author considers to be the most important of these predictions.

Continued Growth

Bobbitt et al. (1998) have predicted that managed behavioral health care will continue to grow, both in the commercial market as well as in the public sector. Accompanying this growth will be further decline of traditional indemnity insurance. However, it is this author's opinion that growth will be achieved through an easing of some of the constraints that MBHOs have imposed upon patients and payers. Part of this loosening of restrictions in care will be the result of government intervention, yet another part will be come about naturally as a result of the a heightening of competition among MBHOs for what Cummings (2000) sees as the shrinking behavioral health care dollar.

Continued Influence of Patients, Providers, and Advocacy/Accreditation Groups

Related to the reasons just given is the continued influence of various stakeholders in the health care process. Bobbitt et al. (1998) specifically refer to advocacy groups such as the National Alliance for the Mentally Ill (NAMI) and professional organizations such as the American Psychological Association who will continue their efforts to influence behavioral health care delivered through managed care systems. Moreover, accreditation organizations such as the National Committee for Quality Assurance (NCQA) and the Joint Commission on Accreditation of Healthcare Organizations (JCAHO) will continue to provide and refine standards that will help ensure that patients both have a say in and are the recipients of quality care from MBHOs. The MBHO standards published by each of these two accrediting bodies are relatively new offerings, with each set of standards having its own benefits and drawbacks to the MBHO. Which set of standards will emerge as the most "popular" among MBHOs is yet to be seen, but it is likely to be the one that allows the MBHO the most flexibility in the way it strives to deliver the highest quality of care.

Continued Mergers

Both Bobbitt et al. (1998) and Cummings (2000) predict continued acquistions and merging of MBHOs, to the point that leads Cummings to predict that eventually only a few giants will dominate the health care industry. However, mergers present many challenges. Observations of mergers that have taken place in the 1990s reveal the difficulties encountered in combining the operations of two or more MBHOs. Merging companies may have to maintain their separate identities and modes of operation under the corporation banner to continue to be successful. This will most likely be the case when the merging MBHOs have established themselves in different regional markets or with different types of customers (e.g., health plans vs. employer groups) with different needs and service expectations.

Contracting with Group Practices

MBHOs will show a preference for contracting with group practices rather than solo practitioners (Bobbitt et al., 1998; Cummings, 1995; Kent & Hersen, 2000). According to Kent and Hersen, this trend reflects the fact that group practices are more likely to handle risk-sharing contracts, are more capable of conducting quality improvement activities, and more easily managed than individual practitioners are. At the same time, Bobbitt et al. feel that there will be opportunities for solo practitioners who have skills for a particular niche service, are particular expert in dealing with culturally diverse groups, or are competent in the health psychology.

Further Development of Practice Guidelines

Without question, the development and proliferation of clinical practice guidelines will continue (Bobbitt et al., 1998; Cummings, 2000; Kent & Hersen, 2000). One will see efforts toward standardizing guidelines for the treatment of specific disorders coming from governmental agencies (e.g., Health Care Financing Administration, or HCFA), professional organizations (e.g., American Psychiatric Association), and MBHOs themselves. Perhaps part of this trend has to do with the industry's move toward accountability and the focus on improving the outcomes of treatment. Although many practitioners would object to this level of intrusion into professional lives, Kent and Hersen make the point that MBHOs do have some right to dictate the type of service provided to their patients because they are, in fact, paying for those services. Logically, one would be hard-pressed to make a case against any treatment based on scientifically proven efficacious and effective approaches and techniques. Nevertheless, practitioners' acceptance of guidelines will not be an easy goal to achieve. As Beutler (2000) explains,

> those who practice psychosocial treatments have held themselves to exceedingly low but implicit standards based on so-called clinical evidence. Shared, strong beliefs and the personal sincerity of those who advocate these beliefs have been held as sufficient evidence to ensure the truth of a treatment recommendation. Treatment practices have been validated by reference to clinical experience, but the nature of this experience has usually been unstated, and the beliefs that are attributed to it have varied widely among similarly experienced clinicians. Extensive research evidence supports the conclusion that, among clinicians, personal beliefs, thus developed, are almost always given greater credence than scientific evidence and are considered to be the real or moral truth when the two sources of evidence are at variance.... Accepting scientifically credible approaches may well mean relinquishing any commitment to the truth of some theories that have been constructed wholly from clinical experience. (p. 999)

medical necessity and level of care (LOC), as well its guidelines for treatment of specific types of mental health and substance abuse disorders (e.g., major depression, schizophrenia, ADHD). Knowledge of these two sets of guidelines is critical for navigating through any MBHO on the behalf of patients. It can facilitate the authorization of appropriate services while limiting or eliminating the frustration that is frequently reported by providers in their dealings with managed care.

Beyond this, there are a number of other things that psychologists can do to help develop and maintain a good working relationship with MBHOs. Stout (1997), drawing on the work of Anderson and Berlat, recommends that psychologists work toward providing accurate diagnoses and cost-effective treatment of their patients' conditions. Diagnosis, of course, can be facilitated by the use of psychological tests (see chapter 2). Ensuring cost-effective treatment may require providing episodic treatment over an extended period of time (perhaps what Cummings et al. [1998] refer to as "brief intermittent psychotherapy throughout the life cycle") or referring the patient to another provider. Consistent with Kiesler's (2000) observations is the recommendation for psychologists to incorporate CQI activities into their practices. Stout also points to the importance of understanding the difference between *utilization review*, which focuses on exclusion of unnecessary services for reimbursement, and *case management*, which focuses on making sure that patients receive the most effective and appropriate care. Related to this is Kiesler's recommendation for psychologists to develop their own review mechanisms in order to avoid utilization review problems with the MBHO. This is where knowledge and application of LOC and treatment guidelines can be helpful. In addition, Shueman (1997) notes the importance of documenting treatment and routinely assessing its outcomes as other means of preparing to deal with MBHOs.

Developing New Approaches to Treatment and Assessment

Many experts and observers of the evolution of managed behavioral health care (e.g., Cummings, 1995; Cummings et al., 1998; Kiesler, 2000) would probably agree with this author's contention that if there is one clinical area in which psychologists should become skilled, it is brief psychotherapy. With limitations on the number of outpatient sessions that are prevalent in many health plans, treatment through MBHOs has required the implementation of problem-oriented, goal-focused treatment (Shueman, 1997) that yields clinically significant results over relatively short periods of time. Training in brief therapy was, at least at one time, not common. Cummings et al. cited the results of Levenson and Davidivitz's national survey of mental health professionals in which they reported that less than 30% of the 65% of the respondents who were working in managed care had any training in brief therapy, with 94% of that 30% indicating that their training had been inadequate. However, this author's experience suggests that training in brief therapy though graduate school experiences, internships, fellowships, and continuing education opportunities is probably more common than it was at the time of the Levenson and Davidivitz survey, which was presented at the 1995 APA convention. However, development of skills in brief therapeutic approaches continues to be needed by all mental health professions.

Some experts have also proposed extensions to the brief psychotherapeutic approach to mental health problems. After first pointing out the large, underserved population of people with mental health problems and the long-term costs of providing inadequate, *too short* treatment to those who do receive services, Kiesler (2000) offers the following for consideration:

> If one accepts the notion that the population of untreated patients is substantial, one quickly gets to the concept of *good enough treatment*. This concept implies that (a) the treatment is not ideal, (b) perhaps with more substantial treatment better outcomes could be obtained, but (c) with the pressures of the payer's requirements, the press of untreated cases, and the capitation level, treatment sufficient to avoid relapse and return is good enough under the circumstances. (p. 485)

Good enough treatment represents a part of Kiesler's recommendation for psychologists to become generalists, with skills that would allow them to deal with a wide range of problems. Just like any form of brief therapy, it would require training that should begin during the psychologist's graduate school training and continue through internship and continuing education experiences.

As for psychological testing and assessment, psychologists need to develop both a new attitude and a new set of skills if they are to function efficiently, effectively, and with less frustration in MBHO systems. There are several actions that psychologists can take in order to achieve these goals. First, psychologists need to accept the fact that not everyone needs to be tested, especially in an environment where a typical episode of care is only 4 to 6 sessions long and the expectation is that approach taken will be problem-oriented and focused on achieving an attainable, measurable goal. In addition, when testing is called for (e.g., for diagnostic rule-out or clarification), an extensive battery of tests is not always required. In many cases, the results from one well-selected test that is relevant to answering the referral question along with data obtained from patient and collateral interviews and chart reviews, can provide all the information necessary to answer the question that led the MBHO to authorize the testing in the first place. In addition, learning to use many of the good, validated, public-domain or low-cost instruments that are available can lower the psychologist's overhead for testing activities and thus make psychological assessment a more profitable enterprise. Finally, one can acquire the expertise that is required for nontraditional applications of psychological testing in MBHO systems. Use of testing in outcomes management programs is a prime example, given the emphasis that MBHOs now place on outcomes assessment activities.

Diversifying Practice Activities

Independent practitioners do not appear to engage in much professional activity beyond the traditional services of psychotherapy and psychological assessment. The CAPP survey (Phelps et al., 1998) revealed that on average, 76% of the professional time of nearly 8,000 independent practitioners involved these two clinical activities. Even within these traditional activities, there is room for diversification beyond standard mental health service delivery in traditional behavioral health care settings. Hersch (1995) points out opportunities that can be derived in working with various health care specialties, including primary care physicians, internists, family physicians, pediatricians, OB-GYNs, other medical specialties, and allied health professionals (e.g., dentists, physical therapists).

The areas of consultation, teaching, and research—areas in which psychologists have received training—also may provide additional opportunities for psychologists to expand their professional lives and income (Phelps et al., 1998). Hersch (1995) recommended that psychologists look at health promotion activities rather than illness-oriented activities as a means of diversification. One area in which he identified opportunities for engagement in health-oriented activities is in business and industry. Not only is there potential for engaging in activities geared to improve the health and well-being of workers but with additional education and skill development, psychologists may be able to expand their practices to include consultation to improve aspects of business and industry such as team work, productivity, and leadership development.

SUMMARY

The growth of managed care as the predominant form of general health care delivery has had an enormous impact not only on patients but practitioners, insurers, employers, and other parties that have a stake in the care and well-being of patients. Although it may manifest itself in many forms (HMOs, PPOs, IPAs, etc.), its focus remains the same: the employment of any number of strategies (e.g., case management, utilization review) to provide high quality care in the most cost-effective manner possible. Managed care has been present in one form or another since the early part of the century. It is only within the past couple of decades—when health care costs began to skyrocket—that it really came into its own and began to influence the way medical and related health care services are delivered. Only after gaining a strong foothold did managed *behavioral* health care emerge as a means by which mental health and substance abuse treatment could be delivered independent of general medical services.

Many benefits have accrued as a result of the introduction of managed behavioral health care. Aside from the documented cost savings, there has been a greater focus on the measurement of the outcomes of treatment and on the improvement of the quality of care. However, the transition from an indemnity-based system of health care to a system of managed behavioral health care has not been an easy one for behavioral health care professionals, particularly psychologists. In addition to the restrictions on length of treatment, the focus on a therapeutic approach in which most psychologists have not been trained (i.e., brief therapy) and the increased time spent on administrative tasks (e.g., requesting authorization for services for their patients), psychologists have seen dramatic restrictions imposed upon the use of psychological testing. Not only have these restrictions resulted in a substantial decrease in income but also, and more importantly, a loss of freedom to exercise professional judgment in the assessment and treatment of their patients. Needless to say, the results of surveys of psychologists' views of and attitudes toward managed care are less than positive as a consequence.

Contrary to early predictions, managed care is not a fad and it will not be going away any time soon. In fact, continued growth is expected, including greater extension into the public sector market. Masters-level professionals will provide most of the mental health and substance abuse treatment services; independent practitioners will continue to form group practices; and MBHOs will continue to merge into larger MBHOs. Many may view the continuation of managed care and these predictions with a sense of fear and foreboding. However, they should take heart in the positive aspects of the future. Patients, providers, advocacy groups, accrediting bodies, and other stakeholders in the health care delivery system will continue to influence the operation of and benefits that are managed by MBHOs. There will be a continued focus on the development of empirically based guidelines, the measurement and management of outcomes, and quality of care in general. Moreover, one can expect that behavioral health care services will once again be integrated into general health care services.

For some, psychology's future in managed behavioral health care systems may appear bleak. And indeed, the future will be bleak for those practitioners who fight to continue to practice their profession the same way it was practiced 20 or 30 years ago. Those days are gone. However, psychologists who are willing to work within the constraints of the policies and procedures of MBHOs, to develop new approaches to psychological assessment and treatment, and to diversify their practices to include nontraditional activities should find the practice professionally satisfying and rewarding. The opportunities are and will be there for those who are willing to evolve as this country's health care system evolves. It is hoped that the information in this book will facilitate that evolution.

A FINAL NOTE

Throughout this book, this author has chosen to use terminology that may appear unclear or inconsistent with terminology expressed in other parts of the book, or with terminology that the reader uses in his professional interactions. Thus, clarification of terms that might be problematic is warranted at this point.

A particularly important point of clarification that needs to be made is use of the terms *psychological testing* and *psychological assessment*. Using the distinction made by Meyer, Finn, Eyde, Kay, Kubiszyn, Moreland, Eisman, and Dies (1998), psychological *testing* can be defined as the administration of one or more psychological tests for the purpose of obtaining a score or set of scores. Psychological *assessment*, on the other hand, involves the integration of these test-derived data with data from other sources information (e.g., clinical and collateral interviews, review of medical and other historical documentation, behavioral observations) into a "cohesive and comprehensive understanding of the person being evaluated" (p. 8). In other words, psychological testing is a component of psychological assessment, and the term "psychological assessment" always implies the use of psychological testing. For this reason, the term "testing" is used in the title of and throughout this book to emphasize the usefulness of this clinical activity to MBHOs for both assessment (as defined before) and nonassessment purposes, such as screening and treatment monitoring; however, it does not preclude the incorporation of information from other sources for particular purpose being described. In fact, it is rare that test scores are used or interpreted in isolation from any other assessment data. The term "assessment" will be used to refer to that clinical activity just described, and at those times when it the term is used as part of common parlance, even though true assessment might not actually be taking place (e.g., "outcomes assessment").

The use of two other terms also might be troublesome to a few readers. Throughout the book, persons receiving behavioral health services are referred to as "patients." Some prefer to use the term "clients" or even "consumers," finding the term "patient" pejorative or otherwise negatively descriptive of those seeking mental health or substance abuse services. This author considers the term "patient" as an appropriate reference for anyone seeking health care (medical or behavioral) services. Those other commonly used terms are viewed as more offensive because they convey a sense of limited importance of the person's concerns and their treatment, relegating the person to the same category as, for example, someone seeking interior decorating services or purchasing a laptop computer.

Finally, this author has chosen to use the term "psychologist" to refer to the person who administers, scores, and/or interprets tests or conducts assessments, or provides the supervision thereof. He recognizes, however, that there are indeed some individuals from the other behavioral health care professions (e.g., psychiatrists, licensed professional counselors) who are qualified both legally and through training to conduct and oversee the testing activities described herein. The term "psychologist" is used because this book is being written primarily for psychologists and psychology graduate students, and (consequently) because psychologists are thought to represent the largest portion of those who will read this book. The term is not meant to discourage other qualified professionals from using the information that is presented.

Potential Applications
of Psychological Testing

In what ways are MBHOs most likely to find value in psychological testing? The answer to that question will vary according to the MBHO and the types of services it offers. However, this author's experience in the MBHO industry indicates that there are many ways in which psychological assessment can contribute value to the quality of services offered by the organization. Moreover, MBHOs are beginning to recognize this fact. This chapter presents a discussion of potential applications of as well as considerations and issues related to their implementation.

SCREENING

One of the most apparent ways in which psychological testing can contribute to the development of an economic and efficient behavioral health care delivery system is using it to screen potential patients for the need for behavioral health care services, and/or to determine the likelihood that the problem being screened is a particular disorder of interest. Probably the most concise, informative treatment of the topic of the use of psychological tests in screening for behavioral health care disorders is provided by Derogatis and Lynn (1999). In this work, these authors turn to the Commission on Chronic Illness (1957) to provide a good working definition of health care screening in general, that being:

> the presumptive identification of unrecognized disease or defect by the application of tests, examinations or other procedures which can be applied rapidly to sort out apparently well persons who probably have a disease from those who probably do not. (p. 45)

Derogatis and Lynn (1999) further clarify the nature and the use of screening procedures, stating that the screening process represents a relatively unrefined sieve that is designed to segregate the cohort under assessment into "positives," who presumably have the condition, and "negatives," who are ostensibly free of the disorder. Screening is not a diagnostic procedure per se. Rather, it represents a preliminary filtering operation that identifies those individuals with the highest probability of having the disorder in question for subsequent specific diagnostic evaluation. Individuals found negative by the screening process are not evaluated further. (p. 42)

The most important aspect of any screening procedure is the efficiency with which it can provide information useful to clinical decision-making. In the area of clinical psychology, the most efficient and thoroughly investigated screening procedures involve the use of psychological testing instruments. As implied by the foregoing, the power or utility of a psychological screener lies in its ability to determine, with a high level of probability, which respondent does or does not have a particular disorder or condition, or whether he is or is not a member of a group with clearly defined characteristics. In daily clinical practice, the most commonly used screeners are those designed specifically to identify some aspect of psychological functioning or disturbance or to provide a broad overview of the respondent's point-in-time mental status. Examples of problem-specific screeners include the Beck Depression Inventory-II (BDI-II; Beck, Steer, & Brown, 1996) and State–Trait Anxiety Inventory (STAI; Spielberger, 1983). Examples of screeners for more generalized psychopathology or distress include the Brief Symptom Inventory (BSI; Derogatis, 1992) and the Symptom Assessment-45 Questionnaire (SA-45; Strategic Advantage, Inc., 1998).

Research-Based Use of Psychological Screeners

The establishment of a system for screening for a particular disorder or condition involves determining what it is one wants to screen in or screen out, at what level of probability one feels comfortable at making that decision, and how many incorrect classifications one is willing to tolerate. Once one decides what he wishes to screen for, he then must turn to the instrument's classification efficiency statistics for the information necessary to determine if a given instrument is suitable for the intended purpose(s).

Classification efficiency is usually expressed in terms of the following statistics: *sensitivity* (the proportion of those individuals with the characteristic of interest who are accurately identified as such), *specificity* (the proportion of individuals not having the characteristic of interest who are accurately identified as such), *positive predictive power* (PPP, the proportion of a population identified by the instrument as having the characteristic of interest who actually do have the characteristic), *negative predictive power* (NPP, the proportion of a population identified by the instrument as not having the characteristic of interest who actually do not have the characteristic), and *overall classification rate* (the proportion of a population that is accurately classified as having or not having the characteristic of interest). These statistics provide the clinician with empirically based information that is useful in the type of decision-making requiring the selection of one of two choices. The questions answered are typically those of the "yes/no" type, such as "Is the patient depressed or not?" or "Does the patient have a psychological problem significant enough to require treatment?" The reader is referred to Baldessarini, Finkelstein, and Arana (1983) for a discussion of issues related the use of these statistics.

The cutoff score, index value, or other criterion used for classification can be adjusted to maximize either sensitivity or specificity. However, maximization of one will necessarily result in a decrease in the other, thus increasing the percentage of false positives (with maximized sensitivity) or false negatives (with maximized specificity). Stated differently, false positives will increase as specificity decreases, whereas false negatives will increase as sensitivity decreases (Elwood, 1993).

Another approach is to optimize both sensitivity and specificity, thus yielding a fairly even balance of true positives and true negatives. Although optimization might seem to be the preferable approach in all instances, there are situations in which a maximization approach is more desirable. For example, a psychiatric hospital with an inordinately high rate of inpatient suicide attempts begins to employ a screener designed to help identify patients with suicide potential, as part of its admission procedures. The hospital adjusts the classification cutting score to a level that identifies *all* suicidal patients in the screener's normative group (maximization of sensitivity). This cutting score is then applied to all patients being admitted to the hospital for the purpose of identifying those warranting a more extensive evaluation for suicide potential. This not only increases the number of true positives, but it also decreases the specificity and increases the number of false positives. However, the trade-off of identifying more suicidal patients early while having more nonsuicidal patients receiving suicide evaluations would appear worthwhile for the hospital's purposes. In other situations, maximization of specificity may be the preferred approach.

Based on the work of Koenig, Meador, Cohen, and Blazer (1988), Shah, Phongsathorn, Bielawska, and Katona (1996) offer suggestions pertinent to the selection of a cutoff scores:

> A cutoff score that maximizes sensitivity (thus minimizes false negatives) should be used for tests that screen for a disease with high morbidity, have little risk associated with screening and are inexpensive. A cutoff score that maximizes specificity should be used where screening leads to significant side-effects, has serious consequences, is expensive and is used to detect a less serious disease. Moreover, for common illnesses, the object is to exclude the illness and thus maximize sensitivity. However, for rare diseases, the specificity is more important as the disease needs to be confirmed. (p. 917)

Hsiao, Bartko, and Potter (1989) note that "a diagnostic test will not have a unique sensitivity and specificity. Instead, for each diagnostic test, the relationship between sensitivity and specificity depends on the cutoff point chosen for the test" (p. 665). The effect of employing individual classification cutoff points can be presented via the use of receiver operating characteristic (ROC) curves, a sophisticated application of these diagnostic/classification efficiency statistics. These curves result from the plotting of the resulting true positive rate (sensitivity) against the false positive rate for each classification cutoff score that might be employed with a test. This allows for a graphical representation of what may be gained and/or lost by shifting cutoff scores. The resulting area under the curve (AUC) provides an indication of how well the test performs. Development of ROC curves from available data for a test being considered for screening purposes is recommended. Excellent discussions of these curves and their utility can be found in Hsiao et al., a series of articles by Mossman and Somoza (1991a, 1991b; Somoza & Mossman 1990, 1991), as well as by Fombonne (1991), Harber (1981), Metz (1978), Richardson (1972), and numerous others.

In day-to-day clinical work, an instrument's PPP and NPP can provide information that is more useful than sensitivity and specificity. As Elwood (1993) has pointed out,

> Although sensitivity and specificity do provide important information about the overall performance of a test, their limitation in classifying individual subjects becomes evident when they are considered in terms of conditional probabilities. Sensitivity is $P (+/d)$, the probability (P) of a positive test result $(+)$ given that the subject has the target disorder (d). However, the task of the clinicians in assessing individual patients is just the opposite: determining $P (d/+)$, the probability that a patient has the disorder given that he or she obtained an abnormal test score. In the same way, specificity expresses $P (-/-d)$, the probability that a patient will have a negative test result given that he or she does not have the disorder. Here again, the task confronting the clinician is usually just the opposite: determining $P (-d/-)$, the probability that a patient has the disorder given a negative test result. (p. 410)

A note of caution is warranted when evaluating the two predictive powers of a test. Unlike sensitivity and specificity, both PPP and NPP change according to the prevalence or base rate at which the condition or characteristic of interest (i.e., that which is being screened by the test) occurs within a given setting. As Elwood (1993) reports, the lowering of base rates result in lower PPPs while increasing base rates result in higher PPPs. The opposite trend is true for NPPs. He notes that this is an important consideration because clinical tests are frequently validated using samples in which the prevalence rate is .50, or 50%. Thus, it is not surprising to see a test's PPP drop in "real-life" applications where the prevalence is lower.

Derogatis and Lynn (1999) indicate that a procedure referred to as "sequential screening" may provide at least a partial solution to the limitations or other problems that low base rates may pose for the predictive powers of an instrument. Sequential screening essentially involves the administration of *two screeners*, each of which measures the condition of interest, and *two phases of screening*. In the first phase, one screener is administered to the low base-rate population. The purpose of this is to identify those individuals without the condition, thus requiring relatively good specificity. These individuals are eliminated from involvement in the second phase, resulting in an increase in the prevalence of the condition among those who remain. This group is then administered another screener of equal or better sensitivity. With the increase prevalence of the condition in the remaining group, the false positive rate will be much lower. As Derogatis and Lynn point out,

> Sequential screening essentially zeros in on a high-risk subgroup of the population of interest by virtue of a series of consecutive sieves. These have the effect of eliminating from consideration individuals with low likelihood of having the disorder, and simultaneously raising the base rate of the condition in the remaining sample. (p. 68)

The sequential screening process is presented in Fig. 2.1.

In summary, PPP and NPP can provide information that is quite valuable to those making important clinical decisions, such as determining need for behavioral health care services, assigning diagnoses, or determining appropriate level of care. However, clinicians must be cognizant of the manner in which the predictive powers may change with the population to which the test or procedure is applied. As well, no diagnosis or other treatment decision should be made on the basis of screening results alone. Once identified, those screening positive by either of the preceding methods should be re-

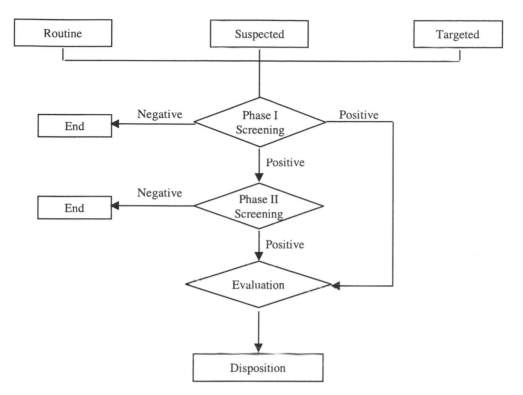

FIG. 2.1. Flow chart for a sequential screening process.

ferred for a more comprehensive evaluation and appropriate disposition. Thus, a referral system must be in place before any screening program is implemented.

Screening in Behavioral Health Care Settings

The screening process just described is one which can be generalized and be useful to just about any behavioral health care setting that provides services to patients covered by MBHOs—staff model HMOs, community mental health and counseling centers, private or group outpatient practices, inpatient or partial hospitalization facilities. Anything that would help providers quickly identify or further clarify significant behavioral health problems that have led a patient to seek treatment at a particular point in time should help reduce health care costs. Obviously, knowing which problem(s) to target as soon as possible allows the clinician to develop and implement the most appropriate, effective treatment for the patient. This can lead to a lessening of unproductive treatment sessions and thus the total number of sessions required to return to the patient to an acceptable level of functioning.

All of this seems pretty straightforward and rational, indicating that screening all patients routinely instead of only those suspected of having a particular type of disorder is always appropriate and therefore should be reimbursable. However, what clinicians and others may see as being obviously useful to the treatment of the patient and likely to result in cost savings probably will not be viewed by the MBHO as justification for automatically authorizing routine screening or screening of strongly suspected cases. A "Trust me, it works" or "Isn't it obvious?" attitude is not going to influence an MBHO's decision about whether to reimburse providers for screening of mental health or substance abuse problems. This will require a demonstration of quality of care improvement and/or cost-effectiveness. A more extensive discussion of this issue is presented in chapter 3.

Screening in Primary Care Settings

Screening of the more traditional behavioral health populations—that is, mental health and substance abuse outpatients—is important. MBHOs may find it to be less of an interest than its use with primary care populations. Here is where real opportunities lie. There are several reasons for this. The first is the high prevalence of mental health and substance abuse disorders in primary care populations. Second, the ability of primary care physicians to detect behavioral health disorders in their patients is inadequate. And when detected, treatment of the behavioral health problem is frequently inadequate. The cost implications for undetected or poorly treated behavioral health conditions can be staggering. Finally, for the past several years, there has been a strong movement toward the integration of primary and behavioral health care services. A more detailed discussion of these and related matters is presented in chapter 8 of this book as well as in Maruish (2000b).

Screening in Disease Management Programs

Beyond the primary care setting, the medical populations for which screening is useful is quite varied and may even be surprising to some. As Todd (1999) has observed, "Today, it is difficult to find any organization in the healthcare industry that isn't in some way involved in disease management. . . . This concept has quickly evolved from a marketing strategy of the pharmaceutical industry to an entrenched discipline among many managed care organizations" (p. xi). It is here that opportunities for the application of psychological screening are just beginning to be realized.

What is *disease management* or (as some prefer) *disease state management*? Gurnee and Da Silva (1999) described it as

> an integrated system of interventions, measurements, and refinements of health care delivery designed to optimize clinical and economic outcomes within a specific population. . . . [Such] a program relies on aggressive prevention of complications as well as treatment of chronic conditions. The program is created with a clear understanding of the natural course of a disease in a population and the effect of interventions at critical points to delay or prevent morbidity and mortality. (p. 12)

Further, Klinkman (1999) distinguishes disease management from "health management" in that it is "disease-centered, with clear disease-specific clinical boundaries and outcomes . . . [It] is characteristically a top-down process, in which a managed care plan or a group of advocates creates a guideline and imposes it on the system. As a result, the disease or disorder is managed in isolation. . . ." (p. S785)

The focus of these programs is on a systems approach that treats the entire disease rather than its individual components, such as is the case in the more "traditional" practice of medicine. The payoff comes in both improvement in the quality of care offered to participants in the program as well as real cost savings.

Where does psychological screening fit into these programs? At some MBHOs, for example, there is a drive to work closer with health plan customers in their disease management programs for patients facing diabetes, asthma, and recovery from cardiovascular diseases. This has resulted in a recognition on the part of the health plans of the value that MBHOs can bring to their programs, including the expertise in selecting or developing screening instruments and developing an implementation plan that can help identify medical patients with comorbid behavioral health problems. These and other medical disorders are frequently accompanied by depression and anxiety that can significantly affect the patient's quality of life, morbidity, and, in some cases, mortality. Early identification and treatment of comorbid behavioral health problems in patients with chronic medical diseases thus can dramatically impact the course of the disease and the toll it takes on the patient.

Implementation of Psychological Screening into the Daily Work Flow

The utility of a screening instrument is only as good as the degree to which it can be integrated into an organization's daily regimen of service delivery. This, in turn, depends on a number of factors. The first is the degree to which the administration and scoring of the screener is quick and easy, and the amount of time required to train the provider's staff to successfully incorporate the screener into the daily work flow.

The second factor relates to the instrument's use. Generally, screeners are developed to assist in determining the likelihood that the patient does or does not have the specific condition or characteristic the instrument is designed to identify. Use for any other validated purpose (e.g., assigning a diagnosis based solely on screener results, determining the likelihood of the presence of other characteristics) only serves to undermine the integrity of the instrument in the eyes of staff, payers, and other parties with a vested interest in the screening process.

The third factor has to do with the ability of the provider to act on the information obtained from the screener. It must be clear how the clinician should proceed based on the information available.

The final factor is staff acceptance and commitment to the screening process. This comes only with a clear understanding of the importance of the screening, the usefulness of the obtained information, and how the screening process is to be incorporated into the organization's daily work flow.

DIAGNOSIS

Key to the development of any effective plan of treatment for mental health and substance abuse patients is an accurate diagnosis of the problem(s) for which the patient is seeking intervention. As in the past, assisting in the differential diagnosis of psychiatric disorders continues to be one of the major functions of psychological assessment (Meyer et al., 1998). In fact, MBHOs are more likely to authorize reimbursement of testing for this purpose than for most other reasons. Assessment with well-validated, reliable psychological test instruments can provide information that might otherwise be difficult (if not impossible) to obtain through psychiatric or collateral interviews, medical record reviews, or other clinical means. This is generally made possible through the inclusion of (a) test items representing diagnostic criteria from an accepted diagnostic classification system, such as the fourth edition of the Diagnostic and Statistical Manual of Mental Disorders (DSM-IV; American Psychiatric Association, 1994) or (b) scales that either alone or in combination with other scales have been empirically tied (directly or indirectly) to specific diagnoses or diagnostic groups.

In most respects, considerations related to the use of psychological testing for diagnostic purposes are the same as those when considering their use for screening. In fact, information obtained from screening can be used to help determine the "correct" diagnosis for a given patient. As well, information from either source should be used only in conjunction with other clinical information to arrive at a diagnosis. The major differentiation between the two functions is that screening generally involves the use of a relatively brief instrument for the identification of patients with a specific diagnosis, a problem that falls within a specific diagnostic grouping (e.g., "affective disorders"), or a level of impairment that falls within a problematic range. Moreover, it represents the first step in a process designed to separate those who do not exhibit indications of the problem being screened for, from those with a higher probability of experiencing the target problem and who thus warrant further evaluation for its presence. Diagnostic instruments generally tend to be lengthier, differentiate among multiple disorders or broad diagnostic groups (e.g., anxiety disorders vs. affective disorders), and/or are administered further along in the evaluation process than is the case with screeners. In many cases, these instruments also allow for a formulation of description of personality functioning.

Psychological testing can provide important diagnostic information, particularly when tests designed to identify and discriminate among particular types of diagnoses are used. Examples of such tests are the Millon Clinical Multiaxial Inventory-III (MCMI-III; Millon, 1994) and the Millon Adolescent Clinical Inventory (MACI; Millon, 1993). However, with the brevity of episodes of care and the problem-focused approach to treatment that are found in MBHOs, routine use of psychological testing to answer diagnostic questions is a thing of the past. As discussed in chapter 3, exceptions are sometimes made. Some examples of reimbursable diagnostic testing MBHOs might authorize include personality testing that can help resolve a differential diagnostic question; achievement and intellectual testing to rule out a learning disability; neuropsychological testing when organic involvement is suspected or needs to be ruled out; and rating scale and continuous performance testing for ADHD or similar types of disorders.

One population for which the use of psychological testing may be viewed more positively than with others are patients with severe forms of mental illness. Bedell, Hunter, and Corrigan (1997) note that MBHOs are increasingly focusing on providing services to individuals with specific types of mental illness, such as the schizophrenic and schizoaffective disorders, bipolar and delusional depressive disorders, and pervasive developmental disorders (also see Staton, 1991). Because of this focus, Bedell et al. point to the importance of developing the skills necessary to identify these people. This includes relevant psychological testing skills. They note that "skills using standardized psychological assessments should ensure the accuracy and reliability of psychologists' categorical diagnosis" (p. 219). They particularly mention developing skills in the use of structured diagnostic interview instruments such as the Structured Clinical Interview for the DSM-IV (SCID-IV; First, Spitzer, Gibbon, & Williams, 1995).

MBHOs are not inclined to authorize psychological testing for any reason without the patient or the patient's family having first been seen by a clinician. Only when a clinician can provide adequate justification for psychological testing, based on interview and other findings, will requests for testing be considered. Obtaining authorization for using psychological testing for diagnostic (or other) purposes might be perceived by the clinician as a barrier to the treatment of his or her patients, or as an insult to their professional judgment. However, elimination of routine testing is a very appropriate cost-saving effort that is intended to eliminate unnecessary and wasteful testing practices from the past.

TREATMENT PLANNING

Treatment planning can be facilitated by the availability of results from psychological tests that are designed to aid in such tasks. However, their utility would be most valued in situations that require *quickly* obtaining important information for planning targeted, effective treatment — information that might otherwise take several sessions to obtain, thus extending the episode of care and increasing costs to the MBHO.

Problem identification through the use screening instruments is only one way in which psychological testing can facilitate the treatment of behavioral health problems. When employed by a trained clinician, psychological testing also can provide information that can greatly facilitate and enhance the planning of a specific therapeutic intervention for the individual patient. It is through the implementation of a tailored treatment plan that the patient's chances of problem resolution are maximized.

The role that psychological testing can play in planning a course of treatment for behavioral health care problems is significant. Butcher (1990) indicated that information available from instruments such as the MMPI-2 not only can assist in identifying problems and establishing communication with the patient, it also can help ensure that the plan for treatment is consistent with the patient's personality and external resources. In addition, psychological testing may reveal potential obstacles to therapy, areas of potential growth, and problems of which the patient may not be consciously aware. Moreover, both Butcher and Appelbaum (1990) viewed testing as a means of quickly obtaining a second opinion. Other benefits of the results of psychological testing identified by Appelbaum include assistance in identifying patient strengths and weaknesses, identification of the complexity of the patient's personality, and establishment of a reference point during the therapeutic episode.

The type of treatment-relevant information that can be derived from patient testing and the manner in which it is applied are quite varied. Regardless, Strupp (see Butcher, 1990) probably provided the best summary of the potential contribution of psychological testing to treatment planning, stating that "careful assessment of a patient's personality resources and liabilities is of inestimable importance. It will predictably save money and avoid misplaced therapeutic effort; it can also enhance the likelihood of favorable treatment outcomes for suitable patients" (pp. v–vi).

There are several ways in which psychological testing can assist in the planning of treatment for behavioral health care patients. The more common and evident contributions can be organized into five general categories. Probably the most common use of psychological testing in the service of treatment planning is for *problem identifica-*

tion. Often, the use of psychological testing per se is not needed to identify what problems the patient is experiencing. He either will tell the clinician directly without questioning, or he will admit his problem(s) while questioned during a clinical interview. However, this is not always the case. The value of psychological testing becomes apparent in those cases where the patient is hesitant or unable to identify the nature of his or her problems. With a motivated and engaged patient who responds openly and honestly to items on a well-validated and reliable test, the process of identifying what led the patient to seek treatment can be greatly facilitated. Note that the type of problem identification described here is different from that conducted during screening. Whereas screening is usually focused on determining the possible presence or absence of a single, specific problem, problem identification generally takes a broader view and investigates the possibility of the presence of *multiple problem areas*.

Psychological testing can often assist in the *clarification of a known problem*. Through tests designed for use with populations presenting problems similar to those of the patient, aspects of identified problems can be elucidated. Information gained from these tests can improve the patient's and clinician's understanding of the problem, and lead to the development of a better treatment plan. The three most important types of information that can be gleaned for this purpose are the severity of the problem, the complexity of the problem, and the degree to which the problem impairs the patient's ability to function in one or more life roles.

The identification and clarification of the patient's problems are of key importance in planning a course of treatment. However, the *identification of other important patient characteristics*, not specific to the identified problem, can be useful in planning treatment. These can be facilitated through the use of psychological test instruments. The vast majority of treatment plans are developed or modified with consideration to at least some of these nonpathological characteristics. The exceptions are generally found with clinicians or programs that take a "one size fits all" approach to treatment. Probably the most useful type of information not specific to the identified problem that can be gleaned from psychological testing is the identification of important patient characteristics that can serve as assets or areas of strength for the patient to draw on in working to achieve his or her therapeutic goals.

Moreland (1996), for example, pointed out how psychological testing can assist in determining if the patient deals with problems through internalizing or externalizing behaviors. He noted that all things being equal, internalizers would probably profit most from an insight-oriented approach rather than a behaviorally oriented approach. The reverse would be true for externalizers. Through their work over the years, Beutler and his colleagues (Beutler & Clarkin, 1990; Beutler, Goodrich, Fisher, & Williams, 1999; Beutler, Wakefield, & Williams, 1994; Beutler & Williams, 1995; Fisher, Beutler, & Williams, 1999) have identified several other patient characteristics that are important to matching patients and treatment approaches for maximized therapeutic effectiveness.

An important consideration in the development of a treatment plan has to do with the likely outcome of treatment. In other words, how likely is it that a given patient with a given set of problems or level of dysfunction will benefit from any of the treatment options that are available? Or in some cases, what is the probability that the patient will significantly benefit from *any* type of treatment? In many cases, psychological test results can yield an empirically based *prediction of outcomes* that can assist in answering these questions. In doing so, the most effective treatment can implemented immediately, saving time, health care benefits, and potential exacerbation of problems that might result from implementation of a less than optimal course of care.

The ability to predict outcomes varies from test to test and even within individual tests, depending on the population being tested and what one would like to predict. For example, Chambless, Renneberg, Goldstein, and Gracely (1992) were able to detect predictive differences in MCMI-II-identified (Millon, 1987) personality disorder patients seeking treatment for agoraphobia and panic attacks. Patients classified as having an MCMI-II avoidant disorder were more likely to have poorer outcomes on measures of depression, avoidance, and social phobia than those identified as having dependent or histrionic personality disorders. Also, paranoid personality disorder patients were likely to drop out before receiving 10 sessions of treatment. In another study, Chisholm, Crowther, and Ben-Porath (1997) did not find any of the seven MMPI-2 scales they investigated to be particularly good predictors of early termination in a sample of university clinic outpatients. However, they did find that the Depression (DEP) and Anxiety (ANX) content scales were predictive of other treatment outcomes. Both were shown to be positively associated with therapist-rated improvement in current functioning and global psychopathology, with ANX scores also being related to therapist-rated progress toward therapy goals.

Similar to Chisholm et al., Clark (1996) did not find the MMPI-2 Negative Treatment Indicators (TRT) content scale, or its two subscales (TRT1 and TRT2) to be good indicators of premature termination in a group of male chronic pain inpatients. However, high scores on TRT or TRT1 (reflecting apathy and perceived inability to change, respectively) were found to be predictive of greater improvement in BDI scores and less improvement in physical capacities. Higher TRT scores were also predictive of greater STAI scores and lower physical capacities posttreatment. In another group of chronic pain patients, Vendrig, Derksen, and de Mey (1999) found that several selected MMPI-2 anxiety, depression, and somatic discomfort scales and subscales to be predictive of subjectively experienced pain and self-reported disability. At the same time, they were not found to be predictive of physical outcome, nor of categorical outcomes (return to full-time work, no use of pain medication, no medical treatment during a 6-month follow-up period). The reader is referred to Meyer et al. (1998) for an excellent overview of the research supporting the use of objective and projective test results for outcomes prediction as well as for other clinical decision-making purposes.

Finally, information obtained from repeated testing during the treatment process can help the clinician to *monitor treatment progress along the path of expected improvement*. This can help the clinician determine if the treatment plan is appropriate for the patient at a given point in time. If not, adjustments can be made. Treatment monitoring as a major application is discussed later in this chapter.

These foregoing points are consistent with how Butcher (1997) feels psychological testing can help control factors that may interfere or limit the progress a patient might achieve from psychological therapy. Also related to some of these points is the compelling evidence presented by Ben-Porath (1997) supporting the advantages and benefits of psychological testing over nonstandardized clinical interviews for treatment planning in MBHOs. He concluded that test data are more valid and reliable, and lend themselves to automated interpretation. These data also provide objective and accurate information that can be used to monitor patient progress during treatment. Moreover, they can later be used to determine the effectiveness of both providers and different modalities or approaches to treatment.

PSYCHOLOGICAL ASSESSMENT AS A TREATMENT INTERVENTION

Psychological testing has been found useful as a therapeutic adjunct and thus can have benefit in this regard to the MBHO. Probably the best known work in this area is that which has been published by Steve Finn, Mary Tonsager, and their associates involving the use of the MMPI-2. Essentially, in what is referred to as *therapeutic assessment,* the patient becomes a partner in the assessment process, which consequently results in therapeutic and other benefits beyond meeting the American Psychological Association's ethical principles (1992) for providing feedback. It seems that this process would be most beneficial, and might be more easily authorized with patients presenting with rather nebulous problems, where benefits are limited and a comprehensive assessment is warranted.

The use of psychological assessment as an adjunct to or means of therapeutic intervention in and of itself has received more than passing attention during the past several years (e.g., Butcher, 1990; Clair & Prendergast, 1994; Fischer, 1970). Therapeutic assessment with the MMPI-2 has received particular attention primarily through the work of Finn and his associates (Finn, 1996a, 1996b; Finn & Martin, 1997; Finn & Tonsager, 1992). Finn's approach appears to be applicable with instruments or batteries of instruments that provide multidimensional information relevant to the concerns of patients seeking answers to questions related to their mental health status. The approach espoused by Finn thus is presented here as a model for deriving direct therapeutic benefits from the psychological assessment experience.

What Is Therapeutic Assessment?

In discussing the use of the MMPI-2 as a therapeutic intervention, Finn (1996b) describes an assessment procedure whose goal is to "gather accurate information about clients . . . and then use this information to help clients understand themselves and make positive changes in their lives" (p. 3). Elaborating on this procedure and extending it to the use of any test, Finn and Martin (1997) describe therapeutic assessment as

> . . . collaborative, interpersonal, focused, time limited, and flexible. It is . . . very interactive and requires the greatest of clinical skills in a challenging role for the clinician. It is unsurpassed in a respectfulness for clients: collaborating with them to address *their* concerns (around which the work revolves), acknowledging them as experts on themselves and recognizing their contributions as essential, and providing to them usable answers to their questions in a therapeutic manner. . . .
>
> The ultimate goal of therapeutic assessment is to provide an experience for the client that will allow him/her to take steps toward greater psychological health and a more fulfilling life. This is done by (a) recognizing the client's characteristic ways of being, (b) understanding in a meaningful, idiographic way the problems the client faces, (c) providing a safe environment for the client to explore change, and (d) providing the opportunity for the client to experience new ways of being in a supportive environment. (p. 134)

Simply stated, therapeutic assessment may be considered an approach to the assessment of mental health patients in which the patient is not only the primary provider of information needed to answer questions, but also is actively involved in formulating the questions that are to be answered by the assessment. Feedback regarding the results of the assessment is provided to the patient and is considered a primary, if not *the* primary element to the assessment process. Thus, the patient becomes a partner in the assessment process; as a result, therapeutic and other benefits accrue. More specifically, Finn and Tonsager (1997) believe this approach is therapeutic because it addresses the patient's motives for *self-verification* (confirmation that others share their view of themselves and their world), *self-enhancement* (wish to be loved, praised and thought well of by themselves and others), and *self-efficacy/self-discovery* (need for mastery, control, and exploration).

The Therapeutic Assessment Process

Finn (1996b) has outlined a three-step procedure for therapeutic assessment using the MMPI-2. As indicated before, it should work equally well with other multidimensional instruments or test batteries that one might select. Finn describes this procedure as one to be used in those situations in which the patient is seen *only* for assessment (i.e., not to be treated later by the assessing clinician). From this author's standpoint, the procedures are equally applicable for use by clinicians who assess patients whom they later treat. With these points in mind, Finn's three-step procedure is summarized next.

Step 1: The Initial Interview. According to Finn (1996b), the initial interview with the patient serves multiple purposes. It provides an opportunity to build rapport, or to increase rapport if a patient–therapist relationship already exists. The assessment task is presented as a collaborative one, and the patient is given the opportunity to identify questions that he or she would like answered using the assessment data. Background information related to the patient-identified questions is subsequently gathered. Any reservations about participating in the therapeutic assessment process (e.g., confidentiality, past negative experiences with assessment) are dealt with in order to facilitate maximum involvement in the process.

After responding to the patient's concerns, Finn (1996b) recommends that the clinician restate the questions posed earlier by the patient. This ensures the accuracy of what the patient would like to have addressed by the assessment. The patient also is encouraged to ask questions of the clinician, thus reinforcing the collaborative context or atmosphere that the clinician is trying to establish. Step 1 is completed as the instrumentation and its administration, as well as the responsibilities and expectations of each party, are clearly defined and the particulars of the process (e.g., date and time of assessment, date and time of the feedback session, clinician fees) are discussed and agreed on.

Step 2: Preparing for the Feedback Session. On completion of the administration and scoring of the instrumentation used during the assessment, the clinician first outlines all results obtained from the assessment, including those not directly related to the patient's previously stated questions. Finn (1996b) presents a well-organized outline for the types of information that the trained user can extract from MMPI-2 data. Unfortunately, clinicians who do not or cannot use the MMPI-2 or other well-researched, multidimensional instruments or batteries will not have the same amount or type of data available to them. (This should not preclude them from identifying the types of valid and useful information that can derived from the instruments and organizing it into a usable form for presentation to the patient.)

As a final point in this step, Finn (1996b) indicates that the clinician must determine what is the best way to present the information to the patient so that he can accept and integrate it while maintaining his sense of identity and self-esteem. This also is a time when the clinician can identify information that he or she may not wish to reveal to the patient because it is not important to answering the patient's questions, and doing so may negatively affect the collaborative relationship. In addition, the clinician may want to prepare for presenting those aspects of feedback that he feels will be most problematic for him (i.e., the clinician) by role-playing with a colleague.

Step 3: The Feedback Session.   As Finn (1996b) states: "The overriding goal of feedback sessions is to have a therapeutic interaction with clients" (p. 44). Thus, the initial tasks of the feedback session are focused on setting the stage for this type of encounter. This is accomplished by allaying any anxiety the patient may have about the session, reaffirming the collaborative relationship, and familiarizing him with the presentation of the test results (e.g., explaining the profile sheet on which the results are graphed, discussing the normative group to which he or she will be compared, providing an explanation of standard scores).

When the session preparation is completed, the clinician begins providing feedback to the patient (Finn, 1996b). This is centered on answering the questions posed by the patient in during Step 1. Beginning with a positive finding from the assessment, the clinician proceeds first to address those questions that the patient is most likely to accept. He then carefully moves to the findings that are more likely to be anxiety-arousing for the patient and/or challenge his self-concept. A key element to this step is to have the patient verify the accuracy of each finding and provide a real-life example of the interpretation that is offered. Alternately, the clinician asks the patient to modify the interpretation to make it more in line with how he sees himself and his situation.

Finn (1996b) recommends that the session end by responding to any additional questions the patient may have; having the patient confirm that he has accurately understood the information that was presented; giving permission for the patient to contact the clinician should further questions arise; and (in the assessment-only arrangement) termination of the relationship. Throughout the session, the clinician maintains a supportive stance with regard to any affective reactions to the findings.

Additional Steps.   Finn and Martin (1997) indicate two additional steps that may be added to the therapeutic assessment process. The purpose of the first additional step, referred to as an *assessment intervention session*, essentially is to clarify initial test findings through the administration of additional instruments. The other step discussed by Finn and Martin (1997) is the provision of a *written report of the findings* to the patient. In addition to summarizing both the test results and the answers to the patient's questions, it also attempts to elicit feedback and reactions from the patient about the assessment.

Empirical Support for Therapeutic Assessment.   Noting the lack of direct empirical support for the therapeutic effects of sharing test results with patients, Finn and Tonsager (1992) investigated the benefits of providing feedback to university counseling center clients regarding their MMPI-2 results. Their experimental group consisted of 32 subjects who underwent therapeutic assessment and feedback procedures similar to those just described while on the counseling center's waiting list. Another 28 subjects were recruited from the same waiting list to serve as a control group. There were no significant differences between the two groups on any important demographic or examiner–contact interval variables.

Instead of receiving feedback, Finn and Tonsager's (1992) control group received nontherapeutic attention from the examiner. However, they were administered the same dependent measures as the experimental group at the same time as the experimental group received feedback. They also were administered the same dependent measures as the experimental group 2 weeks later (i.e., 2 weeks after the experimental group received the feedback) to determine if there were differences between the two groups on those dependent measures. These measures included a self-esteem questionnaire, a symptom checklist (i.e., the SCL-90-R), a measure of private and public self-consciousness, and a questionnaire assessing the subjects' subjective impressions of the feedback session.

The results of Finn and Tonsager's (1992) study indicated that compared to the control group, the experimental group demonstrated significantly less distress at the 2-week postfeedback follow-up, and significantly higher levels of self-esteem and hope at both the time of feedback and the 2-week postfeedback follow-up. In other findings, feelings about the feedback sessions were positively and significantly correlated with changes in self-esteem from testing to feedback, both from feedback to follow-up and from testing to follow-up among those who were administered the MMPI-2. In addition, change in level of distress from feedback to follow-up correlated significantly with private self-consciousness (i.e., the tendency to focus on the internal aspects of oneself) but not with public self-consciousness.

Newman and Greenway (1997) provided support for Finn and Tonsager's findings in their study of 60 Australian college students. Clients given MMPI-2 feedback reported an increase in self-esteem and a decrease in psychological distress that could not be accounted for by the completion of the MMPI-2. At the same time, changes in either of these two variables were found to be unrelated to both their attutudes toward mental health professionals and level or type of symptomatology. Unlike Finn and Tonsager, general satisfaction scores were not associated with change in self-esteem nor change in symptomatology, nor was private self-consciousness found to be related to changes in symptomatology. Recognizing the limitations of their study, Newman and Greenway's recommendations for future research in this area included examination of the components of therapeutic assessment separately, and the use of different patient populations and means of assessing therapeutic change (i.e., use of both patient and therapist/third party report).

Feedback Consultation

A lesser known approach to providing feedback to patients regarding assessment results is what Quirk, Strosahl, Kreilkamp, and Erdberg (1995) refer to as *feedback consultation*. It is viewed as a means to facilitate closure of a case and improve outcomes, and is described as being "particularly useful . . . when a shared understanding between the therapist and the patient has been difficult to acquire or when the initial evaluation indicates that clinical or cost outcomes could be enhanced with this addition" (p. 28). In this approach, the "examining psychologist" is typically someone other than the individual treating the patient. Also, the consultation is provided both to the therapist and the patient.

There are three basic elements to feedback consultation (Quirk et al., 1995). *Paradigm thinking* refers to the "each personality assessment measure possessing an underlying schema that can enrich our understanding of the client and that correspondingly influences the client's perceptions" (p. 28). *Data sampling* refers to the vast amount of data that assessment can provide to assist in the therapeutic process. The last element is the patient's *active participation*, which is thought to bring the benefits of both paradigm thinking and data sampling to the process of psychotherapy. The patient's participation may also help him to accept the findings of the assessment. The reader is referred to Quirk et al., as well as Erdberg (1979) and Fischer (1985) for more detailed information about feedback consultation.

TREATMENT MONITORING

Monitoring how treatment is progressing with psychological test instruments can provide value to MBHOs, especially with those patients who are seen over relatively long periods of time. If the treatment has not resulted in the expected effects, changes in the treatment plan can be formulated and deployed. These adjustments may reflect the need for (a) more intensive or aggressive treatment (e.g., increased number of psychotherapeutic sessions each week, addition of a medication adjunct), (b) less intensive treatment (e.g., reduction or discontinuation of medication, transfer from inpatient to outpatient care), or (c) a different therapeutic approach (e.g., changing from analytic therapy to cognitive-behavioral therapy). Regardless, any modifications require later reassessment of the patient to determine if the treatment revisions have impacted patient progress in the expected direction. This process may be repeated any number of times. These "in-treatment" reassessments also can provide information relevant to the decision of when to terminate treatment.

General Process

Figure 2.2 presents as a general process for treatment monitoring. In this particular paradigm, the screening process may serve as the source of the baseline data against which data obtained at other points in treatment can be compared. This assumes, of course, that the screening measure is what one wants to use to monitor treatment progress.

Once baseline data is obtained, those organizations with the necessary resources in place can generate an expected recovery curve for the patient. This curve will enable the clinician to determine if the patient is on the expected track for recovery through the episode of care. Deviations noted on remeasurement should lead the clinician to consider modifying his treatment strategy (see "Monitoring Treatment" later).

How Often to Measure

The goal of monitoring is to determine whether treatment is "on track" with expected progress at a given point in time. When and how often one might test the patient is dependent on a number of factors. The first is the expected length of treatment. Implementing a monitoring protocol with patients who are only seen for four or five

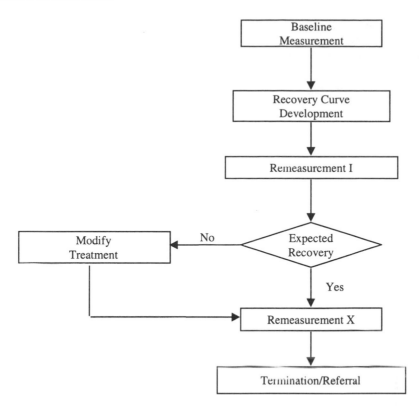

FIG. 2.2.   Flow chart for a treatment monitoring process.

sessions is not cost-effective and probably will not contribute any tremendously useful information. With patients who are likely to be seen for several sessions — for example, eight or more — implementing a plan for regular, scheduled retesting during the episode of care can provide the clinician with information about whether the patient is adequately progressing toward recovery, given clinical expectations.

The second is the instrumentation. Many instruments are designed to assess the patient's status at the time of testing. Items on these measures are generally worded in the present tense (e.g., "I feel tense and nervous," "I feel that my family loves and cares about me"). Changes from one day to the next on the construct(s) measured by these instruments should be reflected in the test results. Other instruments, however, ask the patient to indicate if a variable of interest has been present, or how much or to what extent it has occurred during a specific time period in the past. The items usually are asked in the context of something like "During the past month, how often have you . . ." or "During the past week, to what extent has. . . ." Readministration of these interval-of-time-specific measures or subsets of items within them should be undertaken only after a period of time that is equivalent to or longer than the time interval to be considered in responding to the items. For example, an instrument that asks the patient to consider the extent to which certain symptoms have been problematic *during the past 7 days* should not be re-administered for at least 7 days. The responses from a readministration that occurs less than 7 days after the first administration would include the patient's consideration of his or her status during the previously considered time period. This may make interpretation of the change of symptom status (if any) from the first to the second administration difficult, if not impossible.

The third consideration is the frequency at which the clinician finds monitoring activities useful. This can be dependent on any number of factors, such as expectations for improvement based on clinical judgment, perceived impact of a critical event (e.g., death of a spouse, loss of employment) on the patient's recovery, past experience with monitoring similar patients, and the patient's reactions to repeated measurement of their psychological status. Because of the subjective nature of these variables, determination of the desired frequency of patient monitoring for any given patient is likely to vary from one clinician to another.

Finally, there are financial considerations. What will be the cost of retesting any given patient? And how many retestings is the MBHO willing to reimburse (or is the clinician willing to foot the bill) for any given patient? This may be more important to consider than the other three factors when determining how often to retest a patient, because multiple retestings can be quite time-consuming and expensive. They can also can significantly impact the patient's available benefits.

Howard's Phase Model of Psychotherapy: Implications for Treatment Monitoring

Beyond generic monitoring models that are not tied to any particular therapeutic orientation, one might also consider a potential model that can be tied to Howard and his colleagues' *phase model of psychotherapy* (Howard, Lueger, Maling, & Martinovich, 1993; Howard, Moras, Brill, Martinovich, & Lutz, 1996). The phase model proposes a standard patient progression through distinct phases of psychotherapy. These phases occur in a consistent sequence. The successful accomplishment of one phase permits the patient to move to the next phase and, consequently, efficiently and effectively through the entire therapeutic process.

The first phase identified by Howard et al. (1993, 1996) is *remoralization*. As the patient begins treatment, he is demoralized, seeing himself as a failure in terms of meeting his or others' expectations of him, unable to cope with problems, stuck in a situation that he feels incapable of changing. The therapist's establishing a sense of trust with the patient, helping him or her identify their problem, instilling a sense of hope, and thus increasing his sense of well-being are key at this phase of treatment. This is usually accomplished within the first few sessions.

The second phase of psychotherapy is *remediation* (Howard et al. 1993, 1996). With a renewed sense of confidence in his ability to cope, therapy can begin to focus the patient on overcoming the symptoms that led to his sense of demoralization. This is a much longer progress. Kopta, Howard, Lowry, and Beutler (1994), using the SCL-90-R results of 685 adult outpatients, demonstrated that the length of time needed for clinically significant symptomatic recovery can vary greatly, depending on the type of symptoms the patient is experiencing. They found that 50% of their sample recovered after 11 weekly treatment session whereas 58 weekly sessions were needed for 75% of the sample to recover.

Feeling better about himself and his capabilities, and with his symptomatology improving, the patient can move into the last stage of therapy, the *rehabilitation* phase (Howard et al. 1993, 1996). Here, the focus is on improving those aspects of the patient's functioning that are impaired. These may be related to functioning within the family or social groups, on the job or at school, or in some other life role. Progress in this phase will come at a much slower pace than during the remediation phase and will vary according to the type and severity of problematic area of functioning. What are the implications of this model? As Howard et al. (1993) point out,

> From a psychotherapy practice standpoint, the phase model suggests that different change process (and thus certain classes of interventions) will be appropriate for different phases of therapy and that certain tasks may have to be accomplished before others are undertaken. It also suggests that different therapeutic processes may characterize each phase. Therapeutic interventions are likely to be most effective when they focus on changing phase-specific problems when those problems are most accessible to change. (p. 684)

Further, Howard et al. (1996) assert that: "To the extent that these three phases are distinct, they imply different treatment goals and, thus, the selection and assessment of different outcome variables to measure progress in each phase" (p. 1061).

An additional implication of this model of psychotherapy and therapeutic change is that phase-relevant, objective test data can be used to support decisions regarding the focus of therapeutic endeavors throughout the course of treatment. Treatment monitoring can be directed toward measuring the psychological domain that is or should be most likely to change during any of the three phases of psychotherapy. Monitoring the patient's feeling of well-being during the first phase—using assessment instruments developed for this purpose—can provide the type of information needed to decide whether the patient needs to continue working on "remoralizing" himself and preparing to work toward the goal of the second phase of treatment, symptom "remediation." Similarly, monitoring the patient's symptomatology and/or general level of distress during the second phase—using a symptom scale or other measure of psychological disturbance—can help determine when the patient is optimally prepared for the therapeutic work of the third phase, that is, "rehabilitation" of problematic areas of life functioning. During this phase, ongoing assessment of functioning can provide information necessary for determining the appropriateness and need for continued treatment.

Monitoring Change

Methods for determining if statistically and clinically significant change has occurred from one point in time to another have been developed and can be used for treatment monitoring. Many of these methods are the same as those that can be used for outcomes assessment and are discussed in chapter 6. In addition, the reader is also referred to an excellent discussion of analyzing individual and group change data in Newman and Dakof (1999) and Newman and Tejeda (1999). However, another approach to monitoring therapeutic change can prove to be more valuable than looking at simple changes in test scores from one point in time to another.

Patient profiling is yet another contribution stemming from the work of Howard and his colleagues. It is the product of two of their theories: the phase model of psychotherapy (described before) and *dosage model of psychotherapeutic effectiveness* (Howard, Kopta, Krause, & Orlinsky, 1986). The dosage model theorizes "a lawful linear relationship between the log of the number of sessions and the normalized probability of patient improvement" (Howard et. al., 1996, p. 1060). Howard and his colleagues thought that a log-normal model fit because the target of improvement changes during the course of treatment. In fact, this line of thinking led to the their conceptualization of the phase model of psychotherapy. Using session-by-session data rather than mathematical extrapolations of pre- and posttreatment data, Kadera, Lambert and Andrews (1996) derived dose-effect curves that were more conservative that those generated Howard et al. Those readers considering the use of dose-effect curves or patient profiling are encouraged to also take note of the Kadera et al. findings.

Patient profiling essentially involves the generation of an expected curve of recovery over the course of psychotherapy along any measurable construct dimension that the clinician or investigator may choose (Howard et al., 1996; Leon, Kopta, Howard, & Lutz, 1999). Individual profiles are generated from selected patient clinical characteristics (e.g., severity and chronicity of the problem, attitudes toward treatment, scores on treatment-relevant measures) present at the time of treatment onset. Simply put, the measure of the construct of interest is modeled as a log-linear function of the session number, based on data from a large sample of therapy patients on the same clinical characteristics. Howard et. al. (1996) used scores from the Mental Health Index (MHI; Howard, Brill, Lueger, O'Mahoney, & Grissom, 1993; Sperry, Brill, Howard, & Grissom, 1996), a composite of scores from three instruments measuring well-being, symptomatology, and life functioning, to demonstrate the generation and tracking of individual patient profiles. (The MHI was developed to reflect the important dimensions of the Howard's phase theory and thus provides an excellent measure for profiling purposes. However, one could choose to profile the patient only on a single domain, such as symptomatology, or other global constructs using other appropriate instrumentation.) Hierarchical linear modeling is used to predict the course of improvement during treatment. Multiple administrations of the measure during the course of treatment allow a comparison of the patient's actual score with that expected from similar individuals after the same number of treatment sessions. The therapist thus knows when the treatment is working and when it is not working so that necessary adjustments in the treatment strategy can be made.

The Effects of Providing Feedback to the Therapist

Intuitively, one would expect that having the type of information that Howard and his colleagues demonstrated would result in positive outcomes for the patient. But is this really the case? Lambert, Whipple, Smart, Vermeesch, Nielsen, and Hawkins (2001) sought to answer this question by conducting a study that they hoped would show that patients whose therapists receive feedback about their progress would have better outcomes and better treatment attendance (an indicator of cost-effective psychotherapy) than those patients whose therapists did not receive this same type of feedback.

Approximately half of the 609 patient participants in the Lambert et al. (2001) study were assigned to the feedback (experimental) group while the other half comprised the no-feedback (control) group. The feedback provided to the experimental group's therapists came in the form of a weekly updated numerical and color-coded chart based on the baseline and current total scores of the Outcome Questionnaire (OQ-45; Lambert, Hansen, Umphress, Lunnen, Okiishi, Burlingame, Huefner, & Reisinger, 1996) and the number of sessions that the patient had completed. The feedback report also contained one of four possible color-related interpretations of the patient's progress: (a) functioning in the normal range, consider termination; (b) adequate change being made, no treatment plan changes recommended; (c) rate of change inadequate, consider altering treatment plan, patient may achieve no significant benefit from treatment; or (d) not making expected level of progress, may have negative outcome or drop out of treatment, consider revised or new treatment plan, re-assess readiness for change. Predictions of patients leaving treatment early or being at risk for a negative treatment outcome were based on algorithms developed by Lambert (1998).

The findings from this study were mixed. Although the outcome (i.e., post-treatment OQ-45 scores) for those cases that were predicted to not benefit from or to drop out therapy ("signal cases") was better for those whose therapists received feedback, the difference was not significant. However, two other findings are noteworthy. First, the percent of signal cases with feedback who demonstrated statistically or clinically significant change (Jacobson & Truax, 1991) was twice that of signal cases for whom no feedback was provided (26% vs. 13%). Surprisingly, the deterioration rates for the two signal groups were approximately the same. Moreover, signal cases with feedback received significantly more sessions than their nonfeedback signal counterparts, whereas nonsignal patients with feedback received significantly fewer sessions than nonsignal, no-feedback subsample. Lambert et al. (2001) felt that the results did not support the routine use of their predictive algorithms. Possibly this was due to the fact that therapists did not systematically seek consultation for signal cases when the feedback report recommended it. Also, there apparently was no way of determining whether the report led to changes in type or intensity of treatment provided by the therapist. They did see the session attendance findings as being appropriate. When feedback on patient progress was positive, patients were seen for fewer sessions; when it was negative, patients were seen for more sessions.

The Lambert et al. (2001) study lends partial support for benefits accruing from the use of assessment-based feedback to therapists. It also suggests that information provided in a feedback report alone is not sufficient to maximize its impact on the quality of care provided to a patient. The results would suggest that the information must be put to use. The use of feedback to therapists appears to be beneficial, but further research in this area is called for.

Notwithstanding whether it is used as fodder for generating complex statistical predictions or for simple point-in-time comparisons, psychological test data obtained for treatment monitoring can provide an empirically based means of determining the effectiveness of mental health and substance abuse treatment during an episode of care. Its value lies in its ability to support ongoing treatment decisions that must be made using objective data. Consequently, it allows for improved patient care while supporting efforts to demonstrate accountability to the patient and interested third parties.

SUPPORT FOR TREATMENT AUTHORIZATION REQUESTS

Aside from its obvious treatment value, treatment monitoring data can support MBHO care management decisions regarding requests for authorization for additional treatment. This holds true whether the data is nothing more than a set of scores from a relevant measure (e.g., a symptom inventory) administered at various points during treatment, or they are actual and expected recovery curves obtained by

Howard et al.'s (1986) patient profiling method. Expected and actual data obtained from patient profiling can easily point to the likelihood that additional sessions are needed or would be significantly beneficial for the patient. Combined with clinician impressions, these data can make a powerful case for the patient's need for additional treatment sessions or to terminate treatment.

As well as the need for supporting additional sessions for patients already in treatment, there are indications that patient profiling may also be useful in making initial authorization decisions. (This assumes that the MBHO routinely tests all patients at the beginning of treatment.) Leon, Kopta, Howard, and Lutz (1999) sought to determine whether patients whose actual response curve matched or exceeded (i.e., performed better) the expectancy curve could be differentiated from those whose actual curve failed to match their expectancy curve, could be identified on the basis of pretreatment clinical characteristics. They first generated patient profiles for 821 active outpatients and found a correlation of .57 ($p < .001$) between the actual and expected slopes. They then used half of the original sample to develop a discriminate function that was able to significantly discriminate ($p < .001$) patients whose recovery was predictable (i.e., those with consistent actual and expected curves) from those whose recovery was not predictable (i.e., those with inconsistent curves). The discriminant function was based on 15 pretreatment clinical characteristics (including MHI subscales and items) and was cross-validated with the other half of the original sample. In both subsamples, lower levels of symptomatology and higher levels of functioning were associated with those in the predictable group of patients.

The implications of these findings are quite powerful. According to Leon et al. (1999),

> The patient profiling-discriminant approach provides promise for moving toward the reliable identification of patients who will respond more rapidly in psychotherapy, who will respond more slowly in psychotherapy, or who will demonstrate a low likelihood of benefiting from this type of treatment.
>
> The implications of these possibilities for managed mental health care are compelling. . . . [A] reliable prediction system—even for a proportion of patients—would improve efficiency, thereby reducing costs in the allocation and use of resources for mental health care. For instance, patients who would be likely to drain individual psychotherapeutic resources while achieving little or no benefit could be identified at intake and moved into more promising therapeutic endeavors (e.g., medication or group psychotherapy). Others, who are expected to succeed but are struggling could have their treatment reviewed and then modified in order to get them back on track. . . . Patients who need longer term treatment could justifiably get it because the need would be validated by a reliable, empirical methodology. (p. 703)

OUTCOMES ASSESSMENT

The 1990s have witnessed accelerating growth in the level of interest and development of behavioral health care outcomes programs. Cagney and Woods (1994) attribute this to four major factors. First, behavioral health care purchasers are asking for information regarding the value of the services they buy. Second, there is an increasing number of purchasers who are requiring a demonstration of patient improvement and satisfaction. Third, MBHOs need data that demonstrate that their providers render efficient and effective services. And fourth, outcomes information will be needed for the "quality report cards" that MBHOs anticipate they will be required to provide in the future. In short, fueled by soaring health care costs, there has been an increasing need for providers to demonstrate that what they do is effective. And all of this has occurred within the context of the CQI movement, in which there has been similar trends in the level of interest and growth. Consequently, probably one of the most important applications of psychological assessment in MBHOs today is that for the assessment of treatment outcomes.

What Are Outcomes?

"Outcomes" is a term that refers to the results of the specific treatment that was rendered to a patient or group of patients. Along with structure and process, outcomes is one component of what Donabedian (1980, 1982, 1985) refers to as "quality of care." Taking a much broader perspective, outcomes holds a different meaning for each of the different parties who has a stake in behavioral health care delivery; what is measured generally depends on the purpose(s) for which outcomes assessment is undertaken. As is shown here, these vary greatly. As Migdail, Youngs, & Bengen-Seltzer (1995) have observed:

> Outcomes measures are being redefined from a vague "Is the patient doing better?" to more specific questions, such as, "Does treatment work in ways that are measurably valuable to the patient in terms of daily functioning level and satisfaction, to the payer in terms of value for each dollar spent, to the managed care organization charged with administering the purchaser's dollars, and to the clinician charged with demonstrating value for hours spent?" (p. 1)

This is discussed in more detail in chapter 6.

Outcomes Assessment: Measurement, Monitoring, and Management

Just as it is important to be clear about what is meant by outcomes, it is equally important to clarify the three general purposes for which outcomes assessment may be employed. The first is outcomes *measurement*. This involves nothing more than pre- and posttreatment measurement of one or more variables to determine the amount of change that has occurred (if any) in these variables as a result of therapeutic intervention.

A more useful approach is that of outcomes *monitoring*. This refers to "the use of periodic assessment of treatment outcomes to permit inferences about what has produced change" (Dorwart, 1996, p. 46). Like treatment monitoring, outcomes monitoring involves the tracking of changes in the status of one or more outcomes variables at multiple points in time. Assuming a baseline measurement at the beginning of treatment, remeasurement may occur one or more times during the course of treatment (e.g., weekly, monthly), at the time of termination, and/or during one or more periods of posttermination follow-up. Whereas treatment progress monitoring is used to determine deviation from the expected course of improvement, outcomes monitoring focuses on revealing aspects about the therapeutic process that seem to affect change.

The third, and most useful purpose of outcomes assessment, is that of outcomes *management*. Dorwart (1996) defines outcomes management as "the use of monitoring information in the management of patients to improve both the clinical and administrative processes for delivering care" (pp. 46–47). Whereas Dorwart appears to view outcomes management as relevant to the individual patient, this author views it as a means to improve the quality of services offered to the *patient population(s)* served by the provider, not to any one patient. This population-based perspective is one that is consistent with meeting the cost-containment demands in the era of managed care (Schreter, 1997). Information gained through the assessment of patients can provide the organization with indications of what works best, with whom, and under what set of circumstances, thus helping to improve the quality of services for all patients. In essence, outcomes management can serve as a tool for those organizations with an interest in implementing a CQI initiative (see next).

General Process

In the outcomes assessment process, a baseline measurement is taken (see Fig. 2.3). In some cases, this may be followed by the treatment monitoring process discussed earlier. Frequently, the patient is assessed at the termination of treatment, although this may not always be the case. Posttreatment follow-up measurement may occur, with or without measurement at the termination of treatment. This may involve more than one remeasurement at various points in time. Commonly used intervals include 3 months, 6 months, and 12 months posttermination.

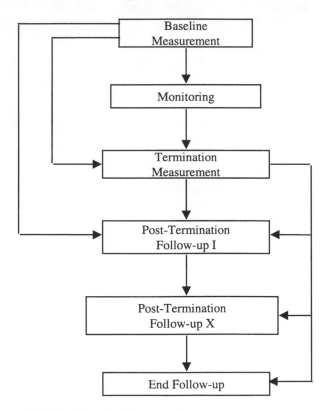

FIG. 2.3.   Flow chart for an outcomes assessment process.

The interesting thing about outcomes measurement like this is that it does not really impact the outcomes of the the patient who provides the data. The results from those participating in follow-up remeasurement are usually combined with those of other individuals for group data analysis. The information that is gleaned from this analysis gives the psychologist or organization a sense of what has worked with whom. This information can be used to guide treatment practices with other patients in the future. Outcomes assessment provides a learning experience for the psychologist or organization, not the patient providing the data.

The requirements for producing and using outcomes data that are imposed on MBHOs by internal forces (e.g., CQI committees) and/or external forces (e.g., accrediting and regulatory bodies) make this an area in which psychologists and others trained in measurement can contribute and add real value to the organization. Chapters 6 and 7 are devoted to the topic of outcomes assessment, so it will not be discussed in any further detail at this point. For now, suffice it to say that tremendous opportunities and financial reward may await those who can develop and implement a practical, useful outcomes system for use in an MBHO.

The demand to demonstrate the outcomes of treatment is pervasive throughout the health care industry. Regulatory and accreditation bodies are requiring that providers and provider organizations show that their services are having a positive impact on the people they treat. Beyond that, the behavioral health care provider also needs to know whether what he does works. Outcomes information derived from psychological testing of individual patients allows the provider to know the extent to which he has helped each patient. At the same time, in aggregate, this information can offer insight about what works best for whom under what circumstances, thus facilitating the treatment of future patients.

RISK MANAGEMENT

Psychological testing can assist in managing risks that certain types of patients may pose to MBHOs. This might include using test results to help identify those who may be a threat to themselves or others; those who are more likely to be high utilizers of psychiatric or medical services over time; those who are likely to be litigious or complain about the quality of service they receive; or those who may be problematic in other ways. Early identification of patients who are likely to become problematic later on can allow the MBHO to begin early on focused interventions that reduce the likelihood of the appearance of these behaviors.

In general, the use of psychological assessment for risk management purposes is an extension of several of the previous described applications of psychological assessment. For example, screening using any of several commonly used depression screeners, scales, or inventories can assist in the identification of patients who have the potential to be suicidal. At the same time, there are instruments such as the Adult Suicidal Ideation Questionnaire (ASIQ; Reynolds, 1991) that were specifically designed to assess suicide potential. Psychometrically based findings such as initial (intake) level of psychological disturbance or distress—either alone or in combination with other patient data—could be shown to be associated with or predictive of overutilization of medical or behavioral health care services. As was shown by Leon et al. (1999) and Lambert et al. (2001), assessment data might also be used to generate patient profiles or predictive algorithms to identify and monitor patients who are likely to experience problems in their treatment or who are in danger of dropping out of treatment altogether. Knowing this information early on can help therapists increase the chances of a successful treatment experience by applying approaches that work well with these types of patients. And of course, outcomes data might be used to determine what treatment does work well with various types of problematic patients.

SUPPORT OF DEMONSTRATION OF COST OFFSET FROM BEHAVIORAL HEALTH CARE SERVICES

One of the major arguments supporting the current push toward the integration of primary and behavioral health care services is related to the reports of overall, long-term medical cost savings that occur when patients with mental health and substance abuse problems, who are seen in primary care settings are identified early on and receive appropriate treatment. Following is a sample of the data cited in the literature supporting this contention:

- Locke (1997) reported average annual savings of $428 for patients participating in an HMO's program to teach somaticizers appropriate means of dealing with their symptoms.
- A Southwest mental health program reported that a program of early diagnosis and treatment of depression led to an annual savings in charges of more than $2 million, or $749 per patient ("Lovelace, Patients Reap Rewards from Primary Care Intervention in Depression," 1997). These savings were realized primarily as a result of decreased utilization of medical visits rather than hospitalization.
- In one of two studies of primary care patients by Simon, Von Korff and their colleagues (cited in Academy of Psychosomatic Medicine, 1997), the average annual health care costs for 6,000 patients with depression was $4,246 while the average health care costs for the same number of patients without depression were $2,371. In a smaller study, the average annual cost of patients with either anxiety or depression was $2,390, as compared $1,397 for patients without either disorder.
- Millman & Robertson and Staywell Health Management Systems (cited in Melek, 1996) conducted a study of the effects of health habits on auto workers' medical claims. The results indicated that the costs for individuals with "elevated mental health" risks were 13% higher than those individuals with low mental health risks. Similarly, the costs of elevated stress-risk individuals were 24% higher than those of low stress-risk individuals.

Another major area in which cost offset can be realized is related to workplace productivity. According to the American Psychological Association (1996), the health conditions most limiting to the ability to work are mental disorders. It therefore is not surprising that major depression resulted in $23 billion in lost workdays in 1990; and that in 1985, behavioral health problems resulted in over $77 billion in lost income. Also, the National Depressive and Manic-Depressive Association (as cited in "Depression Still Undertreated Despite Efforts to Redress," 1997) reported that depression costs employers $4,200 per depressed worker, or $250 per employee, with only

28% of these costs going toward actual treatment. As indicated by Sturm and Wells' (1996), the importance of improving the *quality* of treatment currently being delivered by primary care practitioners is relevant to worker productivity:

> High-quality care leading to better health outcomes creates many benefits to other parties not involved in healthcare. These positive rewards are not realized by health plans and providers but accrue to the employers of better-treated patients through reduced absenteeism and high productivity, to family members and friends through burdens of care for sick individuals, and to government agencies through fewer transfer payments (welfare, unemployment, disability). [Thus,] improved functioning through better care increases family income over time by much more than the additional treatment costs. (p. 66)

Although Sturm and Wells were specifically addressing the need to improve the quality of treatment for depression, one can assume that the same conclusions are also applicable to other behavioral health disorders.

These and several other similar findings have been used to support the assertions that the costs associated with the identification and treatment of behavioral health problems is money well spent. At the same time, it would appear that the case may not be as clear-cut as one might think, at least as far as *medical* cost offset is concerned. In fact, based on their review of over 25 mental health offset cost studies published between 1965 and 1995, Sperry et al. (1996) determined that

> The only conclusion to come from research on cost-offset due to mental health treatment is that there is no clear-cut indication of cost savings. Studies that claim such an effect are often methodologically flawed. The same design problems also cast doubt on the findings of studies that claim to find no cost-offset effect. Future research needs stronger methodology to be considered valid. (pp. 205–206)

To the extent that provision of behavioral health services can be demonstrated to result in cost savings through decreasing medical expenses or improving work productivity, support for the demonstration of medical cost-offset in an integrated system of managed care is yet another way in which psychological testing can prove useful to the MBHO. Here, the data can help show that early problem identification and effective behavioral health treatment — as illustrated through test results — are associated with decreased use of costly medical resources and/or improved worker performance. It might also be shown that the use of testing for treatment planning may result in less *behavioral* health care services over the long term, aside from any demonstration of other forms of cost-offset.

MEETING ACCREDITATION AND REGULATORY REQUIREMENTS

Psychological testing can play an important role as the method by which a particular clinical service need can be demonstrated, or a change therein can be measured in quality improvement studies. These types of studies are required by accreditation organizations such as the National Committee for Quality Assurance (NCQA) and the Joint Commission on Accreditation of Healthcare Organizations (JCAHO), as well as by regulatory bodies that accredit or license MBHOs. With increased pressures to obtain and maintain accreditation from one or more of these oversight bodies, MBHOs are at a point where the knowledge and training possessed by those skilled in clinical psychological testing and related research could significantly contribute to both the quality of services and the financial viability of the organization. Following are a few examples of how that might occur.

NCQA

NCQA began the development of its Managed Behavioral Health Accreditation Program in 1995, using its standards for MCO Accreditation (for health plans) as a template for developing standards for MBHOs (NCQA, 1999). The standards were completed in 1996 and, beginning in 1997, were subsequently used to guide the surveys of those MBHOs applying for NCQA accreditation under the Program. These standards have undergone revision, with the 2001 standards (NCQA, 2000b) being the most recent set at the time of this writing. To be sure, future revisions will be made to reflect the changing standards of health care as the field evolves.

Psychological testing can help meet two major sets of NCQA's 2001 standards required for accreditation or re-accreditation under the Managed Behavioral Health Accreditation Program. The first set of standards is that for Quality Management Improvement (QI), which require the MBHO to "continuously assess and improve the quality of clinical care and service provided to its members . . . to implement a QI process centered on structure, process and outcome, and to use this process to demonstrate improvements in the care and service its members receive" (NCQA, 1999, p. 2). The potential contributions of psychological testing can be of particular relevance toward an MBHO's meeting the QI 10A–QI 11 standards (NCQA, 2000b).

QI 10A–QI 11 require the MBHO to identify at least three clinical issues that are particularly relevant to the MBHO's health plan members (NCQA, 2000b). Two of these have to deal with high-volume (e.g., major depressive disorder patients) or high-risk (e.g., dual diagnosis patients) populations, whereas the third must address a clinical issue pertaining to inpatient, partial hospitalization or ambulatory services. For each type of issue, the MBHO must implement a quality improvement initiative or program requiring a baseline measurement related to the problematic area, implementation of an intervention, remeasurement, analysis of the remeasurement data, further intervention, remeasurement, and so on, until an established performance goal is met. Use of instrumentation that gathers valid and reliable information is an integral part of the process. Thus, use of psychological testing in either a screening, monitoring, or outcomes assessment mode can become key to the success of these improvement efforts.

The other set of NCQA standards that psychological testing can help an MBHO meet are the Preventive Behavioral Health Services (PH) standards. These standards set forth expectations for MBHOs to develop programs "to prevent the [targeted] event or to detect [a behavioral health problem] in its earliest stage possible and to provide the appropriate therapeutic or supportive intervention" (NCQA, 2000b, p. 355). Under this set of standards, psychological testing can be most useful with regard to activities covered under PH 1 (Preventive Behavioral Health Programs) and PH 5 (Performance on Preventive Health Programs) (NCQA, 2000b). These program activities can be primary, secondary, or tertiary in nature. Among other things, psychological tests can be used to screen plan members for the presence or likelihood of

developing relatively common problems (e.g., substance abuse) or to monitor identified conditions to prevent worsening of the condition (e.g., regularly monitoring
schizophrenic patients with a history of not complying with medication regimens).
This same data can be used to evaluate the effectiveness of the prevention program.

JCAHO

Following the lead of NCQA, JCAHO also has established an accreditation program
for MBHOs with sets of standards that require the type of measurement that psychological testing can facilitate (JCAHO, 1997, 1999). Of particular note are the Assessment (PE) and Improving Delivery System Performance (PI) standards. Generally,
the goal of the PE standards is to ensure appropriate care through assessment of each
patient at appropriate times during the course of treatment. In this regard, psychological testing could be used for any of several required assessment tasks, including:
screening for appropriate initial level of care for mental illness that is life-threatening
or serious enough to affect the course of treatment; emotional and behavioral assessment that may include personality, neuropsychological, and/cognitive functioning;
systematically gathering information that could become legal evidence in cases of alleged or suspected abuse or neglect; comprehensive and subsequent annual assessment with patients with mental retardation or other developmental disabilities, including cognitive testing; and "regular assessment using mutually agreeable and
reliable measures of the member's choices, goals, strengths, symptoms, and behavioral patterns" (p. 211) for the purpose of informed decision making.

The PI standards (JCAHO, 1997) also present opportunities for psychological testing to help meet the JCAHO requirements. Psychological measures can serve many
functions, including being the source of data for: systemwide performance measurement and improvement activities; information related to the care of patients; improvement priorities and continuing measurement; outcomes related to prevention,
functional status and psychological comfort of patients; risk-management activities;
and internal and external comparison of provider performance over time.

QISMC

Independent accreditation organizations are not the only not-for-profit bodies requiring quality improvement activities. There are numerous government-sponsored
programs for which quality improvement standards have been developed and, consequently, in which psychological testing can play a major role in meeting. For example, the federal government's Health Care Financing Administration (HCFA) has recently developed standards and guidelines to be used by HCFA as a means of
satisfying their quality assurance provisions of the Balanced Budget Act of 1997
(BBA) (HCFA, 1999a). These standards and guidelines are contained in the Quality
Improvement System for Managed Care (QISMC), a HCFA initiative designed to ensure that managed care organizations, including MBHOs, "protect and improve the
health and satisfaction of Medicare and Medicaid clients" (HCFA, 1999a, 1999b).

The QISMC guidelines are divided into four domains: Enrollee Rights, Health Services Management, Delegation, and the Quality Assessment and Performance Improvement (QAPI) Program. One of the basic requirement for the QAPI domain is
that the managed care organization annually initiate a number of outcome-oriented
projects in which performance improvement is expected (HCFA, 1998). The foci of

these projects are on both clinical areas (e.g., care of acute or chronic conditions, high-risk or preventative services) and nonclinical areas (e.g., availability, accessibility, complaints). Some of the topical areas of investigation and related performance measures are selected by HCFA; other topical areas may be selected by the MBHO. It is within the QAPI requirements and those projects with a clinical focus that opportunities may lie for the application of psychological testing.

Obviously, there are many other governmental and nongovernmental accreditation and regulatory bodies that require MBHOs and other managed care organizations to demonstrate accountability using outcomes-based performance measurement. This will likely open up many opportunities in MBHO settings for individuals with knowledge and training in the use of clinical assessment tools and solid grounding in research methodology. The requirements being made by these oversight bodies will likely not go away, nor will the need for trained psychologists who can capitalize on the opportunities they present.

SUPPORT FOR CONTINUOUS QUALITY IMPROVEMENT PROGRAMS

Implementing a regimen of psychological testing for planning treatment and/or assessing its outcome has a place in all organizations where the delivery of cost-efficient, quality behavioral health care services is a primary goal. However, additional benefits can result from psychological testing when it is incorporated into an ongoing program of service evaluation and CQI.

Although espoused by Americans, the CQI philosophy was initially implemented by the Japanese in rebuilding their economy after World War II. Today, many U.S. organizations have sought to balance quality with cost by implementing CQI procedures. Simply put, CQI may be viewed as a process of continuously setting goals, measuring progress toward the achievement of those goals, subsequently re-evaluating them in light of the progress made, and implementing revised procedures and/or goals. Underlying the CQI process are a few simple assumptions. First, those organizations that can produce high quality products or services at the lowest possible cost have the best chance of surviving and prospering in today's competitive market. Second, it is less costly to prevent errors than to correct them, and the process of preventing errors is continuous. Third, it is assumed that the workers within the organization are motivated and empowered to improve the quality of their products or services based on the information they receive about their work.

The continuous setting, measurement, and re-evaluation of goals that is characteristic of the CQI process is being employed by many health care organizations as part of their efforts to survive in a competitive, changing market. At least in part, this move also reflects what InterStudy (1991) described as a "shifting from concerns about managing costs in isolation to a more comprehensive view that supplements an understanding of costs with an understanding of the quality and value of care delivered" (p. 1). InterStudy defines quality as a position or view that should lead all processes within a system. In the case of the health care system, the most crucial of these processes is that of patient care. InterStudy pointed out that with a CQI orientation, these processes must be well-defined, agreed on, and implemented unvaryingly when delivering care. They also should provide measurable results that will subsequently lead to conclusions about how the processes might be altered to improve the results of care. InterStudy considered CQI as implying ". . . a system that articulates the connections between inputs and outputs, between processes and outcomes . . . , a way of organizing information in order to discover what works, and what doesn't" (p. 1).

In behavioral health care, as in other arenas of health care, CQI is concerned with the services delivered to customers. In a sense, the "customer" may include not only the patient being treated, but also the employer through whom the health care plan is offered and the third-party payer who selects/approves the service providers who can be accessed by individuals seeking care under the health care plan. From the discussion presented throughout this chapter, it should be evident that psychological testing can help the provider focus on delivering the most efficient and effective treatment in order to satisfy the needs of all "customers." Consequently, it can contribute greatly to the CQI effort.

Perhaps the most apparent way in which testing can augment the CQI process is through its contributions in the area of treatment monitoring and outcomes assessment. Through the repeated administration of tests to all patients at intake and later at one or more points during or after the treatment process, an organization can obtain a good sense of how effective individual clinicians, treatment program/units, and/or the organization as a whole are in providing services to their patients. This testing might include the use of not only problem-oriented measures but also measures of patient satisfaction. Considered in light of nontest data, this may result in changes in service delivery goals such as the implementation of more effective problem identification and treatment planning procedures. For example, Newman (1991) offers a graphic demonstration of how data used to support treatment decisions can be extended to indicate how various levels of depression (as measured by the Beck Depression Inventory) may be best served by different types of treatment (e.g., inpatient vs. outpatient).

A CAVEAT

Before concluding this chapter, there is one important fact that must addressed. This has to do with the funding that MBHOs have budgeted for psychological testing services. It is difficult to imagine that any given MBHO would not find value in at least one or two of the previously described testing applications for their organization. The issue becomes whether there are budgeted funds for these applications. This might include funds for testing materials, reimbursing network providers or other third-party contractors (e.g., disease management companies) for the testing they perform, an in-house staff position to conduct or oversee the implementation of this work, or a combination of the three. Regardless, it is highly unlikely that any MBHO is going to spend money on any service that is not considered essential for the proper care of patients *unless that service can demonstrate either short-term or long-term money savings or cost-offset*. The current restrictions for authorizing assessment (as discussed in chapter 3) are a reflection of this fact.

All of the applications of psychological testing that were discussed in previous sections of this chapter may seem obviously beneficial to both patients and MBHOs — if one is looking at the issue from the perspective of a clinician. Frequently, this perspective has been influenced by academic and internship training in which cost considerations have taken a back seat to teaching the student the art and skills of the profession. In some instances, even lack of empirical support for the validity and/or usefulness of a particular test, technique or application has been overlooked for the sake of teaching the student clinician what the instructor feels has been useful for him in the past, or at least what he feels every student should know. And unfortunately, this flawed line of thinking is commonly propagated by these same students during their professional career, perhaps as teachers themselves.

Use of invalid and otherwise useless instruments and wasteful procedures (e.g., testing every patient seeking services) are among the many practices that contributed to the health care crisis. These are just the types of things that MBHOs and the health care industry are now trying to control. Thus, MBHOs tend to view things from the perspective of *demonstrated utility and value*. As Dorfman (2000) succinctly stated,

> Until the value of testing can be shown unequivocally, support and reimbursement for evaluation and testing will be uneven with [MBHOs] and frequently based on the psychologist's personal credibility and competence in justifying such expenditures. In the interim, it is incumbent on each psychologist to be aware of the goals and philosophy of the managed care industry, and to understand how the use of evaluation and testing with his or her patients not only is consistent with, but also helps to further, those goals. To the extent that these procedures can be shown to enhance the value of the managed care product by ensuring quality of care and positive treatment outcome, to reduce treatment length without sacrificing that quality, to prevent overutilization of limited resources and services, and to enhance patient satisfaction with care, psychologists can expect to gain greater support for their unique testing skill from the managed care company. (pp. 24–25)

One way to win support for reimbursable psychological assessment is to use it in the most cost-effective ways. Groth-Marnat (1999b) has provided a set of rationally derived guidelines for demonstrating the financial efficacy of clinical assessment to MBHOs. He recommends that clinicians:

1. Focus on those domains that are most relevant for treatment planning and optimizing patient outcomes. In particular, one should address referral questions and relevant diagnostic issues and patient characteristics.
2. Use formal assessment to reduce legal risk to both the clinician and the MBHO. Patients presenting with danger to themselves or others, or those with complex differential diagnostic questions are examples here.
3. Assess those conditions which will most likely result in the greatest cost savings. Being able to identify and refer somatizing patients to appropriate treatment, for example, could result in tremendous cost savings.
4. Use computer-assisted assessment that will result in time savings in administration and/or interpretation of test instruments. Time savings will consequently lead to cost savings.
5. Along the same line of reasoning, use instruments that require less clinician time. Many such instruments are discussed in chapters 5 and 8.
6. Provide a close linkage between assessment, feedback, and intervention. Finn's (1996b) therapeutic assessment procedure is a good example.
7. Provide a close linkage between assessment undertaken at the time of treatment initiation with that conducted for the purpose of treatment monitoring and outcomes measurement.

One will note the consistency of Groth-Marnot's guidelines with what is discussed in this and other chapters of this book. Many of these recommendations are consistent with those provided by Belar (1997). In addition, Belar stressed the importance of being able to demonstrate empirically the value-added aspect of testing, considering the potential negative side effects of testing, becoming involved in the development of health policy, and improving one's research skills.

In Ficken's (1995) discussion of the role of assessment in an MBHO environment, he concludes that the difficulties clinicians are experiencing in demonstrating the utility of psychological assessment to payers lies in the fact the instruments and objectives of traditional psychological assessment are not consistent with the needs of MCOs. The solution to the problem appears simple:

> . . . the underlying objectives of testing must be aligned with the values and processes of [MBHOs]. In short, this means identifying decision points in managed care processes that could be improved with objective, standardized data. There are two avenues in which these can be pursued: through facilitation/objectification of clinical-decision processes and through outcome assessment. (p. 12)

Failing an attempt to convince an MBHO of the utility of a particular test or a specific application of a program of testing (e.g., screening all new MBHO patients for the presence of a substance abuse problem), clinicians still can administer a specific test or initiate a program of testing for their patients. The difference, of course, is that they may not be reimbursed for their efforts. Some clinicians might not offer any clinical service unless it is reimbursed. Others may feel that what they want to do is important for the quality of care and will go ahead and test patients with no guarantee of reimbursement. It is for especially for these individuals that we have drawn the reader's attention to the Groth-Marnat (1999b) guidelines. For this same reason we have limited the discussion of individual tests in chapters 5 and 8 to no-cost or low-cost instrumentation. In these cases, the clinician may not be reimbursed for his or her time, but at least implementation of testing will not involve any large outlay of money for the instruments and associated materials necessary to do what the clinician thinks to best for the patient.

SUMMARY

The health care revolution has brought mixed blessings to those in the behavioral health care professions. It has limited reimbursement for services rendered and has forced many to change the way they practice their profession. At the same time, it has led to revelations about the cost savings that can accrue from the treatment of mental health and substance use disorders. This has been the bright spot in an otherwise bleak picture for some behavioral health care professionals. For psychologists and others trained in psychological assessment procedures, the picture appears to be somewhat different. They now have additional opportunities to contribute to the positive aspects of the revolution and to gain from the "new order" it has imposed. By virtue of their training and through the application of appropriate instrumentation, they are uniquely qualified to support or otherwise facilitate multiple aspects of the therapeutic process.

The intent of this chapter was to present an overview of the various ways in which psychological testing can be used to facilitate the selection, implementation, and evaluation of appropriate therapeutic interventions in managed behavioral health care settings. Generally, psychological testing can assist the clinician in three important clinical activities: clinical decision-making, treatment (when used as a specific therapeutic technique), and treatment outcomes evaluation. Regarding the first of these activities, three important clinical decision-making functions can be facilitated by psychological testing: screening, treatment planning, and treatment monitoring. The first of these can be served by the use of brief instruments designed to identify (with a high degree of certainty) the likely presence (or absence) of a particular condition or characteristic. Here, the diagnostic efficiency of the instrument used (as indicated by their positive and negative predictive powers) is of great importance. Through their ability to identify and clarify problems as well as other important treatment-relevant patient characteristics, psychological test instruments also can be of great assistance in planning treatment. Moreover, treatment monitoring, or the periodic evaluation of the patient's progress during the course of treatment, can be served well by the application of psychological measures.

Second, psychological assessment may be used as part of a therapeutic technique. In what Finn (1996b) calls "therapeutic assessment," situations in which patients are evaluated via psychological testing are used as opportunities for the process itself to serve as a therapeutic intervention. This is accomplished through involving the patient as an active participant in the assessment process, not just as the object of the assessment.

Third, psychological testing can be employed as the primary mechanism by which the outcomes or results of treatment can be measured. However, use of testing for this purpose is not a cut-and-dry matter. Issues pertaining to what to measure, how to measure, and when to measure require considerable thought prior to undertaking a plan to assess outcomes. Guidelines for resolving these issues are presented in later in chapters 6 and 7, as is information on how to determine if the measured outcomes of treatment are indeed "significant." The role that outcomes assessment can have in an organization's CQI initiative and in meeting regulatory and accreditation requirements also was discussed.

There is no doubt that psychological testing has been dealt a blow by MBHOs within recent years. However, as this chapter hopefully has shown, clinicians trained in the use of psychological tests and related instrumentation have the skills to take these powerful tools, apply them in many different ways that will benefit those suffering from mental health and substance abuse problems, and demonstrate their value to patients and payers.

Authorization of Psychological Testing and Assessment

Throughout this book, the reader is exposed to numerous nontraditional and innovative ways in which psychological testing can benefit MBHOs and the services they offer. However, there will always be the need for the "basic service," that is, testing patients that present particularly difficult diagnostic or treatment challenges. Obtaining authorization for reimbursable, traditional, down-in-the-trenches psychological testing in systems of managed behavioral health care has become somewhat of a challenge itself — or at least more of a challenge than had previously been the case in the past under indemnity insurance plans. The purpose of this chapter is to provide the reader with information that will better prepare him for this challenge and thus facilitate the testing authorization process. Before doing so, an overview of the typical service delivery process will be presented, followed by a discussion of how MBHOs view traditional psychological testing, the potential contribution of testing to the treatment of its patients, and the value it offers to its customers. This will provide a context for the more salient aspects of the chapter.

STANDARD SERVICE DELIVERY PROCESS

Requesting and authorizing psychological testing for an MBHO patient are not isolated activities. They are conducted within a standard process of care management and service delivery. Becoming familiar with other important aspects of this process will facilitate the test request and authorization process and help increase the chances that such requests will be approved.

General Process

The standard service delivery process will vary from one MBHO to another. However, Fig. 3.1 shows a fairly generic process that probably can be observed in most MBHOs, with some organization-specific modifications. Here, one can see that the

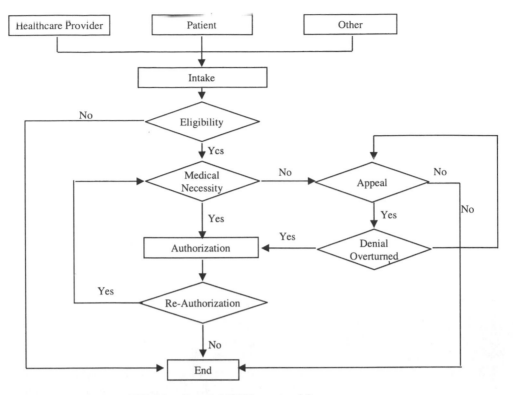

FIG. 3.1.   Generic MBHO service delivery process.

process begins when the health plan member, their health care provider, or another collateral (e.g., spouse, parent) contacts the MBHO requesting services. The provider could be a nonpsychiatric physician (e.g., the patient's primary care provider) who has determined that the patient needs to be evaluated for the presence and/or treatment of a mental health or substance abuse problem. Basic information regarding the patient's clinical status is obtained at the point of intake. This might be done by an intake coordinator (usually bachelor's or master's level) or a care manager (master's or doctoral level), depending on how the MBHO is staffed. Based on this information and on verification of covered health care benefits, a decision about *medical necessity* is made. Generally, medical necessity requires that symptoms that support or potentially support an Axis I diagnosis be present, and that the symptoms or diagnosis be amenable to treatment. A discussion of medical necessity is presented later.

Assuming a determination of medical necessity, the patient is authorized for the services at an appropriate level of care (LOC) and then, if requested, referred to an appropriate network or in-house provider for those services. In a typical case, the patient will be referred to an outpatient provider who will schedule the patient for an initial appointment within a contractually specified time (e.g., 10 working days). The patient will be seen much sooner if the situation is judged to be emergent or urgent, thus requiring more immediate attention.

Typically, only a limited amount of service is initially authorized, for example, 5 to 10 outpatient treatment sessions or 2 to 4 days of inpatient treatment. Authorization for additional treatment beyond that initially authorized may be granted upon request from the provider. At the time of the request, the provider usually must indicate the continued presence of the presenting problem, some evidence that movement toward the treatment goals has been made, and the expectation of continued progress will be made with additional treatment. Denial or noncertification of requests for either initial or continued services (other than denials based on health plan benefits limitations) may, if requested by the patient or his provider, undergo a review by a peer of the person denying the request. If the reviewer upholds the initial denial, the decision may be appealed through different levels of appeal that are required either by accreditation bodies, regulatory agencies, or both.

Determination of Medical Necessity and LOC

In general, the LOC that the MBHO authorizes for the patient is determined by the symptoms that the patient is experiencing at the time of the request, the type of treatment that is effective and most appropriate for his symptom intensity level, and the availability of that treatment. There are several levels of care that may be available through a given MBHO. The more restrictive levels are used for stabilization of the patient and/or to help ensure the safety of the patient or others. MBHOs will vary in the number and types of LOCs they offer, based on the needs of the particular health plan memberships that they serve. This is evident if one peruses the LOC guidelines for some of the largest MBHOs in the United States. However, generally there is a large overlap in the LOCs that are offered and their associated medical necessity criteria. Among the commonly offered LOCs are 23-hour bed, inpatient, partial hospitalization, intensive outpatient (IOP), and outpatient care for mental health treatment. Similar but separate LOCs and medical necessity criteria are established for substance abuse treatment and, sometimes, child and adolescent patients.

Following is a broad overview of the more commonly offered LOCs for mental health problems, based on the medical necessity criteria that are found in the UBH (2000) and CIGNA (1999) guidelines. Note that accompanying the determination of the most appropriate LOC for a given patient is the assumption that there is a DSM-IV Axis I diagnosis present, the assigned LOC can provide the type of treatment the patient needs at that point in time, and that it is the least restrictive LOC for a particular patient to receive that treatment.

23-Hour Bed. The 23-hour bed is intended as a means of assessing and stabilizing patients who are not in *clear* need of acute psychiatric inpatient treatment. This LOC provides a treatment environment that offers quick, intensive intervention for patients in crisis situations of significant proportions (e.g., acute, serious deterioration in functioning, expressed suicidal or homicidal ideation or threats) and determination of the most appropriate disposition on discharge. The disposition here may be admission into an inpatient unit or discharge to a lower LOC (e.g., partial hospitalization).

Inpatient. Precertification for admission into an inpatient facility or unit typically requires that the patient's symptoms either present a serious and imminent risk of harm to self or others; are serious and accompanied by acute deterioration in functioning; or have caused a severe disturbance in the patient's affect, behavior, judgment, or thought processes. In these cases, appropriate treatment requires the type of daily oversight and close monitoring and supervision that an inpatient stay provides and that less restrictive LOCs cannot. Family involvement is an important component for effective inpatient treatment.

For the inpatient LOC, a stay of 1 to 3 days is typically authorized. However, this can be extended if the symptomatology is shown to necessitate continued stay. Additional inpatient days may be authorized if, upon concurrent review of the case (i.e., while the patient is still hospitalized), it is found that the admission criteria is still present; the patient has been actively participating in the treatment plan; and the patient's status suggests that he likely to deteriorate if discharged to a lower LOC. Authorization for additional extended periods of stay might also be granted upon one or more subsequent reviews with a physician.

Partial Hospitalization/Day Treatment. Generally, this LOC is intended for patients who are experiencing symptoms or deterioration in functioning at a level of severity that requires regular monitoring that cannot be provided at lower levels of care, but does not require the same level of monitoring and intervention that is offered through the inpatient LOC (e.g., patient can contract for safety while not attending the program). In cases such as these, the patient might be authorized to attend a hospital-based or free-standing partial hospitalization or day treatment programs 5 hours a day, 4 or 5 days a week until changes in the patient's condition warrant transfer to a lower or higher LOC.

Intensive Outpatient. This LOC is similar but less intense than partial hospitalization, with the patient attending the IOP program perhaps only 3 days a week, 3 hours a day. It is appropriate when more structure, monitoring, and intervention are required than can be offered through standard outpatient services, but the intensity of intervention that is needed is less than that provided in a partial hospitalization program.

Outpatient. Outpatient treatment is appropriate and warranted if the patient exhibits clinical symptoms or behaviors and impairment or deterioration in functioning, all of which are due to a psychiatric illness. Treatment at this level is appropriate when there is no serious risk of harm to self or others; there are clear, focused, and objective treatment goals; and there is linkage with some form of community support. Initially, a set number of outpatient sessions (e.g., 4 or 5) are usually authorized, but additional sessions may be requested and granted if, upon concurrent review, the patient's symptoms are still present and he is actively engaged in treatment.

MBHOs may also offer additional mental health and substance abuse LOCs depending on the contracts they have with specific employers or health plans. Examples may include inpatient detoxification, substance abuse halfway house, home health care services, custodial care, and residential care of children and adolescents.

In general, guidelines for authorization for *continued* treatment at an assigned LOC usually require that the criteria for admission to the current LOC continue to be met, the patient has been actively participating in treatment, the treatment remains appropriate to the problem, the patient is likely to deteriorate if transitioned to a lower level of care or all care is withdrawn, and progress has occurred or treatment has been changed to account for the lack of measurable progress. Guidelines for discharge from an assigned LOC generally require that either the guidelines for that assigned LOC are no longer applicable, appropriate treatment is available at a lower LOC, or the patient is in no longer is in need of behavioral health care services.

CURRENT STATUS OF MEASUREMENT IN MANAGED CARE SETTINGS

Given their day-to-day processes for authorizing and managing the care of their covered lives, where does psychological testing fit into the priorities of MBHOs? The results of the surveys discussed in chapter 1 bear out the de-emphasis that MBHOs have placed on psychological testing as part of the routine care offered to those seeking services. Usually, reimbursable psychological testing requires special or separate authorization, something that is not given unless specific criteria are met. But the de-emphasis on individual, clinically related testing does not mean that all measurement is relegated to the back burner of MBHO priorities.

MBHOs' Primary Interests

Even though it is not always apparent, MBHOs do indeed rely on and value psychological testing and measurement for many purposes. As it happens, however, the purposes for which MBHOs are most interested in testing and find it most useful are not the same as those generally valued by their network psychologists. MBHOs generally view psychological test data from groups of patients rather than individual patients as more useful in helping to assure that the people they serve are receiving quality services. This is consistent with a move toward a population-based focus in the delivery of behavioral health care (Schreter, 1997).

Measurement of Population-Based Clinical and Service Quality Performance Indicators. Today, MBHOs are dedicating considerable financial and manpower resources to measurement activities. The focus here is directed more toward population-based measurement of structure and process indicators of both clinical and service quality, rather than to the measurement of the symptomatology, functioning, etc, of the individual patient. These indicators provide the organization with gauges of its ability to meet both clinical and nonclinical needs of its covered lives. Thus, this type of measurement is typically tied to formal and informal quality improvement activities. Common types of clinical and service monitors are discussed in subsequent chapters of this book.

Meet Internal and External Demands for Process and Outcomes Performance Measures. In addition, these and other measurement-required activities help the organization fulfill external requirements. For example, JCAHO and NCQA both require accredited MBHOs to conduct studies aimed at improving the quality of their clinical and nonclinical services. Here again, measurement has a population focus, but individual testing may play an important role in studies or programs in which identification of patients with specific characteristics or symptoms is a key component.

Measurement activities are also needed for externally driven requirements to demonstrate treatment outcomes. The sources of these requirements may be the purchasers of the services, regulatory/accrediting bodies, market demands, or other forces. Measuring outcomes is becoming a common requirement these days and one in which psychologists have a potentially tremendous opportunity to capitalize on with their particular skills and training. For this reason, chapters 6 and 7 are devoted to a discussion of this topic.

Program Development.   Another area in which this author has observed a growth in testing in MBHO settings is that of program development, that is, testing is frequently becoming a part of specialized programs that MBHOs are developing. What particularly comes to mind is increasing MBHO interest in developing behavioral medicine programs or supporting disease management programs being developed by health plans with which they contract. In disease management programs, screeners are administered to individuals upon entry into the program to assist in identifying program participants who may have a comorbid mental health disorder—such as depression—that might interfere with the patient's treatment and, more importantly, may directly have an impact on the morbidity and mortality of these patients. In essence, it is used to support case-finding efforts.

As an example of such programs, some MBHOs have become involved with health plans in the design and implementation of a number of cardiovascular risk-reduction programs. These programs seek to reduce the rate of short-term morbidity and mortality in patients recovering from a cardiac event such as a myocardial infarction (MI), by screening these patients for depression. The literature is replete with studies showing that post-MI patients who are depressed are considerably more likely to relapse or die during the 6 months following the event than those who are not depressed. Thus, identifying depressed cardiac patients early on—using a brief depression screener followed by a clinical assessment of those screening positive—and providing appropriate intervention can lead to both an increase in the health and well-being of these patients as well as significant cost savings.

The preceding observations are consistent with those of Ambrose (1997) who has stated,

> Ideally, if an objective personality measure can deal with one of the three primary problems the [MBHO] has as a part of its everyday existence [i.e., demonstrating value, extending benefits, increasing treatment outcomes], there is a greater likelihood that the service will be included in the basic overall benefit package that the company offers its customers, and, as such, it will become a given rather than a negotiated service. (pp. 65–66).

Although Ambrose speaks specifically to the use of objective personality measures, the same comments hold true for the use of measures of other important domains of interest to MBHOs (e.g., social functioning, well-being, role functioning).

MBHOs' Secondary Interests

It is both interesting and unfortunate that psychologists' unique knowledge, skill, and experience base in psychological testing is related to applications that most MBHOs would probably consider secondary in utility to those that just discussed. Routine testing of patients for diagnostic and treatment planning purposes is essentially a thing of the past. Only in specific circumstances are MBHOs likely to consider authorizing reimbursable testing, the most common of these being for diagnostic and treatment planning purposes.

Testing to Assist in Diagnosis.   It is probably safe to say that most people seeking mental health or substance abuse services present with problems that are fairly clear-cut. What the psychologist is likely to encounter the vast majority of the time are affective and anxiety disorders that are relatively easy to diagnose and generally responsive to psychotherapeutic (e.g., individual psychotherapy) and/or psychopharmacologic interventions. There are those times, however, when the picture the patient presents is unclear, containing signs and symptoms that might be indicative of more than one type of disorder. Even with extensive data gathered from collateral interviews, a review of medical charts and contacts with other potential sources of information, a determination of exactly what is going on with the patient can remain elusive. In a behavioral health care system that is oriented toward problem-focused treatment, an accurate diagnosis may not always be as important as the resolution of the presenting problem. However, the accuracy of the diagnosis at the onset of treatment can have a tremendous impact on the treatment that is provided to the patient and, consequently, the outcomes of that treatment. Table 3.1 presents some of the more common differential diagnostic questions that Schaefer, Murphy, Westerveld, and Gewirtz (2000) have identified in their dealings with MBHO systems. Note some of the possible treatment implications for each.

It is when just these sorts of diagnostic questions arise that MBHOs are more likely to see the value of psychological testing. One of the fortes of several psychological test instruments is the empirically based support for their use to assist in answering differential diagnostic questions. One of the most popular psychological tests is the Minnesota Multiphasic Personality Inventory-2 (MMPI-2; Butcher, Dahlstrom, Graham, Tellegen, & Kaemmer, 1989). Although not specifically developed to answer differential diagnostic questions, the amount of empirical research available on various diagnostic groups can provide an otherwise unavailable source of support for the psychologist's diagnostic decision (see, for example, Graham, 2000b; Greene, 2000). An instrument that was developed more for the purpose of answering those difficult diagnostic questions is the MCMI-III (Millon, 1994). With its base rate and diagnostic efficiency data (sensitivity, specificity, positive and negative predictive powers) and its tie to DSM-IV disorders, the MCMI-III can be invaluable in helping the psychologist make difficult differentiations that can impact the patient's treatment. Other similarly designed instruments also are available to assist in answering diagnostic questions.

Whereas personality assessment is typically used to help resolve the more common diagnostic questions, other types of testing also may be authorized for this purpose. For example, neuropsychological testing might be authorized to help differentiate "functional" from "organic" problems. Authorization for evaluation of patients suspected to have attention deficit hyperactivity disorder (ADHD), which likely includes the completion of rating scales by teachers and other collaterals, is not uncommon. Moreover, cognitive (achievement and intellectual) testing could be authorized to help determine the presence of a learning disability. In the case of a suspected learning disability in a child or adolescent, however, the MBHO may contend that this type of assessment is the responsibility of the patient's school system.

TABLE 3.1
Implications of Differential Diagnostic Questions

Referral Question	Implications
Attention deficit hyperactivity disorder (ADHD) vs. anxiety	• Stimulant vs. anxiolytic or selective serotonin reuptake inhibitor (SSRI) • Structured therapy vs. insight-oriented
ADHD vs. posttraumatic stress disorder (PTSD)	• Emphasis on external/environmental controls vs. capacity for internal control
Psychosis vs. anxiety Psychosis vs. PTSD	• Neuroleptic vs. anxiolytic or SSRI • Supportive and structured treatment vs. insight-oriented and/or cognitive–behavioral (e.g., desensitization)
Psychosis vs. major depressive disorder (MDD), psychotic features	• Supportive/structured treatment vs. interpersonal therapy (adolescent) vs. insight-oriented
Psychosis vs. pervasive developmental disorder (PDD)	• Neuroleptic vs. skills training • Prognosis; long-term management
Psychosis vs. bipolar Psychosis vs. language/cognitive	• Neuroleptic vs. mood stabilizer • Choice and level of intervention (educational, social skills, psychotherapy) • Treatment modality
Bipolar/unipolar vs. borderline traits	• Medication indications • Therapeutic (e.g., dialectic behavioral therapy vs. cognitive behavioral therapy, insight-oriented) • Selection of treatment program (individual/group, level of intensity)
PDD vs. anxiety	• Anxiolytic vs. SSRI • Treatment modality and setting • Selection of treatment program
Antisocial traits vs. intermittent explosive	• Impulsivity vs. character, therapeutic and disorder prognosticators • Indication for medication • Level of containment
Mood vs. oppositional defiant disorder	• Medication indications • Therapeutic modality (structured vs. supportive vs. insight-oriented)

Note.   From *Psychological Assessment and Managed Care: Guidelines for practice with Children and Adolescents,* by M. Schaefer, R. Murphy, M. Westerveld, & A. Gewirtz. Continuing education workshop presented at the annual meeting of the American Psychological Association, August, 2000. Copyright 2000 by authors. Adapted with permission.

Testing to Assist in Treatment Planning.   Another way in which MBHOs have found testing useful is in the assistance it can provide in developing a treatment plan for patients who are not making the expected progress toward their treatment goals. In these cases, testing may be able to elicit insight into barriers to progress that might not otherwise be available to the patient's care provider or MBHO care manager. For example, a patient being treated successfully for anxiety may be found to be experiencing a hitherto unknown comorbid depressive disorder that has prevented him from returning to his previous level of functioning. In other instances, neuropsychological, cognitive, and ADHD evaluations may be authorized to determine the extent to which associated deficits may interfere with both the patient's functioning and ability to benefit from therapeutic interventions. As in the case of differential diagnosis, the value-added aspect of psychological testing for treatment planning lies in the empirical research that enables access to information that may not be easily accessible even to experienced clinicians.

Reasons for Decline in Psychological Assessment in MBHOs

It is quite apparent that the introduction of managed care has affected one of psychologists' identifying skills and activities. The profession needs to do much work in order to reclaim the level of acceptance and value that psychological testing was held at in previous years. To step back for a moment, it is important to ask why MBHOs are hesitant to authorize testing of their covered health plan members. Understanding this question will be the key to regaining psychological testing's former status as an invaluable component of behavioral health care services.

General Emphasis on Streamlining Interventions and Containing Costs. First and foremost among the reasons for the decline of psychological testing in MBHOs is the general emphasis on streamlining interventions and containing costs. In doing so, they have adopted what Schreter (1997) refers to as the *principle of parsimony*, which holds that "each patient should receive the least intensive, least expensive treatment at the lowest level of care that will permit a return to health and function" (p. 653).

It is important to keep in mind that the managed care movement arose from the need to control health care costs. Managed care was and will continue to be (at least in the foreseeable future) a viable solution to runaway costs. It is therefore incumbent on managed care organizations to trim as much unnecessary cost from its expenses as is possible without compromising quality of care. One way of reducing costs is to eliminate services unnecessary for patient improvement. Given MBHOs' questions surrounding the validity and cost-effectiveness of testing (see next), as well as psychologists' sometimes indiscriminant or inappropriate use of testing in the past, it is not surprising that psychological testing has come under close scrutiny and is authorized by MBHOs only under certain circumstances. Moreover, with limited benefits and the fact that the typical patient terminates treatment after only 5 to 10 sessions anyway, it frequently does not make sense to devote an authorized visit or hour of time to an activity that may yield no long-term benefit for the patient. This is particularly the case when, for the reasons just cited, treatment tends to be problem-focused.

MBHOs' Attitude Toward Psychological Testing. Ambrose (1997) summarizes what the American Psychological Association's Psychological Assessment Work Group (PAWG; Kubiszyn, Meyer, Finn, Eyde, Kay, Moreland, Dies, & Eisman, 2000) concluded to be the typical attitude of MBHOs toward psychological assessment:

> Typically, when a clinician is asked why third-party payers should pay for personality assessment measures, their response generally falls into one of the following categories:
> - It improves diagnosis.
> - It improves treatment outcomes.
> - It shortens treatment.
> - I have children in college, and I need the money.
>
> While these responses appear to be logical, there is no conclusive, unequivocal research that demonstrate that objective personality assessment in and of itself does any of the above. Intuitively, we anticipate that the more information we gather about a patient, the better likelihood we will be able to improve diagnosis. With a better diagnosis, we can increase treatment outcomes and shorten treatment durations. Yet, most research

has never been aimed at a cost benefit analysis of objective personality assessment. Instead, most research is based on a goal of diagnostic or triage verification. (p. 66)

This is consistent with Schaefer et al.'s (2000) observation that MBHOs find limited evidence for the claims that are made about the utility of psychological assessment. However, the PAWG (Kubiszyn et al., 2000) contests the claims made by Ambrose (1997), stating that

considerable empirical support exists for many important clinical health care applications of psychological assessment instruments. For such applications psychological assessment can enhance diagnosis and treatment. Health care cost savings would be expected to follow from enhanced diagnosis and treatment, an outcome that third-party payers would be expected to be seriously interested in. (p. 120)

They then cite several studies and meta-analyses supporting their claims for the validity and utility of psychological testing for several applications. The applications that are noted include symptom description and differential diagnosis; description and prediction of role functioning; prediction of health, medical outcomes, mental health, psychotherapeutic, and forensic outcomes; identification of characteristics that can affect the outcomes of treatment; and psychological assessment as a treatment technique.

Certainly, this author is in agreement with the PAWG. Why then do the findings reported in the professional literature seem to fall on deaf ears? The PAWG members contend that the profession has not done a good job of educating MBHOs and other third-party payers about the empirical support that exists for psychological testing and assessment. Taking some license with that famous saying from the movie *Jerry Maguire*, MBHOs are asking psychologists to *SHOW ME THE DATA!*

Cost-Effectiveness and Value of Assessment not Empirically Demonstrated.   One major point made by the PAWG that this author disagrees with is its contention that psychological testing is cost-effective (Kubiszyn et al., 2000). There really has not been an *empirical* demonstration of the direct value and (most importantly) the cost-effectiveness of psychological testing and assessment in MBHOs. This claim is not new and, to the best of this author's knowledge, cannot be disputed at this time. Even the PAWG stops short of disputing the claim, making statements that only indicate the possibility or likelihood of cost-effectiveness. For example, the PAWG indicates that "Health care costs *would be expected* to follow from enhanced diagnosis and treatment" (p. 120) stemming from psychological assessment; "Neuropsychological tests . . . are useful . . . for *facilitating accurate diagnosis toward cost-effective treatment*" (p. 120); and "psychological assessment instruments can identify patients who are likely to utilize health care services more often than average," and "health care utilization *clearly influences* third-party payer 'bottom line' decision making" (p. 124) [italics added]. But MBHOs are crying, "*SHOW ME THE MONEY!*" The industry will not accept a "trust me, it works" attitude by psychologists, particularly when other behavioral health care professionals render effective treatment without it. Psychologists must show actual cost and/or treatment effectiveness *beyond* what treatment yields *without* using the same assessment process.

Why has the cost-effectiveness never been proven? One reason has to do with the difficulty in implementing the type of methodology that would have to be employed—particularly with regard to controlling for variables related to psychologists' skill, patients' symptoms, the instrumentation used, and the therapy process employed. As Ambrose (1997) has stated,

As distasteful as it sounds, the question that all health care providers face in this new health care environment is, "Why should managed care pay for these traditional services?"—especially since it is the responsibility of [the MBHOs] to ensure that benefits are expended in an appropriate fashion on behalf of the members they serve. While it is fairly easy to document benefits of the extrication of a cancerous tumor from the human body, or the utilization of an advanced radiological technique to identify cerebral malfunction, it is much more difficult to present a uniform cause–effect relationship between the uses of objective personality assessment, and treatment outcomes, given the uniqueness of instrument client–clinician variables. (p. 62).

A well-controlled study is not impossible, but it would be very difficult and quite costly. Assuming the ability to implement the necessary methodology, the question then becomes one of who would bear the cost of such a study. One can be fairly certain that it would not be the MBHOs. To be sure, this is an important issue that would be more appropriately dealt with by the American Psychological Association or other professional groups that represent the practicing psychologists and promote their work to individuals, businesses, and organizations outside of the profession.

Use of Medication Trials to Arrive at Diagnoses. Another PAWG report (Eisman, Dies, Finn, Eyde, Kay, Kubiszyn, Meyer, & Moreland, 1998, 2000) identified an increase in the use of medication trials as one reason for the decline in psychological testing—at least for diagnostic purposes. Here, the fact that positive reactions to certain medications are expected in certain disorders but not in others might be used to differentiate between those disorders. A good example might be the use of Ritalin to differentiate ADHD from other possible disorders, such as anxiety, depression, or a psychotic disorder. However useful this might seem, the PAWG pointed out the downside of such a practice, for example, the possibility of developing serious medication side effects, or delaying or restricting a patient's access to other more appropriate types of treatment, such as psychotherapy.

AUTHORIZATION OF PSYCHOLOGICAL TESTING

Despite the complaints and fears psychologists have about its place in the current system of behavioral health care, MBHOs do authorize psychological testing services—just not every time it is requested. Sometimes authorization denials are based on a clear lack of justification for the testing and thus are quite appropriate. Sometimes they reflect idiosyncrasies of a particular reviewer's clinical judgment. At other times, however, denials may come about not as the result of inappropriate requests or lack of knowledge on the part of a particular care manager, but rather as a consequence of various factors that are unrelated to a real need for the benefits that testing can bring. This frequently reflects a lack of knowledge, errors, or oversights on the part of the psychologist during the authorization request process—variables that are clearly within his control.

The sections that follow present information intended to provide the reader with an understanding of the general reasoning behind and processes associated with the authorization of psychological testing services in MBHO settings. Also included are suggestions about how one should go about submitting an authorization request. There are no guarantees that this knowledge will result in authorization for testing, but it should help improve the chances that a request for authorization will be approved.

What MBHOs Want to Know About Providers of Testing Services

In order to receive authorization for testing, the psychologist typically must be member of the MBHO's provider panel or otherwise be known to the MBHO. Stout (1997) recommends that psychologists wishing to contract with MBHOs for their testing services should be prepared to provide the organization with specific information. First, in addition to the general information that is gathered as part of the MBHO's credentialing process, MBHOs may want to know basic access and availability information, such as what the psychologist's ability is to take on new referrals, his appointment availability, ability to return calls in a timely manner, and the geographic areas that he services. Professionally, they may inquire about the psychologist's professional status at local hospitals, the number of provider panels he is a member of, and his liability history.

As for information more specifically related to testing, Stout (1997) indicates that the psychologist may be asked about his testing philosophy; his fee structure by Common Procedural Terminology (CPT) code, specific procedure or test, and battery type (e.g., psychological, neuropsychological); and the degree to which his testing services are automated (e.g., use of PC- or Internet-based administration or scoring software). In addition, he also may be asked to provide the MBHO with samples of psychological reports written for various clinical populations (e.g., children, adult inpatients, neuropsychological or geriatric patients).

Even if this or similar information is not specifically required, the psychologist seeking testing authorizations and referrals from an MBHO may wish to provide it anyway. There are two reasons for this. First, the psychologist becomes a known entity. Having this type of information enables the MBHO to match the skills and credentials of the psychologist to particular populations and situations in which the need for testing arises. Knowing the psychologist and his areas of expertise can make MBHO staff feel more confident about necessity of testing being requested by the psychologist and the person who will actually be doing the testing. Second, providing this information may help stave off any misconceptions or unrealistic expectations about the psychologist's skills. This in turn may help prevent potentially conflictual situations with the MBHO from arising in the future.

Authorization Process

Like everything else, the process for submitting, evaluating, and approving requests for psychological testing varies among MBHOs. However, there are several aspects of the process that probably generalize across many of these organizations. Based on the experience of Schaefer et al. (2000) and that of this author, the following is a likely scenario that is consistent with the operation of many MBHOs:

1. A member of the MBHOs provider network has completed an initial evaluation of a patient, or has begun treating a patient, and has determined the need for psychological testing.

2. The provider submits a written request to the MBHO for psychological testing.

3. The request is reviewed for a determination of medical necessity for the testing by a designated MBHO staff member. In most cases, the reviewer will be an MBHO

staff psychologist with the appropriate training and credentials to make a determination of medical necessity. However, it is possible that the determination will be made by someone other than a psychologist (Ambrose, 1997).

4. Based on an evaluation of the information provided to the reviewer against the MBHO's criteria for medical necessity, a decision is made to approve or not approve the request. A request may be approved for the administration of all requested tests or for a portion thereof.

5. Upon request, a peer-to-peer (the requesting provider-to-MBHO reviewer) review of the case may take place prior to the decision.

6. The provider making the request is notified of the decision regarding the request.

7. If the request is approved in full or part and the requesting provider is a qualified psychologist, the psychologist may proceed with and be reimbursed for the testing that was approved. If the requesting provider is not a psychologist qualified to conduct the testing that has been approved, the patient is referred to a qualified psychologist for the approved testing.

8. If the request was denied in full or in part, the requesting provider is notified of his right to appeal the decision and the process by which to do so. Upon appealing the original decision but barring an overturn of that decision, the requesting provider is notified of the next level of appeal that is available to him and the process by which to initiate this second level of appeal. Depending on state regulations, applicable accreditation standards, health plan delegation agreement and the rights and responsibilities specified in the patient's health plan certificate of coverage, other levels of appeal also may be available should the original decision continue to be withheld at the second level. Such an appeal may be forwarded to an agency external to the MBHO for final disposition.

Determination of Medical Necessity for Testing

Generally, an MBHO's criteria for determining the medical necessity of any requested testing is consistent with the orientation of a system providing care that is typically brief in duration, problem-focused, and oriented to optimizing the resources that are available to it. Consequently, MBHOs do not view testing as a standard part of the services they offer but as a tool to assist its network providers in the treatment of the more difficult or complex cases.

Criteria for Authorization of Testing. Again, based on the experiences of this author and Schaefer et al. (2000), the criteria for approving a request for psychological testing in an MBHO system will likely include most if not all of the following:

- The patient for whom the testing is requested has been evaluated and/or treated by a psychologist or other qualified provider.
- Based on the provider's evaluation or treatment of the patient,
  (a) the patient is not responding to treatment in the expected manner, or there is a differential diagnostic question that has a significant bearing on the treatment of the patient; and
  (b) the results of the testing will help resolve the diagnostic question and/or clarify the appropriate course of treatment.

- The questions to be answered by the testing are clearly stated and can be answered by the results of the specific tests that are being proposed for that purpose.
- The results of the testing will indicate either a diagnosis or mode of treatment that is covered under the patient's health plan certificate of coverage.
- All the tests that are requested are necessary for answering the evaluation questions.
- The psychologist who is requesting authorization for testing is qualified to conduct the proposed testing, or another psychologist qualified to conduct the testing is available for referral.

It is possible that a request may be partially approved. For example, instead of authorizing a request to administer the MMPI-2, MCMI-III, and Rorschach for a differential diagnostic question, the MBHO may determine the questions can be answered by the results of the MMPI-2 alone. In this example then, only the MMPI-2 would be authorized.

Requests for authorization for neuropsychological testing are frequently considered separately from requests from the more "standard" requests. Under some certificates of coverage, neuropsychological testing is covered under medical benefits rather than behavioral health benefits. Depending on the patient's health plan then, requests for neuropsychological testing may be referred to the health plan for review and an authorization decision. According to Schaefer et al. (2000), when neuropsychological testing is requested, it may not be necessary for the patient to have been evaluated first by a qualified provider, to have a DSM-IV Axis I or Axis II diagnosis (an Axis III diagnosis may suffice), or to display evidence of functional impairment. Moreover, the purpose of the testing may be for a reason other than the development or modification of a treatment plan. For instance, it may also be used to determine the patient's ability to live independently or to monitor the progression of the disease or disorder.

Criteria for Noncertification of Testing.   The experiences of this author and others (Schaefer et al., 2000; E. A. Nelson, personal communication, November 22, 1999) suggest that requests for authorization for psychological testing are likely to be denied for any of a number of reasons, including:

- The answer to the testing question can be obtained or inferred from other sources of data (e.g., medical chart review, collateral interview).
- The testing results will be used only to *confirm* or cross-validate an already answered diagnostic question.
- The results of the testing will be used to determine the presence of a diagnosis or the appropriateness of a treatment that is not covered in the patient's certificate of coverage.
- Psychological testing for the purpose specified by the referring provider is not part of the patient's covered health plan benefits.
- A qualified provider has not yet assessed the patient at the time of the request.
- Testing has been requested as routine part of a psychologist's assessment of all patients.

- The request is for

  (a) a reason other than to assist in the formulation of a diagnosis of or a treatment plan for a psychiatric disorder (e.g., achievement testing for appropriate grade placement in school; intellectual or vocational interest assessment as part of career exploration), or

  (b) the purpose of specifying the aspects of the patient's problem beyond the point of actually impacting the treatment plan.

- The patient's level of stress and/or associated functional impairment is related to obvious current stressors.

- The tests requested do not have empirical support for addressing the issues that have prompted the request for authorization.

- The psychological testing can be appropriately performed by another organization (e.g., the public school system).

- The testing is court-ordered but unrelated to the determination of a diagnosis or development of a treatment plan (e.g., determination of competency to stand trial).

Reimbursement Considerations

Like every other aspect of the business, the rate at which authorized testing is reimbursed varies from one MBHO to another. It may be based on an established per test or per battery rate, or on a set hourly rate based on the time spent in approved testing activities (administration, scoring, interpretation, report by individual, and/or feedback to the patient). Alternately, the MBHO may reimburse the psychologist a percent (e.g., 75%) of his standard fee for the type of testing that has been authorized. In other instances, the psychologist may be permitted to use a certain number of the total sessions authorized for the patient's treatment for the purpose of completing the psychological assessment. Reimbursement is then made at the standard per session rate.

In most cases, authorization is for a licensed psychologist to perform the testing. There may be exceptions, depending on what is permitted by the state in which the patient receives services and the conditions specified in the patient's certificate of coverage. Reimbursement may be denied if the testing was conducted by someone other than the provider who received the authorization (e.g., psychological assistant/technician).

Improving the Chances of Obtaining Authorization: What to Do

As anyone who has gone through the process knows, obtaining an MBHO's authorization to conduct psychological testing on one of its covered lives is neither a "gimme" nor a *pro forma* exercise. MBHOs want to make sure that the requested testing is necessary for the care of the patient in question. It therefore is important for the psychologist to do all that he can to maximize the chances that his request will be approved by the MBHO. Following are several positive actions that should be helpful in this regard.

Learn to Work and Deal With Managed Care. The best thing that any MBHO provider can do to help ensure his patients receive the appropriate and necessary services is to learn to work within the system. This is true whether the services in question involve psychological testing, inpatient or outpatient mental health treatment, residential care, or any other services that are available through the MBHO. Based on a survey of managed care organizations regarding what they saw as training needs for their providers, Schreter (1997) has identified six core sets of essential skills that psychologists and other providers need to master in order to adequately address their patients' needs in MBHO systems.

The first core skill set identified by Schreter (1997) is *clinical care skills*. These include providing goal-focused, problem-oriented treatment that is organized around treatment guidelines and preferred practices, yields the greatest return for the time and resources that are invested, and returns the patient to adequate health and functioning. Also included here are the use of couples, family, group, and other alternative treatment modalities, and knowing when to make appropriate use of the inpatient services.

The second set of core skills is classified as *clinical management skills* (Schreter, 1997). In this case, clinical management involves providing services at the appropriate level and intensity of care. This includes making use of community resources, as appropriate. Related to this is the coordination of care with the patient's primary care provider and other health care providers, and the facilitation of the work of the MBHO's care managers. Other important clinical management skills include knowing how to deal with personality-disordered patients and being able to organize clinical and management services within a CQI framework.

Clinical knowledge encompasses the third set of core skills (Schreter, 1997). This entails providing treatment using the primary care model of brief, symptom-focused treatment within the context of a long, continuous provider–therapist relationship. Tied to this is knowing the most effective and efficacious treatment approaches, including when to incorporate psychopharmacologic interventions. Knowledge and use of preventative strategies within a population model of health care also are important.

The fourth core set is *skills with special populations*. In particular, Schreter (1997) identified traditionally underserved populations (e.g., children, adolescents, elderly, disabled), patients referred from employee assistance programs (EAPs), and worker's compensation/disabled patients. He also pointed to the need to develop and implement innovative programs for patients with special needs (e.g., substance abusers with AIDS). Moreover, providers must be able to differentiate substance abuse and mental health problems and, as needed, refer elsewhere for appropriate treatment.

Administrative competence is the fifth core skill set identified by Schreter (1997). Although the least *clinically* relevant of the identified skill sets, it is nonetheless important. This skill set essentially represents knowing the "rules of the game" and how to play. Included here are knowing the MBHO's medical necessity criteria and their implications for treatment; conforming to the MBHO's administrative procedures, such as those pertaining to requesting pre-authorization, additional services (e.g., psychological testing), appealing authorization denials, and billing; and documenting treatment according to the MBHO's standards. Another facet of the administrative competence skill set is knowing and understanding the patient's benefit plan. This is particularly important when the benefit in question is psychological testing.

Schreter's (1997) sixth and final core skill set is *ethical care management*. Here, he refers to the need to place the patient first when conflicts between potential clinician benefit and the patient's well-being arise, to advocate to the MBHO for the what is in the patient's best interest, and to manage the patient with the available resources across the continuum of care. Also included here is Schereter's warning, that "If you don't want to see it in the newspaper, don't do it" (p. 657). An extensive discussion about dealing with ethical issues is presented in chapter 9.

Educate Care Managers About Testing. Ambrose (1997) mentions several ways to influence the decision about the psychologist's testing request. One is to develop a good working relationship with the MBHO such that testing becomes a win–win proposition for both parties. In other words, the psychologist should work toward demonstrating his skills and value to the MBHO while helping the MBHO to demonstrate its value to its customers and other stakeholders in the care process. Depending on the person, this may first require educating the nonpsychologist care manager about the value of testing. This may involve discussing topics such as situations when testing is appropriate, types of questions testing can help answer, the advantages and strengths of various types of tests, and the effect of client variables on test results. Providing sample reports will also prove helpful in educating care managers, as will explaining how psychological testing can help meet the MBHO's goals of demonstrating value, extending benefits to patients, and improving outcomes. The psychologist also should be sensitive to the care manager's desire to have the explanation for testing and the resulting findings presented in simple, concise terms. Overall, demonstrating his ability to cooperate with the MBHO and be an effective provider and problem solver will help establish the psychologist with the MBHO. With time, the MBHO will begin to view him as a resource requiring less scrutiny when he submits requests for services.

For those just beginning their relationship with an MBHO, it will be helpful to have other nonpsychologist providers (e.g., psychiatrists, clinical social workers) vouch for their services and the value they can bring to the MBHO and its patients (Ambrose, 1997). As well, providing the MBHO with evidence of positive feedback that the psychologist has received from employers (who are the purchasers of the behavioral health service and the MBHO's ultimate customers) and employees about the usefulness of psychological testing can go a long way in promoting its benefits.

Know the Patient's Benefits. As might be surmised from the earlier discussion, not only is it important to know the specific criteria that are used to evaluate requests for testing, it also is important to know if a particular type of testing is even covered by the patient's benefit plan. As indicated earlier, neuropsychological testing may be a reimbursable benefit under the patient's medical benefits but not under his behavioral health benefits. Alternately, it may not be a covered under either set of benefits. And asking the patient about his benefits probably is not the best way to determine what they actually are. Ambrose (1997) offered sage advice about this matter, stating that

> a clinician is best served by assuming little about a potential client's level of benefits. In particular, one should never assume that the client fully understands the extent of the mental health benefit package they possess unless they have verified them by reviewing their benefit booklet information or have discussed benefit limits with the parent company Customer Service [or Provider Relations] Department. (p. 63)

Ambrose (1997) goes on to recommend that the psychologist document all contacts with either of these two MBHO departments. Documentation of each contact should include the date and time of the contact, the name of person with whom they spoke, the issue that was discussed, and the information that was supplied. Having this type of documentation may prove to be valuable should related issues arise in the future.

Provide the Necessary Support for the Request. An important step to obtaining approval of a request for psychological testing is providing the MBHO the information it needs to make an informed decision about the request. Many MBHOs require the completion of a standard form designed to elicit the particular information that they use in making decisions about requests for psychological testing. Others allow a less formal means of submitting such a request. For those MBHOs that fall into this latter category, this author recommends providing the information that the testing request form developed by Schaefer et al. (2000) elicits. This includes the following:

- *Current DSM-IV Axis I and Axis II diagnoses.* One should include working diagnoses but not rule-out, provisional, or differential diagnoses. If present, these would be indicated in one of the sections that follow.
- *Reason for referral.* Typically, the reason for referral will be because the patient has failed to progress as expected in treatment, or there is a question concerning the patient's diagnosis. The diagnostic question commonly arises from symptom complexity or conflicting diagnoses from multiple providers and facilities that had treated the patient in the past.
- *History of present illness.* The information presented here should include those current and past symptoms related to the patient's presenting illness, including a description of the onset, duration, and precipitants of each.
- *Treatment history.* This section should include a history of current and past episodes of care. For each episode, the following should be specified: LOC, therapeutic modality, pharmacotherapy (if any), provider's discipline, frequency of care, duration of care, and response to treatment.
- *Previous testing.* A summary of relevant psychological testing that was previously performed should be provided in this section. For each incidence of psychological testing, there should be a summary that includes the relevance to the reason for referral, date of testing, the person performing the testing, purpose of testing, test findings and recommendations, and the outcomes of that testing.
- *Referral question.* This will commonly be for differential diagnosis or to rule out a diagnosis, or to make a clinical or functional distinction that will impact the patient's treatment.
- *Treatment implications.* Here, one would indicate how the findings from the testing will affect the treatment that the patient receives. For example, the differential diagnosis favoring an affective disorder over an anxiety disorder will have pharmacotherapeutic implications. Similarly, a differential diagnosis favoring a psychotic disorder over an affective disorder would have implications for the type of therapy that would be employed (supportive vs. cognitive–behavioral).
- *Tests required.* All requested tests and procedures, including clinical interview, collateral interviews (e.g., teacher, spouse, parent), and the test feedback session should be listed.
- *Total hours requested.* The time involved for each requested test or procedure, as well as the total time, also should be indicated. The time taken to administer,

score, and/or interpret a given test or procedure can be a bone of contention between the psychologist and the MBHO. One way of averting arguments over time required for testing is refer to the findings from Camara et al.'s (2000) test usage survey of clinical psychologists and neuropsychologists. Data from this survey include the mean, standard deviation, and median time (in minutes) for each of the separate administration, scoring, and interpretation activities for the 50 test and procedures that were most frequently being used by their subsample of 179 clinical psychologists.

These data are reproduced in Table 2.2. (Similar data is available for the neuropsychologist subsample in Camara et al.)

Things to Recognize When Requesting Authorization. Ambrose (1997) offers some final advice under the category of what one might do to improve the chances of testing authorization. The first is to recognize that for at least those MBHOs who use a nonpsychologist to review testing requests, it may be easier for that person to deny authorization than to wade through issues such as is the request appropriate, who is qualified to perform the testing, and which instruments are most appropriate for the questions the requested testing would be trying to answer. One can also add to this the fact that "Because it is not uniformly accepted that all mental health providers offer these services, it is easy to conclude that they are not uniformly necessary" (p. 68). Second, the psychologist should keep the intended audience in mind when writing the report of the test findings. Although personality issues and characteristics should be highlighted, the report should be clear, concise, and focused on the conclusions and recommendations. Failure in this regard weakens its value and usefulness in the eyes of the patient's care manager. Third, the psychologist should not rely too much on computerized assessment, especially to the point that the MBHO may begin to wonder about the incremental value that the psychologist himself brings beyond the computer-generated report.

Use Clinical and Personal Skills in Dealing With MBHOs. All MBHOs are different, so they need to be treated differently. Ambrose (1997) recommends that when dealing with MBHOs, the psychologist use the same skills that he uses in clinical and personal settings. He does not explain exactly what he means by this, but to this author the implication is pretty clear. The approaches and techniques that have serve the psychologist well in his work and personal life are the ones that will also likely serve him well in dealing with MBHOs. The psychologist must help the MBHO maintain a state of "well-being" while at the same time maintaining his own sense of well-being.

Maximizing the Chances of Authorization: What Not to Do

The recommendations just presented represent positive actions that psychologist can do to help ensure that requests for testing will be approved by the MBHO. By the same token, there are a number of errors which, if avoided, will also increase the chances of authorization of testing.

What Not to do With Care Managers. One of the most important things that a psychologist can do when requesting testing or any other type of service for his patient is avoid entering into an adversarial relationship with the patient's care man-

TABLE 3.2.

Minutes Required by Clinical Psychologists to Administer, Score and Interpret Individual Tests

Tests	No.[1]	Minutes to Administer			Minutes to Score			Minutes to Interpret		
		M	SD	Mdn	M	SD	Mdn	M	SD	Mdn
Aphasia Screening Test	27	24.8	11.9	20.0	11.4	7.3	10.0	14.1	9.9	10.0
Beck Depression Inventory	53	11.1	10.0	10.0	8.2	7.2	5.0	12.5	14.0	10.0
Bender Visual Motor Gestalt Test	112	15.7	7.9	15.0	11.3	7.5	10.0	12.3	8.9	10.0
Boston Naming Test	13	18.8	11.8	15.0	8.8	7.4	5.0	9.6	7.4	10.0
California Verbal Learning Test	18	30.6	11.9	30.0	16.7	8.6	15.0	34.6	69.8	17.5
Category Test	20	43.0	13.5	45.0	13.1	8.7	10.0	20.3	16.9	15.0
Child Behavior Checklist	29	13.1	17.9	10.0	20.0	11.2	20.0	23.3	16.1	20.0
Children's Apperception Test (CAT-A)	38	36.2	18.5	30.0	19.2	21.1	15.0	29.7	29.0	27.5
Children's Depression Inventory	14	11.6	8.0	10.0	9.6	5.0	10.0	10.4	6.5	10.0
Conners' Parent and Teacher Rating Scales	37	11.2	15.6	10.0	12.2	7.3	10.0	14.7	11.2	10.0
Developmental Test of Visual–Motor Integration	20	19.2	24.2	15.0	13.0	12.5	10.0	12.3	9.0	10.0
FAS Word Fluency Test	17	15.1	27.5	7.0	8.3	14.1	5.0	7.6	7.5	5.0
Finger Tapping Test	22	12.5	9.6	10.0	6.2	3.2	5.0	7.8	6.1	5.0
Grooved Pegboard Test	12	8.5	4.1	10.0	4.7	2.4	5.0	4.9	2.0	5.0
Halstead–Reitan Neuropsychological Battery	27	237.8	135.5	240.0	57.3	36.5	60.0	81.9	74.7	60.0
Hand Dynamometer	12	6.3	3.1	5.0	4.9	2.7	5.0	5.3	2.6	5.0
House-Tree-Person Projective Technique	60	17.3	7.7	15.0	11.0	10.6	10.0	15.0	8.5	15.0
Human Figures Drawing Test	49	14.7	8.1	15.0	12.3	13.8	10.0	14.1	9.6	10.0
Kaufman Assessment Battery for Children	19	70.3	23.9	60.0	27.1	24.5	20.0	37.1	30.2	30.0
Kinetic Drawing System for Family and School	25	14.0	6.3	15.0	8.1	11.3	5.0	13.3	10.0	10.0
Luria–Nebraska Neuropsychological Battery	14	126.8	62.1	120.0	34.3	23.6	30.0	53.9	33.8	52.5
Memory Assessment Scales	12	53.8	19.9	50.0	17.5	5.0	15.0	21.3	8.6	20.0
Millon Adolescent Clinical Inventory	38	14.8	17.3	10.0	16.0	13.8	15.0	32.4	17.8	30.0
Millon Clinical Multiaxial Inventory	53	19.4	21.6	10.0	18.8	16.2	15.0	29.3	17.3	25.0
Minnesota Multiphasic Personality Inventory (MMPI-2)	138	29.8	37.0	10.0	21.9	16.5	20.0	36.1	32.9	30.0

Myers–Briggs Type Indicator	10	14.0	12.6	10.0	18.0	12.1	17.5	46.0	47.7	27.5
Peabody Picture Vocabulary Test–Revised	34	22.9	10.5	20.0	12.4	6.5	10.0	15.4	10.9	15.0
Personality Inventory for Children	10	5.5	7.2	2.5	21.5	15.6	20.0	20.5	13.4	15.0
Rey Complex Figures Test	25	19.9	8.8	20.0	14.9	8.3	10.0	24.2	60.0	10.0
Reynolds Adolescent Depression Scale	11	16.8	16.5	10.0	12.3	7.2	10.0	17.3	18.1	10.0
Roberts Apperception Test for Children	25	39.8	17.4	35.0	21.6	15.9	20.0	33.8	22.8	30.0
Rorschach Inkblot Test	124	45.3	20.6	45.0	44.8	31.7	37.5	50.6	45.7	30.0
Rotter Incomplete Sentences Blank	45	16.6	12.2	15.0	12.1	12.2	10.0	17.8	12.1	15.0
Symptom Checklist-90-Revised	12	15.2	16.4	12.5	10.3	8.8	10.0	22.5	18.5	15.0
Sentence Completion Test	40	15.3	10.5	15.0	12.0	10.2	10.0	21.8	17.6	15.0
Shipley Institute of Living Scale	11	15.9	13.0	10.0	10.5	7.6	10.0	18.4	18.7	15.0
Sixteen Personality Factor Questionnaire	15	36.1	36.7	30.0	16.3	8.3	15.0	25.0	17.9	20.0
Stanford–Binet Intelligence Scale	22	68.8	31.1	60.0	22.6	11.0	20.0	31.3	21.5	30.0
Strong Interest Inventory (4th ed.)	15	25.0	23.5	15.0	137.7	349.3	5.0	30.0	19.9	20.0
Stroop Neuropsychological Screening Test	19	15.3	6.1	15.0	10.5	6.9	10.0	13.9	8.4	10.0
Test of Visual-Motor Integration	25	15.5	4.3	15.0	11.6	4.7	10.0	12.9	11.4	10.0
Thematic Apperception Test	107	38.4	19.2	30.0	19.5	19.9	15.0	34.2	29.4	30.0
Trail Making Test A&B	52	14.3	8.7	12.5	9.5	10.3	5.0	13.8	25.7	10.0
Vineland Adaptive Behavior Scales	37	51.1	19.7	45.0	25.7	12.4	30.0	26.6	16.9	30.0
Vineland Social Maturity Scale	13	24.6	10.7	20.0	15.4	14.2	10.0	13.2	10.1	10.0
Wechsler Adult Intelligence Test-Revised	151	78.6	22.1	75.0	22.9	15.7	20.0	35.3	40.1	30.0
Wechsler Intelligence Scale for Children-Revised and III	135	82.4	25.7	80.0	24.7	18.5	20.0	39.2	44.1	30.0
Wechsler Memory Scale-Revised	58	48.7	25.3	45.0	19.6	11.2	15.0	23.5	14.5	20.0
Wide Range Achievement Test-Revised	86	31.9	20.2	30.0	15.7	11.4	15.0	17.7	14.5	15.0
Wisconsin Card Sorting Test	19	31.3	12.6	30.0	20.4	16.0	15.0	19.3	14.1	15.0
Woodcock-Johnson Psycho-Educational Battery-Revised	30	90.5	68.6	72.5	33.4	22.9	30.0	36.9	28.2	30.0

Note. From "Psychological Test Usage: Implications in Professional Psychology," by W. J. Camara, J. S. Nathan, and A. E. Puente, 2000, *Professional Psychology: Research and Practice, 31,* p. 151. Copyright 2000 by the American Psychological Association. Adapted with permission.

[1]Number of psychologists reporting.

ager. Ambrose (1997) offers a few sound suggestions regarding this matter. First, one should not become defensive when asked to justify his reasons for requesting the testing. This behavior is self-defeating and only prolongs doing what must be done to obtain the necessary approval. Keep in mind that the unquestioning approval of requests for sometimes-unnecessary testing and therapeutic services in the past has contributed to the current state of behavioral health care today. It is fiscally irresponsible to both the consumer (i.e., the patient) and the customer (i.e., the payer) of the service to rubber stamp requests for testing. It may be frustrating to have to repeatedly go over the reasons for requesting testing with the care manager. At the same time, if presented in a manner that educates the care manager, this will help to establish a positive relationship that should lead to less need for time-consuming explanations and justifications in the future.

Second, one should avoid using technical terms and jargon in place of clear, concise communication with the care manager (Ambrose, 1997). Spouting "psychobabble" to intimidate the care manager may accomplish nothing more than limiting the amount of information that can be used to support the psychologist's request while inciting or contributing to antagonism between the two parties. Finally, do not threaten that a crisis and its inevitable consequences (e.g., an expensive inpatient admission) will ensue if testing is not performed. This, too, can contribute to an adversarial relationship unless such claims are back by some form of verification.

In the spirit of promoting a good relationship with its care managers, it also is unwise to continually bombard the MBHO with testing authorization requests. Despite how one may have been trained, every patient does *not* need to be tested, nor does every other patient, nor every third patient. Requests should be made with this in mind, and with the knowledge that approaching the MBHO for authorization for testing only when it is really needed (not just desirable) will help the psychologist build credibility with care managers and increase the chances for approval of these requests.

Common Clinical Mistakes in Requesting Authorization.   Schaefer et al. (2000) identified several *clinical* mistakes that are commonly made in requesting authorization for psychological testing. These mistakes are as follows:

1. Testing is requested before the patient has undergone an evaluation or begun treatment. In other words, testing is requested as a routine part of the services that the psychologist provides rather than as a means to resolve a difficult diagnostic or treatment question.
2. The only rationale for testing is the patient's history. What has happened with the patient in the past (e.g., previous treatment, sexual abuse as a child, past history of substance abuse) is no justification in and of itself for a psychological assessment in the present.
3. The referral question does not clearly indicate why testing is deemed important at this particular time.
4. The psychologist is unfamiliar with the background and other details of the case, including previous test findings. This can convey a sense that the psychologist has not done a thorough evaluation that could help answer the referral question, before making his request.
5. The primary reason for testing is to determine the most appropriate LOC. As was discussed earlier in this chapter, LOC decisions are based on MBHO-

specific criteria that are not directly unrelated to test findings. This is aside from the fact that very few psychological tests are developed to answer such questions.

6. The implications of testing for the patient's treatment are vague and unrelated to the referral question.

There is another clinical error that can be added to this list. It is an extension of what was just touched on in Item 5, that is, requesting authorization to administer tests that are not designed to answer the referral question. For example, it is highly unlikely that an MBHO will approve a request for the administration of the Rorschach to rule out the presence of brain dysfunction; nor will the administration of a WAIS-III be authorized to answer a differential diagnostic question of an anxiety disorder versus an affective disorder.

Note that all of these clinical errors can be preempted if the psychologist takes the time to think carefully about what he is asking for and why he is asking for it now. The conclusion he reaches may be that a request for testing is not justified for this patient at this particular time. This, in turn, may prevent the submission of a request that not only is denied but also may lead the MBHO to be less receptive to (or at least to more closely scrutinize) future requests from the psychologist. In essence, exercising good clinical judgment now can avert problems with credibility and questions of the psychologist competency later on.

Common Administrative Mistakes. MBHOs must adopt a complicated system of policies and procedures in order to meet regulatory, accreditation, and business needs and remain competitive in the behavioral health care market. These set the "rules of the game" for the organization and, consequently, for those in the organization's provider network. Thus, not conforming to required procedures with regard to requesting and billing for psychological testing services can only lead to delays or denials in the authorization or reimbursement process. In addition to the clinical mistakes just mentioned, Schaefer et al. (2000) identified several *administrative* mistakes that commonly occur with regard to the test authorization process. They include the following:

1. *Failure to complete the psychological testing request/authorization form.* One needs to make sure that if a specific test authorization request form is required by the MBHO, it is completed in full and according to the MBHO specifications. Similarly, all of the information the MBHO requires for making a testing authorization decision requested should be provided if there is no form to complete.

2. *Billing the wrong carrier.* Sometimes, neuropsychological testing and other testing should be billed to the health plan that is responsible for the patient's medical care. A good rule of thumb may be that if it is a medical diagnosis, bill to the medical carrier. The MBHO would be able to clarify the matter if there is any question.

3. *Submission of an incorrect claim form.* The MBHO will be able to provide the correct claim form to use when submitting a claim for testing.

4. *Use of incorrect billing codes.* The MBHO will also be able to verify the correct CPT or other codes to use for the testing itself (e.g., CPT 96100) or services related to the assessment (e.g., initial interview, CPT 90801).

5. *Failure to heed provider restrictions.* Errors here can range from performing procedures that are not covered under psychological services (e.g., EEG testing as part of a

neuropsychological evaluation) to the use of technicians or assistants for the administration, scoring, and/or interpretation of tests. This latter point may be particularly important to neuropsychologists, who frequently use technicians to administer and score lengthy neuropsychological test batteries. The best rule of thumb is to verify with the MBHO care manager what, if any, authorization restrictions exist.

6. *Failure to consider the requirement for a written report.* The MBHO may require a written report of test findings as a condition of the approved request, so it is best to clarify this ahead of time. One should also clarify what the MBHO would like to see in terms of report content, format, and/or special reporting requirements. Moreover, if a report is required, this fact should be made known to the patient so that the appropriate release of information can be obtained.

7. *Failure to obtain a referral from the patient's primary care provider (PCP).* In some MBHOs, authorization for psychological testing requires a referral from the patient's PCP. Obviously, before making any requests for testing, the psychologist should determine if this is the case with the MBHO(s) he serves. If so, it would be important for the psychologist to establish some means of facilitating the referral process with PCPs.

SUMMARY

Many aspects of psychological testing have changed since the managed system of behavioral health care delivery began to gain prominence. Obtaining authorization for reimbursable testing is just one of those aspects, but an important one, to be sure. As with other services, MBHOs have processes for requesting and authorizing testing that are part of a larger system of service authorization and care management. It is a system that psychologists and other behavioral health care professionals often find frustrating, but it is also a system that enables the MBHO to meet the demands of multiple stakeholders — patients, providers, payers, regulatory and accrediting bodies — while remaining fiscally solvent and working to demonstrate value, extend benefits to patients, and improve the outcomes of care.

Partly as a consequence of meeting these requirements, the use of psychological testing in the more "traditional" way has taken a back seat to other purposes that the MBHOs view as primary. These days, testing of individual patients for diagnostic and/or treatment planning purposes is viewed as secondary in utility to its use in measuring clinical performance indicators, assessing treatment outcomes, or developing programs for specific patient populations. There are several reasons for this, including MBHOs' emphasis on brief treatment, its skepticism of claims pertaining to the value and cost-effectiveness of psychological testing, and the use of medication trials for diagnostic purposes. Also, one should not forget the occurrences of unnecessary and sometimes inappropriate use of psychological testing that psychologists have been guilty of in the past — occurrences that have contributed to MBHOs' skepticism about testing's true value to the treatment of behavioral health problems.

MBHOs typically have a separate process for requesting and authorizing testing services for those whose care they are responsible. The psychologist is asked to provide information that justifies the request. Based on this information and the MBHO's established criteria, the request is either approved or denied. An appeals process provides the patient and/or psychologist a means of recourse when the request is denied.

There are several things the psychologist can do to facilitate the approval of the testing requests that he submits. The first is learning how to work with the MBHO in a manner that promotes good relations and prevents the development of an adversarial relationship between the two parties. This includes knowing the criteria for testing authorization. Also, educating the care manager who reviews testing requests about the use and benefits of testing (if necessary), knowing the patient's benefits, and providing all the information the MBHO requires for making a decision can go a long way toward being successful in receiving authorization for testing. In addition, there are a number of clinical errors (e.g., requesting testing before the patient has undergone an initial assessment) and administrative errors (e.g., failure to complete a testing authorization request form) that, if avoided, can also serve to facilitate the authorization process.

Psychological Test Instruments, Technology, and Criteria for Their Selection

Several types of instruments could be used in MBHO systems for the general assessment purposes described in chapter 2. For example, neuropsychological instruments might be used to assess memory deficits that could impact the clinician's decision to perform further testing, the goals established for treatment, and the approach to treatment that is selected. Tests designed to provide estimates of level of intelligence might be used for the same purposes. Similarly, many test formats and automated delivery systems for administering, scoring, and reporting the results of these instruments are available to assist in the testing process. In general, applications of the same technology that touches many aspects of our lives have been developed to assist in testing activities, thus enabling psychologists to be more efficient and cost-effective in providing services within MBHO and other health care systems.

It is beyond the scope of this chapter (and this book) to address, even in the most general way, all of the types of tests, rating scales, instrumentation, and technologies that might be employed in an MBHO environment. Instead, the focus here will be on general classes of instrumentation and technologies that have the greatest applicability in the service of patient screening and diagnosis, as well as in the planning, monitoring, and evaluation of psychotherapeutic interventions. To a limited extent, specific examples of instruments and technology are presented. This is followed by a brief overview of criteria and considerations that will assist psychologists and MBHOs in selecting the best instrumentation and technological application(s) for their intended purposes. Instruments that this author has identified as being particularly useful for assessment in MBHO systems are discussed at length in chapters 5 and 8.

INSTRUMENTATION FOR PSYCHOLOGICAL TESTING IN MANAGED BEHAVIORAL HEALTH CARE SYSTEMS

The instrumentation required for any testing application will depend on (a) the general purpose for which the testing is being conducted and (b) the level of informational detail that is required for that purpose. Generally, one may classify the types of instrumentation that would serve the testing purposes in MBHO systems into one of five general categories. Other types of instrumentation are frequently used in clinical settings for therapeutic purposes. However, the present discussion will be limited to those instruments that are more commonly used for screening, diagnosis, treatment planning, treatment monitoring, and outcomes assessment in MBHO settings.

Psychological/Psychiatric Symptom Measures

Probably the most frequently used instrumentation for each of the five stated purposes are measures of psychopathological symptomatology. These are the types of instruments on which the majority of the clinician's training in psychological testing has likely been focused. These instruments were developed to help assess the problems that typically prompt people to seek treatment in MBHOs and other behavioral health care settings.

Comprehensive Multidimensional Measures. These are typically lengthy, multiscale instruments that measure and provide a graphical profile of the patient on several symptom domains (e.g., anxiety, depression) or disorders (schizophrenia, antisocial personality). Also, summary indices sometimes are available to provide a more global picture of the individual with regard to his or her psychological status or level of distress. Probably the most widely used and/or recognized of thse measures are the Minnesota Multiphasic Personality Inventory (MMPI; Hathaway & McKinley, 1951) and its restandardized revision, the MMPI-2 (Butcher, Dahlstrom, Graham, Tellegen, & Kaemmer, 1989), the MCMI-III (Millon, 1994), and the Personality Assessment Inventory (PAI; Morey, 1991).

Multiscale instruments of this type can serve a variety of purposes that facilitate therapeutic interventions. They may be used on initial contact with the patient to screen for the need for service and, at the same time, yield information that is useful for diagnosis and treatment planning. Indeed, some such instruments (e.g., the MMPI-2) may make available supplementary, content-related, and/or other special scales or indices that can assist in addressing specific treatment considerations (e.g., motivation to engage in treatment). As noted in chapter 2, discussion of the results of these instruments with the patient can serve as a therapeutic intervention. Other multiscale instruments might be useful in identifying specific problems that may be unrelated to the patient's chief complaints (e.g., low self-esteem). Multiscale instruments also can be administered numerous times during the course of treatment to monitor the patient's progress toward achieving established goals and to assist in determining what adjustments (if any) must be made to the therapeutic approach. Moreover, use of such instruments in a pre- and posttreatment fashion can provide information related to the outcomes of an individual patient's treatment. At the same time, data obtained in this fashion can be analyzed with the results of other patients to evaluate the effectiveness of an individual therapist, a particular therapeutic approach, individual service delivery units, or the MBHO staff as a whole.

Abbreviated Multidimensional Measures. These are quite similar to the comprehensive multidimensional measures in many respects. First, by definition, they contain multiple scales for measuring a variety of symptom domains or disorders. They also may allow for the derivation of an index of the patient's general level of psychopathology or distress. In addition, they may be used for screening, diagnostic, treatment planning and monitoring, and outcomes assessment purposes just like the lengthier comprehensive instruments. The distinguishing feature of the abbreviated instrument is its length. These instruments are relatively short, and easy to administer and (usually) to score. Their brevity does not allow for an in-depth assessment of the patient and his or her problems, but this is not what these instruments are designed to do.

Probably the most widely used of these brief instruments are the Derogatis family of symptom checklist instruments. These include the original Symptom Checklist-90 (SCL-90; Derogatis, Lipman, & Covi, 1973) and its revision, the SCL-90-R (Derogatis, 1983). Both of these instruments contain a checklist of 90 psychological symptoms that score on the instruments' nine symptom scales. For each of these instruments an even briefer version has been developed. The first is the Brief Symptom Inventory (BSI; Derogatis, 1992), which was derived from the SCL-90-R. In a health care environment that is cost-conscious and unwilling to make too many demands on a patient's time, this 53-item instrument is gaining popularity over its longer 90-item parent instrument. Similarly, a brief form of the original SCL-90, the SA-45, has been developed (Strategic Advantage, Inc., 1998). Its development did not follow Derogatis' approach to the development of the BSI; instead, cluster analytic techniques were used to select five items to assess each of the same nine symptom domains found on the three Derogatis checklists.

The major strength of the abbreviated multiscale instruments is their ability to broadly and very quickly survey several psychological symptom domains and disorders relative to the patient. Their value is most clearly evident in settings such as MBHOs, where both the time and dollars available for assessment services are quite limited. These instruments provide a lot of information quickly. Also, they are much more likely to be completed by patients than their lengthier counterparts. This last point is particularly important if one is interested in monitoring treatment or assessing outcomes, both of which require two or more testings of the patient to obtain the necessary information.

Unidimensional Measures.   By definition, these instruments assess only one type of disorder or symptom domain and thus are of limited utility. They are most useful in situations in which only a single symptom domain or disorder is of interest, such as in clinical drug trials or treatment programs focused on the alleviation of only one type of symptomatology. Most are brief and are generally used when one wishes to screen for or monitor a particular type of psychopathology. Good examples are the BDI-II, Beck Anxiety Inventory (BAI; Beck, Epstein, Brown, & Steer, 1988; Beck & Steer, 1990), the STAI, and the Geriatric Depression Scale (GDS; Brink, Yesavage, Lum, Heersema, Adey, & Rose, 1982; Yesavage, Brink, Rose, Lum, Huang, Adey, & Leirer, 1983).

Diagnosis-Specific Instruments.   There are many instruments available that have been specifically designed to help identify patients with one or more disorders that meet a diagnostic classification system's criteria for the presence of these disorder(s). Recall that one of the most common reasons for an MBHO to authorize psychological testing is to assist in the diagnosis of complicated cases. In the vast majority of the cases, these types of tests have been designed to detect individuals meeting the diagnostic criteria of DSM-IV or the tenth edition of the International Classification of Diseases (ICD-10; World Health Organization, 1992). Excellent examples of such instruments include the MCMI-III, the Primary Care Evaluation of Mental Disorders (PRIME-MD; Spitzer, Williams, Kroenke, Linzer, duGruy, Hahn, Brody, & Johnson, 1994), the Patient Health Questionnaire (PHQ, the self-report version of the PRIME-MD; Spitzer, Kroenke, Williams, & the Patient Health Questionnaire Primary Care Study Group, 1999), and the Mini-International Neuropsychiatric Interview (M.I.N.I.; Sheehan, Lecrubier, Sheehan, Amorim, Janavs, Weiller, Thierry, Baker, & Dunbar, 1998).

Like many of the instruments developed for screening purposes, most diagnostic instruments are accompanied by research-based diagnostic efficiency statistics — sensitivity, specificity, positive and negative predictive powers, and overall classification rates — that provide the user with estimates of the probability of accurate classification of those having or not having one or more specific disorders. One typically finds classification rates of the various disorders assessed by this type of instrument to vary considerably. For example, the positive predictive power (PPP) for those disorders assessed by the PRIME-MD (Spitzer et al., 1999) range from 19% for minor depressive disorder to 80% for major depressive disorder. For the self-report version of the M.I.N.I. (Sheehan et al., 1998), the PPNs ranged from 11% for dysthymia to 75% for major depressive disorder. Generally, negative predictive powers (NPPs) and overall classification rates are found to be relatively high and significantly less variable across diagnostic groups. For the PRIME-MD, overall accuracy rates ranged from 84% for anxiety not otherwise specified (NOS) to 96% for panic disorder, while M.I.N.I. NPPs ranged from 81% for major depressive disorder to 99% for anorexia. Generally, it would appear that one can feel more confident in the results from these instruments when they indicate that the patient does *not* have a particular disorder. For diagnostic instruments such as these, it therefore is important for the user to be aware of what the research has revealed to be the instrument's classification accuracy for *each individual disorder*, as this may vary quite a bit within and between measures.

It is important to keep in mind the difference between "screeners" and "diagnostic tests." As Volk, Pace, and Parchman (1993) point out:

> A screen is a test used with otherwise unspecified groups, in the absence of other clinical data, that when positive suggests further action be taken, either in the form of diagnostic testing or treatment. . . . It is meant to be brief, practical, and raise suspicion when positive. A diagnostic test allows the [clinician] to make treatment decisions based on the likelihood of disease and is meant to provide a look at a problem that is as good as is technically or economically feasible, given the particular disease. (p. 180).

Regardless of the psychometric property of any given instrument for any disorder or symptom domain evaluated by that instrument, or whether it was developed for diagnostic purposes or not, one should never rely on test findings alone when assigning a diagnosis. As with any other types of psychological test instruments, diagnosis and other clinical conclusions should be based on findings from the test and from other sources, including findings from other instruments, patient and collateral interviews, reviews of psychiatric and medical records (when available), and other pertinent documents.

Other Measures Used for Diagnostic Purposes. There are a number of instruments that, although not specifically designed to arrive at a diagnosis, can provide information that is suggestive of a diagnosis or diagnostic group (e.g. affective disorders), or that can assist in the differential diagnosis of complicated cases. These include multiscale instruments that list symptoms and other aspects of psychiatric disorders, and ask the respondent to indicate if or how much they are bothered by each of these, or whether certain statements are true or false as they apply to them. Generally, research on these instruments has found elevated scores on individual scales, or patterns or "profiles" of multiple elevated scores to be associated with specific disorders or diagnostic groups. Thus, when present, these score profiles are suggestive of the presence of the associated type of pathology and bear further investigation. This information can be used either as a starting place in the diagnostic process or as additional information to support the hypothesis of an already suspected problem.

Probably the best known of this type of instrument is the MMPI-2. It has a substantial body of research indicating that certain elevated scale and subscale profiles or code types are strongly associated with specific diagnoses or groups of diagnoses (see Graham, 2000b and Greene, 2000). For example, an 8-9/9-8 highpoint code type (Schizophrenia and Hypomania scales being the highest among the significantly elevated scales) is typically associated with schizophrenia, while the 4-9/9-4 code type is commonly associated with a diagnosis of antisocial personality disorder. Similarly, research on the PAI has demonstrated typical patterns of individual and multiple-scale configurations that also are diagnostically related. For one PAI profile cluster — prominent elevations on the Depression (DEP) and Suicidal Ideation (SUI) scales with additional elevations on the Schizophrenia (SCZ), Stress (STR), Nonsupport (NON), Borderline Features (BOR), Somatic Complaints (SOM), Anxiety (ANX), and Anxiety-related Disorders (ARD) scales — Morey (1991, 1999) found the most frequently associated diagnoses to be major depression (20%), dysthymia (23%), and anxiety disorder (23%). Sixty-two percent of those with a profile cluster consisting of prominent elevations on Alcohol Problems (ALC) and SOM with additional elevations on DEP, STR, and ANX were diagnosed with alcohol abuse or dependence.

In addition, there are a number of other well-validated, single- or multiscale symptom checklists also can be useful for diagnostic purposes. They provide means of identifying symptom domains (e.g., anxiety, depression, somatization) that are problematic for the patient, thus providing diagnostic clues and guidance for further exploration to the psychologist. The BDI-II and STAI are good examples of well-validated, single-scale symptom measures. Multiscale instruments include measures such as the SCL-90-R and two of its related instruments, the BSI and the SA-45.

Measures of Role Functioning

The term "functioning" can cover numerous activities and other aspects of life that are related to one's ability to cope with the demands of living and make it from one day to the next. Symptomatology, or the lack thereof, reflects one type of functioning, that is, psychological or emotional functioning. Here, the other major aspects of day-to-day functioning are being referred to.

One such aspect is that related to satisfactory performance on the job or, in the case of children or college students, at school. Of course, school performance can also be an issue for adults. Employers are quite interested in their employees returning to or maintaining a satisfactory performance level on the job. Thus, in cases where employers have a vested interest in the service that is provided to their employees, such as those services provided through EAPs or self-insured plans, data on employment-related variables (e.g., number of days tardy, days sick or absent from work, relationships with supervisors or coworkers, work productivity) become particularly relevant and important.

Improvement in one's marital relationship in general, as well as sexual performance, parenting skills, and other identified marital/family problem areas can all be important indicators of positive treatment-related changes. Improvement in relationships outside of the family, such as with friends, teammates, neighbors or anyone else whom the patient has to deal with on a regular basis, can also be a good indicator of psychological improvement. This is especially the case when one considers the degree to which almost any psychological disorder or impairment affects one's ability to appropriately interact with those whom we come in contact.

Except in the case of severely impaired patients, improvement in daily living skills, such as managing money, meeting one's basic survival needs (food, clothing and shelter) and caring for one's self, is not likely to be a major concern. When it is, however, measurement of this aspect of functioning may become tantamount to any other concern about the patient's functioning.

Role functioning has recently gained attention as an important variable to address in the course of assessing the impact of a physical or mental disorder on an individual's life functioning. How the person's ability to work, perform daily tasks, or interact with others is affected by a psychological disorder is important to consider in developing a treatment plan and monitoring progress over time. There are several measures of role functioning that are currently available, including the Katz Adjustment Scales (Katz & Lyerly, 1963; Katz & Warren, 1997). However, this and similar instruments generally tend to be too lengthy for use in MBHO systems. Often, one will find the use of a few very general items, either as part of an intake assessment or as a component of an outcomes measurement system. In other instances, general health status measures that incorporate questions tapping into broad aspects of role functioning will be used to help assess this domain. As will be discussed later, the 36-item SF-36 Health Survey (SF-36; Ware, Snow, Kosinski, & Gandek, 1993; Ware & Sherbourne, 1992) and the 39-item Health Status Questionnaire 2.0 (HSQ; Radosevich, Wetzler, & Wilson, 1994) both address these issues with scales designed for this purpose.

Measures of General Health Status

During the past decade, there has been an increasing interest in the measurement of health status in medical and behavioral health care delivery systems. Initially, this interest was shown primarily within those organizations and settings focused on the treatment of physical diseases and disorders. In recent years, MBHOs and behavioral health care providers have recognized the value of evaluating the patient's general level of health.

It is important to recognize that the term "health" means more than just the absence of disease or debility; it also implies a state of well-being throughout the individual's physical, psychological, and social spheres of existence (World Health Organization; as cited in Stewart & Ware, 1992). Dickey and Wagenaar (1996) note how this concept of health recognizes the importance of eliciting the patient's point of view in measuring health status. They also point to similar conclusions reached by Jahoda (1958) that are specific to the area of mental health. Here, an individual's report of his mental health status relative to *how he feels it should be* is an important component of "mental health."

Measures of health status and physical functioning can be classified into one of two groups: *generic* and *condition-specific*.

Generic Health Status Measures. Probably the most widely used and respected generic health status measures are the SF-36 and HSQ. Aside from minor variations in the scoring of one of the instruments' scales (i.e., Bodily Pain) and the HSQ's inclusion of three depression screening items, the two measures essentially are identical. Each measures eight dimensions of health—four addressing mental health-related constructs and four addressing physical health-related constructs—that reflect the WHO concept of "health."

In response to concerns that even these two relatively brief objective measures are too lengthy for regular administration in clinical and research settings, a 12-item, abbreviated version of each has been developed. The SF-12 Health Survey (SF-12; Ware, Kosinski, & Keller, 1995) was developed for use in large scale, population-based research where the monitoring of health status at a broad level is all that is required. Also, a 12-item version of the HSQ, the HSQ-12 (Radosevich & Pruitt, 1996), was developed for similar uses. (It is interesting that despite being derived from essentially the same instrument, there is only 50% item overlap between the two abbreviated instruments.)

Condition-Specific Measures. Condition-specific health status and functioning measures have been utilized for a number of years. Most have been developed for use with physical rather than mental disorders, diseases, or conditions. However, condition-specific measures of mental health status and functioning are available. A major source of this type of instrumentation is the Center for Outcomes Research and Effectiveness (CORE) at the University of Arkansas for Medical Sciences. CORE also serves as the distributor/clearinghouse for these instruments and associated scoring and information services. The available instruments that would be most useful to behavioral health care practitioners through CORE include those developed for use with schizophrenic, depressive, alcohol/substance use, and adolescent disorders. Measures for other specific psychological disorders are currently under development at CORE.

Quality of Life Measures

Frisch (1999), drawing on the words of others, describes quality of life as "the degree of excellence in life (or living) relative to some expressed or implied standard of comparison, such as most people in a particular society" (p. 1279). In their brief summary of this area, Andrews, Peters, and Teesson (1994) indicate that most of the definitions of the "quality of life" (QOL) describe a multidimensional construct encompassing physical, affective, cognitive, social, and economic domains. *Objective measures* of QOL focus on environmental resources required to meet one's needs and can be completed by someone other than the patient. The *subjective measures* of QOL assess the patient's satisfaction with the various aspects of his life and thus must be completed by the patient.

Andrews et al. (1994) indicate other distinctions in the QOL arena. One has to do with the differences between *QOL* and *health-related quality of life*, or HRQL; and (similar to the case with health status measures) the other has to do with the distinction between *generic* and *condition-specific* measures of QOL. QOL instruments differ from

HRQL instruments in that the former attempts to measure the whole "fabric of life" while the latter measures quality of life as it is affected by a disease or disorder or by its treatment. The generic measures are designed to assess aspects of life that are generally relevant to most people; condition-specific measures are focused on aspects of the lives of particular disease/disorder populations. However, as Andrews et al. point out, there tends to be a great deal of overlap between generic and condition-specific QOL measures.

There are several instruments available that specifically measure for QOL. One example is the Quaility of Life Inventory (QOLI; Frisch, 1994a, 1994b), a 36-item instrument on which the respondent rates the importance of and his satisfaction with 16 aspects of life (e.g., friends, play, work). However, measures of other constructs are frequently used or referred to as sources of information about QOL. For example, one may see references to the SF-36 or SF-12 as being an indicator of QOL. Thus, one should be discerning when investigating potential measures of QOL. The reader will find Frisch's (1999) insights into the matter to be particularly helpful in this regard.

Measures of Well-Being

Within the context of behavioral health assessment, there probably has been no other time in which there has been as great of an interest in subjective well-being (more commonly referred to as "well-being") as now. This probably reflects society's relatively recent focus on maintaining good health and preventing disease and illness, in both the physical and psychological realms. This, in turn, has led to the identification of well-being as an important aspect of psychological health, one that should be attended to and promoted, and, consequently, one that should be measured. Also, recall how Howard and his colleagues view the re-establishment of well-being as an important phase of psychotherapy, and how a quantification well-being is used to generate treatment recovery curves or patient profiles (see chapter 2).

What is "well-being"? Well-being is one of those nebulous constructs that are difficult to define or describe, even though we all have a good sense of what it is. Most clinicians and researchers in this area probably agree that it has to do with the way a person feels about himself and about his capacity to deal with problems and maintain control over his life. Diener (2000) describes *subjective well-being* as "people's evaluations of their lives—evaluations that are both affective and cognitive. People experience abundant [well-being] when they feel engaged in interesting activities, when they experience many pleasures and few pains, and when they are satisfied with their lives" (p. 34). However, Frankish, Herbert, Milsum, and Peters (1999) define the term in a manner that probably is more consistent with or important in a psychotherapeutic context:

> While well-being is associated with health, a consensus is emerging that the term well-being implies a wider emphasis than does health on the individual's sense of wholeness, in all its physical, mental, emotional, social and spiritual aspects. It expresses the individual's capacity to cope with stress without losing effective functioning. . . . A conceptual model of well-being necessarily overlaps that of health, and encompasses an ongoing process dimension rather than representing the specific end-state or outcome measure. (pp. 41–42)

It should be noted that many (including this author) would argue with the last sentence of this quote, contending that well-being is indeed a legitimate outcomes measure.

It is difficult to identify examples of well-known and/or widely used instruments that were develop to measure *psychological* well-being. Typically, well-being is equated with quality of life, and it is quality of life measures that are commonly cited. And indeed, the relationship between the two constructs can be a bit unclear. As with the case of measures of role functioning, what this author is familiar with and employs are sets of small numbers of items that tap into one's feeling of contentment with life and their ability to cope. Examples of such items include "I can deal with my problems," "I am satisfied with my life," and "I am able to maintain control over my life." These could be responded to using a 5-point agree–disagree Likert rating scale or a simple true/false format.

Service Satisfaction Measures

With the expanding interest in assessing the outcomes of treatment for the patient, it is not surprising to see an accompanying interest in measuring the patient's satisfaction with the services received. In fact, many professionals and organizations view satisfaction as an outcome, and frequently they consider it *the* most important outcome.

Just like other health care organizations, MBHOs probably have a greater interest in measuring patient satisfaction than any other potential domain of interest. If they have to pick just one thing to measure, this would probably be it. In a survey of 73 behavioral health care organizations, 71% of the respondents indicated that their outcomes studies included measures of patient satisfaction (Pallak, 1994). For the most part, service satisfaction data provide clear information about what customers like about the organization and what they do not like, making it relatively easy for the MBHO to know what it needs to work on. Published satisfaction results may also play a large role in the patient's decision about what health plan or provider they wish to receive services from.

Although service satisfaction is frequently viewed as an outcome, it is this author's contention that it should not be classified as such. As Eisen (1996b) notes, "assessment of satisfaction addressees structures and processes. Clinical outcomes assessment is clearly differentiated from the structure and processes of care" (p. 72). Thus, it should be considered a measure of an organization's structure and treatment processes, encompassing the patient's perception of how and where the service was delivered, the capabilities and attentiveness of the service provider, the benefits derived from the service, and any of a number of other selected aspects of the service he received. Patient satisfaction surveys *don't* answer the question, "What was the result of the treatment rendered to the patient?"; they do answer the question, "How did the patient feel about the treatment he or she received?" Consequently, these surveys serve an important program evaluation/improvement function. Moreover, they are generally required by a number of regulatory and accrediting bodies.

Service satisfaction is a multidimensional construct that encompasses multiple aspects of service that were received or encountered during the patient's episode of care. There are many aspect of service satisfaction. Sometimes, it may not always be necessary to measure satisfaction with all aspects of care or service. Two aspects of service that should always be surveyed by providers coming under the scrutiny of accrediting bodies are *access* and *availability*. Availability has to do with having enough providers of the appropriate type and geographical distribution to meet the needs of the covered lives. Access refers to the patient having access to available services when they need it, including both telephone and appointment access.

Obtaining patient feedback regarding satisfaction with other aspects of care probably would be rated more relevant and important to many providers. Here, examples include such things as the perceived understanding of the patient's problems by the care provider and his staff, the perceived competence and technical expertise of the care provider, and perceived improvement in the patient's functioning as a result of treatment.

Other important aspects of care are the physical environment where the services were rendered, and how safe the patient felt in the place where the episode of care was administered. This latter concern is most relevant in settings other than outpatient settings. It is not unusual for some psychiatric inpatients to complain of the unsafe conditions, whether related to the facilities or staff themselves, or to other patients whom they perceived as having posed a threat to their well-being and safety during their stay.

Satisfaction surveys, of course, are generally administered at the end of treatment. This might be at the time of discharge, or perhaps several months later. There are advantages to each point of administration, although the closer to the time of discharge or termination, the more accurate the results probably will be. Moreover, one can measure satisfaction from the viewpoint of either or both the patient and a family member or close friend. Satisfaction of this "other" is most conspicuously important in cases where the patient is a child or an adult functioning at such a severe level of impairment that valid and/or meaningful information cannot be elicited. Sometimes it is helpful to elicit input from both parties, because there may be a tendency for one to differ from another and this difference itself may be informative.

The instruments used to measure satisfaction with care are almost as numerous as the institutions that employ them. This reflects a tendency for organizations to develop their own instruments from scratch, or to customize existing instruments for their own needs. Use of nonstandardized instruments is sometimes driven by marketing departments looking for the most powerful data that can be used to sell their particular product. This, in turn, reflects a response to outside demands to "do something" to demonstrate the effectiveness of their services. Often, this "something" has not been evaluated to determine its basic psychometric properties. As a result, there exist numerous survey options that one may choose from; however, only very few of these have demonstrated their validity and reliability as measures of service satisfaction. Unfortunately, these nonstandardized instruments do not allow the consumer to make informed comparisons among MBHOs or other service providers.

Fortunately, there are a patient satisfaction survey instruments that have been investigated for their psychometric integrity. Probably the most widely used and researched patient satisfaction instrument designed for use in behavioral health care settings is the eight-item version of the Client Satisfaction Questionnaire (CSQ-8; Attkisson & Greenfield, 1999; Attkisson & Zwick, 1982; Nguyen, Attkisson, & Stenger, 1983). The CSQ-8 was derived from the original 31-item CSQ (Larsen, Attkisson, Hargreaves, & Nguyen, 1979), which also yielded two longer 18-item alternate forms, the CSQ-18A and CSQ-18B (LeVois, Nguyen, & Attkisson, 1981). The more recent work of Attkisson and his colleagues at the University of California at San Francisco is the Service Satisfaction Scale-30 (SSS-30; Greenfield & Attkisson, 1989, 1999). The SSS-30 is a 30-item, multifactorial scale that yields information about several aspects of satisfaction with the services received, such as perceived outcome and manner and skill of the clinician.

Outcomes Measurement Systems

The decade of the 1990s saw a proliferation in the development of what might be termed "outcomes measurement systems." Fueled by the growing interest in implementing CQI initiatives, along with increasing need to demonstrate the outcomes of behavioral health treatment for any number of reasons, entrepreneurs seized the opportunity to develop systems of instrumentation, processes of implementation, and the technology to capitalize on both. The result was a number of products that were marketed in trade papers and at trade shows, as well as other products that were developed by and proprietary to MBHOs and other large health care organizations. Probably the best known of the commercial outcomes measurement systems are the COMPASS products for inpatient, outpatient, and partial hospitalization settings (Coughlin, 1997), as well as the COMPASS for Primary Care (COMPASS-PC; Grissom & Howard, 2000) version of the system. These are based on Howard's dose–response and phase theories of psychotherapy and recovery (see chapter 2). Other systems were developed for proprietary use within health care systems, such as the DecisionCare System developed for use within the Charter Behavioral Health System of psychiatric facilities.

All of these outcomes systems are different in one way or another, but they also share a lot in common. Generally, the instrumentation is developed to satisfy the specific purposes and features that the developers feel the potential market want to have addressed. It typically includes patient self-report measures of various domains, such as symptomatology, well-being, social/work/school functioning, substance use and dependence, and patient satisfaction. Clinician-completed assessment tools also are commonly included. This is packaged with technology such as faxback, IVR, and Internet solutions, alone or in combination, for administration, scoring, and/or reporting the results of the instrumentation. A benchmark database is also a part of the system, as is sophisticated statistical capabilities for performing such functions as risk adjustment of patient data. The market for these systems is usually MBHOs and large provider organizations that looking for a means of obtaining consistent, useful data within and across provider networks. Consequently, the data is useful for several activities, including screening, treatment planning and monitoring, outcomes measurement and management, provider profiling, and marketing purposes.

These measurement systems are not usually designed for or marketed to individual providers or small provider groups. They can be quite costly and are typically purchased by MBHOs or other health care organization. MBHO staff or network providers typically have cost-free access to them because their use of this system is often a critical component to the success of the organization's outcomes measurement initiative.

GUIDELINES FOR THE SELECTION OF PSYCHOLOGICAL TEST INSTRUMENTS

Test publishers and other developers of psychological measures (e.g., universities, government agencies) regularly release new instrumentation that can facilitate and evaluate behavioral health care treatment in MBHO settings. Thus, availability of instrumentation for these purposes is not an issue. However, selection of the *appropriate* instrument(s) for one or more of the purposes described in chapter 2 is a matter requiring careful consideration. Inattention to instrument's intended use, its demonstrated psychometric characteristics, its limitations, and other aspects related to its practical application can result in misguided treatment and potentially harmful consequences for a patient.

General Considerations for Instrument Selection

Regardless of the type of instrument one might consider using in an MBHO system, psychologists frequently must choose between many product offerings. What are the general criteria for the selection of any instrument for psychological testing? What should guide the clinician's selection of an instrument for a specific therapeutic purpose? As part of their training, psychologists and appropriately trained professionals from related specialties have been educated about the psychometric properties that are important to consider when determining the appropriateness of an instrument for its intended use. However, this is just one of several considerations that should be taken into account in evaluating a specific instrument for a specific clinical application. Following are criteria that are recommended for the selection of tests and other assessment instruments for use within MBHO systems, regardless of their intended purpose. Some of these may seem obvious, but one would be surprised how easily some of these considerations can be overlooked.

Brevity. One of the most important characteristics of any instrument being considered for use in MBHOs is that it is brief. Lengthy instruments do not fit well in a behavioral health care delivery system where time-limited, problem-oriented intervention is the primary approach to patient treatment. In addition, to maximize the patient's cooperation with the testing process, the length of the instrument should be acceptable to most patients. Keep in mind that what psychologists consider "short" for a test may seem unreasonable long to the patient. The use of lengthy, expensive instruments or batteries of instruments that either provide little useful information or represent overkill with a patient being seen for an average of four or five sessions is of little value in MBHO settings. An exception may be found in outcomes assessment systems. Generally, however, the shorter the instrument the better, as long as acceptable levels of reliability and validity are maintained.

Psychometric Integrity. Brevity is meaningless unless the instrument is valid and reliable. In fact, the briefer the instrument, the more one should be concerned with its psychometric properties given that brief instruments tend to be less valid and reliable than longer instruments. Thus, although the psychometric characteristics of all psychological instruments used in MBHO and other settings should be carefully evaluated, particular scrutiny is called for with short measures of any construct.

In selecting a test, one must ask, "Is the instrument a valid and reliable measure of what it purports to measure?" In addition, should specific aspects of validity and reliability be attended to more than others when evaluating psychological measures? There is no one clear answer to this question. All relevant aspects of validity and reliability are important to consider in selecting a test, but depending on the intended use, particular types of validity and/or reliability might be given more weight in the decision. For example, if the intended use is treatment monitoring, one would like to see empirical data demonstrating good test–retest reliability. When used for screening, one should closely consider the instrument's criterion validity and accompanying diagnostic efficiency statistics. The reader is referred to the *Standards for Educational and Psychological Testing* (American Educational Research Association, American Psychological Association, & National Council on Measurement in Education, 1999) for further guidance on this matter. Also, Cicchetti (1994) provides guidelines for evaluating the validity and reliability of psychological measures being considered for clinical use.

Relevancy to Intended Purpose of Assessment.   Validity and reliability are important considerations with regard to the next desired test characteristic — relevancy to the intended purpose of administering the instrument. Administering a Beck to screen for levels of general distress is not the most appropriate way to accomplish the task — unless, of course, it has been empirically shown to be effective when used this way. Regardless of its psychometric integrity, a measure lacking empirical support for the MBHO's or the provider's intended use should not warrant any further condsideration.

Availability of Relevant Normative Data.   Tied to the relevancy and psychometric soundness of the instrument is the issue of whether normative data are available for the particular population(s) with whom the measure will be used. Using the GDS to screen geriatric patients for depression is quite appropriate. However, use of this same instrument with patient populations consisting primarily of young adults and adolescents should be avoided unless its use with other populations has been demonstrated to be valid.

Cost.   Cost is always a factor. When testing is authorized, one does not want to write-off a great deal of the reimbursement to expensive testing forms or scoring services. Fortunately, valid, reliable and useful instruments are becoming more available for little or no cost. Some of these are instruments that have been in the public domain for a number of years; other cost-free instruments have become available only during the past few years. Others, such as the Behavior and Symptom Identification Scale (BASIS-32; Eisen & Culhane, 1999; Eisen, Grob, & Klein, 1986) and SF-12, are provided by their developers for a nominal licensing fee.

In addition, some instrumentation is available from the MBHO at no charge. This is likely to be the case when the MBHO wishes to implement a program that will, in the end, provide improved service for the patient and/or cost savings to the organization. For example, as part of a project undertaken by one MBHO, patients are administered a brief instrument via an IVR system, with a copy of the results being sent to the patient's care provider and/or care manager.

Reading Level.   For instruments that are completed via a paper-and-pencil or on-line computer administration format, reading level is a major consideration. In general, developers of tests and other assessment instruments have become more sensitive to the issue of reading level vis-á-vis the intended patient population's reading level. Part of this may be due to the fact that software is available to easily determine the reading level of material, thus providing a means of identifying problematic text. However, one is still amazed at the reading level of some instrumentation that is intended for a general patient audience. MBHOs cater to the care of patients with various levels of education, so the recommendation is to try to select an instrument with a reading level no higher than eighth grade. Tests requiring no more that a sixth-grade reading level are preferable, but these may be difficult to find. Alternatives, of course, are those instruments that have available an oral administration mode, such as by audiotape or an interactive voice response (IVR) system.

Instrument Content. Aside from meeting an issue related to validity, the content of the test—what the test is asking the patient to report on—is also important in achieving acceptability to the patient. Asking questions that are not considered relevant by the patient (i.e., face invalidity) or that are informative but potentially offensive should be avoided. Patients' perceptions of what is appropriate or useful to inquire about can have a direct bearing on the probablility that they will give a valid response to any or all of the questions being asked.

Ease of Use. One selection criterion that many professionals may overlook, or at least minimize in their importance, is the ease at which the test is administered and scored by themselves or (in cases where the psychologist is not going to be engaged in these activities) other staff members. Considerations here can include how easily the person who will be administering, scoring, and/or interpreting the instrument can become skilled in its use. It also extends to how acceptable it is to the MBHO, that is, the degree to which the MBHO sees the value in and is willing to reimburse for its use.

Comprehensibility of Results. Another often overlooked criterion in instrument selection is how easily the test results can be understood by the MBHO care management staff or other relevant individuals, such as the patient and their family. Aside from the fact that authorization for appropriate treatment may hinge on a care manager's fully comprehending the implications of the test findings, the psychologist should be able to easily explain the results to the patient and/or his family in order that they more clearly understand the patient's problems and the implications they have for his day-to-day functioning. In some cases, the results may reveal areas of strength, which, if understood by the patient, may facilitate efforts to facilitate positive change. Comprehensibility of results is particularly important when the psychologist utilizes Finn's (1996b) therapeutic assessment technique during the course of treatment.

Application-Specific Considerations

In addition to these general considerations, the selection of test instruments for specific purposes will sometimes require other considerations.

Considerations for Instrumentation for Screening and Diagnosis. Screening for the likelihood of the presence of disorders or (more generally) for the need for additional assessment requires considerations that do not necessarily apply to instruments when they are used for the other therapeutic assessment purposes addressed in chapter 2. When selecting tests for use in screening for the presence of general psychopathology or specific disorders, there are a number of considerations related to sensitivity and specificity that must play into the decision. In general, Ficken's (1995) requirements of instruments used for screening were noted to include

(a) high levels of sensitivity and specificity to DSM-IV or ICD diagnostic criteria;
(b) a focus on hard-to-detect (in a single office visit) but treatable disorders that are associated with imminent harm to self or others, significant suffering, and a decrease in productivity;
(c) an administration time of no more than 10 minutes; and
(d) an administration protocol that easily integrates into the organization's work flow.

Much like Derogatis and Lynn's (1999) sequential screening process, cases testing "positive" on the screener would be administered one or more "second tier" instrument(s) to establish severity and a specific diagnosis. Ficken feels that if they are to be accepted by MBHOs, these second tier instruments should meet the requirements of screeners and either specify or rule out a diagnosis.

The issue of sensitivity and specificity are only two components of a much more encompassing consideration, that is, criterion validity. Although broadly included in the construct of "validity," it bears particular attention when evaluating instruments for screening purposes. What is being referred to here is classification accuracy or efficiency, which is discussed in detail in chapter 2.

Considerations for Instrumentation for Treatment Monitoring. Tests that are used for ongoing monitoring of treatment progress over time require other considerations, all of which are related to the fact that the instrument will be completed two or more times during the course of an episode of care. Thus, cost becomes a particularly important factor in the selection of a measure to be used for this purpose.

Next, given that the purpose of repeated testing is to detect change in a patient's status on one or more domains of functioning, it is important that the selected instrument is sensitive to change that has occurred over time. Here, good test–retest reliability is a key indicator of this sensitivity. Lambert and his colleagues (Burlingame, Lambert, Reisinger, Neff, & Mosier, 1995) indicate that the minimum acceptable reliability should be about .70. Ideally, one would want to see reported reliability coefficients that are based on a demographically relevant "normal" or community sample. It is difficult to tell what a stated reliability coefficient based on patient sample really means. Is a low to moderate reliability on a given measure (based on a patient sample) due to true change in the patient as a result of intervention, or is it a reflection of error variance that is built into the instrument? And what does a high, patient-based reliability mean? Does it indicate that the instrument is insensitive to change, or was it based on a sample who truly did not change as a result of intervention? From this author's perspective, one should feel confident with instruments with good community sample-based reliabilities.

In some cases, using a test with alternate forms might be advisable. For instance, if there is a likelihood that the results of subsequent administrations of a given test may reflect a memory or learning effect, it would be helpful to have a different set of questions that have been empirically demonstrated to yield results comparable to those of the original. Unlike achievement and ability tests, it will be rare to find frequently used treatment monitoring instruments for which there is validated alternate form.

Considerations for Outcomes Instruments.   Generally, outcomes measurement might be considered an extension or variant of treatment monitoring. It is, in effect, the monitoring of the results of treatment at or beyond the end of treatment. For this reason, those additional test-selection considerations for treatment monitoring also apply when tests are being considered for use in outcomes measurement.

Probably the most thorough and clinically relevant guidelines for the selection of instruments for outcomes measurement purposes comes from the National Institute of Mental Health (NIMH) supported work of Ciarlo, Brown, Edwards, Kiresuk, and Newman (1986). A synopsis of Newman, Ciarlo, and Carpenter's (1999) updated summary of this NIMH work is presented here.

Newman et al. (1999) describe 11 criteria for the selection of outcomes assessment instruments, each of which can be grouped into one of five types of considerations. The first consideration is that of *relevance to the target group*. The instrument should measure those problems, symptoms, characteristics, and so forth that are common to the population to whom it will be administered. The more heterogeneous the population, the more chance that modifications will be required and that these will alter the standardization and psychometric integrity of the instrument. Related to relevance is the degree to which the results obtained from the instrument's administration is independent of the type of treatment that is offered to the population being tested.

The second set of general considerations is that of *methods and procedures* (Newman et al., 1999). Several selection criteria are related to this group. The first is that administration of the instrument is simple and easily taught. Generally, this is more of an issue with clinician rating scales than self-report scales. In the case of rating scales, concrete examples or objective referents at each rating level should be provided to the user. The second criterion is that the instrument should allow input not from just the patient but also from other sources (e.g., the clinician, collaterals). The benefits of this include the opportunities to obtain a picture of the patient from many perspectives, to validate reported findings and observations, and to promote honesty in responding from all sources (given that all parties will know that others will be providing input also). The third methods and procedures criterion is that the instrument provide information relevant to understanding how the treatment may have affected change in the individual.

The last two methods and procedures criteria, if adhered to, would significantly limit the number of instruments that could be used for outcomes assessment. Neither of the two appears to be critical for use in MBHO settings at this point in time. Consequently, one may not wish to place too much weight on their consideration unless there are specific reasons for doing so.

Newman et al.'s (1999) third set of considerations has to do with the *psychometric strengths* of the instruments. Consistent with what was stated earlier, the NIMH panel of experts indicated that outcomes measures should (a) meet the minimum psychometric standards for reliability (including internal consistency, test–retest reliability, and as appropriate, interrater reliability) and validity (content, construct, and concurrent validity); (b) be difficult to "fake bad" or fake good"; and (c) be free from response bias and not be reactive or sensitive to factors unrelated to the constructs that are being measured (e.g., physical settings, behavior of the treatment staff). These criteria obviously also apply to other psychological instruments used for purposes other than outcomes assessment.

The fourth group of considerations concerns the *cost* of the instruments. Newman et al. (1999) point out that how much one should spend on assessment instrumentation and associated costs (e.g., staff time for administering, scoring, processing, and analyzing the data) will depend on how important the data gathered are to assuring a positive return on the functions they support. In the context of the NIMH undertaking, Newman et al. felt that the data obtained through treatment outcomes assessment would support screening/treatment planning, efforts in quality assurance and program evaluation, cost containment/utilization review activities, and revenue generation efforts. However, this should probably be considered the ideal. At this point, the number and nature of the purposes that would be supported by the obtained data will depend on the individual organization. The more purposes the data can serve, the less costly the instrumentation is likely to be, at least from a value standpoint. In terms of actual costs, Ciarlo et al. (1986) estimated that 0.5% of an organization's total budget would be an affordable amount for materials, staff training, data collection, and processing costs related to outcomes assessment. At the same time, be mindful that the recommendation was made over 15 years ago and may not reflect changes in policies, regulatory and accreditation requirements, rate of inflation, and attitudes related to the use of psychological test instruments since that time.

The final set of considerations in instrument selection has to do with the *utility* of the instrument. Newman et al. (1999) posit four criteria related to utility. First, the scoring procedures and the manner in which the results are presented should be comprehensible to all with a stake in the treatment of the organization's patients. This would include not only the patient, his or her family, the organization's administrative staff and other treatment staff, but also third party payers and legislative and administrative policymakers. Related to this is the criterion is that the results of the instrument be easily interpreted by those with a stake in them. Another utility-related criterion is that the instrument be compatible with a number of clinical practices and theories that are employed in the behavioral health care arena. This should allow for a greater range of problem applicability and greater acceptance by the various stakeholders in the patient's treatment.

Also important to consider with regard to utility is that "the instrument support[s] the clinical processes of a service with minimal interference" (Newman et al., 1999, p. 166). There are two issues here. The first has to do with whether the instrument can support the screening, planning, and/or monitoring activities in addition to the outcomes assessment activities. In other words, are multiple purposes served by the instrument's results? The second issue is one has to do with the extent to which the organization's staff is burdened with the collection and processing of assessment data. How much will the assessment process interfere with the daily work flow of the organization's staff? An extensive discussion of this issue is presented in chapter 7. Equally important is whether the benefits that accrue from the use of the instrument justify the cost of implementing an assessment program for whatever purpose(s).

Other Criteria for Outcomes Assessment Instruments.   Although the work of Newman and his colleagues provides more extensive instrument selection guidelines than most, others who have addressed the issue have arrived at recommendations that serve to reinforce and/or compliment those found in the NIMH document. For example, Gavin Andrews' work in Australia has led to significant contributions to the body of outcomes assessment knowledge. As part of this, Andrews et al. (1994) have identified six general "qualities of consumer outcome measures" that are generally concordant with those from the NIMH study. First, the measure should meet the criterion of *applicability*. In other words,

... it should address dimensions which are important to the consumer (symptoms, disability, and consumer satisfaction) and useful for the clinician in formulating and conducting treatment, yet the measure should be one which can have its data aggregated in a meaningful way so that the requirements of management can be addressed. (p. 30)

Multidimensional instruments yielding a profile of scores on all dimensions of interest are viewed as a means of best serving the interests of all concerned.

Acceptability, that is, being both brief and user-friendly, is another desirable quality identified by Andrews et al. (1994). Closely associated with this is the criterion of *practicality.* It might be viewed as a composite of those NIMH criteria related to matters of cost, ease of scoring and interpretation, and training in the use and interpretation of the measure. Again in agreement with the NIMH work, the final three criteria identified by Andrews et al. relate to *reliability, validity,* and *sensitivity to change.* With regard to reliability, Andrews et al. specify what they consider to be the minimum levels of acceptable internal consistency reliability (.90 for long tests), interrater reliability (.40), and construct and criterion validity (.50). They also stress the importance of an instrument's face validity in helping to ensure cooperation from the patient, as well as the importance of self-report instruments having multiple response options rather then just "yes/no" options. This, of course, would increase the sensitivity of an instrument to small but relevant changes in the patient's status over time. Ficken's (1995) requirements for "successful" outcomes assessment instruments are consistent with those of Andrews and his colleagues.

Based on the work of Vermillion and Pfeiffer (1993), Burlingame et al. (1995) recommended four criteria for the selection of outcomes measures that also reveal consistency in the thinking of other experts in the field. The first is acceptable "technical features," that is, validity and reliability. Specifically, these authors recommended that instruments have an internal consistency of at least .80, test-retest reliability of at least .70, and concurrent validity of at least .50. The second criterion is "practicality features." These include brevity, ease of administration and scoring, and simplicity of the reporting of results. Third, the instrumentation should be "suitable" for the patients that are seen within the setting. Thus, because of the nature of most presenting problems in mental health settings, it should assess symptomatology and psychosocial functioning. The fourth criterion is sensitivity to "meaningful" change over time, allowing for a differentiation of *symptomatic* change from interpersonal/social role *functional* change.

In addition to some already mentioned criteria (acceptable validity, reliability, affordability, ease of administration, and ease of data entry and analysis), Sederer, Dickey, and Hermann (1996) discuss technological considerations that warrant attention in selecting outcomes measures for specific situations. These include automation capabilities related to availability of software for data analysis and reporting, compatibility with the organization's existing information system, and the ability to enter data via an optical scanner. They provide additional advice that should help guide the user in selecting the appropriate instrumentation:

A plan should be developed that addresses the following questions: which patients will be included in the study? What outcomes will be most effected by the treatment? When will the outcomes be measured? Who is going to read (and use) the information provided by the outcomes study? The more specific the answer to these questions, the better the choice of outcome instrument. (p. 4)

These issues tie into more general issues related to the design of outcomes management programs. As such, they are discussed in more detail in chapter 6. In addition, Sederer et al.'s recommendations would appear equally applicable when selecting instruments for other purposes.

Schlosser (1995a) proposed a rather nontraditional approach to outcomes assessment. In what he refers to as a "patient-centric" view, assessment information is gathered and used *during the course of therapy* to bring about change before treatment has ended. Essentially, this equates to what has been referred earlier as treatment monitoring. In this model, Schlosser feels that this type of assessment requires "elements regarding very specific, theoretically derived, empirically validated areas of functioning" (p. 66). These would involve the use of both illness and well-being measures that assess the patient on emotional, mental/cognitive, physical, social, life direction, and life satisfaction dimensions. Many of Schlosser's (1995a) considerations for selection of such measures are not unique (e.g., having "acceptable" levels of reliability and validity, brief, low-cost, and sensitive). However, for the purposes described, Schlosser also indicates that they should also (a) have "paradigmatic sensibility" (i.e., key words have the same meaning across instruments), (b) be designed for repeated administration for feedback or self-monitoring purposes, and (c) provide "actionable information."

Actionable information generally refers to information that one can do something with, that is, information that gives the provider and/or the MBHO direction about how to improve the quality of services offered to patients. During the ongoing monitoring of an individual's progress in treatment, information that is actionable can be used to indicate when therapy is not working as well as to suggest the changes that need to be made. However, as alluded to earlier, the patients who provide the *outcomes* data that yield actionable information frequently do not benefit from that information because they are no longer in treatment. Instead, the information that they provide can lead to changes from which future patients will benefit.

An excellent example of actionable information is the information that is commonly obtained from patient satisfaction surveys. These surveys are almost always administered to patients at the end of an episode of care. Their assessment of specific aspects of the quality and helpfulness of the provider's services, the access to and availability of those services, the professionalism of the clinical and support staff, and other aspects of the quality of the services they received will help the provider and the MBHO see where improvement can be made that will result in a more beneficial experience for those patients seen at a later point in time. Similarly, aggregated outcomes data from a multidimensional symptom inventory may show that a clinician does quite well in treating depression but his efforts yield minimal results with anxiety disorders. As a result, the clinician may decide to obtain more supervised training in the treatment of anxiety disorders or, alternatively, limit his practice to depressive disorders.

Slade, Thornicroft, and Glover (1999) identified *feasibility* as another desirable criterion for outcomes instrumentation. In this context, they defined feasibility as "the extent to which [the instrument] is suitable for use on a routine, sustainable and meaningful basis in typical clinical settings, when used in a specified manner and for a specified purpose" (p. 245). Feasibility actually is comprised of six characteristics, five of which—brevity, availability, relevance, simplicity, acceptability—are generally comparable to criteria identified earlier by others. What is unique in this conceptualization is the sixth criterion, *value*. Value is said to occur when the benefits of using the instrument exceed the costs associated with learning how to use the instrument, implementing its use, and analyzing, presenting and interpreting the resulting data.

Finally, Blankertz, Cook, Rogers, and Hughes (1997) outlined criteria for selecting outcomes measures for use with individuals with severe and persistent mental illness (SPMI). Referred to as "The Five 'Cs' of Choice," these five requirements or concepts reflect the important variables that should be considered when evaluating the outcomes of treatment provided to this particular population. In summary, outcomes measures selected for use with SPMI should:

- Reflect *changes* in "real-world" behaviors. In the more popular parlance, the measure should have "ecological validity" and reflect changes that can occur over long periods of time.
- Remain *constant*, thus allowing for the measurement of true changes, not artifacts of changes in instrumentation. If instrumentation changes must occur, this should be performed in increments that will permit the benchmarking of new data against previously gathered data.
- Be *comparable* to measures used by other providers or organizations. This will enable comparison of performance of one provider to another, or performance of one organization to another.
- Be *client-oriented*, that is, provide data that is at the level of the individual patient and is considered the most useful by all stakeholders.
- Reflect the *consequences* of both the mental illness and the efforts at rehabilitation. Measurement should focus not only on the those outcomes that are the primary goals of treatment, but also on the more long-term, secondary outcomes that can accrue from treatment (e.g., vocational, quality of life, legal).

Moreover, Blankertz et al. recommend that the instrumentation that is selected reflect the main focus of the organization's activities. This focus may be identified or defined by the goals that are most valued by the organization's stakeholders, by its mission statement, or the areas in which the majority of its services are offered.

TECHNOLOGY FOR PSYCHOLOGICAL ASSESSMENT

Looking back to the mid-1980s and early 1990s, the cutting edge technology for psychological testing at that time included desktop personal computers linked to optical mark reader (OMR) scanning technologies. There also were those "little black boxes" that facilitated the per-use sale and security of test administration, scoring, and interpretive reports for test publishers, while making computer-based testing convenient and available to practitioners. As has always been the case, someone has had the foresight to develop applications of current technological advances that we use everyday, to the practice of psychological testing. Just as at one time the personal computer held the power of facilitating the assessment process, the Internet, fax machine, and interactive voice response (IVR) technologies are being developed to make the assessment process easier, quicker, and more cost-effective. These technologies support the increasing use and popularity of *telehealth*, "the use of electronic and communications technology to accomplish health care over distance" (Jerome, DeLeon, James, Folen, Earles, & Gedney, 2000, p. 407). In addition to assessment, telehealth can enable or support the provision of other clinical services, including crisis response, triage, treatment planning, care management, and even psychotherapy.

Internet Technology

The Internet has changed the way we do many things, so application of this technology for the administration, scoring, and interpretation of psychological instruments should not be a surprise to anyone. An Internet-based process is straightforward. The clinician accesses the Web site on which the desired instrumentation resides. The desired test is selected for administration, and then the patient completes the test online. There may also be an option of having the patient complete a paper-and-pencil version of the instrument and then have administrative staff key-enter the responses into the program. The data is scored and entered into the Web site's database, and a report is generated and transmitted back to the clinician through the web. Turn around time for receiving the report can be only a matter of minutes. The archived data can later be used for any of a number of purposes, such as regularly scheduled reporting of aggregated data to the MBHO or psychologist. Data from repeated testing can be used for treatment monitoring and report card generation. These data can also be used for psychometric test development or other statistical purposes.

A good example of an Internet-based outcomes management system is that available through CORE at the University of Arkansas. The NetOutcomes Solutions system is one that provides a complete package of behavioral health outcomes tools that can benefit not only the MBHO or organization in its mission, but also the individual clinician in the delivery of quality services to the individual patient (see *http://www.netoutcomes.net/NO_Solutions/NO Main/NO_Home.asp?menu=nethome*, retrieved May 5, 2000). At the time of this writing, CORE was making available to MBHOs and providers its outcomes "modules" for depression, schizophrenia, substance abuse, and adolescent assessment through the NetOutcomes Solutions system. This includes capabilities for administration, scoring, and reporting during baseline and multiple follow-up assessments. These instruments can be administered online, or data from completed paper forms of the instruments can be key-entered into the system through the Internet.

The NetOutcomes System can generate an individual patient report with tabular and graphical summaries of the data and transmit it back to the provider almost immediately. Results from any previous assessments of the patient are presented along with the current findings, thus assisting in the determination of the progress the patient has made over time and enhancing their overall clinical utility. The system also enables the creation of quarterly reports that are generated from the aggregation of data from patients seen by a given provider or data from all patients seen by all providers in a program or multiple programs in one facility. Included in the reporting is case mix adjustment and disease severity indexing that enhances the meaningfulness of the information. Benchmarking also is possible through the system's database capabilities.

The advantages of an Internet-based assessment system are clear-cut. It allows for online administration of tests, which include branching logic for item selection. Instruments available through a Web site can be easily updated and made immediately available to users. This is in contrast with disk-distributed software, where updates and fixes are sometimes long in coming. The results of an Internet-based test administration can be made available almost immediately. In addition, data from multiple sites can easily be aggregated and used for the purpose of normative comparisons, test validation, risk adjustment, benchmarking, generating recovery curves, and any number of other statistically based activities that require large data sets.

There are only a few major disadvantages to an Internet-based system. The first and most obvious is the fact that it requires access to the Internet. In this day and age, many would probably be surprised to know that by some estimates, less than 50% of clinicians have computers in their offices. And it is probably safe to say that the percent that have access to the Internet in their offices is even less. This percent will increase over time. The second disadvantage has to do with the general Internet data security issue. Again, with time, this will likely become less of a concern as advances in Internet security software and procedures continue to take place. Finally, as Tsacoumis (2000) has noted, Internet-based testing can be costly, especially when one takes into account fees for Internet access, test administration scoring and reporting services from a reputable vendor, and equipment maintenance and upgrading. How costly this may become will vary from one provider or organization to another, depending on the particular services and vendors that are used.

Faxback Technology

The development of facsimile and faxback technology that has taken place during the last decade has made available an important application for psychological testing. At the same time, it probably has dealt a huge blow to the low-volume customer base of scanning technology companies.

The process for implementing faxback technology is fairly simple. A paper-and-pencil answer sheet for a test available through the faxback system is completed by the patient. In those systems in which several tests are available, the answer sheet for a given test contains numbers or other types of code that tell the scoring and reporting software which test is being submitted. When the answer sheet is completed, it is faxed in — usually through a toll-free number that the scoring service has provided — to the central scoring facility where the data is both entered into a data base and then scored. A report is generated and faxed back to the clinician within a few minutes, depending on the number of phone lines that vendor has made available and the volume of submissions at that particular time of day. At the scoring end of the process, the whole system remains paperless. Later, the stored data can be used in the same ways as those gathered by an Internet-based system.

Like Internet-based systems, faxback systems allow for immediate access to software updates and fixes. They also can incorporate the same statistical and benchmarking capabilities. Like the PC-based testing products that are offered through most test publishers, their paper-and-pencil administration format allow for more flexibility as to where and when a patient can be tested. In addition to the types of security issues that come with Internet-based testing, the biggest disadvantage of or problem with faxback testing centers around test identification and linkage of data obtained from an individual patient. Separate answer sheets are required for each instrument that can be scored through the faxback system. The system must also be able to link data from multiple tests or multiple administrations of the same test to a single patient. At first glance, this may not seem to be a very challenging task for 21st century technology. But there are issues related to the sometimes conflicting needs to maintain confidentiality while ensuring the accuracy of patient identifiers that link data over a single or multiple episodes of care, that may be difficult to resolve. If data cannot be linked, then it will be limited in its usefulness. Overcoming this challenge can therefore be the key to the success of any faxback system.

An example of how faxback technology can be implemented for screening purposes can be found in a project described by Maruish, Bershadsky, and Goldstein (1998) and Goldstein, Bershadsky, and Maruish (2000). In this project, the SA-45 and SF-12 were scored and reported in a primary care practice through the use of faxback technology. This study is interesting from several standpoints, not the least of which are the barriers to successful implementation that arose during the course of the project.

IVR Technology

One of the more recent applications of new technology to the administration, scoring, and reporting of results of psychological tests can be found in the use of interactive voice response, or IVR, systems. In essence, IVR test administration is similar to the automated online, desktop administration of psychological measures. However, as Kobak, Greist, Jefferson and Katzelnick (1996) point out, the advantages of IVR over PC-based testing include the patients' comfort with the technology (i.e., touch-tone telephone), easy availability and access to that technology, and the ability of the patient to complete the administration outside of the practitioner's office at any time of the day or week.

Everyone is familiar with IVR technology. When one calls to order products, address billing problems, find out the balance in his checking account or conduct other phone-enabled activities, one is often asked to provide information to an automated system in order to facilitate the meeting of our requests. This is IVR, and its applicability to test administration, data processing, and data storage is simple. What may not be obvious is how the data can be accessed and used.

An example of the use of an IVR system for data gathering and reporting for the purpose of improving the quality of care can be seen in a project that was conducted by one MBHO. Patients were asked to take an intake assessment tool at the time of treatment initiation. The instrument used was one that was designed by the MBHO staff and its external project partner to assess the key aspects of functioning identified by Howard and his colleagues: well-being, symptomatology, and social and work functioning. The CAGE-AI (Brown & Rounds, 1995) was also included as part of the instrument. All items were either taken from public domain instruments or were developed in-house. When calling in to the MBHO, the patient was either connected directly to the IVR system by the intake coordinator, or was given a toll-free number and patient code to access the system at their convenience later on, 7 days a week, 24 hours a day.

After the patient completed the questionnaire, the data was processed and a report was generated and faxed to the patient's care provider. This report could give the clinician a head start on the assessment of the patient's problems and needs, even before the first therapy session. As adequate data were collected, recovery curves were supposed to be generated to give the provider an idea of the amount and length of recovery that he could expect for the patient, based on data from similar patients that were stored in the system. A copy of the report was also automatically e-mailed to the patient's care manager. This was intended to assist the care manager in making utilization and other care-related decisions about the patient.

The system was set up such that 6 weeks after the initial assessment, the patient was sent a notice that it was time for him to complete the assessment instrument again. The notice contained the dial-up number and patient-specific code that allowed the patient to access the system once again. The patient code also tied the patient's data from the current follow-up administration to those of previous administrations of the IVR instrument. Using the same process, the patient was re-assessed again 6 months after the initial assessment. These outcomes data could be used for predictive modeling, generation of recovery curves, or as simply outcomes information to fulfill JCAHO, NCQA, or QISMC standards.

IVR technology's utility as a test delivery system has been reported in a number of published studies. Over the years, Kobak and his colleagues have conducted several studies that have employed the use of IVR technology for administration of various types of psychological instruments. In their review of 10 studies that included the administration of both clinician- and IVR-administered versions of the Hamilton Depression Rating Scale (HDRS; Kobak, Reynolds, Rosenfeld, & Greist, 1990), Kobak, Mundt, Greist, Katzelnick, and Jefferson (2000) found the IVR system to generally yield comparable or better psychometric properties than the clinician version. The combined data across all 10 studies yielded an overall correlation of .81 ($p < .001$) between the scores resulting from the administration of the HRSD in both formats. In another study, Kobak, Taylor, Dottl, Greist, Jefferson, Burroughs, Katzelnick, and Mandell (1997) found support for the overall validity and use of both IVR and desktop-computer administered versions of the PRIME-MD as instruments for gathering information from behavioral health patients. Here, the results from the clinician-administered SCID-IV were used as the diagnostic gold-standard criteria. Findings from this study are discussed in greater detail in chapter 8.

Moreover, in their HRDS and other studies, Kobak et al. (2000) reported that up to 90% of patients being assessed by IVR systems reported moderate to very strong acceptance as it related to clarity and ease of use. These, in turn, are consistent with Kobak et al.'s (1997) findings in the PRIME-MD study. Findings from these and other studies led Kobak, Taylor, Dottl, Greist, Jefferson, Burroughs, Mantle, Katzelnick, Norton, Henk, and Serlin (2000) to observe that "several decades of research have shown that people often report more problems of greater severity to computer applications than to clinicians, especially when such problems concern personally sensitive topics" (p. 152). Millard and Carver (1999) arrived at similar findings in their comparison of results obtained from the administration of the SF-12 via the IVR and live telephone interview formats.

IVR technology is attractive from many standpoints. It requires no extra equipment beyond a touch-tone telephone for administration. It is available for use 24 hours a day, 7 days a week. One does not have to be concerned about the patient's reading ability, although oral comprehension levels need to be taken into account when determining which instruments are appropriate for administration via the IVR (or other audio) administration format. As with faxback- and Internet-based assessment, the system is such that branching logic can be used in the administration of the instrument. Updates and fixes are easily implemented system wide. Also, the ability to store data allows for comparison of results from previous testings, aggregation of data for statistical analyses, and all the other data analytic capabilities available through faxback- and Internet-based assessment.

Moreover, Kobak et al. (2000) have indicated the following methodological benefits of IVR:

1. Completely standardized, structured assessment,
2. Elimination of interrater unreliability,
3. Remote patient evaluation 24 hours a day, 7 days a week,
4. Thorough and complete error checking of data at the time of collection,
5. Elimination of possible data transcription or scoring errors,
6. Immediate real-time access to analyzable data,
7. Patient-determined pace of assessment,
8. Increased honesty on sensitive questions, and
9. Independent, reliable assessments that cannot be influenced by exogenous information, such as functional unblinding of human raters. (p. 153)

As for the downside of IVR assessment, probably the biggest issue is that in many instances the patient must be the one to initiate the testing. Control of the testing is turned over to a party that may or may not be interested in or otherwise amenable to psychological testing. With less cooperative patients, this may require costly follow-up efforts to encourage full participation in the process.

Considerations for Technology Selection

As noted, each of the previously described assessment technologies has its own set of advantages and disadvantages. How does one determine which technology is best for his particular needs? For the individual MBHO network psychologist, there may not be a choice. The MBHO for which the practitioner provides services may have an assessment system in place—instrumentation, delivery system, and associated reports—and the practitioner may be required to use it. Alternately, the practitioner may be free to employ (at his own expense) any automated test delivery system that best meets his needs. Regardless of whether the decision-maker is the MBHO or the psychologist, there are several points that should be considered when selecting from among the available technologies.

Cost. Just as it is for test instrumentation, the cost of a system that will administer, score, and/or report the results of psychological measures is a major consideration. In addition to any up-front equipment purchase or development costs, one must also consider the associated costs. Depending on the delivery system, additional expenses may result from ongoing technical support, maintenance contracts, system upgrades, adding new measures to the system, and ongoing phone line and Internet provider fees, just to mention a few. These costs will vary from one MBHO to another, or from one psychologist to another, depending on the resources that may already be available to the purchaser.

Clinical Utility. In Gray's (1999) discussion of factors to consider in selecting a clinical outcomes system, he discusses clinical utility. In this context, clinical utility refers to "the ability to provide the clinician with real-time feedback" (p. 9). Thus, one should ascertain how quickly assessment information is accessible once the measures are completed. This can be an extremely important consideration in evaluating systems that will be used to support screening, treatment monitoring, and other clinical activities involving real-time clinical decision-making. Information that is not immediately available to the clinician may prove to be of little or no value.

Availability/Accessibility. The technologies discussed earlier are all relatively new and therefore may not available to or accessible by all involved parties. A good example here is the Internet. Although it seems that everyone has a computer and access to the Internet, this certainly is not the case. An MBHO wishing to initiate a web-based outcomes management system should therefore determine how many of its network providers and/or potential patients have access to the Internet before completing the decision-making process. Faxback and IVR would therefore seem to be less problematic for providers and/or patients to access, but this should not be assumed without any evidence to this effect.

Consistency With Existing IS&T Initiatives. The presence of existing or planned information systems and technologies or initiatives within an organization or practice should certainly have a bearing on which technology one selects for psychological testing purposes For example, although an IVR may be appealing to an MBHO for many reasons, the organization's plans to develop a multifunction Web site would suggest that an Internet-based test delivery system would be more practical and cost effective, all other considerations being equal. For a small individual or group practice office with no existing Internet access, faxback, IVR, and Internet solutions may be equally viable.

Ease of Implementation. Regardless of who the decision-maker is, one must consider how easy it will be to implement this assessment delivery technology in daily clinical practice. How receptive will the clinical and support staff be to the selected technology? How easy will it be to train them in its use? What demands will its use make on them? Where will its use be inserted into the daily work flow? How receptive will patients be to this technology? How difficult will it be for patients to understand how to complete an assessment via this technology? These all are important questions and should have a strong bearing on any decision related to the selection of technology for the purpose of test administration and reporting. Especially in the case of outcomes assessment, the success of an assessment program can hinge on the degree to which a workable plan of implementation—including technology-related aspects—can be developed.

Patient Affordability. Situations in which testing is not fully covered by an MBHO make the costs incurred by the patient worthy of careful consideration. This is particularly true if there is a per use fee for the instrument(s) being administered and a separate charge for the use of the automated system. The full or copay charge incurred by the patient will be made more acceptable if he can see value in both the need for testing and the use of the system. If the benefits of the test delivery are not obvious to the patient, this may negatively impact the relationship with the provider and, consequently, the outcomes of treatment.

Access to Measures Selected for Use. No matter how sophisticated the technology is, it will be of limited utility if the instrumentation that the psychologist or MBHO wishes to use are not available or cannot be developed (e.g., due to copyright restrictions) for use with it. Here, one must consider not only what the current needs are but also what they are likely to be in the future. Anticipating future needs for assessment information can be difficult to do. But when it is possible, one should evaluate the potential of having the desired measures available on each type of technology being considered, in light of such factors as test software publishers' histories of developing new applications for their products, copyright issues, and changes in the technology itself.

Logistics of Re-administration of Measures.   This becomes an issue when psychological testing is part of a system of treatment monitoring or outcomes assessment. Obtaining a baseline measure of a patient's status is not that difficult when he is in-office or (in the case of IVR assessment) on the phone line going through a psychologist's or MBHO's intake procedures. At intake, patients generally more amenable to taking psychological test instruments. Either later during treatment or after the episode of care has been completed, the interest or willingness to complete the baseline measure one or more times again is usually on the wane.

A provider's monitoring of treatment progress while the treatment is ongoing is facilitated by the fact the patient can be re-tested while he is in the office. After treatment has been completed, the ability to conduct a follow-up remeasurement for outcomes management purposes becomes more difficult since the psychologist and MBHO no longer have ongoing contact with the patient. Thus, there must be a feasible means of conducting a "long distance" follow-up assessment of the patient. This would include being able to cost-effectively contact the patient for retesting, provide him with a means of easily completing the measures in question, and having the data returned for analysis. For some, this problem may be solved through the use of an IVR system. As was described earlier, the psychologist or (more likely) the MBHO would send the patient a letter at a specific time following the termination of treatment, asking him to retake the baseline measure. Included in the letter would be a toll-free, phone-in number and personal identification number to access the system. One might increase his response rate by also enclosing a written copy of the instrument and giving the patient the option of using the IVR system or completing the paper form and mailing it back. A similar method might be used if the psychologist's or MBHO's Internet assessment system is accessible to patients.

Flexibility.   Flexibility refers to the degree to which any number of test administration and reporting options are available through the technology. For example, faxback and IVR technologies only allow for data input via one means, that is, through either completion and faxing of a paper-and-pencil form or through telephone keypad entry, respectively. Internet-based testing (along with the more common in-office PC-based assessment) allows for online administration and data entry, as well as key-entry, or in some cases, optical scanning of data gathered from a pencil-and-paper test form. Flexibility will not be an important consideration in many cases. However, in those cases where maximization of data collection or meeting a minimum quota of tested individuals is critical (e.g., surveying the satisfaction of a specified minimal number of members from a given heath plan), having the means of gathering data by more than one means can help increase the chances of success in the endeavor.

SUMMARY

Overall, the developments in instrumentation and technology that have taken place over the past several years suggest two major trends in MBHO settings. First, there will always be a need for the commercially published, multidimensional assessment instruments on which most psychologists received training. However, use of these types of instruments will become the exception rather than the rule in day-to-day, "down-in-the-trenches" clinical practice. Instead, brief, valid, problem-oriented instruments whose development and availability were made possible by public or other grant money will gain prominence in the psychologist's armamentarium of psychological measures. As for the second trend, it is this author's contention that the Internet will eventually become the primary medium for automated test administration, scoring, and reporting. MBHOs' development of Internet-based tools and access to the Internet by both psychologists and patients will soon become universal. This will expand the possibilities for in-office and off-site assessment and make test administration simple, convenient, and cost-effective for patients and those responsible for their treatment.

Choosing the right measures and technology for psychological assessment can be a difficult task. This author has tried to convey various criteria, features, and issues that he and other recognized experts feel are important to consider in selecting psychological measures and the technology to support their use in MBHO (and non-managed care) systems. In reality, there is no one set of criteria which either instrumentation or technology must or should meet. Instead, decision makers must decide what to measure, why they want to measure it, and how they plan to use the resulting information. Based on the answers to these questions, determining the importance and necessity (if any) of each of the considerations presented in this chapter as it pertains to the MBHO's goals or the psychologist's needs will be a relatively simple task.

5

Useful Psychological Measures for Managed Behavioral Health Care Systems

The previous chapters contain references to a number of commercially available psychological measures that might be used in behavioral health care settings for any number of purposes. However, not all of them are *generally* recommended for regular use in MBHO systems. Matters related to their availability; the cost for their use on an ongoing basis (particularly if the psychologist is not being adequately reimbursed for their use); the time it takes to administer, score, or interpret them; the usefulness of the information they yield for achieving the goals of short-term treatment; lack of widespread professional acceptability; and other factors do not make a number of good, psychometrically sound instruments the best choices for instrumentation for use with patients seen through MBHOs. Based on this author's knowledge of psychological measures and employment in a large MBHO system, a number of other instruments that were named earlier, as well as some that were not identified, stand out as potentially excellent tools for use by psychologists and other appropriately trained behavioral health care professionals.

The purpose of this chapter is to identify and discuss many of those instruments believed by this author to be useful and feasible to implement in MBHO and other health care systems where cost and other constraints in the use of psychological testing exist. For this reason, instruments that are published and/or distributed by the large commercial psychological test publishing houses *generally* have been omitted from the discussion in this chapter. Included with the discussion of each of the identified instruments is a broad overview of the instrument's development, how its results are generally interpreted, and some general validity and reliability information. Note that the psychometric information that is presented does not represent a summary or conclusions related to an exhaustive, critical review of the existing literature. That is beyond the scope of this chapter. Rather, an attempt has been made to present some basic findings that have been reported in either original sources or published reviews of the literature. Those considering any of the instruments discussed in this chapter are urged to conduct a more thorough review of the literature on these instruments for themselves. This will assist them in determining the appropriateness of each instrument for the MBHO system which they serve.

Accompanying the test descriptions that follow are partial or complete copies of several of these instruments. These reproductions are presented with the written permission of the instrument's copyright owner. Readers wishing to reproduce any of these instruments for their own use must secure the permission of the copyright owner.

MEASURES OF GENERAL DISTRESS

As discussed in chapter 6, researchers and service providers have started to look past symptomatology and have become more aware of the importance of measuring improvement in family, social, and/or work functioning in determining if an intervention has been beneficial. These variables are also used in determining such things as the value of treatment and cost-offset. However, contrary to what some experts suggest, many patients, providers, and third-party payors still consider level of symptomatology the primary and most important domain on which outcomes data should be gathered.

In evaluating psychiatric symptomatology, one can take either of two approaches. One may consider the patient's general level of distress or disturbance, or measurement can be limited to the presence or level of one or more specific types of symptomatology. Either approach is acceptable, but each has its own benefits and drawbacks that must be considered in the measurement selection process.

Measures of general distress have the advantage of not being limited to the examination of one particular type of psychopathology. This is a huge advantage in settings where one wishes to measure the outcomes of treatment on a population that presents with a wide range of symptoms and problems spanning the entire range of severity. A major drawback here is that instruments that are developed for this purpose are likely to be longer than symptom-specific instruments, in that they attempt to measure the patient's level of distress on multiple symptom dimensions. Another drawback may occur in certain settings — such as in specialty clinics or even other general treatment settings — where only one or two types of patients are usually seen.

Conversely, brevity is likely to be the biggest advantage of symptom-specific measures, as are its limited yet relevant symptom focus in settings that usually treat only one type of presenting problem. At the same time, brevity may limit a measure's reliability, and the narrow focus may result in a failure to detect the presence of other significant problems and/or their improvement resulting from intervention.

Fortunately, there are many cost-free or inexpensive multidimensional and symptom-specific measures of distress that are available to the clinicians. Many of these are currently being used in MBHO settings and thus have the added advantage of being managed-care friendly. Following are discussions of many of those instruments that this author considers particularly useful for multiple assessment purposes.

OQ-45

Over the past decade, the Outcomes Questionnaire, or OQ-45 (Lambert et al., 1996) has gained widespread acceptance and popularity in MBHOs and other behavioral health care settings as a useful tool for identifying, tracking, and measuring the outcomes of behavioral health treatment. Contributing to this acceptance is its brevity, low cost, and focus on multiple areas of functioning that are generally deemed important in evaluating those seeking behavioral health care services.

Development.   The 45 items selected for inclusion in the OQ-45 were chosen because they "addressed commonly occurring problems across a wide variety of disorders . . . tap the symptoms that are most likely to occur across patients, regardless of their unique problems . . . [and] measure personally and socially relevant characteristics that effect the quality of life of the individual" (Lambert & Finch, 1999, p. 832). These items are presented in the reproduction of the OQ-45 form in Fig. 5.1 and comprise three scales of this instrument.

The *Symptom Distress (SD)* scale consists of 25 items that measure the presence and severity of anxious and depressive symptomatology (Lambert & Finch, 1999). These symptom domains were selected because of their prevalence in one large epidemiological study as well as in diagnostic data from one large MBHO. Because research has shown these two types of symptomatology are not easily separated, there was no attempt by the test authors to distinguish them in the OQ-45. In addition to anxiety and depression items, there are also two of the items that screen for substance abuse.

The *Interpersonal Relations (IR)* scale is comprised of 11 items dealing with satisfaction with and problems in interpersonal relations. Lambert & Finch (1999) point to research that indicates that interpersonal problems are the most commonly addressed in therapy. The IR items measure marriage, family, friendships, and life relationships.

The nine items on the *Social Role (SR)* scale assess "a patient's level of dissatisfaction, conflict, distress, and inadequacy in tasks related to their employment, family roles, and leisure" (Lambert & Finch, 1999, p. 833). Inclusion of these types of items demonstrates a recognition of and the importance in measuring how intrapsychic problems can effect a patient's ability to perform both personal tasks (e.g., leisure activities) and societal tasks (e.g., work).

Each of the 45 items includes five Likert-type response choices that the patient uses to indicate the degree or frequency ("Never" to "Almost always") at which the content of the item has been present during the previous week. Each of the five response choices are weighted so that the score for each of the three scales is computed by summing the weights of the response choices selected for the items that score on that scale. A Total score also is calculated by summing response weights from all 45 items. An important feature of the OQ-45 is the normative data that are available for use with scored results. Lambert et al. (1996) report individual sets of normative data for community, employment assistance (EAP), university counseling center, community mental health, and inpatient psychiatric samples, as well as for three samples of undergraduate students. Because the OQ-45 does not transform raw data into standardized or other types of scores, the norms are reported as raw score values for each of the Total scale and three subscales.

Interpretation of Results.   The availability of different norm sets increases the applicability and utility of the instrument. However, the interpretation of the results is based on the use of the community sample norms. A Total raw score of 63 (approximately 1 standard deviation from the mean of the community sample) or greater makes it more likely that the respondent belongs to a patient sample than a community (nonpatient) sample (Lambert et al., 1996). For the subscales, similar interpretations are made using cutoff scores of 36 for the SD subscale, 15 for the IR subscale,

Outcome Questionnaire (OQ®-45.2)

Instructions: Looking back over the last week, including today, help us understand how you have been feeling. Read each item carefully and mark the box under the category which best describes your current situation. For this questionnaire, work is defined as employment, school, housework, volunteer work, and so forth. Please do not make any marks in the shaded areas.

Name:_____ Age:____ yrs.

Sex

ID#_____ M ☐ F ☐

Session #_____   Date___/___/___

	Never	Rarely	Sometimes	Frequently	Almost Always	SD IR SR *DO NOT MARK BELOW*
1. I get along well with others.	☐	☐	☐	☐	☐	
2. I tire quickly.	☐	☐	☐	☐	☐	
3. I feel no interest in things.	☐	☐	☐	☐	☐	
4. I feel stressed at work/school.	☐	☐	☐	☐	☐	
5. I blame myself for things.	☐	☐	☐	☐	☐	
6. I feel irritated.	☐	☐	☐	☐	☐	
7. I feel unhappy in my marriage/significant relationship.	☐	☐	☐	☐	☐	
8. I have thoughts of ending my life.	☐	☐	☐	☐	☐	
9. I feel weak.	☐	☐	☐	☐	☐	
10. I feel fearful.	☐	☐	☐	☐	☐	
11. After heavy drinking, I need a drink the next morning to get going. (If you do not drink, mark "never")	☐	☐	☐	☐	☐	
12. I find my work/school satisfying.	☐	☐	☐	☐	☐	
13. I am a happy person.	☐	☐	☐	☐	☐	
14. I work/study too much.	☐	☐	☐	☐	☐	
15. I feel worthless.	☐	☐	☐	☐	☐	
16. I am concerned about family troubles.	☐	☐	☐	☐	☐	
17. I have an unfulfilling sex life.	☐	☐	☐	☐	☐	
18. I feel lonely.	☐	☐	☐	☐	☐	
19. I have frequent arguments.	☐	☐	☐	☐	☐	
20. I feel loved and wanted.	☐	☐	☐	☐	☐	
21. I enjoy my spare time.	☐	☐	☐	☐	☐	
22. I have difficulty concentrating.	☐	☐	☐	☐	☐	
23. I feel hopeless about the future.	☐	☐	☐	☐	☐	
24. I like myself.	☐	☐	☐	☐	☐	
25. Disturbing thoughts come into my mind that I cannot get rid of.	☐	☐	☐	☐	☐	
26. I feel annoyed by people who criticize my drinking (or drug use). (If not applicable, mark "never")	☐	☐	☐	☐	☐	
27. I have an upset stomach.	☐	☐	☐	☐	☐	
28. I am not working/studying as well as I used to.	☐	☐	☐	☐	☐	
29. My heart pounds too much.	☐	☐	☐	☐	☐	
30. I have trouble getting along with friends and close acquaintances.	☐	☐	☐	☐	☐	
31. I am satisfied with my life.	☐	☐	☐	☐	☐	
32. I have trouble at work/school because of drinking or drug use. (If not applicable, mark "never")	☐	☐	☐	☐	☐	
33. I feel that something bad is going to happen.	☐	☐	☐	☐	☐	
34. I have sore muscles.	☐	☐	☐	☐	☐	
35. I feel afraid of open spaces, of driving, or being on buses, subways, and so forth.	☐	☐	☐	☐	☐	
36. I feel nervous.	☐	☐	☐	☐	☐	
37. I feel my love relationships are full and complete.	☐	☐	☐	☐	☐	
38. I feel that I am not doing well at work/school.	☐	☐	☐	☐	☐	
39. I have too many disagreements at work/school.	☐	☐	☐	☐	☐	
40. I feel something is wrong with my mind.	☐	☐	☐	☐	☐	
41. I have trouble falling asleep or staying asleep.	☐	☐	☐	☐	☐	
42. I feel blue.	☐	☐	☐	☐	☐	
43. I am satisfied with my relationships with others.	☐	☐	☐	☐	☐	
44. I feel angry enough at work/school to do something I might regret.	☐	☐	☐	☐	☐	
45. I have headaches.	☐	☐	☐	☐	☐	

+   +

Total=

FIG. 5.1. OQ-45 test form. Copyright © 1996 American Professional Credentialing Services, LLC. All rights reserved. Licensure required for all uses: e-mail: apcs@erols.com; web site: www.oqfamily.com. Reproduced with permission.

and 12 for the SR scale. Lambert and Finch (1999) latter recommended adjusting the subscale cutoffs to 30, 15, and 15, respectively. Elevated subscale scores can provide clues as to what aspects of functioning are particularly problematic for the patient when his Total scale score is 63 or greater. Individual item analysis also will enable a more specific determination. In general, an elevated Total scale score suggests problems in one or more of the general areas associated with the subscales. An elevated SD score suggests that the patient is bothered by symptoms associated with anxiety, affective, adjustment, and stress-related disorders. A high IR scores suggests loneliness and problems in the patient's relationships with spouse, family, or others, whereas a high SR scores points to problems in the patient's role as worker, homemaker, and/or student.

The OQ-45 was developed not only as an outcomes instrument to be administered at the beginning and end of treatment, but also as an instrument that can be used to track the progress of patients during the course of treatment. To assist in the monitoring of patient status over time, Lambert et al. (1996) provide the reliable change index (RCI) values for the each of the Total scale and the three subscales. Based on the work of Jacobson and Truax (1991), the RCI values are 14 for the Total scale, 10 for SDS, 8 for IR, and 7 for SR. Thus, a change in the Total scale score or any of the subscale scores between any two points in time by at least their respective RCI values is considered a reliable change. Improvement is indicated if the difference value is reliable and reflects a decrease in the Total or subscale score from one point in time to another. If the difference value is reliable and reflects an increase in the score from one point in time to another, a worsening of the patient's condition is indicated.

Reliability.   Lambert et al. (1996) report internal consistency (alpha coefficient) reliabilities for the four scale/subscales, ranging from .70 to .92 for a university student sample, and from .71 to .93 for a EAP patient sample. For both samples, the Total and SD values were in the low .90s whereas the IR and SR values were in the low .70s. Test–retest reliabilities derived from the student sample were less variable, ranging from .78 for the SR scale to .84 for the Total scale. Weekly administration of the OQ-45 to 56 undergraduates over a 10-week period yielded gradually diminishing but expected retest correlations. The correlations between the first week's Total score and that for each of the subsequent 9 weeks ranged from .82 (Week 1 and Week 2) to .66 (Week 1 and Week 10). Lambert and his colleagues cautioned that because of the possible influence of several earlier administrations, these reliabilities are not "true" test–retest reliabilities. At the same time, they do lend support for the stability of the instrument and its utility in monitoring patient change over time.

Validity.   The validity of the OQ-45 has been investigated using a variety of approaches that provide evidence that is typically associated with an instrument's concurrent and construct validity. First, using student sample data, Lambert et al. (1996) found both the Total score and the SD score to correlate significantly ($p < .01$) with various measures of general and domain-specific symptomatology (e.g., SCL-90-R GSI, BDI, STAI). The Total score also correlated significantly with the Inventory of Interpersonal Problems (IIP; Horowitz, Rosenberg, Baer, Ureno, & Villasenor, 1988) and the Social Adjustment Scale–Self-Report version (SAS-SR; Weissman & Bothwell, 1976). Significant correlations also were found between the OQ-45 IP subscale and the IIP, and between the SR subscale and the SAS.

Umphress, Lambert, Smart, Barlow, and Clouse (1997) investigated both concurrent and construct validity of the OQ-45 using the data obtained from four samples:

community subjects, university counseling center clients, community clinic patients, and inpatients. In addition to the OQ-45, all subjects completed the SCL-90-R. IIP, and SAS-SR. Concurrent validity was investigated by correlating the scores of each of these three measures with each of the four OQ-45 measures (Total, SD, IR, SR) separately for the counseling center, outpatient mental health, and inpatient samples. Correlations between all OQ-45 and all criterion measures were significant ($p < .01$) within all three samples. Generally, the scores of both the Total and the SD scales correlated higher with the SCL-90-R GSI score than with the IIP or SAS-SR scores, whereas the SR score correlated higher with the SAS-SR score than with the GSI or IIP score. Unexpectedly, the correlation of the IR subscale did not show the highest correlation with the IIP, except in the case of the community mental health clinic sample.

The data gathered by Umphress et al. (1997) also permitted an investigation of the OQ-45's construct validity through several means. First, the correlations between the four OQ-45 measures, computed separately for the counseling center, outpatient mental health and inpatient samples, revealed that the Total scale to be highly and significantly correlated with the other three subscales (from .72 to .96; all $ps < .01$). In all three samples, the highest correlation was with the SD subscale (.96–.98). With the exception of the IP and SR correlation, all other correlations between the other variables were significant. Second, the scores of those community clinic sample members assigned a DSM disorder were significantly higher ($p < .001$) than those with a V-code assignment on all but the IR subscale of the OQ-45. Third, with few exceptions, there were between-sample differences in the scores on each of the four OQ-45 scales. Generally, the score for each of the four subscales tended to increase significantly from one sample to the next in a manner that would be expected for a measure that purports to be sensitive to various levels of distress and changes therein. For example, the Total scale score for the community sample was significantly lower than that for the counseling center sample, which was significantly lower than that for the community clinic sample, which was significantly lower than that for the inpatient sample.

As suggested previously, a demonstration of pre- to posttreatment changes in scores for the four OQ-45 scales would support the instrument's claims of construct validity. This is what Lambert and his colleagues found with a group of 40 patients who were seen for at least 7 sessions in an outpatient clinic (Lambert et al., 1996). Here, the scores on all of the scales decreased significantly ($p < .001$). Similarly, support for the OQ-45's construct validity can be found in the decreasing Total scores for Kadera et al.'s (1996) group of 64 community clinic patients as they progressed through treatment over a period of 7 weeks.

Mueller, Lambert, and Burlingame (1998) investigated the OQ-45's construct validity as a multidimensional instrument through the use of confirmatory factor analysis (CFA). Using the OQ-45 results of a mix of 1,085 community "normals," college students, EAP patients and community mental health patients in a split-sample, cross-validation design, Mueller et al. examined one-, two-, and three-factor models of the instrument. The goodness-of-fit indexes for three models were all poor, although the fit for the three-factor model (reflective of the dimensions purported to be measured by the DS, IR, and SR subscales) was significantly better than the indexes for the other two models.

In further investigating the construct validity of the instrument, Vermeesch, Lambert, and Burlingame (2000) examined the OQ-45's sensitivity to change at the item, subscale, and full-scale levels. For the purpose of this study, the OQ-45 results from 1,176 individual psychotherapy patients and 284 controls were employed. At each of three levels, sensitivity to change was considered to be present if two criteria were met: change on an item/scale/full scale reflected improvement over the course of treatment, and patient improvement on the item/scale/full scale was significantly greater for patients than nonpatients. With the exception of eight items and the IR subscale, the OQ-45 generally met the criteria on all levels across heterogeneous patient samples.

Comment.   The OQ-45 was designed to meet the needs of MBHOs and other behavioral health care providers and organizations. It has been shown to be a valid and reliable instrument that lends itself to one or more re-administrations during the course of an episode of care. The Total scale score represents a combination of items designed to measure three dimensions of patient functioning that are thought to be important in the conceptualization of mental disorders (American Psychiatric Association, 1994). Support for the independence of the subscales that measure these dimensions (SD, IR, SR) has not been strong. However, as Mueller et al. (1998) state,

> Whereas the domains of symptom distress, interpersonal relationships, and social role functioning, as measured with the OQ, appear at the present time to be so highly correlated that they effectively represent a single factor, they also represent distinct and important psychological constructs that merit concern and investigation by researchers and practitioners alike. Thus, clinical use of the OQ may continue to utilize the scales that have been developed. . . . [T]he content groupings of these subscales may provide clinicians with valuable information regarding various aspects of their patients' lives in a manner clinicians can readily incorporate into treatment. (p. 260)

Umphress et al. (1997) see the OQ-45 as a measure of psychological distress with interrelated domains that allow for a more complete picture of a patients overall functioning. This view is consistent with those of Mueller et al. (1998) and Lambert et al. (1996) in recommending the use of only the Total subscale score for tracking clinically significant change. Indeed, the simultaneous assessment of symptomatology and social/role functioning is attractive to MBHOs who need to demonstrate to patients, employers, and payers a level of patient improvement that is much broader than can be indicated by decreased symptomatology alone.

BASIS-32

Another instrument that is gaining acceptance as an outcomes measure is the Behavior and Symptom Identification Scale, or BASIS-32 (Eisen, Dill, & Grob, 1994; Eisen, 1996a; Eisen & Culhane, 1999). It can be distinguished from most other outcomes measures from three perspectives. It was developed on an inpatient psychiatric sample; it includes an assessment of problematic symptoms and functioning; and its content reflects the patient's perspective, that is, it addresses problems that are meaningful to the patient. Like the OQ-45, this is a brief, inexpensive instrument that provides for a measure of multiple domains of patient functioning. A reproduction of the BASIS-32 is presented in Fig. 5.2.

Development.   The BASIS-32 was initially constructed as a clinician-administered interview (Eisen et al., 1994). Development of this instrument began with evaluating the reports of 354 psychiatric inpatients concerning the problems that led them to inpatient treatment. The 897 identified problems were categorized and then further re-

BASIS-32™ (Behavior And Symptom Identification Scale)

Instructions To Respondent: Below is a list of problems and areas of life functioning in which some people experience difficulties. Using the scale below, fill in the box with the answer that best describes how much difficulty you have been having in each area **DURING THE PAST WEEK.**

0 = No Difficulty
1 = A Little Difficulty
2 = Moderate Difficulty
3 = Quite A Bit of Difficulty
4 = Extreme Difficulty

Please do not leave any questions blank. If there is an area that you consider to be inapplicable, indicate that it is *0 = No Difficulty*.

IN THE PAST WEEK, how much difficulty have you been having in the area of:

1. **Managing day-to-day life.** (For example, getting places on time, handling money, making everyday decisions)..........1

2. **Household responsibilities.** (For example, shopping, cooking, laundry, cleaning, other chores)................................2

3. **Work.** (For example, completing tasks, performance level, finding/keeping a job)...3

4. **School.** (For example, academic performance, completing assignments, attendance)...4

5. **Leisure time or recreational activities.**...5

6. **Adjusting to major life stresses.** (For example, separation, divorce, moving, new job, new school, a death)...............6

7. **Relationships with family members.**..7

8. **Getting along with people outside of the family.**..8

9. **Isolation or feelings of loneliness.**...9

10. **Being able to feel close to others.**..10

11. **Being realistic about yourself or others.**..11

12. **Recognizing and expressing emotions appropriately.**..12

13. **Developing independence, autonomy.**..13

14. **Goals or direction in life.**..14

15. **Lack of self-confidence, feeling bad about yourself.**...15

16. **Apathy, lack of interest in things.**..16

17. **Depression, hopelessness.**...17

18. **Suicidal feelings or behavior.**..18

19. **Physical symptoms.** (For example, headaches, aches and pains, sleep disturbance, stomach aches, dizziness)..........19

20. **Fear, anxiety, or panic.**...20

21. **Confusion, concentration, memory.**...21

FIG. 5.2. *(Continued)*

0 = No Difficulty
1 = A Little Difficulty
2 = Moderate Difficulty
3 = Quite A Bit of Difficulty
4 = Extreme Difficulty

IN THE PAST WEEK, how much difficulty have you been having in the area of:

22. Disturbing or unreal thoughts or beliefs..22

23. Hearing voices, seeing things..23

24. Manic, bizarre behavior..24

25. Mood swings, unstable moods..25

26. Uncontrollable, compulsive behavior. (For example, eating disorder, hand-washing, hurting yourself)..............26

27. Sexual activity or preoccupation...27

28. Drinking alcoholic beverages...28

29. Taking illegal drugs, misusing drugs...29

30. Controlling temper, outbursts of anger, violence..30

31. Impulsive, illegal, or reckless behavior..31

32. Feeling satisfaction with your life...32

For the following questions, please write the response code in the appropriate box.

33. How old were you on your last birthday? (age in years)...33

34. What is your sex?   1 = Male   2 = Female..34

35. What is your race?   1 = Black/African American   3 = Asian/Pacific Islander   5 = Other
                           2 = White/Caucasian   4 = American Indian/Alaskan....................35

36. Are you Hispanic or Latino?   1 = Yes   2 = No..36

37. What is your marital status?   1 = Never married   3 = Separated   5 = Widowed
                                     2 = Married   4 = Divorced....................................37

38. How much school have   1 = 8ᵗʰ grade or less   3 = High school graduate/GED   5 = 4-year
    you completed?   2 = Some high school   4 = Some college   college graduate.....38

39. In the past 30 days, what were   1 = Alone   3 = With family/partner 5 = Shelter/street
    your usual living arrangements?   2 = Halfway house/   4 = With non-relative   6 = Other...........39
                                       group home/hospital

40. In the past 30 days, were you working at a paid job?   1 = Yes   2 = No.........................40

41. If yes, how many hours per week?   1 = 1-10 hours   3 = 21-30 hours
                                         2 = 11-20 hours   4 = More than 30 hours...................41

42. In the past 30 days, were you a student attending a high school,
    vocational training program, college or graduate degree program?   1 = Yes   2 = No...............42

43. Today's date...43   Month / Day / Year

FIG. 5.2.   Behavior and Symptom Identification Scale (BASIS-32). Copyright © McLean Hospital Department of Mental Health Services Research. All rights reserved, Reproduced with permission. An annual site license is required to use the BASIS-32. Requests for permission to reproduce or a site license for the BASIS-32 should be addressed to Susan V. Eisen, Ph.D., Department of Mental Health Services Research, McLean Hospital, 115 Mill Street, Belmont, MA 02478.

122

duced by cluster analysis, resulting in the derivation of the final 32 items. Then, 387 inpatients were administered the items via clinician interview within 1 week of their admission for inpatient treatment. In addition, a paper copy of the questionnaire was mailed to each of these patients 6 months later in order to obtain follow-up data needed to validate the instrument. Two hundred forty-seven (64%) of the subjects from the initial sample completed the follow-up questionnaire.

Factor analysis of the data obtained during the clinician interviews at the time of admission yielded five factors that have become the BASIS-32 scales: Relation to Self and Others, Daily Living/Role Functioning, Depression/Anxiety, Impulsive/Addictive Behavior, and Psychosis. Patients respond to the 32 BASIS items by indicating how much they have been bothered by the each of the 32 listed problems during the past week using a Likert-type scale of 0 ("No difficulty") to 4 ("Extreme difficulty"). The score for each scale is computed by averaging all rating values assigned to each of items contained within the given scale. In addition to the average rating for the five scales, an overall mean response score is computed.

Interpretation of Results.　　There are no specific guidelines for interpreting the BASIS-32 results. As with the OQ-45 and many other multiscale instruments, interpretation can take place on the item, subscale, and overall severity/impairment level. At each of these levels, one can establish a rating criterion for determining the presence of problems that he considers "significant" and requires intervention or, at the least, further investigation. Certainly, an item or scale/overall average rating of 4 ("Extreme difficulty") should be cause for concern, but one may also wish to attend to item ratings or scale averages of 2 ("Moderate") or 3 ("Quite a bit").

Alternately, one can use normative data to guide decisions about the severity of problems and/or the necessity of attending to them. Originally, the BASIS-32 was developed for use in inpatient settings. As part of their development efforts, Eisen et al. (1994) published inpatient normative data based on the 387 patients who completed the BASIS-32 (via interview) at or about the time of their admission. Since then, the use of the BASIS-32 in outpatient settings has been investigated, resulting in the availability of outpatient normative data (Eisen, Wilcox, Leff, Schaefer, & Culhane, 1999; Eisen, Wilcox, Schaefer, Culhane, & Leff, 1997).

Reliability.　　Eisen et al. (1994) found the internal consistency (alpha coefficient) reliabilities for the interview version of the BASIS-32 to range from .71 to .80 for all subscales except Psychosis (α = .63). The alpha coefficient for the entire 32-item instrument was .89. Generally, Eisen et al.'s findings were the same for another sample of 144 patients, except that the alpha coefficient for Psychosis dropped to .43. Two- to 3-day test–retest subscale reliabilities for a separate sample of 40 inpatients ranged from .65 to .81, whereas the full-scale test–retest reliability was .85 (p < .001 for all reliabilities).

Meanwhile, Russo, Roy-Byrne, Jaffe, Ries, Dagadakis, O'Connor, and Reeder (1997), using the self-report version of the BASIS-32 administered to a sample of 361 inpatients within 24 hours of both admission and discharge, found consistently higher coefficients than Eisen et al. (1994). Admission alpha coefficients ranged from .74 to .81 and discharge alphas ranged from .76 to .89. The lowest coefficients at both admission and discharge those for the Psychosis subscale. Russo also obtained admission-to-discharge change score correlations ranging from .58 for the Psychosis score to .92 for the full-scale score.

The Eisen et al. (1999) study of 399 outpatients tested at the initiation of outpatient treatment and again 30 days thereafter provided additional reliability data. This study (described in more detail later) used the self-report version of the BASIS-32. The full-scale internal consistency was .95. The alpha coefficients for the Psychosis and Impulsive/Addictive Behavior subscales were .65 and .66, respectively, and those for the other three subscales ranged from .87 to .89. Further, three of the Impulsive/Addictive Behavior items and two of the Psychosis items failed to meet the minimum standard (.40) for item–scale correlations.

In a study that sought to validate earlier BASIS-32 findings, Hoffman, Capelli, and Mastrianni (1997) administered the instrument to a group of 462 adult (19–85 years old) psychiatric inpatients and 244 adolescent (12–18 years old) inpatients at admission, discharge, and at 6 months postdischarge. Hoffman et al. obtained full-scale alpha coefficients of .91 and .92, respectively, for the adult and adolescent samples. Adult subscale alphas ranged from .65 for Psychosis to .80 for Self/Others, and adolescent subscale alphas ranged from .56 for Psychosis to .81 for Depression/Anxiety.

Validity.   In addition to reliability information, the three preceding investigations also provided much information about the construct validity of the BASIS-32. First, Eisen et al. (1994) found that at 6-month remeasurement, there was a significant trend on the full-scale and all subscales except the Impulsive/Addictive Behavior subscale for still-hospitalized inpatients to score higher (i.e., complain of more problematic behavior) than patients who had been rehospitalized but had since been discharged. This group, in turn, scored higher that those who had not been rehospitalized. Overall, there were significant decreases (i.e., improvement; $p < .007$) on each of the six BASIS-32 measures for these patients from the initial admission to follow-up 6 months later. Eisen et al. also found that unipolar depressive, psychotic, and substance abuse patients scored higher on each of the respective BASIS-32 scales than members of other diagnostic subgroups. Finally, while intercorrelations among the five subscales were all significant ($p < .01$), the Psychosis and Impulsive/Addictive Behavior subscales were found to be more independent of each other and the other three scales.

Russo et al. (1997) sought to validate Eisen et al.'s (1994) findings for the clinician-interview version of the BASIS-32 with the patient self-report version. Their data supported Eisen et al.'s findings regarding the instrument's factor structure, the relationship among its subscales, and its ability to discriminate among diagnostic groups. They also found significant ($p < .001$) intake-to-discharge score decreases for all six BASIS-32 measures, with effect sizes ranging from .43 for the Psychosis score to 1.24 for the full-scale score. The relationships between clinician ratings of functional and satisfaction aspects of quality of life (QOL), cognitive functioning, and symptomatology and related BASIS-32 subscales varied according to what was being rated and subscales being considered. In general, the results supported the use of both clinician-rating and patient self-report measures in the assessment of psychiatric inpatients.

Hoffman et al. (1997) also used a self-report version of the BASIS-32 with their adult and adolescent inpatient samples in their attempt to replicate the validity findings of Eisen et al. (1994). Although the adult sample factor structure was found to be congruent with the original structure, the same was not true for the factor structure that resulted for the adolescent sample. As with the original BASIS-32 findings, intercorrelations among the five subscales yielded moderate to strong correlations among the Self/Others, Daily Living, and Depression/Anxiety for both adult and adolescent samples. Unlike the adult and original sample, however, the adolescent sample also showed moderate to strong correlations between the Impulsive/Addictive and Psychosis subscales, and between each of these subscales and the remaining subscales.

In other validity-related analyses, Hoffman et al. (1997) found both the total average (mean of response to all items) and overall intensity (mean of all items for which some difficulty was identified) measures for both the BASIS-32 and the SCL-90 to correlate significantly ($p < .01$) for both a subsample of the adults (.73 and .75, respectively; $n = 211$) and a subsample of adolescents (.88 and .82, respectively; $n = 122$). Low but significant correlations (.20, .40, and .19) were found between three BASIS-32 subscales (Depression/Anxiety, Impulsivity/Addiction, and Psychosis, respectively) and three similar scales from the Child and Adolescent Functional Assessment Scale (CAFAS; Hodges, 1994) for a subsample of 88 adolescents. BASIS-32 intensity ratings at both discharge and 6-month follow-up were found to be significantly higher ($p < .05$) for those adults who had been rehospitalized during that time; only the discharge score differences reached significance for the adolescent sample. ANOVAS revealed that the Impulsivity/Addiction scale differentiate both adolescents and adults with a substance abuse diagnosis from those without no such diagnosis ($p < .0001$). However, while the Depression/Anxiety scale at admission differentiated adult patients with major depression from other adult patients ($p < .001$), the same was not found for adolescents. Finally, both adults and adolescents reported significant differences ($p < .01$) from admission to discharge and admission to follow-up on all BASIS-32 subscales and the overall intensity level, with the exception of Role Functioning for adolescents from admission to follow-up ($p < .05$).

Eisen et al. (1999) also sought to replicate the Eisen et al. (1994) inpatient findings with a group of 399 outpatients who were administered the both the BASIS-32 and the SF-36 at intake. Fifty-six percent completed the instruments again during a 30-day follow-up assessment. Confirmatory factor analysis of the outpatient data validated the original factor structure derived from the 1994 inpatient data, but ability to discriminate among diagnostic groups on relevant subscales was confirmed only for those patients with anxiety or depressive disorders. As expected, the mean intake scores on all six BASIS-32 measures were significantly lower than those for a group of 949 inpatients ($p < .001$; effect sizes = .21-.43). Also as expected, those 223 patients who completed the follow-up assessment had significantly lower follow-up scores on the six measures ($p < .001$; effect sizes = .31-.53).

The Eisen et al. (1999) study also yielded important concurrent validity information through correlations of the six BASIS-32 measures with three SF-36 domains (mental health, physical health, and physical/mental health), each of which were comprised of two or three of the eight SF-36 scales. All correlations between the two sets of measures were significant ($p < .001$). Correlations of the BASIS-32 measures with the SF-36 mental health measure ranged from −.35 to −.70; from −.27 to −.54 with the mental/physical health measure; and from −.21 to −.38 with the physical health measure. The pattern and degree of the correlations between the BASIS-32 and SF-36 measures were as expected, given the nature of the content of each of the measures from the two instruments.

Comment. The BASIS-32 has the advantage of yielding not only symptom-related information, but also information related to social and day-to-day functioning. It has a large range of applicability, having been originally designed for use with psychiatric inpatients, but now it also has empirical backing and gaining wide acceptance for use in outpatient and partial hospital programs. Generally, research to this point supports its use in outpatient settings as a measure of outcomes in a variety of important symptomatic and functional domains. The overall scale mean is particularly useful as a summary measure in both clinical and research applications. The psychometric properties of the Psychosis and Impulsive/Addictive Behavior subscales frequently have been shown to be relatively weak in various analyses, perhaps warranting more caution in their use as clinical or research measures. Based on the findings of Hoffman et al. (1997), one should also exercise caution in its use with adolescents.

BPRS

Unlike the other instruments discussed in the chapter, the Brief Psychiatric Rating Scale (BPRS; Overall & Gorham, 1962, 1988) is a clinician-completed instrument. It has been used in numerous studies of the severely mentally ill (e.g., schizophrenic patients) and the effectiveness of pharmacological interventions for these types of populations. It was originally developed for use with psychiatric inpatients, but it also has demonstrated its usefulness in a variety of other settings.

Development.   Overall and Gorham (1962) indicated that the purpose of designing the BPRS was to make available "a highly efficient, rapid evaluation procedure for use in assessing treatment change in psychiatric patients while at the same time yielding a rather comprehensive description of major symptom characteristics. It is recommended for use where efficiency, speed, and economy are important considerations. . . ." (p. 799). They later reported that it was developed to meet the needs of psychopharmacological research (Overall & Gorham, 1988). The original version of the BPRS consisted of 16 rating items reflecting symptom constructs derived from the factor analyses of other rating scales. Later, 2 additional symptom constructs were added to increase its utility, yielding a total of 18 rating constructs (see Faustman & Overall, 1999). The 18 rating constructs are: Somatic Concerns, Anxiety, Emotional Withdrawal, Conceptual Disorganization, Guilt Feelings, Tension, Mannerisms and Posturing, Grandiosity, Depressive Mood, Hostility, Suspiciousness, Hallucinatory Behavior, Motor Retardation, Uncooperativeness, Unusual Thought Content, Blunted Affect, Excitement, and Disorientation.

Each of the constructs is rated on a 7-point Likert scale, with rating options ranging from "Not present" to "Extremely severe." Some use a 0–6 numerical assignment for the rating categories, while others use a 1–7 assignment system. For this reason, Faustman and Overall (1999) recommend reporting which convention is used, particularly in reporting the results for research purposes. There does not appear to be a clear recommendation of one convention over the other. An example of the BPRS form is presented in Fig. 5.3.

Overall and Klett (1972) proposed an additional source of organizing BPRS data based on the results of factor analyses that had been conducted. They identified four factor dimensions, each of which is scored by summing the unweighted ratings for the three rating constructs that comprise the dimension. The four dimensions include Thought Disturbance, Withdrawal–Retardation, Hostile–Suspiciousness, and Anxious Depression.

THE BRIEF PSYCHIATRIC RATING SCALE

Patient _____ Rater _____ No. _____ Date _____	Not Present	Very Mild	Mild	Moderate	Moderately Severe	Severe	Extremely Severe
1. SOMATIC CONERN	1	2	3	4	5	6	7
2. ANXIETY	1	2	3	4	5	6	7
3. EMOTIONAL WITHDRAWAL	1	2	3	4	5	6	7
4. CONCEPTUAL DISORGANIZATION	1	2	3	4	5	6	7
5. GUILT FEELINGS	1	2	3	4	5	6	7
6. TENSION	1	2	3	4	5	6	7
7. MANNERISMS and POSTURING	1	2	3	4	5	6	7
8. GRANDIOSITY	1	2	3	4	5	6	7
9. DEPRESSIVE MOOD	1	2	3	4	5	6	7
10. HOSTILITY	1	2	3	4	5	6	7
11. SUSPICIOUSNESS	1	2	3	4	5	6	7
12. HALLUCINATORY BEHAVIOR	1	2	3	4	5	6	7
13. MOTOR RETARDATION	1	2	3	4	5	6	7
14. UNCOOPERATIVENESS	1	2	3	4	5	6	7
15. UNUSUAL THOUGHT CONTENT	1	2	3	4	5	6	7
16. BLUNTED AFFECT	1	2	3	4	5	6	7
17. EXCITEMENT	1	2	3	4	5	6	7
18. DISORIENTATION	1	2	3	4	5	6	7

FIG. 5.3. Brief Psychiatric Rating Scale (BPRS). From "The Brief Psychiatric Rating Scale: Recent Developments in Ascertainment and Scaling," by J. E. Overall & D. R. Gorham, 1988, *Psychopharmacology Bulletin, 24*, 97–99.

Interpretation. Generally, interpretation of the scores is based on a comparison of current rating to the baseline ratings with regard to individual rating constructs, factor dimensions, or the total score (i.e., the sum of all 18 construct numerical ratings). Lachar, Bailley, Rhoades, and Varner (1999) have indicated that a BPRS percent change score (PCS) is often used to determine the effects of medication. This same approach can be used for monitoring change occurring from one point in time to an-other, regardless of the type of intervention that has occurred (medication, psycho-therapy, ECT, etc.). The PCS is calculated by subtracting the score from the latest BPRS rating from the previous score, dividing the difference by the score from that previous rating, and multiplying the result by 100.

Reliability. For the original 16-item version, Overall and Gorham (1962) re-ported interrater reliabilities ranging from .56 for Tension to .87 for Hallucinatory Be-havior and Guilt Feelings for a group of newly admitted schizophrenic patients. In addition, Faustman and Overall (1999) cite Hedlund and Viewig's (1980) findings from a review of the literature, indicating that the BPRS total score interrater reliabil-ity is generally high—fluctuating around .85—whereas those for individual concep-tual items can fall into the lower ranges.

Validity. In their brief overview of the some of the work supporting the validity of the scale, Faustman and Overall (1999) indicate the following:

- The BPRS and its factor subscales have been shown to be sensitive to the effects of antipsychotic medications in schizophrenic patients.
- In two cited studies, the BPRS depression items have been shown to correlate at about .80 with the total score from the HAM-D in schizophrenic inpatients.
- The Scale for the Assessment of Negative Symptoms (SANS; Andreasen & Olsen, 1982) has been found to correlate with a factor analytically derived cluster of items that measure withdrawal/retardation, as well as with other BPRS items groupings indicative of negative symptoms, at about the level of the BPRS's interrater reliability.
- Work to date suggests that using the results of schizophrenic patients, the factor structure of the BPRS may vary depending on whether the patient is medicated or not.

Possibly more interesting and useful information from an MBHO standpoint are findings from studies investigating the relationship between MMPI and BPRS vari-ables. For instance, Ward and Dillon (1990) correlated the BPRS ratings and MMPI scale scores for a group of 123 outpatients. They found the following significant scale correlations: MMPI Masculinity–Femininity with BPRS Guilt Feelings ($r = .23$, $p < .01$), Anxiety ($r = .32$, $p < .01$), and Depressed Mood ($r = .27$, $p < .01$); MMPI Hypochondriasis with BPRS Somatic Concern ($r = .43$, $p < .001$); MMPI Psychasthenia with BPRS Anxiety ($r = .36$, $p < .001$); MMPI Depression with BPRS Depressed Mood ($r = .45$, $p < .001$); and MMPI Hypomania with BPRS Hostility ($r = .26$, $p < .01$). In an-other MMPI study using data from 588 inpatients, Lewandowski and Graham (1972) determined that those who could be classified into one of 19 different MMPI code types differed significantly ($p < .01$) from the remainder of the sample on a number of potential correlates, including the BPRS scales. A number of expected BPRS corre-lates of MMPI code-type were found, such as more unusual thought content being found with both 48/84 and 68/86 profiles, more somatic concern with 13/31 profiles, and more grandiosity with 46/64 profiles. There were also unexpected findings, such as *less* depression with 12/21 profiles.

Comment. The need for a rating scale like the BPRS will not occur very frequently in MBHO systems. In most cases, self-report measures such as those presented in this chapter will be more than adequate to meet the type of evaluation demands that MBHOs are likely to have. They will also be more cost-effective because they require little clinician time to obtain the results. However, there are situations in which a clinician-rating scale will provide information that might not otherwise be obtained. Patients who cannot read or are too disturbed to complete self-report measures are examples of these types of situations. There also are times when clinician ratings are desired *in addition to* patient self-report information. This is not uncommon in some systems of outcomes management. In these cases, the BPRS is among the best available options. However, one should be warned that to be truly useful, it will be important for raters to receive adequate training, such as that described by Faustman and Overall (1999).

SA-45

With a need for an inexpensive, brief, multidimensional measure that could serve as a preliminary screener, treatment outcomes indicator and general purpose research tool, Strategic Advantage, Inc. (SAI), a now defunct Minneapolis-based behavioral health care outcomes assessment and consultation group, set out to develop an alternative to the BSI. The original Symptom Checklist-90 (SCL-90; Derogatis et al., 1973) was the logical source from which to derive and further develop a set of items to satisfy SAI's requirements. Using a different approach than that used by Derogatis and his colleagues, SAI researchers selected 45 items from the SCL-90 (five items for each of the nine SCL-90 symptom domains) for inclusion in the Symptom Assessment-45 Questionnaire (SA-45; SAI, 1998).

Development. The approach taken in developing the SA-45 was that of *cluster analysis.* For the purpose of initial item selection, the SCL-90 results of an inpatient sample tested at the time of admission to a large system of private psychiatric hospitals were used. This sample is described in Davison, Bershadsky, Bieber, Silversmith, Maruish, and Kane (1997) as their inpatient intake sample (hereafter referred to as the "development sample").

To examine the structure of the symptom domains, items were intercorrelated and Ward's (1963) method of cluster analysis was applied to the correlation matrix. A nine-cluster solution was forced, with each cluster containing five items. Based on these findings, nine scales matching the symptom domain scales of the SCL-90, SCL-90-R, and BSI were constructed. These include Anxiety, Depression, Hostility, Interpersonal Sensitivity, Obsessive–Compulsive, Paranoid Ideation, Phobic Anxiety, Psychoticism, and Somatization. Each SA-45 symptom domain scale incorporates the five items from the respective parent SCL-90 scale that were identified through the cluster-analytic procedures. Subsequent cluster analyses were performed on five subgroups of adult and adolescent inpatients and nonpatients to examine the degree to which items clustered according to expectations (Davison et al., 1997). The required item response sets needed for this study were extracted from SAI's existing SCL-90 data sets. The number of hits (i.e., items that clustered according to expectation) ranged from 35 (78%) of the 45 items using nonpatient data to 43 (96%) of the items using adult inpatient intake data. In comparison, cluster analyses of SCL-90 intake data and BSI item responses extracted from that same SCL-90 data yielded hits for 51 (61%) of the 83 scored SCL-90 items, and for 42 (86%) of the 49 scored BSI items.

SAI's experience with the SCL-90 and BSI indicated that two summary indices found on both instruments — the Positive Symptom Total (PST) and the Global Severity Index (GSI) — were useful as descriptors of overall level of psychopathology or symptomatology. The PST index is the total number of symptoms reported by the respondent to be present to any degree during the previous seven days. The GSI represents the average item response value (ranging from 1 to 5) for all items on the SA-45 and thus provides a good indication of the respondent's overall level of distress or disturbance. A sample of items from the SA-45 is presented in Fig. 5.4. Nonpatient normative data for the SA-45 items were extracted from SCL-90 data sets gathered on separate samples of adult and adolescent males and females. Recognizing that being able to compare a patient's results to those of inpatients might enhance the interpretation of results, SCL-90 data sets for large separate samples of adult and adolescent male and female inpatients were rescored to arrive at inpatient normative data for each of the 11 SA-45 scales and indices.

Interpretation.   At the core of the SA-45 data are the area T scores and percentiles derived from the *nonpatient* normative data for the 11 symptom domain scales and summary indices. Separate nonpatient norms are available for use with male and female adult and adolescent groups. As a general rule, an area T score of 60 or greater on a given scale or index (i.e., one standard deviation above the nonpatient normative group's average area T score of 50) indicates a problem area warranting further

Sample of SA-45 Questions

Instructions: Below is a list of problems and complaints that people sometimes have. Please read each one carefully. After you have done so, circle the number on the right that best describes *how much that problem has bothered or distressed you during the past 7 days, including today.* Circle only one number for each problem, and do not skip any items.

	Not at all	A little bit	Moderate -ly	Quite a bit	Extreme- ly
2. Feeling blue.	1	2	3	4	5
10. Suddenly scared for no reason.	1	2	3	4	5
12. Feeling afraid to go out of your house alone.	1	2	3	4	5
15. Feeling that people are unfriendly or dislike you.	1	2	3	4	5
21. Difficulty making decisions.	1	2	3	4	5
29. Feeling weak in parts of your body.	1	2	3	4	5

FIG. 5.4. Sample questions from the Symptom Assessment-45 Questionnaire (SA-45). Copyright © 1998, Strategic Advantage, Inc., under exclusive license to Multi-Health Systems Inc. All rights reserved. In the USA, 908 Niagara Falls Blvd., North Tonawanda, NY 14120-2060, 1-800-456-3003. In Canada, 3770 Victoria Park Ave., Toronto, ON M2H 3M6, 1-800-268-6011. Internationally +1-416-492-2627. Fax +1-416-492-2243. Reproduced by permission.

investigation. SA-45 area T scores and percentiles based on a mixed psychiatric inpatient sample also are available. This additional information enables the clinician to compare the respondent's SA-45 results to both nonpatient and inpatient reference groups. This can to be quite useful, particularly when evaluating a respondent with known psychological problems. The combination of these two sets of findings may have implications in triaging a person to the appropriate level of care, arriving at a diagnosis, or planning treatment should inpatient psychiatric treatment be indicated. Maruish (1999a) provides a 5-step approach to the interpretation of SA-45 results that incorporates overall, scale-level, and item-level findings.

Reliability. The internal consistency reliability of each of the nine symptom domain scales was evaluated using Cronbach's coefficient alpha for each of four adult samples and four adolescent samples (Davison et al., 1997). The coefficients for the adult samples were computed from the results of separate, large samples of adult and adolescent (a) mental health or chemical dependency inpatients who took the SCL-90 at the time of treatment intake; (b) intake patients who took the SCL-90 again at treatment termination; (c) intake patients who took the SCL-90 again 6 months following treatment termination; and (d) nonpatients. The alpha coefficients for the adult samples ranged from 0.71 for the Psychoticism scale for the follow-up sample to 0.92 for the Depression scale for the termination sample. For the adolescent samples, the alphas ranged from 0.69 for the Psychoticism scale for both the termination and follow-up samples to 0.90 for the Depression scale for the intake sample. In general, the SA-45 coefficients are comparable to those for the BSI but, as would be expected, the coefficients of the much longer SCL-90 are greater than both.

In another examination of internal consistency, each of the SA-45's items was correlated with the total raw score for each of the nine symptom domain scales. In those instances in which an item was correlated with the scale of which it is a member, that item was removed from the scale before the scale score and correlation were calculated. For the combined adult and adolescent development sample, it was determined that the highest correlations of 42 of the 45 items (93%) were with the scale to which each item belongs. For 19 of these 42 items (45%), the correlations were at least 0.10 greater than the correlation of these items with any other scale. Data from a large inpatient cross-validation sample yielded similar findings. Overall, the results of these two analyses compare quite favorably to those obtained by Boulet and Boss (1991) in a similar analysis of the BSI items.

One-to-two-week test–retest data were gathered on separate groups of adult and adolescent nonpatients. The adult, raw score-based correlations were generally in the .80s, with notable exceptions for the Somatization scale (.69) and Anxiety scale (.42). These findings are somewhat lower but generally in line with the BSI 2-week test–retest reliabilities reported by Derogatis (1993) for a group of 60 nonpatients. For the adolescent nonpatient sample, the raw score–based correlations were quite variable, ranging from 0.51 for the Hostility scale to .85 for the Psychoticism scale. Consistent with the adult findings, the Anxiety scale coefficient (.58) was the next to the lowest of the coefficients. Area T-score changes from the first to second testings remained relatively stable, dropping on an average only 1.12 points for the nine symptom domain scales and 2.27 points for the two summary indices.

Validity. To cross-validate the item composition of the nine symptom domain scales, SA-45 item responses were extracted from SCL-90 intake data for four large samples of psychiatric inpatients and submitted to the same cluster-analytic procedures used to derive the scales. For each group, the percent of correct classifications was 98% for the adult patient group, 71% for the adolescent patient group; and 96% for each of the male and female patient groups. Overall, the findings support the cluster solution originally derived for the SA-45. However, as will be shown later, the psychometric data for adolescents is not as strong as those for adults.

The SA-45's construct validity has been demonstrated through various approaches. One approach was an investigation of the instrument's interscale correlations. Using the SCL-90 item responses of more than 1,300 adult inpatients, the SA-45 interscale correlations were found to range from 0.38 between the Phobic Anxiety and Hostility scales, to 0.75 between the Interpersonal Sensitivity and Depression scales, suggesting a substantial degree of shared variance (14%–56%) and a lack of clear independence among these nine scales. Similar analyses were conducted on the interscale correlations for the inpatient adolescent sample, resulting in findings that were similar to those for the adult sample. At the same time, additional analyses of the same SCL-90 data indicated that the SA-45 scales are statistically more distinct than those in the SCL-90 for both adults and adolescents; and with one exception, the distinction between the SA-45 scales is equal to or better than that for the BSI for both age groups.

An instrument developed to assess the presence and intensity of normal personality or psychopathological constructs should yield results that differentiate groups possessing varying degrees of those constructs. In the case of psychiatric inpatients, one would expect them to report more severe symptomatology at the time of admission than at the time of discharge or several months thereafter. One also would expect nonpatients to report less symptomatology than psychiatric inpatients at the time of admission, and also to report a level of symptomatology that would be no more (and probably less) than inpatients at the time of their discharge and on postdischarge follow-up. Results reported by Davison et al. (1997) generally revealed these expected group differences for adults. The results were somewhat different for the male and female adolescent subsamples but generally supported the SA-45's ability to discriminate among groups of different symptom severity levels.

Related to the contrasted group comparisons is the SA-45's ability to accurately classify a respondent as belonging or not belonging to inpatient and nonpatient samples (i.e., sensitivity and specificity) using a single score or set of scores. In establishing cutoffs for maximized sensitivity and specificity, a 90% rate of correct classification of inpatients and nonpatients, respectively, was used to match the prevalence or base rate of inpatients within the total available sample. Preliminary findings revealed that the use of scores from a subset of the SA-45 scales in a derived logistic regression equation was superior to the GSI score alone for classification purposes. Analyses revealed relatively high sensitivity and specificity values for both adult gender samples with the female values (.87 and .87, respectively) being somewhat higher than those for the males (.78 and .86, respectively) when optimized classification cutoffs were applied. For the two adolescent groups, the values for optimized classification showed a substantial drop, with the sensitivity and specificity values being 0.73 and 0.69, respectively, for the females and 0.57 and 0.68, respectively, for the males.

Because the SA-45 items were derived from the SCL-90 in a manner that retained the structure and representativeness of the symptom domains of the parent instrument, the SA-45's scales and global indices should correlate highly with those of the SCL-90. To demonstrate this, the SCL-90 results of the adult and adolescent inpatient development samples were scored using standard SCL-90 scoring procedures and then rescored to obtain SA-45 data. The correlations between the scales and indices of the two instruments for these large samples of adult and adolescent inpatients generally were found to be .95 or higher. Of course, the relationship between the two sets of scales was probably maximized due to the fact that the SA-45 data were derived from the same SCL-90 data with which it was correlated.

Because 35 of the SA-45's items are identical to items scored on the BSI, one also would expect scales from these two brief symptom measures also to be highly correlated. Because all scored BSI items are contained in the SCL-90, scores for the nine BSI symptom domain scales were derived from the SCL-90 data sets used for the SA-45 development. Correlations between the SA-45 and BSI were similar to those found between the SA-45 and the SCL-90.

Comment. Using a different approach than that employed by Derogatis and his colleagues, SAI researchers selected 45 items from the original SCL-90 (five items for each of the nine symptom domains) for inclusion in the SA-45. Separate gender-based norms were developed for both adolescents and adults from both inpatient and nonpatient populations, and the requisite validity and reliability studies were completed. The SA-45 became a key component of the instrumentation employed by SAI in its behavioral health care outcomes research for a large behavioral health care system. Having demonstrated its psychometric properties and utility, the SA-45 is now commercially available. Certainly, one would like to see more published literature on the instrument. Regardless, when called for, it is an economical means of performing multidimensional screening, as well as assisting in planning, monitoring, and assessing the outcomes of treatment. In addition to be useful in MBHOs, its utility has also been demonstrated in primary care settings (Goldstein et al., 2000; Maruish et al., 1998; Maruish, 2000a).

One of the attractive aspects of the SA-45 is the availability of norms and other psychometric data supporting the use of the SA-45 for both adult and adolescent populations. However, one needs to be mindful that the data presented here and in the test manual (SAI, 1998) suggest that this instrument probably is not as robust as measure of psychological distress in adolescents as it is in adults. Caution (i.e., a more conservative interpretation of the data) therefore should be exercised when the testing adolescents.

MEASURES OF SPECIFIC SYMPTOMATOLOGY

There are numerous low- or no-cost symptom-specific scales that are available for use. These include the Zung depression and anxiety scales, the University of Arkansas D-ARK measures, the Geriatric Depression Scale, and others. Measures of depression and anxiety are specifically mentioned because in the vast majority of instances, these are the symptoms or problems MBHO patients are most likely to present. If one must measure something, he is on pretty safe ground measuring either or both of these. For this reason, several of the instruments discussed in this section are those that were designed to detect and assess the severity level of these types of symptomatology. However, other types of instrumentation are also included here.

Zung Self-Rating Depression Scale (SDS)

One of the more commonly used depression screeners is Zung's Self-Rating Depression Scale (SDS; Zung, 1965). It has a long history of use as both a clinical and research instrument, particularly in primary care and other medical settings. It was developed to meet the need for an instrument to assess depression as a psychiatric disorder. In describing its development, Zung indicated that

> We were interested in having a scale for assessing depression in those patients whose primary diagnoses were that of depressive disorder, which would fulfill the following: it should be all inclusive with respect to symptoms of the illness, it should be short and simple, it should quantitate rather than qualitate, and it should be self-administered and indicate the patient's own response at the time the scale is taken. (p. 63)

Development.   Zung (1965) began development of the SDS by first identifying commonly found traits or characteristics of depression (pervasive affect, physiological equivalents, psychological equivalents) and their associated symptoms, and then devising items representative of those symptoms, using recorded patient interview material. Ten of the resulting 20 items were worded in a symptom positive manner, and the other 10 were worded in a symptom negative manner. Four response choices (ranging from "A little of the time" to "Most of the time," with response weightings ranging from 1 to 4) are included for the patient to indicate how the item content applied to them at the time of the testing. The current version uses a previous 2-week time frame for responding (Zung, 1995). The SDS index is computed by dividing the sum of the response weightings by 80 (the maximum response weight summation) and multiplying by 100. The SDS items are presented in Fig. 5.5.

Interpretation.   Less than a decade after the first publication on the measure, Zung (1973b) provided a summary of the literature that serves as a good guide to the interpretation of the SDS results. It states that:

> the distribution of SDS indices showed that patients with global ratings of mild to moderate depressions had SDS indices of between 50 to 59, patients with moderate to severe depressions had indices of 60 to 69, and patients globally rated as severely depressed had indices of 70 and over. In addition, it is to be noted that there is usually some depressive symptomatology present in almost all of the psychiatric disorders. Thus, the SDS results in the various studies have demonstrated scores of 50 or above for psychiatric patients with diagnoses other than depression. (p. 335)

Reliability.   Zung (1972) reported an odd–even split-half reliability of .73 ($p <$ .01). DeForge and Sobal (1988) obtained an alpha coefficient of .68 in their sample of 78 elderly people with osteoarthritis; however, studies with 113 Dutch depressed and nondepressed psychiatric outpatients (DeJonghe & Baneke, 1989) and 268 Chinese primary care patients (Leung, Lue, Lee, & Tang, 1998), each obtained alpha coefficients of .82. In the DeJonghe and Baneke study, the split-half reliability was .79. Item–total correlations ranged from .14 to .64 in the Leung et al. study, seven of which were less than .30.

Validity.   Using the 50 or greater (50+) index cutoff as the criterion, Baer, Jacobs, Meszler-Reizes, Blais, Fava, Kessler, Magruder, Murphy, Kopans, Cukor, Leahy, and O'Laughlen (2000) obtained sensitivities of .97 and .89 and specificities of .88 and .53,

Instructions

Read each sentence carefully. For each statement, check the bubble in the column that best corresponds to how often you have felt that way during the past two weeks.

For statements 5 and 7, if you are on a diet, answer as if you were not.

Please check a response for each of the 20 items.

		None or a little of the time	Some of the time	Good part of the time	Most or all of the time
1	I feel downhearted, blue, and sad	O	O	O	O
2	Morning is when I feel the best	O	O	O	O
3	I have crying spells or feel like it	O	O	O	O
4	I have trouble sleeping through the night	O	O	O	O
5	I eat as much as I used to	O	O	O	O
6	I enjoy looking at, talking to, and being with attractive women/men	O	O	O	O
7	I notice that I am losing weight	O	O	O	O
8	I have trouble with constipation	O	O	O	O
9	My heart beats faster than usual	O	O	O	O
10	I get tired for no reason	O	O	O	O
11	My mind is as clear as it used to be	O	O	O	O
12	I find it easy to do the things I used to do	O	O	O	O
13	I am restless and can't keep still	O	O	O	O
14	I feel hopeful about the future	O	O	O	O
15	I am more irritable than usual	O	O	O	O
16	I find it easy to make decisions	O	O	O	O
17	I feel that I am useful and needed	O	O	O	O
18	My life is pretty full	O	O	O	O
19	I feel that others would be better off if I were dead	O	O	O	O
20	I still enjoy the things I used to do	O	O	O	O

FIG. 5.5.   Zung Self-rating Depression Scale (SDS). Copyright © 1965, 1974, 1991, W. K. Zung. Used with permission of Eli Lilly and Company. All rights reserved.

respectively, for two samples of SCID-confirmed depressed and nondepressed subjects recruited through newspaper ads. Nineteen (38%) of the 50 members of Leung et al.'s (1998) Chinese primary care sample who were evaluated for DSM-IV diagnoses were found to have a DSM-IV diagnosis. Although none were found to have major depression, about half were experiencing some form of minor depression. The sensitivity, specificity, and overall classification rate were found to be 1.0, .71, and .76, respectively, with a 50+ index cutoff; .67, .90, and .86, respectively, with a 55+ index cutoff; and .44, .90, and .82, respectively, for a 60+ index cutoff. Using a DIS-obtained, DSM-III diagnosis of major depressive disorder as the criterion and the standard 50+ SDS cutoff, Zung, Magruder-Habib, Velez, and Alling (1990) obtained an SDS sensitivity of .97, a specificity of .63, a PPP of .77, an NPP of .95, and an overall classification rate of .82 for a group of 206 general medical patients.

In commenting on various findings in the literature, Zung (1973a) noted that depression, at least as defined by the SDS, is not present in the "normal" population. Applying the 50+ index value cutoff to the results of age-matched groups 20- to 64-year-old depressed patients and normal controls would result in the correct identification of 88% of each of the two groups. However, the data suggest that for individuals less than 20 years old or older than 64 years, the cutoff might have to be adjusted upward, in that the baseline index values for "normals" in these age ranges are higher than those in the 20–64 years age range.

In a different type of comparison reported in Zung's original article (1965), he examined the mean SDS index score for four samples: 31 patients admitted and discharged with a diagnosis of depressive disorder (mean = 74 and 39, respectively), 25 patients admitted for depressive disorder but discharged with another disorder (mean = 53), and a normal control group of 100 (mean = 33). As would be expected with known groups such as these, the mean discharge index score for the sample of patients admitted and discharged with a diagnosis of depression was significantly less ($p < .01$) than their score at the time of admission, and greater than the scores of the control and other diagnostic groups. Also, the mean discharge score of the depressive disorders group at discharge was not found to be significantly different from that of the control group. DeJonghe and Baneke's depressed patients scored significantly higher than their nondepressed patients (53 vs. 47; $p < .0004$). Similarly, Senra (1995) administered the SDS to a group 52 Spanish, major depressive-disordered outpatients at admission, and then again after 12 weeks and 24 weeks of treatment with tricyclic antidepressants. Mean scores decreased from 51 to 43 to 38 during the respective measurement periods. Also, effect sizes of 1.34, 1.22, and 1.79 were noted for the 0–12 weeks, 12–24 weeks, and 0–24 weeks time periods, respectively.

In investigating whether an anxiolytic agent can have both antianxiety and antidepressant effects, Zung (1973a) found that SDS pre- and posttreatment scores (61 and 48, respectively) indicated significant ($p < .01$) and expected changes in level of anxiety after 4 weeks of treatment with an anxiolytic agent in a group of 275 patients with a primary diagnosis of an anxiety disorder. The placebo group in this study also showed significant ($p < .01$) SDS changes in pre- and posttreatment scores, but to a lesser degree (62 and 53, respectively).

Burlingame et al. (1995) reported that the SDS score correlated at .88 with both the OQ-45's Symptom Distress and Total scores, yet DeForge and Sobal (1988) reported a correlation at .69 ($p < .001$) with the Center for Epidemiologic Studies Depression Scale (CES-D; Radloff, 1977; see later) in their elderly sample. Using an SDS cutoff of 60, they found that the two scales agreed in their classification of 83% of the total sample as not being depressed; they agreed that 5% of the sample were depressed. In total, the two instruments agreed in their classification of 88% of the sample. In addition, significant correlations ($p < .001$) between the SDS and CES-D psychological symptom indices (.66) and the somatic indices (.50) were reported.

Comment. The SDS ranks among the most popular and time-tested depression screeners. For over 35 years, it has been used in numerous clinical and research applications and is well-known to various specialties within both the behavioral health and medical professions. This recognition makes the SDS an attractive selection for use with many types of patients and in many types of managed care programs. One should exercise caution when using the instrument with younger or older adults, given the data reported by Zung. Higher cutoff scores may be required with these populations.

Zung Self-Rating Anxiety Scale (SAS)

As with the case of depressive disorders, Zung (1971a) identified the need for a self-rating measure of anxiety that reflects the diagnostic criteria of anxiety as a clinical disorder. Actually, he recognized a need for both a self-report measure *and* an observer rating scale that would allow the evaluation of the presence of anxiety from the patient's and clinician's perspectives on the same criteria. The resulting clinician-rating instrument was the Anxiety Status Inventory (ASI). The accompanying self-report measure was the Self-Rating Anxiety Scale (SAS).

Development. Like the SDS, the SAS includes 20 multiple-choice items that are based on the same diagnostic criteria as was used in the development of the ASI (Zung, 1971a). Again, Zung drew upon verbatim patient records in developing items reflective of the 20 anxiety symptoms. A 1-week time frame was the interval of consideration, and the four response choices ("None OR a little of the time" to "Most OR all of the time") were weighted from 1 to 4. Like the SDS, the SAS index score is computed by dividing the sum of the response weightings by 80 and multiplying by 100.

Interpretation. Information presented by Zung et al. (1990) indicate the following SAS index score interpretive ranges for the presence and severity of anxiety: less than 45, none; 45–59, mild; 60–74, moderate; 75–80, severe. In addition, Zung (1973a) has noted that although the mean score of normal controls between 20 to 64 years old is 34, a higher mean score has been obtained for both those under 20 years (45) and over 64 years (40). Thus, as with the SDS, one may wish to use more conservative (i.e., higher) cutoffs with younger and older individuals.

Reliability. Reliability data for the SAS is sparse. In the original study, however, Zung (1971a) reported an odd–even split-half reliability of .71 for his group of 225 psychiatric inpatients and outpatients. Also, item–scale correlations ranged from .27 to .69. The correlation between the ASI and the SAS (a measure of alternate-form reliability) was .66 for the entire patient sample and .74 for patients with a diagnosed anxiety disorder. All correlations were significant ($p < .01$).

Validity. For the same patient group, Zung (1971a) obtained a correlation of .30 ($p < .01$) between the SAS and the Taylor Manifest Anxiety Scale (TMAS; Taylor, 1953). Bystritsky, Stoessel, and Yager (1993) found the SAS to correlate .76 ($p < .05$)

with the Four-Dimensional Anxiety Scale (FDAS; Bystritsky, Linn, & Ware, 1990), a 75-item, multidimensional measure of anxiety. The SAS also correlated significantly ($p < .05$) with each the FDAS subscales: Emotional (.68), Physical (.75), Cognitive (.66), and Behavior (.41). The SAS correlation with the Rand Depression Screener (Burnam, Wells, Leake, & Landsverk, 1988) was .51. Burlingame et al. (1995) reported that the SAS score correlated at .81 with both Symptom Distress and Total scores from the OQ-45.

Mean SAS scores for Zung's (1971a, 1971b) sample of inpatients and outpatients, as well as those for an additional sample of 100 normal controls, varied by diagnostic group in expected directions. The mean scores were 59 for the anxiety disorder patients, 51 for the depressive disorder and personality disorder patients, 46 for schizophrenic patients and transient situational disturbances, and 34 for normal controls. The scores for the anxiety disorder group were significantly greater ($p < .05$) than those of any of the other four patient subgroups, and the normal control group scores were significantly lower ($p < .01$) than any of the five patient groups.

Zung's anxiolytic study (1973a) found that the SAS pre- and posttreatment scores (58 and 45, respectively) indicated significant ($p < .01$) and expected changes in level of anxiety after 4 weeks of treatment with an anti-anxiety agent in a group of 275 patients with a primary diagnosis of an anxiety disorder. The placebo group in this study also showed significant ($p < .01$) changes in pre- and posttreatment scores, but to a lesser degree (57 and 49, respectively). In summarizing earlier findings of normal and patient samples, Zung reported a sensitivity of .89 and a specificity of .92 using the SAS cutoff of 45.

Zung et al.'s (1990) investigation into the comorbidity of anxiety and depression among primary care patients indicated that 98% of those 112 patients who were classified as depressed by the SDS also achieved an SAS index score of 45 or greater. At the same time, application of a cutoff of 60 (moderate to severe anxiety; see above) to these patients' SAS scores indicated that 67% had significant symptoms of a cormorbid anxiety disorder. Spierings and van Hoof (1996) reported that 39% of their headache sufferers and 22% of their controls obtained SAS scores indicating the presence of mild anxiety (45–59). Moderate anxiety (SAS = 60–74) was reported by 9% of the headache group and only 2% of the controls.

Comment.   Interest in exploring the psychometric properties and practical utility of the SAS has not been as great as it has been with its companion instrument, the SDS. Consequently, neither the empirical backing nor popularity of the SAS is as extensive as that of the SDS. However, the evidence that does exist suggests that it may serve as a good first-level screener for the presence of symptomatology related to anxiety disorders when such is called for in general practice or in MBHO disease management programs.

CAGE-AID

One clinical activity that is actively promoted by many MBHOs is the screening of patients for the presence of alcohol or other substance abuse problems. This not only helps the MBHO ensure that appropriate care is being provided to all health plan members, it also may assist the organization in meeting quality improvement requirements placed on it by accreditation bodies such as NCQA and JCAHO. In many MBHOs, network providers are asked to screen adult and adolescent patients for substance abuse problems. Data relating to this may be regularly gathered and reported to facilitate provider performance. Substance abuse screening can be conducted through any number of formal (i.e., standardized screening instruments) or informal (i.e., nonstandardized, interview questions) approaches. Incorporating a formal approach into one's standard assessment protocol provides a means of not only ensuring that screening does take place, but that the results of the screening and the decisions that are based on those data have empirical backing.

There is a number of brief substance abuse screening instruments that are available to providers. Many of these have been developed for the purpose of screening for alcoholism only; they do not include questions inquiring about the use of other drugs. With the prevalence of abuse of many types of substances, it becomes important to ensure that one screens for *all* types of substance abuse. One instrument that has been developed for this purpose is the CAGE-AID (Brown & Rounds, 1995).

Development. The development of the CAGE-AID began with the development of the CAGE alcohol screener by Ewing and Rouse (1970). The CAGE was designed to be a brief, easily administered, sensitive, and valid measure for the detection of alcoholism: in other words, "a questionnaire that promises to correct many of the shortcomings of previous alcohol screening instruments" (Mayfield, McLeod, & Hall, 1974). As first documented by Ewing (1984), the CAGE was developed by contrasting the reponses of 16 alcoholic and 114 nonalcoholic general hospital patients (as identified by their physicians) on a series of questions taken from instruments developed by other research teams. Of the 16 "yes/no" questions found to separate the two subgroups, four were identified as being the minimum number of items that could be administered and still remain useful for discriminating these subgroups. These four items ask about the need to *cut* down drinking, feeling *annoyed* by others' criticism of their drinking, *guilt* over drinking, and needing a drink as an *eye-opener* in the morning; thus the "CAGE" acronym. Subsequently, Ewing and Rouse crossvalidated the ability of the CAGE to discriminate between a group of alcohol rehabilitation patients and another group of nonalcoholic general hospital patients using a cutoff of two or more positive responses as being indicative of alcoholism.

Noting previous research indicating that 20% to 43% of substance abusers use both alcohol and one (or more) other drugs, Brown and Rounds (1995) identified the need for instrument like the CAGE that would screen for both (also see Brown, 1992). They subsequently developed and tested a version of the CAGE questions that were *adapted to include drugs*, or CAGE-AID, on a group of 124 primary care patients using various cutoff scores for the modified instrument. The CAGE-AID questions are presented in Fig. 5.6.

Interpretation. As with any other test designed for screening purposes, the selection of the criterion for distinguishing individuals who are likely to have the problem of interest from those who do not will depend on how important it is to maximize sensitivity, maximize specificity, or optimize both. The research suggests that employing a cutoff of one or more affirmative responses to the CAGE-AID questions should be used in situations that seek to maximize sensitivity, whereas a cutoff of two or more affirmative responses is appropriate for maximizing specificity or optimizing both sensitivity and specificity (see later). As with any type of screening, it is this author's preference to optimize both sensitivity and specificity, and for this reason the *general* recommendation is to use the two or more affirmative responses as the criterion for determining whether the individual should undergo further evaluation for a substance abuse problem. One may wish to increase the cutoff score to three

CAGE-AID

1. Have you ever felt you ought to **C**ut down on your drinking or drug use?
2. Have people **A**nnoyed you by criticizing your drinking or drug use?
3. Have you ever felt bad or **G**uilty about your drinking or drug use?
4. Have you ever had a drink or used drugs first thing in the (**E**ye-opener) to steady your nerves or to get rid of a hangover?

Scoring: Count 1 for each "yes" response.

> FIG. 5.6.   CAGE-AID. From "Conjoint Screening Questionnaires for Alcohol and Other Drug Abuse: Criterion Validity in a Primary Care Practice," R. L. Brown & L. A. Rounds, 1995, *Wisconsin Medical Journal, 94*, 135–140.

or more when screening women, given that the CAGE-AID may be less sensitive to substance abusing women than substance abusing men.

Reliability. As part of their investigation of the efficiency of several substance abuse screeners, Dyson, Appleby, Altman, Doot, Luchins, and Delehant (1998) administered the CAGE-AID to 100 adult psychiatric inpatients at the time of their admission and then again within 48 hours. Results indicated intake (T1) and retest (T2) alpha coefficients of .83 and .84, respectively, and a kappa coefficient of 1.0 for six raters. A kappa of .62 was obtained for the two administrations of the instrument. The T1–T2 correlation was .72 ($p < .001$). Midanik, Zahnd, and Klein (1998) obtained an alpha coefficient of .90 with their sample of 1,147 pregnant women. For the 274 adolescents in the sample, the alpha was .82. All subjects were asked to use the 12 months prior to knowledge of their pregnancy as the referenced time frame. Note that Midanik et al. modified the fourth question ("eye-opener") in their study.

Validity. Initial validity data comes from Brown and Rounds' (1995) study that included an examination of the accuracy and efficiency of the CAGE-AID using various raw score classification cutoffs in their group of 124 primary care patients. The DSM-III-R diagnoses derived from the administration of the alcohol and drug sections of the Diagnostic Interview Schedule-Revised (DIS-R; Helzer, Robins, McEvoy, Spitznagel, Soltzman, Farmer, & Brockington, 1985) were used as the criteria. Brown and Rounds achieved sensitivity, specificity, PPP, and NPP findings of .79, .77, .78, and .78, respectively, when one or more (1+) affirmative responses to the four questions were given. When the affirmative response criterion was raised to two or more (2+), sensitivity decreased (.70) as specificity increased (.85). Using the 1+ criterion led to greater sensitivity to 11 or 14 different patterns of substance-related diagnoses than the 2+ criterion. Brown and Rounds' results also indicated the CAGE-AID was less sensitive to the women in their sample than to the men.

Other studies have investigated the differences in efficiency that come from using different CAGE-AID affirmative response cutoffs. Dyson et al. (1998) used the results from the administration of the Structured Clinical Interview for DSM-III-R (SCID; Spitzer, Williams, Gibbon, & First, 1990) as the criterion for classifying their sample of psychiatric inpatients as having a current (30-day) or lifetime substance use disorder. The results yielded efficiency statistics indicative of better prediction of lifetime disorders than 30-day disorders at both intake and upon remeasurement. Based on the intake CAGE-AID results, respective sensitivities and specificities for lifetime diagnosis were found to be .86 and .87 using the 1+ cutoff, and .75 and .91 using the 2+ cutoff. For 30-day diagnosis, respective sensitivities and specificities for were found to be .88 and .55 using the 1+ cutoff, and .66 and .79 using the 2+ cutoff. The ROC AUCs for lifetime and 30-day diagnosis were .88 and .77, respectively. Using the 2+ cutoff, this same study (reported in Appleby, Dyson, Altman, & Luchins, 1997) demonstrated the CAGE-AID's ability to discriminate between the two cluster analytic-derived groups with substance abuse problems (91% and 78% classified with substance abuse problems) from the third cluster group (19% classified as having minimal substance use problems).

Midanik et al.'s (1998) investigation of changes in classification accuracy were based not only on the cutoff score employed, but also on the age and type of substances used. The two age groups consisted of women 15 to 19 years old and 20 years and older while the substances were grouped as lighter drugs (e.g., stimulants, tranquilizers, pain killers), heavier drugs (e.g., cocaine, heroin, methamphetamine), and marijuana/hashish (used 3+ days per week). For all classes of drugs in each age group, regardless of the cutoff employed, the specificities were at least .94. However, sensitivities did not exceed .37 for either age group for lighter drugs or marijuana/hashish. The CAGE-AID was found to work best in identifying women 20 years and older who used heavy drugs during the 12 months prior to finding out they were pregnant. For this group, the sensitivities, specificities, and ROC AUCs were .84, .98, and .94, respectively, using the 1+ cutoff, and .88, .96, and .92, respectively, when using the 2+ cutoff. For the younger women, these values were .31, .97, and .78, respectively, using the 1+ cutoff, and .56, .97, and .76, respectively, when using the 2+ cutoff.

In another examination of the instrument's validity, Dyson et al. (1998) found that the CAGE-AID correlated with the Drug Abuse Screening Test (DAST; Skinner, 1982) at .61, the Alcohol Severity Index (ASI; McLellan, Luborsky, Woody, & O'Brien, 1980) drug scale at .58, the ASI problem severity at .41, the Chemical Use, Abuse, and Dependence Scale (CUAD; McGovern & Morrison, 1992) drug scale at .40, and the CUAD severity scale at .36. All correlations were significant at $p < .001$.

Comment. Although the available research is limited, the CAGE-AID appears to be a good selection as an initial, high-level screener for the presence of alcohol or other substance abuse problems, or both. However, one may want to exercise caution when screening women, given that at least two studies have shown that it does not seem to be as sensitive with female patients as it is with male patients. As with any screener, positive findings should always be explored through a detailed substance use interview, possibly supplemented with data from a more comprehensive assessment instrument.

CORE Depression Screener and D-ARK

Experts from the University of Arkansas for Medical Sciences (UAMS) and the RAND Corporation developed a set of three depression instruments. In addition to meeting the recommendations of the Agency for Health Care Policy and Research's (AHCPR's) Depression Guideline Panel (1993a, 1993b) for brief, easily scored and sensitive instruments for the detection of primary care patients at high-risk for depression, their use extends from identification of presence of depressive symptomatology to diagnosis and outcomes measurement. These companion instruments (Rost, Smith, Burnam, & Burns, 1992; Smith, Burnam, Burns, Cleary, & Rost, 1994), now available through the UAMS Center for Outcomes Research and Effectiveness (CORE), include the two- or three-item Screener, the 11-item Depression Arkansas Scale (D-ARK), and the in-depth, multicomponent Depression Outcomes Module (DOM). They can be implemented as part of a stepwise, systematic process for screening, monitoring, and assessing the outcomes of depressed patients. Unfortunately, use of the DOM involves a degree of patient and clinician involvement that most MBHOs are not likely to commit to. The Screener and the D-ARK are much more MBHO friendly and thus are discussed here.

Screener Development. The Screener evolved from subsets of data that were gathered as part of the Epidemiologic Catchment Area (ECA) study, in which the Diagnostic Interview Schedule (DIS; Robins, Helzer, Croughan, & Ratcliff, 1981) and DSM-III-R diagnostic information were used to assess for the presence of psychiatric disorders. At one of the ECA sites, the Center for Epidemiologic Studies Depression Scale (CES-D) was also administered. Burnam, Wells, Leake, and Landsverk (1988) developed the original screener, consisting of two DIS items and 6 CES-D items. In an attempt to create a brief screener for predicting recent depression in mental health, medical, and community samples, Rost, Burnam, and Smith (1993) reviewed Burnam et al.'s logistic regression data and subsequently retained the two DIS items and the one CES-D item that contributed the most to the prediction of a depressive disorder (major depression or dysthymia). These items and the scoring criteria for positive findings for both the two- and three-item versions are presented in Fig. 5.7. The three-item version is recommended because of its psychometric properties, particularly its PPP (see later). Note that contrary to what the reference term implies, the "two-item" version of the Screener actually includes three items, and the "three-item" Screener includes four items.

Screener Interpretation. Based on the diagnostic efficiency data provided by Rost et al. (1993), one can be quite certain that the patient does not have a depressive disorder if the results of the three-item Screener yields a negative finding, regardless of the setting in which it is obtained. A positive finding on the instrument indicates the possibility of a recent (during the past year), but not necessarily a current depressive disorder that requires further evaluation for confirmation of presence and type of depression (Kramer & Smith, 2000). Given the fact that one half to one third of the screened population may be misidentified, it is obvious that further evaluation is called for to lower the number of false positives.

Screener Reliability. Reliability data for the three-item Screener has not been investigated apart from its inclusion in the DIS data obtained during the ECA study. As Rost et al. (1993) report, the overall 3-month test–retest agreement of the Screener's two DIS items for lifetime depression was 91% for the 2 years of feeling depressed and 86% for two weeks of feeling depressed.

Screener Validity. The only validity data reported for the Screener comes from the Rost et al. (1993) development study. Here, the investigators reported diagnostic efficiency statistics for the one ECA site (Los Angeles, $N = 3,132$) in which the DIS and CES-D were both administered. Separate statistics were computed for the entire sample, as well as for two subsamples: (a) those who were seen for physical problems during the preceding six months ($n = 212$) and (b) those who were seen for mental

Two- and Three-Item CORE Screener

Instructions: Please answer each question by circling 1 for Yes or 0 for No.

1. In the past year, have you had **2 weeks or more** during which you felt sad, blue or depressed, or when you lost all interest or pleasure in things that you usually cared about or enjoyed? *(Yes = 1, No = 0)*

2. a.   Have you had **2 years or more** in your life when you felt depressed or sad most days, even if you felt okay sometimes? *(Yes = 1, No = 0. If No, skip 2b)*

   b.   Have you felt depressed or sad much of the time **in the past year?** *(Yes = 1, No = 0)*

3. How much of the time **during the past week** did you feel depressed? *(Less than 1 day = 0, 1-2 days = 1, 3-4 days = 2, 5-7 days = 3)*

Two-Item Screener Scoring.   Either Question 1 = 1 or (Question 2a = 1 and Question 2b = 1) in the past year.

Three-Item Screener Scoring. Either Question 1 = 1 or (Question 2a = 1 and Question 2b = 1) in the past year, plus Question 3 = 1 or more as defined above.

FIG. 5.7.   Two- and three-item CORE Screener and scoring criteria. Copyright © 1994 University of Arkansas for Medical Sciences, 4301 West Markham Street, Little Rock, AR 72205. All rights reserved. Reproduced with permission.

health problems during that same time interval ($n = 1,450$). The sensitivity, specificity, PPP, and NPP were .81, .95, .33, and .99, respectively, for the total sample; .82, .87, .49, and .97, respectively, for the mental health subsample; and .80, .95, .33, and .99, respectively, for the medical subsample. In all, 2.8% of the total sample, 13.2% of the mental health subsample, and 3.2% of the medical subsample met the classification criterion. Although the two-item version of the Screener was found to be generally more sensitive for this and two other ECA sites, the PPPs were generally lower, ranging from .14 to .23 for the total sample, .23 to .39 for the mental health subsample, and .17 to .24 for the medical subsample.

D-ARK Development.   Whereas the Screener was designed to identify individuals at high risk for depressive disorders, the D-ARK was developed for both diagnosing and measuring the severity of depression (Kramer & Smith, 2000). It was originally intended for use as part of the DOM but has since established itself as a stand-alone measure. Initially, it was composed of 20 items but later was reduced to 11 items through the elimination of the 9 items that correlated the lowest with the scale's total score. The patient responds to each of the 11 symptoms by indicating how often he or she has been bothered by the symptom during the previous 4 weeks on a 4-point scale ("Not at all" to "A lot"). The D-ARK items and scoring algorithms are presented in Fig. 5.8.

1. How often **in the past 4 weeks** have you felt depressed, blue, or in low spirits for most of the day? *(1 = Not at all, 2 = 1-3 days, 3 = Most days a week, 4 = Nearly every day for at least 2 weeks)*

2. How often **in the past 4 weeks** did you have days in which you experienced little or no pleasure in most of your activities? *(1 = Not at all, 2 = 1-3 days, 3 = Most days a week, 4 = Nearly every day for at least 2 weeks)*

3. How often **in the past 4 weeks** has your appetite been either less than usual or greater than usual? *(1 = Not at all, 2 = 1-3 days, 3 = Most days a week, 4 = Nearly every day for at least 2 weeks)*

4. **In the past 4 weeks,** have you gained or lost weight without trying to? *(1 = No, 2 = Yes, a little weight, 3 = Yes, some weight, 4 = Yes, a lot of weight)*

5. How often **in the past 4 weeks** have you had difficulty sleeping or trouble with sleeping too much? *(1 = Not at all, 2 = 1-3 days, 3 = Most days a week, 4 = Nearly every day for at least 2 weeks)*

6. **In the past 4 weeks,** has your physical activity been slowed down or speeded up so much that people who you know could notice? *(1 = No, 2 = Yes, a little slowed or speeded up, 3 = Yes, somewhat slowed or speeded up, 4 = Yes, very slowed or speeded up)*

7. **In the past 4 weeks,** have you often felt more tired out or less energetic than usual? *(1 = No, 2 = Yes, a little tired, 3 = Yes, somewhat tired out, 4 = Yes, very tired out)*

8. How often **in the past 4 weeks** have you felt worthless or been bothered by feelings of guilt? *(1 = Not at all, 2 = 1-3 days, 3 = Most days a week, 4 = Nearly every day for at least 2 weeks)*

9. **In the past 4 weeks,** have you had trouble thinking, concentrating, or making decisions? *(1 = No, 2 = Yes, a little trouble thinking, 3 = Yes, some trouble thinking, 4 = Yes, a lot of trouble thinking)*

10. How often have you thought about death or suicide **in the past 4 weeks?** *(1 = Not at all, 2 = 1-3 days, 3 = Most days a week, 4 = Nearly every day for at least 2 weeks)*

11. **In the past 4 weeks,** have you thought a lot about a specific way to commit suicide? (1 = No, 2 = Yes)

FIG. 5.8. *(Continued)*

D-ARK Diagnostic Scoring.
For Part A: If the respondent scores Questions 1 or 2 greater than or equal to 2, then
        Part A = 1.
For Part B: Score individual items as follows:
        If Question 1 is greater than or equal to 2, Criterion 1 = 1.
        If Question 2 is greater than or equal to 2, Criterion 2 = 1.
        If Question 3 is greater than or equal to 2, *or*
                Question 4 is great than or equal to 2, Criterion 3 = 1.
        If Question 5-9 are greater than or equal to 3, Criteria 4-8 = 1 each.
        If Question 10 is greater than or equal to 3, *or* Question 11 = 2, Criterion 9 = 1.

If the total of Criteria 1-9 is greater than or equal to 5, then Part B = 1.
If Part A = 1 and Part B = 1, then the respondent meets the criteria for depression.

D-ARK Severity Scoring
Recode Questions 1-10 as 0 to 3. If Question 11 = 1, then Question 11 = 0. If Question
        11 = 2, then Question 11 = 3.
Calculate the mean of Questions 1-11; multiply by 33.33. This product is the severity
        score.
If Question 10 is missing *or* two or more questions are missing, do not score Severity.

FIG. 5.8. D-ARK and scoring criteria. Copyright © 1997 University of Arkansas for
Medical Sciences, 4301 West Markham Street, Little Rock, AR 72205. All rights reserved.
Reproduced with permission.

D-ARK Interpretation.   The D-ARK items assess the symptoms that must be
present for the DSM-IV diagnosis of major depression. As such, the presence major
depression is strongly indicated if the pattern of item endorsement meets the criteria
for major depression (as indicated by the scoring algorithm). The D-ARK also permits the calculation of a symptom severity score that ranges from 0 to 100, with a
score of 70 suggesting severe impairment (Kramer & Smith, 2000). One should always check the responses to last two items that deal with suicidal ideation when employing the instrument.

D-ARK Reliability.   In their investigation of the DOM with 40 patients using an
earlier version of the D-ARK, Rost et al. (1992) reported a value of .87 for both the 1-
week test–retest correlation and the alpha coefficient for the severity score (both $p <$
.0001). The retest reliability of the two-item suicidal measure was only .56. Thirty-one
of the 40 patients participating in this study were diagnosed with major depression
or dysthymia. Zimmerman, Coryell, Corenthal, and Wilson (1986) reported an alpha
coefficient of .92 for their group of 32 depressed and 12 nondepressed mental health
patients. Kramer and Smith (2000), reporting on a study involving 11 nonpatients
along with 29 depressed and 14 nondepressed inpatients and outpatients, obtained
an alpha coefficient of .94.

D-ARK Validity.   In the Rost et al. (1992) study, the D-ARK depression severity
score correlated with clinician ratings on the Hamilton Psychiatric Rating Scale for
Depression (HRSD; Hamilton, 1967) at .41 ($p < .01$), with the number of symptoms
elicited on the DIS interview at .56 ($p < .01$), and with the number of symptoms on the

SCID at .60 ($p < .01$). A nonsignificant tendency ($p < .07$) for decreasing depressive symptomatology in patients receiving "effective" psychopharmacologic treatment also was found. Finally, changes in depressive symptom severity correlated significantly ($p < .01$) with changes in bed days, social functioning, and emotional functioning among their 25 depressed patients who completed the follow-up. No significant symptom severity changes were associated with changes in health perceptions, pain, nor physical functioning.

The data in the study reported by Kramer and Smith (2000) revealed D-ARK findings that were highly concordant with those of the SCID (94%). Also, a kappa coefficient of .89 was obtained. Using the SCID classification as the criterion, the D-ARK achieved a sensitivity of .93, specificity of .96, a PPP of .96, and an NPP of .92. It correlated with the Inventory to Diagnose Depression (IDD; Zimmerman et al., 1986) at .94. It also achieved a concordance rate of 52% and a kappa of .70 with the IDD. The efficiency statistics derived with the IDD results as the criteria were 1.00, .81, .67, and 1.00, respectively. The reported PPP and NPP statistics are at odds with those reported by Zimmerman et al. in their study.

Comments.   Both the Screener and the D-ARK provide means of quickly and easily screening for the presence of depressive disorders. The research supporting the use of either is limited; however, the data that are available, along with the face-valid nature of the items and their straightforward link to DSM-IV, support the use of each of these instruments in day-to-day clinical practice. The Screener can be used to perform a very broad-level screening whereas the D-ARK allows for identifying the presence of diagnostic-specific symptomatology. The D-ARK has the additional advantage of providing a measure of symptom severity that can be useful in tracking treatment-related changes for monitoring and outcomes assessment purposes. Of course, both the Screener and the D-ARK can be used in combination. The complementary use of the Screener and the D-ARK is illustrated in process flow chart presented in Fig. 5.9.

CES-D

An instrument that has become well-known during the last quarter of the last century is the CES-D (Radloff, 1977). One will frequently see this 20-item depression screener listed in the methodology section of published studies, as a means of screening for the presence of depression or as a criterion measure in the validation of other depression screeners. According to Brantley, Mehan, and Thomas (2000), it is a tool that is used predominantly by physicians in medical settings. However, there is nothing to preclude its use in MBHO or other service delivery settings.

Development.   The CES-D was originally developed by the National Institute of Mental Health (NIMH) in response to a need for a self-report measure of the current level of depressive symptomatology for epidemiologic surveys (Radloff, 1977). Twenty items were selected from other depression instruments to represent those broader aspects of depression that were selected to be assessed by the scale (e.g., depressed mood, guilt feelings). A pretest of these items led to some minor revisions, with the revised set then being incorporated into a 300-item structured interview that NIMH later would use in a large-scale community study. Radloff subsequently demonstrated adequate psychometric integrity for the CES-D in samples of psychiatric inpatients and outpatients, as well as in the original sample. The CES-D asks the re-

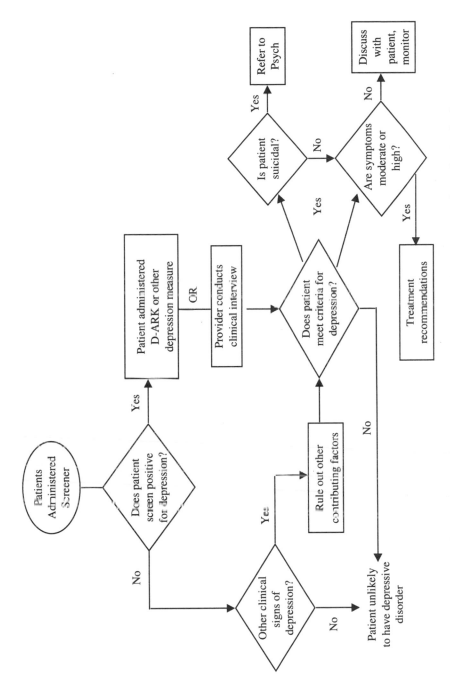

FIG. 5.9. Work flow for integration of the CORE Screener and D-ARK into a process for evaluation for depression. From "Tools to Improve the Detection and Treatment of Depression in Primary Care" (p. 471), by T. L. Kramer & G. R. Smith. In M. E. Maruish (Ed.), *Handbook of Psychological Assessment in Primary Care Settings*, 2000, Mahwah, NJ: Lawrence Erlbaum Associates. Copyright 2000 by Lawrence Erlbaum Associates. Reprinted with permission.

CES-D

Instructions: Circle the number for each statement which best describes how often you felt or behaved this way DURING THE PAST WEEK.

DURING THE PAST WEEK:	**Rarely or none of the time (less than 1 day)**	**Some or a little of the time (1-2 days)**	**Occasion-ally or a moderate amount of time (3-4 days)**	**Most or all of the time (5-7 days)**
1. I was bothered by things that usually don't bother me.	0	1	2	3
2. I did not feel like eating; my appetite was poor.	0	1	2	3
3. I felt that I could not shake off the blues even with help from my family or friends.	0	1	2	3
4. I felt that I was just as good as other people.	3	2	1	0
5. I had trouble keeping my mind on what I was doing.	0	1	2	3
6. I felt depressed.	0	1	2	3
7. I felt that everything I did was an effort.	0	1	2	3
8. I felt hopeful about the future.	3	2	1	0
9. I thought my life had been a failure.	0	1	2	3
10. I felt fearful.	0	1	2	3
11. My sleep was restless.	0	1	2	3
12. I was happy.	3	2	1	0
13. I talked less than usual.	0	1	2	3
14. I felt lonely.	0	1	2	3
15. People were unfriendly.	0	1	2	3
16. I enjoyed life.	3	2	1	0
17. I had crying spells.	0	1	2	3
18. I felt sad.	0	1	2	3
19. I felt that people dislike me.	0	1	2	3
20. I could not get "going."	0	1	2	3

FIG. 5.10.   Center for Epidemiological Studies Depression Scale (CES-D).

spondent to rate the frequency ("Rarely or none of the time [less than a day]" to "Most or all of the time [5–7 days]") at which each of the 20 depression-related symptoms have bothered him during the previous week. A response weight of 0 to 3 is assigned to each response, with the total score being the sum of the weights for the indicated responses. A copy of the CES-D is presented in Fig. 5.10.

Interpretation.   Radloff (1977) demonstrated that a score of 16 or higher discriminated psychiatric patients from nonpatient samples, with 70% of patients having achieved the classification score, yet only 20% of the nonpatient sample met this same criterion. The findings of Zich, Attkisson, and Greenfield (1990) for their primary care sample suggests that this cutoff may have to be adjusted, based on the particular population that is being assessed. In addition, gender-related cutoff adjustments might also have to be made. As reported in Brantley et al. (2000), men achieved a mean CES-D score of 7.1 whereas women obtained a mean scored of 10.0 in national survey of over 3,000 individuals (Sayetta & Johnson, 1980).

Reliability. For community sample and patient groups, Radloff (1977) found respective split-half reliabilities of .76 to .85, Spearman–Brown coefficients of .87 and .92, and overall alpha coefficients of .84 and .90. Alpha coefficients for age, gender, race, and education subsamples of her general population data were all greater than .80. Wong (2000) obtained an alpha coefficient of .89 for her sample of homeless people. Radloff's item–scale correlations ranged from .29 to .79 across samples; however, 80% or more of the items achieved item–scale correlations of .40 or greater in each of the four samples investigated. At the same time, in all but Radloff's patient sample, 75% or more of the items achieved item–item correlations of .30 or less. Results from Roberts, Lewinsohn, and Seeley's (1991) sample of 1,704 adolescents yielded an alpha coefficient of .89.

Radloff (1977) also reported test–retest reliabilities that were based on variables related to differences in retest time interval intervals, method of retest (interview vs. mail-back), and whether significant life events had occurred. All in all, Radloff described the CES-D as generally showing lower test–retest reliabilities as retest intervals increased and if negative life events had occurred before either or both administrations. In all, she indicated that .54 probably represented the "fairest" single estimate of test–retest reliability for the CES-D. This same correlation was obtained from 4-week test–retest data on Radloff's mixed inpatient and outpatient psychiatric sample. Consistent with Radloff's conclusion is Wong's (2000) finding of a test–retest correlation of .56 using retest intervals ranging from 3 months to 1 year. Roberts et al.'s (1991) adolescent data yielded a 1-week test–retest reliability of .61.

Validity. Radloff (1977) found that patients' CES-D total scores correlated .56 with nurse–clinician depression severity ratings. Interviewer ratings of depression correlated with the CES-D from .44 to .54 at admission, and from .69 to .75 after 4 weeks of treatment. Other validity findings from this same study included relatively high correlations with other measures of depression, higher mean scores among community respondents who indicated that they had a recent problem for which they needed help, higher scores for those with the more serious life events during the past year, lower mean scores for a subgroup of outpatients 4 weeks after initiating treatment, and similar four-factor–analytic solutions for three community samples. This structure was subsequently confirmed through a series of studies that were reviewed by Knight, Williams, McGee, and Olaman (1997) for various clinical and community populations; by Zich et al. (2000) for a primary care sample; and by Wong (2000) for a homeless sample. However, Brantley et al. (2000) point out that research suggests the same factor solution may not be appropriate for minority populations. At the same time, the sensitivity of the CES-D to life events was again demonstrated in Wong's (2000) homeless sample (i.e., improvement accompanying the procurement of a domicile).

Feightner and Worrall's (1990) review of studies investigating the relationship of the CES-D and other depression measures using clinical and community samples revealed correlations of .51 to .89 with measures such as the Hamilton scale and the

SCL-90. They also reported findings of sensitivity to depression ranging from 64% for the general population to 91% for depressed patients. Specificity for depressed patients was found to be 56%. DeForge and Sobal (1988) found that the CES-D correlated at .69 ($p < .001$) with the Zung SDS, and that both measures agreed at a high level regarding those among their elderly sample that did and did not have a clinically significant depression. In the Roberts et al. (1991) adolescent sample, the CES-D correlated .70 with the BDI and .48 with the Hamilton Depression Rating Scale (Hamilton, 1960). Sears, Danda, and Evans (1999) obtained a correlation of .68 ($p < .001$) between the CES-D total score and PRIME-MD-determined depression status for a group of low-income rural primary care patients.

Comment. The CES-D is a public domain instrument that has demonstrated its utility as both a research and clinical tool. One drawback is its lack of coordination with the DSM-IV. At the time of this writing, a group at the Johns Hopkins University Prevention Research Center (Eaton, Muntaner, & Smith, 1998) is completing the development of a revised version of the CES-D, the HRCESD-20. This revised version is being developed as a measure that is more closely tied to the DSM-IV criteria for major depression. The proposed items for this revision are presented in Fig. 5.11. Although this revised version shows promise as a much improved and more useful instrument, one should be cautious in its use until studies attesting to its validity and reliability appear in the published literature.

GDS-10

Another instrument that has garnered a great deal of respect over the past two decades is the 30-item Geriatric Depression Scale (GDS; Brink et al., 1982; Yesavage et al., 1983). The impetus for its development came from a realization that many of the existing measures of depression were not adequate for detecting the presence of depression in older adults. According to Scogin, Rohen, and Bailey (2000), among the expressed concerns about the available measures were their assessment of somatic symptoms, a response format (i.e., multiple choice) that frequently is confusing to the elderly, and a lack of norms for this age group.

Yesavage et al. (1983) began the development of the GDS by selecting from among 100 yes/no items that were thought to useful in detecting depression in geriatric populations, the 30 items that correlated the highest with the total score for a mixed group of depressed and nondepressed elderly patients. This set of items was subsequently cross-validated with another mixed group of depressed and nondepressed elderly. This yielded an alpha coefficient of .94 and a 1-week test–retest coefficient of .85. The GDS also was found to correlate .84 with the Hamilton scale and .83 with the Zung. A cutoff score of 11 yielded a sensitivity of 84% and specificity of 95%.

Feeling that a shorter version of the instrument would be better, Yesavage and his colleagues (Sheikh & Yesavage, 1986) later developed a 15-item version GDS (GDS-15). Evidence supporting the use of the GDS-15 can be found in many other studies (e.g., Herrmann, Mittmann, Silver, Shulman, Busto, Shear, & Naranjo, 1996; Shah et al., 1996). In their review of the literature, Scogin et al. (2000) indicated that some investigators (Lesher & Berryhill, 1994; Steiner, Raube, Stuck, Aronow, Draper, Rubenstein, & Beck, 1996) have supported the use of the GDS-15 over the GDS-30. At the

HRCESD-20

Instructions: Below is a list of the ways you might have felt or behaved. Please check the boxes to tell me how often you have felt this way in the past week or so.

DURING THE PAST WEEK:	Not at all *or* less than 1 day	1-2 days	3-4 days	5-7 days	Nearly every day for 2 weeks
1. My appetite was poor.					
2. I could not shake off the blues.					
3. I had trouble keeping my mind on what I was doing.					
4. I felt depressed.					
5. My sleep was restless.					
6. I felt sad.					
7. I could not get going.					
8. Nothing made me happy.					
9. I felt like a bad person.					
10. I lost interest in my usual activities.					
11. I slept much more than usual.					
12. I felt like I was moving too slowly.					
13. I felt fidgety.					
14. I wished I were dead.					
15. I wanted to hurt myself.					
16. I was tired all the time.					
17. I did not like myself.					
18. I lost a lot of weight without trying to.					
19. I had a lot of trouble getting to sleep.					
20. I could not focus on the important things.					

Scoring: Responses in the first, second, and third answer columns are scored 0, 1 and 2, respectively. Responses in either the fourth or fifth answer columns are scored 3.

FIG. 5.11. Proposed items for the revised Center for Epidemiological Studies Depression Scale (HRCESD-20).

same time, others (e.g., Ingram, 1996) report findings that do not support its use as a surrogate for the original 30-item version of the instrument.

Development of the GDS-15 was followed by investigations into 10-, 4-, and 1-item versions of the GDS. In this author's opinion, the 10-item version represents the shortest version of the instrument that should be used while still maintaining acceptable validity and reliability. For this reason, it is the version of the GDS that is recommended for screening geriatric populations in MBHO settings. The GDS-10 items and scoring key are presented in Fig. 5.12.

Development.   Development of the GDS-10 is chronicled in the study by D'Ath, Katona, Mullan, Evans, and Katona (1994). D'Ath et al. administered the GDS-15 to 194 individuals 65 years or older who were being seen by their general practitioners. Applying the standard total scale cut score of 4/5 to each participant's total score, the participants were classified as to their "caseness" or "noncaseness" for depression. The 15 items were then subjected to a logistic regression analysis in which caseness was used as the dependent variable, yielding the three shorter forms of the GDS.

Interpretation.   Based on the findings of D'Ath et al. (1994) and Shah et al. (1996) presented next, geriatric patients obtaining a total score of 4 or greater on the GDS-10 should be evaluated further for the presence of depression. However, one may wish to consider lowering the cutoff to 3 or more if false positives are not a major concern.

Reliability.   D'Ath et al. (1994) validated the GDS-10 (as well as the GDS-4 and GDS-1) using an independent data set containing the results of the GDS-30 and the Geriatric Mental Health Status Schedule (GMS, a structured psychiatric interview for geriatric patients; Copeland, Dewey, & Griffiths-Jones, 1986) for a group of 120 geriatric primary care patients. Subjects were classified for caseness by GMS findings.

Geriatric Depression Scale-10

1. Are you basically satisfied with your life?   Yes/*No*
2. Have you dropped many of your activities and interests?   *Yes*/No
3. Do you feel that your life is empty?   *Yes*/No
4. Are you afraid that something bad is going to happen to you?   *Yes*/No
5. Do you feel happy most of the time?   Yes/*No*
6. Do you often feel helpless?   *Yes*/No
7. Do you feel you have more problems with memory than most?   *Yes*/No
8. Do you feel full of energy?   Yes/*No*
9. Do you feel that your situation is hopeless?   *Yes*/No
10. Do you think that most people are better off than you are?   *Yes*/No

Scoring: Count 1 for each italicized response.

FIG. 5.12.   Geriatric Depression Scale–10 (GDS-10) and scoring key. From "Screening, Detection and Management of Depression in Elderly Primary Care Attenders. I: The Acceptability and Performance of the 15 Item Geriatric Depression Scale (GDS15) and the Development of Short Versions," by P. D'Ath, P. Katona, E. Mullan, S. Evans, & C. Katona 1994, *Family Practice, 11,* 260–266.

Scoring of the GDS data set for the GDS-10 yielded an alpha coefficient of .72. No other reliability findings are reported.

Validity. D'Ath et al. (1994) found that the GDS-10 correlated with the GDS-15 at .97 ($p < .0001$), and with the full GDS-30 at .91 ($p < .0001$). Using the GMS designation of caseness/noncaseness as the criterion, sensitivity, specificity, and NPP were found to be .93, .63. and .94, respectively, when a GDS-10 total score of 3 or more was applied. When the total score cutoff was raised to 4 or more, the statistics changed to .89, .77, and .93, respectively. Moreover, agreement with the GDS-15 caseness classification was 95% with a cutoff of 3 or more and 93% with a cutoff of 4 or more.

Shah et al. (1996) rescored the GDS-10 from a GDS-30 data set for a group of 42 geriatric inpatients. Each patient was classified according to both depression and dementia criteria based on the accompanying data from the Brief Assessment Schedule (BAS), which is part of the Comprehensive Assessment and Referral Evaluation (CARE; Gurland, Kuriansky, Sharpe, Simon, Stiller, & Birkett, 1977). The BAS is a semistructured interview with an organic brain syndrome scale and a depression scale. Sensitivity, specificity, PPP, and NPP were found to be .95, .50, .63, and .92, respectively, when a GDS-10 total score of 3 or more was applied. These statistics changed to .75, .77, .75, and .77, respectively, when the cutoff was raised to 4.

Comment. Available data indicates that the GDS-10 can serve as an excellent means of initial screening for depression in geriatric populations. It correlates highly and has diagnostic efficiency statistics that are comparable with both the original and the 15-item versions of the instrument. One should exercise caution in using the GDS-10 for monitoring change or assessing treatment outcomes over time due to the lack of test–retest reliability data. Steiner et al. (1996) found a 1-week test–retest reliability of .85 for a group of elderly nonpatients on the GDS-15, while Ingram (1996) obtained an 8-week test–retest reliability of .67 ($p < .0001$) for a group of 19 community-dwelling adults 55 to 75 years old. Given the correlation between the GDS-15 and GDS-10, this suggests that the GDS-10 should perform at an acceptable level. However, this is an area for further investigation.

MEASURES OF HEALTH STATUS AND FUNCTIONING

The recognition of the importance of assessing an individual's overall health and ability to function in all aspects of life was discussed earlier (see chapter 2). There are several inexpensive, brief self-report instruments that can provide a good measure of both health status and functioning. However, in terms of professional acceptability and widespread use in MBHO and other medical and behavioral health care systems, probably nothing comes close to the SF-36 Health Survey (SF-36; Ware et al., 1993). There are over 1,200 studies in which the SF-36 has been used (Wetzler, Lum, & Bush, 2000). An abbreviated version of the SF-36, the SF-12 Health Survey (SF-12; Ware et al., 1995), also has gained recognition and is widely used. In addition, at the time of this writing, Ware and his associates are developing an eight-item, abbreviated version of the SF-36.

SF-36

The SF-36 contains 36 items that comprise a total of eight independent scales—four having to do with the patient's physical health and its effects on role functioning, and four having to do with the patient's mental health and its effects on role functioning. Two component summary scales also can be derived to present an overall summary of the patient's responses on the two sets of four scales.

Development.   Comprehensive yet brief overviews of the development of the SF-36 are presented in Ware (1999b) and Wetzler et al. (2000). In summary of these works, development of the SF-36 can be said to have its origins in two large-scale studies. One was the Health Insurance Experiment (HIE), which investigated issues related to health care financing. The other was the often-reference Medical Outcomes Study (MOS), which investigated physician practice patterns and consequent patient outcomes. Both required the use of brief measures of functional and health status. The MOS investigators used a 149-item questionnaire that made use of items from other commonly used instruments, including those used in the HIE. It is from this questionnaire that 36 items were selected to represent the eight health concepts that were considered to be most affected by disease and treatment, and that were also the most widely measured concepts in other instruments. The following scales represent these eight health concepts: Physical Function (PF), Role Physical (RP), Bodily Pain (BP), General Health (GH), Vitality (VT), Social Function (SF), Role Emotional (RE), and Mental Health (MH). Each of the scales is composed of 2 to 10 of the items, and each of the 35 scale-related items (the one general health item is not a scale item) scores on only one of the scales.

Factor analytic work on SF-36 findings from several sources revealed that 80%–85% of the instrument's reliable variance could be accounted for by physical and mental health factors. These factors led to the development of the Physical Component Summary (PCS) and Mental Component Summary (MCS) scales (Ware, Kosinski, & Keller, 1994). The transformed z scores of all eight scales contribute to the computation of the T scores for both summary scales. However, the PF, RP, GH, and BP z scores are multiplied by positively weighted factor coefficients in the computation of the PCS scale. The MH, RE, and SF z scores are multiplied by positively weighted factor coefficients in the computation of the MCS scale. VT contributes to both summary scales through positive factor weightings. The SF-12 (Ware et al., 1995) was later developed as a means of predicting MCS and PCS scores from only 12 items (see later).

Version 2 of the SF-36 was developed in 1996 (see *http://www.qmetric.com/products/assessments/sf36/v2.php3*; retrieved December 11, 2000). Improvements in this version include improved formatting and presentation of the items and instructions, wording changes to improve objectivity and understandability, increased measurement precision through expanded item response choices, norms-based standardized scoring (i.e., T scores), and the development of norms for Version 1 that enable direct comparison with Version 2 results.

There are two instruments that are related and quite similar to the SF-36: the Health Status Questionnaire (HSQ; Radosevich et al., 1994) and the RAND-36 Health Survey (RAND-36; RAND Corporation, 1992). Both contain the same 36 items as the SF-36 with some variations on one or two of the scales. The HSQ also includes the two-item Screener that is part of the Arkansas suite of depression instruments that was described earlier. Although essentially the same instrument, neither the HSQ nor the RAND-36 have gained the same name recognition or widespread use as the SF-36. Moreover, a 12-item version of the HSQ, the HSQ-12, was developed (Health Outcomes Institute, 1996) and includes 6 of the SF-12 items. Similar to the HSQ, it has not gained the same recognition or use as the SF-36-derived abbreviated form. A copy of the SF-36 is presented in Fig. 5.13.

Interpretation.   Initially, scores for each of the eight SF-36 scales represented the percent of the total weighted score that was achieved by the summation of the weights of the responses given to each item scored for the scale, minus the lowest possible score for that scale, times 100. Thus, scores could range from 0 to 100 and could be compared to general nonpatient population normative data (calculated in the same manner) as well as disease-/disorder-specific normative data. (Ware et al., 1993). The lower the score, the worse the impairment in the area measured by the scale. More recently, the approach taken to the interpretation of the eight scales has been the same as that which was developed for interpretation of the PCS and MCS scales, that is, through the conversion of raw scores to T scores (Ware, 1999b). As noted before, means of converting Version 1 normative sets to T scores is part of Version 2 of the SF-36.

Patient-level interpretive information is available. However, consistent with the recommendations of Ware et al. (1993), one can probably feel safe in interpreting SF-36 scale and summary scale scores (original transformed scores or T scores) that are less than one standard deviation below the mean of the appropriate age and gender general population norms as indicating limitations in the construct purported to be measured by the scale in question. Similarly, a score that is one standard deviation above the mean for a scale or summary scale suggests that the individual or group of individuals is reporting functioning in the area that is generally better than that of the normative comparison group. Scores that are based on specific disease or disorder norms are interpreted *relative* to the comparison group's functioning and should not be used to make statements regarding the patient's or group's general level functioning.

Reliability.   Data reported in the SF-36 manual (Ware et al., 1993) indicate that various ranges of alpha coefficients for the eight scales have been reported for different samples of patient and nonpatient samples. For a large, random sample (n = 1,692) of the U.S. population, the coefficients ranged from .63 for the SF scale to .94 for the PF scale, with all but the SF scale having an alpha coefficient of .81 or greater (McHorney, Kosinski, & Ware, 1994). These findings are quite similar to those for a large general population sample (n = 9,332) from the United Kingdom. Across several studies with various patient and nonpatient samples, the PF scale tended to yield the highest alpha coefficients while the SF scale tended to yield the lowest. Moreover, Ware et al. (1994) reported internal consistency reliabilities of .93 for the PCS scale and .88 for the MCS scale for a large American general population sample (n = 2,474). Similar results were obtained from samples from three European countries as well as from a large subsample of the MOS (n = 503) who were clinically depressed.

Two-week test–retest correlations ranged from .60 to .81 on the eight SF-36 scales, and .89 for the PCS scale and .80 for the MCS scale for a group of British general practice patients (Brazier, Harper, Jones, O'Cathain, Thomas, Usherwood, & Westlake, 1992). Six-month test–retest correlations ranged from .43 to .90 for a sample of diabetic patients (Nerenz, Repasky, Whitehouse, & Kahkonen, 1992).

The SF-36™ Health Survey

Instructions for Completing the Questionnaire

Please answer every question. Some questions may look like others, but each one is different. Please take the time to read and answer each question carefully by filling in the bubble that best represents your response.

EXAMPLE

This is for your review. Do not answer this question. The questionnaire begins with the section *Your Health in General* below.

For each question you will be asked to fill in a bubble in each line:

1. How strongly do you agree or disagree with each of the following statements?

		Strongly agree	Agree	Uncertain	Disagree	Strongly disagree
a)	I enjoy listening to music.	○	●	○	○	○
b)	I enjoy reading magazines.	●	○	○	○	○

Please begin answering the questions now.

Your Health in General

1. In general, would you say your health is:

Excellent	Very good	Good	Fair	Poor
○	○	○	○	○

2. **Compared to one year ago**, how would you rate your health in general <u>now?</u>

Much better now than one year ago	Somewhat better now than one year ago	About the same as one year ago	Somewhat worse now than one year ago	Much worse now than one year ago
○	○	○	○	○

Please turn the page and continue.

FIG. 5.13. *(Continued)*

3. The following items are about activities you might do during a typical day.   Does **your health now limit you** in these activities? If so, how much?

		Yes, Limited a lot	Yes, limited a little	No, not limited at all
a)	**Vigorous activities**, such as running, lifting heavy objects, participating in strenuous sports	O	O	O
b)	**Moderate activities**, such as moving a table, pushing a vacuum cleaner, bowling, or playing golf	O	O	O
c)	Lifting or carrying groceries	O	O	O
d)	Climbing **several** flights of stairs	O	O	O
e)	Climbing **one** flight of stairs	O	O	O
f)	Bending, kneeling, or stooping	O	O	O
g)	Walking **more than a mile**	O	O	O
h)	Walking **several blocks**	O	O	O
i)	Walking **one block**	O	O	O
j)	Bathing or dressing yourself	O	O	O

4. During the **past 4 weeks**, have you had any of the following problems with your work or other regular daily activities <u>as a result of your physical health?</u>

		Yes	No
a)	Cut down on the **amount of time** you spent on work or other activities	O	O
b)	**Accomplished less** than you would like	O	O
c)	Were limited in the **kind** of work or other activities	O	O
d)	Had **difficulty** performing the work or other activities (for example, it took extra time)	O	O

5. During the **past 4 weeks**, have you had any of the following problems with your work or other regular daily activities <u>as a result of any emotional problems (</u>such as feeling depressed or anxious)?

		Yes	No
a)	Cut down on the **amount of time** you spent on work or other activities	O	O
b)	**Accomplished less** than you would like	O	O
c)	Didn't do work or other activities as **carefully** as usual	O	O

Please turn the page to continue.

FIG. 5.13.   *(Continued)*

6. During the **past 4 weeks**, to what extent has your physical health or emotional problems interfered with your normal social activities with family, friends, neighbors, or groups?

Not at all	Slightly	Moderately	Quite a bit	Extremely
○	○	○	○	○

7. How much <u>bodily</u> pain have you had during the **past 4 weeks**?

None	Very mild	Mild	Moderate	Severe	Very severe
○	○	○	○	○	○

8. During the **past 4 weeks**, how much did <u>pain</u> interfere with your normal work (including both work outside the home and housework)?

Not at all	A little bit	Moderately	Quite a bit	Extremely
○	○	○	○	○

9. These questions are about how you feel and how things have been with you during the **past 4 weeks**. For each question, please give the one answer that comes closest to the way you have been feeling. How much of the time during the **past 4 weeks**...

	All of the time	Most of the time	A good bit of the time	Some of the time	A little of the time	None of the time
a) did you feel full of pep?	○	○	○	○	○	○
b) have you been a very nervous person?	○	○	○	○	○	○
c) have you felt so down in the dumps nothing could cheer you up?	○	○	○	○	○	○
d) have you felt calm and peaceful?	○	○	○	○	○	○
e) did you have a lot of energy?	○	○	○	○	○	○
f) have you felt downhearted and blue?	○	○	○	○	○	○
g) did you feel worn out?	○	○	○	○	○	○
h) have you been a happy person?	○	○	○	○	○	○
i) did you feel tired?	○	○	○	○	○	○

10. During the **past 4 weeks**, how much of the time has your <u>physical health or emotional problems</u> interfered with your social activities (like visiting friends, relatives, etc.)?

All of the time	Most of the time	Some of the time	A little of the time	None of the time
○	○	○	○	○

11. How TRUE or FALSE is <u>each</u> of the following statements for you?

	Definitely true	Mostly true	Don't know	Mostly false	Definitely false
a) I seem to get sick a little easier than other people	○	○	○	○	○
b) I am as healthy as anybody I know	○	○	○	○	○
c) I expect my health to get worse	○	○	○	○	○
d) My health is excellent	○	○	○	○	○

***THANK YOU* FOR COMPLETING THIS QUESTIONNAIRE!**

FIG. 5.13. SF-36 Health Survey (SF-36). Copyright © Medical Outcomes Trust and John E. Ware, Jr. All rights reserved. Reproduced with permission.

Validity.   It is beyond the scope of this chapter to present a review all of the numerous studies that have been conducted to investigate the validity of the SF-36 scales. However, in addition to the information provided in the SF-36 manual (Ware et al., 1993), the reader is referred to the excellent overviews of the data supporting the validity of the instrument provided by Ware (1999b) and Wetzler et al. (2000). For the purpose of this discussion, suffice it to say that from Ware's review of pertinent validity studies:

- The eight health concepts measured by the SF-36 compare favorably with those of similar generic health status surveys. With the exception of sexual functioning, these concepts correlate substantially with other general health concepts and specific problems that are not addressed by the instrument.
- In studies of known-group validity, the MH, RF, and SF scales (as well as the MCS scale) have been shown to be the most valid SF-36 measures of mental health, whereas the PF, RP, and BP scales (as well as the PCS scale) have been shown to be the most valid SF-36 measures of physical health.
- The MH scale has been useful in screening for mental health disorders.
- SF-36 scales have been shown to be predictive of such variables as health care service utilization, loss of employment, and course of depression.
- As would be expected, pre- to posttreatment changes in PF, RP, and BP have been shown for physical disorders whereas changes in MH, RE, and SF have been shown in the treatment of depression.

The manual for the PCS and MCS scales (Ware et al., 1994) reports evidence for the validity of these scales. Again, numerous sets of data are presented, among which are results indicating the following:

- Mean PCS and MCS T scores vary by patient groups in expected directions. For a group of minor medical patients, both scores were within normal limits; however, the MCS score was 8 T-score points higher. The MCS score remained within normal limits for a group of serious medically ill patients while the PCS score was almost 1.5 standard deviations below the mean. The PCS score was within normal limits for a group of psychiatric patients while the MCS score was over one standard deviation below the mean. Both the PCS and MCS were over one standard deviation below the mean for a small group patients with comorbid psychiatric and serious medical problems.
- Consistent with the previous findings, expected mean difference and effect size (ES) findings were obtained from this same data set in comparisons of serious medical patients, minor medical patients, and psychiatric patients between each other individually or in various mixed medical and mixed medical and psychiatric group combinations.
- The PCS and MCS scales correlated with symptoms assessed during the MOS in a somewhat expected pattern. The MCS scale correlated highest with symptoms of headaches, dizziness, lightheadedness, drowsiness, and sleep difficulties, while the PCS correlated highest with back and chest pains, muscle stiffness/pain, and shortness of breath on exertion.
- Expected patterns of correlations between the MCS and PCS scales and MOS functioning and well-being measures were found. In general, the PCS scale

showed higher correlations than the MCS scale with groups of measures categorized as measures of physical functioning, health perceptions, pain, and physical/psychophysiologic symptoms. The inverse was true for measures of social/family/sexual functioning, psychological distress/well-being, cognitive functioning, sleep, and quality of life. The pattern of correlations with role functioning also differed in the expected direction according to whether role limitations were due to physical problems or emotional problems.

One may refer to an annotated bibliography for the SF-36 developed by Manocchia, Bayliss, Connor, Keller, Shiely, Tsai, Voris, and Ware (1997) for additional sources of information about the validity of the SF-36 scales.

Comment.   Recall that Kiesler (2000) has predicted a trend away from currently popular "carve-out" MBHO services toward behavioral health care services that are "carved-in" to general health care (i.e., integrated care). Consequently, the emphasis on measuring outcomes of treatment will continue but there will be more of a need to incorporate measurement of both physical health and mental health into these initiatives. The SF-36 provides an excellent means of gathering data on both health status and mental health status economically and with minimum burden on both patient and psychologist. Its value for this purpose has been recognized for several years now, and it is likely to grow considerably as integrated care moves toward becoming the norm (see chapter 8). It has a large, solid research base that continues to grow and will likely lead to further innovations in the measurement of health status.

The SF-36 was originally developed as a population- or group-based measure. However, many practitioners use the instrument alone or as part of clinical assessments of individual patients. There are those who contend that the psychometric properties of the instrument are not adequate for use of the instrument in individual assessments. For example, McHorney and Tarlov (1995) argue that neither the SF-36 nor four other general health status surveys they investigated met their six criteria for individual patient applications. These criteria included: (a) practical features (e.g., taking less than 15 minutes to complete), (b) breadth of health measured (e.g., includes scales measuring physical and mental status), (c) depth of health measured (allowing for adequate floor and ceiling), (d) cross-sectional measurement precision (e.g., internal consistency reliability ≥ .90), (e) longitudinal-monitoring measurement precision (e.g., 2–4-week test–retest reliability ≥ .90), and (f) validity (e.g., convergent and divergent validity, sensitivity to change).

According to the data available to the McHorney and Tarlov (1995) at the time, the SF-36 did not meet the stated criteria for ceiling effects and reliability (internal consistency and test–retest). One could (and should) note that their the reliability requirements are too stringent. By these standards, the MMPI-2 would not be considered appropriate for individual testing purposes (see Tables D-1 through D-9 in Butcher et al., 1989). As for the ceiling effects, Ware (1999a) would argue that there is more of a problem with floor effects, and that these more frequently occur with the more severely ill patients. One also might rightly argue that the required "practical features" only come with some sacrifice in other required features, whether it is lowered validity or reliability or limitations in the breadth or depth of measurement. In short, this and many other authors in the field would argue that the SF-36 is certainly more than "adequate" for individual assessment, especially in light of the demands that MBHOs and other health care systems place on such instruments (e.g., brevity, ease of use) if they are to be incorporated into the daily work flow of individual psychologists and provider organizations.

As a final note, the issues raised by McHorney and Tarlov (1995) may be adequately dealt with if basic interpretation of individual patients' results is initially limited to those pertaining to the PCS and MCS scales. Refinement of this initial interpretation of the component summary scales can come through examination of those health concept scales that are associated with a PCS or MCS score that falls outside the "normal" range. In those cases, this approach can provide insight into what aspects of the patient's physical or emotional functioning may be particularly problematic.

SF-12

In their investigations of the SF-36, Ware and his colleagues came across two important findings. One was that physical and mental factors accounted for 80% to 85% of the variance in the SF-36's eight health concept scales, and that the PCS and MCS scales were almost always sensitive to hypothesized differences in independent mental and physical criterion variables (Ware et al., 1995). Together, these findings suggested that the SF-36 could be shortened without losing a substantial amount of information, and subsequently led to the development of the SF-12 Health Survey (SF-12). The SF-12 form is presented in Fig. 5.14.

Development. With the above goal in mind, Ware and his colleagues began exploring ways to develop a survey that could fit on a single page, be administered in 2 minutes, and explain at least 90% of the variance in the PCS and MCS scales (Ware et al., 1995). Using regression methods, the desired abbreviated summary measures were derived from 10 items representing six of the SF-36 health concept scales. Two additional items were added to allow for representation from all eight of the health concept scales. The results yield scores on two scales, the PCS-12 and MCS-12, that represent estimates of the T scores that would have been obtained for the PCS and MCS scales had the full SF-36 been administered.

Interpretation. As noted by Ware et al. (1995), "The high degree of correspondence between SF-36 PCS and MCS summary scores estimated using SF-12 items suggests that PSC-12 and MCS 12 scores will have much the same interpretation as scores estimated using the full SF-36" (p. 18). Thus, this author recommends interpreting T scores of 40 or less as suggestive of significant impairment, and T scores of 60 or greater as suggestive of better than average functioning.

Reliability. Ware et al. (1995) report 2-week test–retest coefficients for the PCS-12 and MCS-12 of .89 and .76, respectively, based on U.S. general population data, and .88 and .79, respectively, based on U.K. population data. On both scales across both samples, the average change in scores from the first to second testing was one point or less. As well, over 85% of both samples scored within the first administration's 95% confidence interval for both the PCS-12 and the MCS-12 during the second administration.

Regarding internal consistency, the correlation between the MCS-12 score and items from the SF-36's RE and MH scales ranged from .78 to .85 while correlations with the items from the SF-36's PF, RP, BP, GH, and VT scales ranged from .03 to .31 (Ware et al., 1995). Conversely, the correlations between the PCS-12 score and the

The SF-12™ Health Survey

Instructions for Completing the Questionnaire

Please answer every question. Some questions may look like others, but each one is different. Please take the time to read and answer each question carefully by filling in the bubble that best represents your response.

EXAMPLE

This is for your review. Do not answer this question. The questionnaire begins with the section *Your Health in General* below.

For each question you will be asked to fill in a bubble in each line:

1. How strongly do you agree or disagree with each of the following statements?

		Strongly agree	Agree	Uncertain	Disagree	Strongly disagree
a)	I enjoy listening to music.	○	●	○	○	○
b)	I enjoy reading magazines.	●	○	○	○	○

Please begin answering the questions now.

Your Health in General

1. In general, would you say your health is:

Excellent	Very good	Good	Fair	Poor
○	○	○	○	○

2. The following items are about activities you might do during a typical day. Does your health now limit you in these activities? If so, how much?

		Yes, Limited A Lot	Yes, Limited A Little	No, Not Limited At All
a.	**Moderate activities**, such as moving a table, pushing a vacuum cleaner, bowling, or playing golf	○	○	○
b.	Climbing **several** flights of stairs	○	○	○

Please turn the page to continue.

FIG. 5.14. *(Continued)*

3. During the **past 4 weeks**, have you had any of the following problems with your work or other regular daily activities <u>as a result of your physical health?</u>

		YES	NO
a.	**Accomplished less** than you would like	○	○
b.	Were limited in the **kind** of work or other activities	○	○

4. During the **past 4 weeks**, have you had any of the following problems with your work or other regular daily activities <u>as a result of any emotional problems (</u>such as feeling depressed or anxious)?

		YES	NO
a.	**Accomplished less** than you would like	○	○
b.	Didn't do work or other activities as **carefully** as usual	○	○

5. During the **past 4 weeks**, how much did <u>pain </u>interfere with your normal work (including both work outside the home and housework)?

Not at all	A little bit	Moderately	Quite a bit	Extremely
○	○	○	○	○

6. These questions are about how you feel and how things have been with you during the **past 4 weeks**. For each question, please give the one answer that comes closest to the way you have been feeling. How much of the time during the **past 4 weeks** . . .

		All of the Time	Most of the Time	A Good Bit of the Time	Some of the Time	A Little of the Time	None of the Time
a.	Have you felt calm and peaceful?	○	○	○	○	○	○
b.	Did you have a lot of energy?	○	○	○	○	○	○
c.	Have you felt downhearted and blue?	○	○	○	○	○	○

7. During the **past 4 weeks**, how much of the time has your <u>physical health or emotional problems</u> interfered with your social activities (like visiting with friends, relatives, etc.)?

All of the time	Most of the time	Some of the time	A little of the time	None of the time
○	○	○	○	○

***THANK YOU* FOR COMPLETING THIS QUESTIONNAIRE!**

FIG. 5.14.   SF-12 Health Survey (SF-12). Copyright © Medical Outcomes Trust and John E. Ware, Jr. All rights reserved. Reproduced with permission.

items from the PF, RP, BP, GH, and VT scales ranged from .44 to .87 while correlations with the items from RE and MH scales ranged from –.14 to +.14. The correlation between the single SF item and each of the PCS-12 and MCS-12 scales was essentially the same (.51 and .54, respectively).

Validity.   Because the SF-12 was developed to yield the same information as the PCS and MCS scales derived from the full administration of the SF-36 using only one third of the items, a demonstration of the comparability of the PCS-12 and MCS-12 findings to those of the PCS and MCS scales is imperative. In support of this demonstration, Ware et al. (1995) reported a correlation of .96 between the PCS and PCS-12 as well as between the MCS and MCS-12 based on a large sample (n = 2,329) of the U.S. population. The correlations derived from MOS data (n = 2,833) were .95 and .97, respectively. Moreover, using data from the same U.S. general population sample, age, gender, and total sample comparisons of mean PCS and MCS T scores with their SF-12 counterparts all yielded less than 1-point difference between mean T scores.

Ware et al. (1995) summarized the findings of other investigations into the validity of the SF-12 as follows:

> [The results of] 16 tests of validity . . . have been compared with the results for summary measures and the eight scales based on the SF-36. . . . In the 12 tests based on criterion variables defining differences in physical health, statistical conclusions based on the PCS-12 agreed with PCS-36 consistently and agreed with the three best SF-36 physical scales (PF, RP, BP) 30 out of 36 times. . . . PCS-36 performed better than PCS-12 in 11 of 12 tests. Conclusions based on the MCS-12 agreed with those based on the MCS-36 in all four comparisons between groups differing in the presence and severity of mental health conditions. In these mental health tests, [relative validity] coefficients . . . were below those for MCS-36 in three of four tests. (p. 48)

Overall, Ware et al. felt the evidence available at that time indicated the empirical validity of the PCS-12 and MCS-12 is about 10% less than that of the SF-36-derived PCS and MCS.

Comment.   Using only 12 items from the SF-36, the SF-12 Health Survey provides a very quick estimate of the Physical and Mental Component summary scales. When should one use the SF-12 instead of the SF-36, and vice versa? Keller and Ware (1996) offer the following recommendations:

> The summary scales for the SF-36 and SF-12 Health Surveys are recommended when there is a need to: (a) limit the number of endpoints being considered; (b) increase the power of the statistical test; or (c) study the effectiveness of the treatment primarily in the physical or mental health domain. . . . In the cases where only the summary measures are of interest the choice of whether to use the 36-item or 12-item short form is largely a practical choice, because the 12-item survey reproduces the summary scales (PCS and MCS) based on the SF-36 as well. . . . When more information is sought regarding why there is a physical or mental health effect or the specific nature of that effect, all eight scales of the SF-36 should be evaluated. . . . When there is interest in examining all eight scales, it is recommended that the 36-item survey be used, as the SF-12 lacks the precision required for this level of analysis. (p. 3)

Thus, the SF-12 is best suited for situations in which brevity is a must and the finer level of discrimination and interpretation offered by the SF-36's eight scales is not required. An excellent example is the use of the PCS-12 and MCS-12 variables for treatment monitoring purposes or as part of an outcomes management program data set. However, this should not preclude considering the instrument for other purposes, such as screening of individual patients at a very high level.

OQ-45 and BASIS-32

Recall that both the OQ-45 and the BASIS-32 incorporate items and scales that assess several areas of functioning. Thus, these instruments have the advantage of measuring multiple realms of functioning — psychological/emotional and social — at the same time, thus possibly eliminating the need for the use of additional outcomes instruments. The reader is referred to the discussion of these two instruments in an earlier section of this chapter.

MEASURES OF PATIENT SATISFACTION

The MBHO industry abounds with measures of patient satisfaction. These measures vary in their length, format (open-ended vs. multiple-choice reponding), content focus, and degree of psychometric integrity. Most of them have been developed by the organization itself, or represent a modification or subset of some established instrument. Relatively few are standardized to allow for comparison of results across organizations. However, there are patient satisfaction instruments that have sought to exercise the developmental rigor and achieve the professional acceptance that is typically sought by developers of other types of psychological instruments. Three of these are presented here.

CSQ-8

Only a few patient satisfaction instruments have gained acceptance and/or been used by several MBHOs and other behavioral healthcare organizations. Probably the best known of these is the eight-item Client Satisfaction Questionnaire (CSQ-8; Attkisson & Greenfield, 1996, 1999; Attkisson & Pascoe, 1983; Rosenblatt & Attkisson, 1993). The CSQ-8 was developed using both theoretical and empirical methods by Clifford Attkisson and his colleagues at the University of California at San Francisco (UCSF; saawww.ucsf.edu/csq). Attkisson considers the CSQ-8 as a *global* measure of satisfaction, that is, one that is comprised of general questions that provide a good overall measure of satisfaction. In situations where this is all that a caregiver or provider organization is looking for, the published research and widespread acceptability of the CSQ-8 make it an excellent choice.

Development. The CSQ-8 is actually one in a family of CSQ instruments that began with the development of a 31-item measure of patient satisfaction, the CSQ-31. As chronicled by Nguyen et al., (1983), development of the CSQ-31 began with the identification of various aspects of service that could be tied to a patient's satisfaction with that service. Through a series of expert rating tasks, an initial pool of items developed to measure each of nine identified service categories was narrowed to a total of 31 questions. Subsequent factor analysis of the CSQ-31 items yielded a single factor that accounted for much of the variance of the instrument. Those items that loaded highly on this factor and showed good item–total and interitem correlations were selected for inclusion in a brief, eight-item form of the scale, the CSQ-8. The CSQ-8 became the basis of two, 18-item parallel versions of the instrument, the CSQ-18A and CSQ-18B. Studies allowing a comparison of the CSQ-8 and CSQ-18 (Form B) indicated that the CSQ-8 performed as well or better than the CSQ-18. Obviously, its brevity without substantial loss of information has led to the CSQ-8's greater attractiveness over the 18-item version.

The CSQ-8 items measure the patient's satisfaction with one of the following aspects of service: physical surroundings, procedures, support staff, kind or type of service, treatment staff, quality of service, outcome of service, and general satisfaction (Attkisson & Greenfield, 1996). Different sets of 4-point response choices, with each set of responses weighted from 1 to 4, are used for each of the items. The CSQ-8 items and response choices are presented in Fig. 5.15. The CSQ-8 is also available in various language translations, including Cambodian, Chinese, Dutch, French, Japanese, Korean, Laotian, Portuguese, Russian, Spanish, Tagalog, and Vietnamese (e.g., see Roberts, Attkisson, & Mendias, 1984).

Interpretation.   The response values for each recorded response are summed to give the total CSQ-8 score. This is consistent with the instrument being designed to be a "global measure" of satisfaction. Assistance in interpreting the obtained scores is provided through Attkisson and Greenfield's (1999) summary of the psychometric properties (see Table 43.2 that work). This tabular summary presents psychometric and normative data for various types of service delivery settings (e.g., mental health, primary care, family services).

Reliability.   Attkisson and Greenfield's (1999) tabular summary of several CSQ-8 studies indicate that obtained alpha coefficients for large and small samples have ranged from .83 to .93. Median item–total correlations ranged from .57 to .69, and median interitem correlations ranged from .40 to .53. Waxman (1996) obtained item–total correlations ranging from .73 to .78 and interitem correlations ranging from .79 to .87 for a sample of 3,500 inpatients.

Validity.   As reported in Attkisson and Greenfield (1999), Larsen (1979) found that for a group of 49 mental health outpatients, those who dropped out of treatment within a month had lower CSQ-8 scores than those that continued treatment ($p < .01$). Among those who remained in treatment, there was a nonsignificant ($p < .06$) trend for the CSQ-8 scores of those who missed a large percentage of scheduled sessions to be lower than the scores of those who missed a smaller percentage of sessions. In this same study, CSQ-8 ratings were found to correlate significantly with a SCL-90-related measure of global improvement ($r = .53; p < .001$), the total score for the BPRS ($r = .44; p < .01$), and therapist ratings of client satisfaction ($r = .56; p < .001$).

In discussing the work of Zwick (1982), Attkisson and Greenfield (1999) point to further evidence of the validity of CSQ-8. In this study, 46 mental health outpatients were administered both the CSQ-8 and the CSQ-18B just 1 month after initiating treatment. The two instruments correlated .93 with each other and were found to have nearly identical average item means and variances. In addition, Zwick's findings supported Larsen's (1979) findings of the relationship of the CSQ-8 scores with both remaining/terminating therapy after 1 month and the number of sessions dur-

CLIENT SATISFACTION QUESTIONNAIRE ©
CSQ-8

Please help us improve our program by answering some questions about the services you have received. We are interested in your honest opinions, whether they are positive or negative. *Please answer all of the questions.* We also welcome your comments and suggestions. Thank you very much, we really appreciate your help.

CIRCLE YOUR ANSWERS

1. How would you rate the quality of service you have received?

4	3	2	1
Excellent	Good	Fair	Poor

2. Did you get the kind of service you wanted?

1	2	3	4
No, definitely not	No, not really	Yes, generally	Yes, definitely

3. To what extent has our program met your needs?

4	3	2	1
Almost all of my needs have been met	Most of my needs have been met	Only a few of my needs have been met	None of my needs have been met

4. If a friend were in need of similar help, would you recommend our program to him or her?

1	2	3	4
No, definitely not	No, I don't think so	Yes, I think so	Yes, definitely

5. How satisfied are you with the amount of help you have received?

1	2	3	4
Quite dissatisfied	Indifferent or mildly dissatisfied	Mostly satisfied	Very satisfied

6. Have the services you received helped you to deal more effectively with your problems?

4	3	2	1
Yes, they helped a great deal	Yes, they helped somewhat	No, they really didn't help	No, they seemed to make things worse

7. In an overall, general sense, how satisfied are you with the service you have received?

4	3	2	1
Very satisfied	Mostly satisfied	Indifferent or mildly dissatisfied	Quite dissatisfied

8. If you were to seek help again, would you come back to our program?

1	2	3	4
No, definitely not	No, I don't think so	Yes, I think so	Yes, definitely

The Client Satisfaction Questionnaire (CSQ) was developed by Drs. Clifford Attkisson and Daniel Larsen in collaboration with Drs. William A. Hargreaves, Maurice LeVois, Tuan Nguyen, Robert E. Roberts and Bruce Stegner. Every effort has been made to publish information and research on the CSQ for widest possible dissemination.

saawww.ucsf.edu/csq

Copyright ©1979, 1989, 1990.
Clifford Attkisson, Ph.D.
Used with written permission. Use, transfer, copying, reproduction, merger, translation, modification, or enhancement, in whole or in part is forbidden without the written permission of Clifford Attkisson, Ph.D.

UCSF

University of California San Francisco

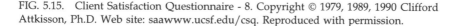

FIG. 5.15. Client Satisfaction Questionnaire - 8. Copyright © 1979, 1989, 1990 Clifford Attkisson, Ph.D. Web site: saawww.ucsf.edu/csq. Reproduced with permission.

ing that month. Unlike Larsen, there was no relationship between satisfaction and the proportion of scheduled appointments that were missed.

Comment. The CSQ-8 is one of the few instruments developed to measure satisfaction with mental health services that also has a relatively strong empirical backing. It provides a quick and easy means of gathering information pertaining to patients' level of global satisfaction with services received. It does not allow for a determination of specific aspects(s) of service that may be problematic, but then again that is not what it was designed to do. For such information one needs to turn to instrumentation that is multidimensional in nature. A good example of this is the SSS-30.

SSS-30

In those situations where a more detailed, multidimensional assessment is desired, Attkisson and his colleagues developed the 30-item Service Satisfaction Scale, or SSS-30 (Greenfield & Attkisson, 1989, 1999). Like the CSQ-8, this instrument was also developed using both theoretical and empirical methods. It provides an excellent "off-the-shelf" tool (in contrast to a site-specific customized tool) for those wishing to assess multidimensional aspects of service satisfaction.

Development.   As chronicled by Greenfield and Attkisson (1999), subsequent to the development of the CSQ-8, the UCSF research team continued their work in satisfaction measurement by dealing with various challenges and problems that were revealed during their earlier work. These included the need to assess specific aspects of service and improve item sensitivity. Based on reviews of the literature, important aspects of care were identified and items related to their measurement were constructed. Response scaling moved from a 4-point to a 5-point system, with response choices ranging from "Delighted" to "Terrible" (as is frequently seen in life satisfaction and quality of life research). The resulting SSS-30 yields scores on four factor-analytically derived subscales, two of which — Practitioner Manner and Skill and Perceived Outcome — have been replicated across diverse types of settings. The other two subscales — Office Procedures and Access — have shown more factor variability across settings but are reported to be useful for management purposes. The SSS-30 items, as well as a key to indicate the subscale they are included in, are presented in Fig. 5.16.

Interpretation.   Interpretation of the SSS-30 can take place at both the subscale level and at the overall satisfaction level. Normative data for diverse samples — mental health, employee assistance program (EAP), student counseling, substance abuse treatment clinic, primary care — are presented for the Practitioner Manner and Skill and Perceived Outcome subscales in Greenfield and Attkisson (1999).

Reliability.   Greenfield and Attkisson's (1999) summary of six studies that utilized the SSS-30 revealed alpha coefficients for the Practitioner Manner and Skill subscale ranging from .85 to .93, median item–total correlations ranging from .56 to .76, and mean interitem correlations ranging from .39 to .59. For the Perceived Outcome subscale, alpha coefficients ranged from .80 to .90, median item–total correlation ranged from .50 to .74, and mean interitem correlations ranged from .33 to .53. Alpha coefficients ranged from .69 to .83 for the Office Procedures subscale and .60 to .76 for the Access subscale. In addition, composite (full-scale) SSS-30 alpha coefficients of .93 and .94 were obtained for samples from a mental health/substance abuse clinic and an EAP program, respectively.

Greenfield and Attkisson (1999) identified two studies that present data related to the test-retest reliability of the SSS-30. In one study, Ruggeri and Dall'Agnola (1993) presented findings from their work on the development of an Italian patient satisfac-

SERVICES EVALUATION (SSS-30 Practitioner Version)

ᴄᴏɴꜰɪᴅᴇɴᴛɪᴀʟ

SUBSCALE KEY

 Please read the following statements carefully. Indicate the answer that best describes your feeling about each aspect of the services you have received. We are interested in your *overall experience* based on all visits or contacts you have had *during the last year*. By "practitioner" we mean the one or more doctors. psychologists. counselors. clinicians. etc.. who have worked with you.

What is your overall feeling about the . . .

M 1. Kinds of services offered

☐ DELIGHTED ☐ MOSTLY SATISFIED ☐ MIXED ☐ MOSTLY DISSATISFIED ☐ TERRIBLE*

M 2. Opportunity to choose which practitioner you see

☐ TERRIBLE ☐ MOSTLY DISSATISFIED ☐ MIXED ☐ MOSTLY SATISFIED ☐ DELIGHTED*

O	3.	Effect of services in helping you deal with your problems
P	4.	Office personnel (receptionists. clerks) on the telephone or in person
P	5.	Office procedures (scheduling. forms. tests. etc.)
M	6.	Professional knowledge and competence of the main practitioner(s)
A	7.	Location and accessibility of the services (distance. parking. public transportation. etc.)
	8.	Appearance and physical layout of the facility (e.g.. waiting area)
M	9.	Ability of your practitioner(s) to listen to and understand your problems
M	10.	Personal manner of the main practitioner(s) seen
W	11.	Waiting time between asking to be seen and the appointment (date and time) given
W	12.	Waiting time when you come to be seen or keep an appointment made
	13.	Availability of appointment times that fit your schedule
	14.	Cost of services to me
O	15.	Effect of services in maintaining well-being and preventing relapse
M	16.	Confidentiality and respect for your rights as an individual
O	17.	Amount of help you have received
O	18.	Availability of information on how to get the most out of the services
O	19.	Prescription (or nonprescription) of medications
	20.	Explanations of specific procedures and approaches used
O	21.	Effect of services in helping relieve symptoms or reduce problems
A	22.	Response to crises or urgent needs during office hours
A	23.	Arrangements made for after hours emergencies or urgent help
M	24.	Thoroughness of the main practitioner(s) you have seen
O. P	25.	Appropriate use of referrals to other practitioners or services when needed
P	26.	Collaboration between service providers (if more than one)
	27.	Publicity or information about programs and services offered
P	28.	Handling and accuracy of your records (as best you can tell)
O	29.	Contribution of services to achievement of your life goals
M	30.	In an overall general sense. how satisfied are you with the service you have received?
	31.	(If applicable) Support of the group as a whole. helpfulness and caring of its members

SUBSCALE KEY

M = Manner and Skill (9-items; average $\alpha = .88$)
O = Perceived Outcome (8-items; average $\alpha = .83$)
P = Procedures (5-items; average $\alpha = .74$)
A = Accessibility (4-items; average $\alpha = .67$)
W = Waiting (2 items, may optionally be combined with Access)

* Note Individual item scale anchors alternate direction throughout scale. scoring reverses every other item.

FIG. 5.16.   Service Satisfaction Survey - 30. Copyright 1986, 1987, 1989, 1990, 1995 T. K. Greenfield, C. C. Attkisson, and G. C. Pascoe. All rights reserved. Web site: saawww. ucsf.edu/csq. Reproduced with permission.

tion scale that includes 29 items from the SSS-30. According to Greenfield and Attkisson, the responses of 40 patients to each of the SSS-30 items showed at least 75% agreement over a retest interval ranging from 7 to 15 days when adjacent responses were considered as evidence for agreement. In the other study, Greenfield and Stoneking (1993) were reported to have obtained 6-month subscale reliabilities ranging from .45 to .67.

Validity.   Greenfield and Attkisson (1999) point to the correlation Greenfield (1989) found between the SSS-30 and the CSQ ($r = .70$; $p < .0001$) for a group of individuals going through a drinking driver program as support for the validity of the instrument as a measure of general patient satisfaction. In addition, findings from Greenfield and Attkisson's (1989) factor analysis of the SSS-30 results from the two samples (mental health and health clinics), as well as those from Greenfield's (1989) drunk driver program and EAP samples, led Greenfield and Attkisson (1999) to conclude that "across four different types of service (studied in independent investigations), the major factors of [Practitioner] Manner and Skill satisfaction and [Perceived] Outcome satisfaction are well confirmed" (p. 1359).

Comment.   The SSS-30 is a good alternative to the CSQ-8 when more a detailed evaluation of satisfaction with behavioral health care services is warranted, as is typically the case in MBHO settings. Although minimal, the variety of setting-specific comparison data that is available for the SSS-30 is likely to be more than one will find from other multifactorial, generic satisfaction instruments that are not a part of a more comprehensive outcomes assessment system. Although initial results are promising, further exploration of the instrument's psychometric properties is encouraged.

GHAA Visit-Specific Satisfaction Questionnaire (VSQ)

Another patient satisfaction instrument that can be of assistance in some MBHO systems is the nine-item, visit-specific questionnaire that was derived from the Group Health Association of America's (GHAA's) Consumer Satisfaction Survey (Davies & Ware, 1991). Unlike most other satisfaction instruments, the Visit-Specific Satisfaction Questionnaire (VSQ; Davies & Ware, 1991; Radosevich, Werni, & Cords, 1994; Rubin, Gandek, Rogers, Kosinski, McHorney, & Ware, 1993; Ware & Hays, 1988) measures aspects of satisfaction that were experienced during a *specific office visit*, assessed at the end of that particular visit. This is contrast to the MBHO satisfaction surveys that elicit the patient's perceptions of multiple aspects of care during an *episode of care*, measured at the end of that episode.

Development.   The VSQ was adapted from the Patient Satisfaction Questionnaire-III (Hays, Davies, & Ware, 1987) and developed for use as part of the Medical Outcomes Study (see Davies & Ware, 1991). It contains nine items taken from the questions related to access to care (appointment wait, office location, telephone access, office wait) and quality of care (time with doctor, explanation of care, technical skills, personal manner, overall care). Each of these aspects of the office visit are rated on a 5-point scale ("Excellent" to "Poor") and each item is treated as a separate scale unto itself. A copy of the VSQ questions is presented in Fig. 5.17.

Visit-Specific Satisfaction Questionnaire

Instructions: Thinking about your visit with the person you saw, how would you rate the following:

	Poor	Fair	Good	Very Good	Excellent
1. How long you waited to get an appointment	1	2	3	4	5
2. Convenience of the location of the office	1	2	3	4	5
3. Getting through to the office by phone	1	2	3	4	5
4. Length of time waiting at the office	1	2	3	4	5
5. Time spent with the person you saw	1	2	3	4	5
6. Explanation of what was done for you	1	2	3	4	5
7. The technical skills (thoroughness, carefulness, competence) of the person you saw	1	2	3	4	5
8. The personal manner (courtesy, respect, sensitivity, friendliness) of the person you saw	1	2	3	4	5
9. The visit overall	1	2	3	4	5

FIG. 5.17. GHAA Visit-Specific Satisfaction Questionnaire (VSQ). Adapted from the GHAA Consumer Satisfaction Survey; Health Outcomes Institute Personal Characteristic Form. Copyright © GHAA/Davies & Ware, 1988, 1991; Health Outcomes Institute, 1993, 1995. All rights reserved. Reproduced with permission.

Interpretation. Davies and Ware (1991) present the number and percentage of the 18,118 MOS respondents who responded to each of the five response choices for each of the nine items. How the findings are interpreted will depend on the situation and what one considers to be important. For instance, in Rubin et al.'s (1993) investigation of the ratings given by patients seen in different types of medical practice with different payment plans, the authors chose to classify a patient's response as either "excellent" or not excellent (i.e., "poor," "fair," "good," or "very good") because "current theories of quality management and improvement recommend comparisons to best practices rather than to minimum standards" (p. 836). However, one could choose another convention, such as including "very good" with the "excellent" response or even grouping the "good" response with these two highest levels of satisfaction.

Reliability and Validity. To this author's knowledge, there have not been studies to investigate the aspects of VSQ's validity and reliability as it may pertain to MBHO settings. However, Rubin et al. (1993) does present validity data that for medical groups that may be of use in determining the appropriateness of the scale for specific settings.

Comment.   The VSQ enables a provider or provider organization to *immediately* determine whether a single patient or sample of patients perceive any problems related to their care, and thus allows these problems to be dealt with sooner. The obvious limitation with the VSQ is the lack of validity and reliability data, as well as the lack of MBHO normative data. It is hoped that large-scale investigations into the use of this instrument in MBHOs will take place in the near future. Regardless, it is a face-valid instrument that any psychologist or MBHO can use and quickly obtain important information about their specific performance and areas of service that require improvement. With regular use, MBHOs can easily and quickly begin to develop their own standards for comparison within their network of providers.

ADDITIONAL RESOURCES FOR IDENTIFYING PUBLIC DOMAIN AND LOW-COST INSTRUMENTS

In addition to those instruments discussed in this chapter, chapter 8 of this book presents several low- or no-cost instruments that either were developed specifically for use in primary care settings or which have their greatest applicability in those settings. Regardless of their originally intended target population, many of these instruments or portions thereof are quite appropriate for use in MBHO settings. A good example is the Primary Care Evaluation of Mental Disorders, or PRIME-MD (Hahn, Kroenke, Williams, & Spitzer, 1999; Spitzer et al., 1994) and its individual modules and derivative instruments.

As has been the case for several decades, the Buros Institute's *Mental Measurements Yearbook* (MMY; Impara & Plake, 1998) and its accompanying supplement (Plake & Impara, 1999) can serve as a good starting place in searching for instruments that meet the particular needs of the practitioner. The MMY provides descriptions, professional reviews, and reference lists for most available instruments. It includes information for only commercially available tests and therefore may be of limited value to those who are looking for no-cost instrumentation. The Buros Institute also publishes the *Tests in Print* series (TIP; Murphy, Impara, & Plake, 1999), which serves as an index and quick reference guide for the instruments reviewed in the MMY.

There are a number of other available resources that can assist the practitioner in identifying other low- or no-cost measures that are "MBHO friendly." One source is the work by Fischer and Corcoran, titled *Measures for Clinical Practice, Volumes 1 and 2* (1994a, 1994b). This two-volume set contains a compilation of test forms and accompanying brief descriptive and psychometric information for what are referred to as *rapid assessment instruments (RAIs)*. Each measure is said to contain less than 50 items and is cross-referenced by problem areas, such as depression, anxiety, family functioning, and eating problems. Volume 1 deals with measures designed for use with children, couples, and families. Volume 2 is limited to measures developed for use with adults. Many of the instruments presented are available at little or no cost, while others are copyrighted and require permission or a fee to use.

Two books edited by this author also discuss several other low- or no-cost instruments in great detail. The first is *The Use of Psychological Testing for Treatment Planning and Outcomes Assessment (2nd ed.)* (Maruish, 1999b). With a focus on their use with the specific application indicated in the title, this work presents individual chapters on both commercial and noncommercial instruments, some of which have been discussed in this chapter. Similar but much less detailed information is presented in Sederer and Dickey's (1996) *Outcomes Assessment in Clinical Practice.*

In another of this author's books, *Handbook of Psychological Assessment in Primary Care Settings* (Maruish, 2000b), the focus is on both commercial and noncommercial measures with specific applications for the screening, treatment planning, and treatment monitoring of psychological symptoms and disorders in general medical practices. Again, detailed discussions of some of the instruments discussed in this chapter are included in the primary care book.

An excellent resource for health risk assessment measures is the Society of Prospective Medicine's *SPM Handbook of Health Assessment Tools* (Hyner, Peterson, Travis, Dewey, Foerster, & Framer, 1999). In addition to the informative chapters on isssues related to "the theoretical and practical framework for designing, selecting, using and evaluating many different kinds of health assessment tools" (p. II-5), the second half of this work is devoted to summaries of and/or acutal test forms for various commercially available and "research" instruments. The types of instruments covered include health risk appraisals, health status assessments, quality of life instruments, and lifestyle-specific health assessments.

There are many Internet Web sites that can provide access to various tests and/or information about them. One such site is Mental Health Net's (2000) *Assessment Resources,* which provides links to psychological assessment resources of both a commercial and noncommercial nature, news groups, and mailing lists. Similar sites likely can be found by conducting standard searches through available web browsers. Additionally, many good literature search services are available. These can make the identification of specific types of instrumentation or information on specific measures of interest relatively easy. A good example is the PsychInfo service offered through the American Psychological Association.

Finally, the interested reader is encouraged to review the Science Directorate of the APA's (1995) guide to finding information about published to unpublished tests for further assistance in locating and using such instruments.

SUMMARY

Limitations imposed by MBHOs on the authorization of psychological testing have had a significant impact on the frequency at which this clinical service is performed. Yet, there are still a number of psychologists who have been reluctant to limit their use of psychological measures to only those situations in which full or partial reimbursement is guaranteed. The information provided by the tools of the trade is so valuable that these psychologists are willing to forgo payment and assume the expenses for the time, effort, and materials spent in psychological testing activities. For them, usual testing costs can be reduced through the use of valid, reliable instrumentation that is available at no cost or at a cost substantially lower than that charged for products that are commercially published and marketed.

Noncommercial instruments of the type discussed in this chapter have been available for many years. Some have been developed out of necessity for specific clinical or research settings or applications, and have been discussed only in professional meetings or obscure publications. However, because of the restrictions on testing benefits offered by health plans and other circumstances that have occurred since the beginning of the last decade (e.g., the push to measure outcomes and patient satisfaction, the willingness for test developers to share their products directly with the professional community), these types of instruments are starting to move to the forefront. Moreover, the need to gain general acceptability by both the professional community and the consumers of MBHO and other health care services has led developers to be more conscientious about ensuring the quality of these measures. These noncommercial developers are now employing standard test development practices and procedures to a much greater extent than has been in the past. As a result, the practitioner now has many excellent product choices beyond those provided by commercial test publishing houses; one can anticipate more such choices in the future.

As with any commercially available test product, the practitioner needs to exercise appropriate caution when selecting from among the types of instruments described in this chapter. The test selection criteria described in chapter 4 will provide guidance in this regard.

6

Issues and Considerations in Developing Test-Based Outcomes Assessment Programs

The interest in and need for behavioral health treatment outcomes measurement/ management and accountability in this era of managed care provides a unique opportunity for psychologists to use their training and skills in testing. However, the extent to which psychologists and other trained professionals become key and successful contributors to outcomes initiatives that are required or encouraged by MBHOs, will depend on their understanding of what "outcomes" and their measurement and applications are all about. This issue is so important that this and the following chapter are devoted to the topic of outcomes assessment. The present chapter focuses on familiarizing the reader with the most important issues and considerations that must be taken into account in developing a test-based outcomes management progam. It also provides a context with which to think about outcomes. This information lays the groundwork for chapter 7, which focuses on matters related to designing and implementing an outcomes assessment program.

This chapter and chapter 7 will address issues that are important from the viewpoints of MBHOs and those responsible for their organization's outcomes assessment system. At the same time, most of these issues and recommendations also relevant to individual practitioners, group practices, and facilities that contract with MBHOs and either (a) are required by the MBHO to establish an outcomes system or participate with other contracted providers in an MBHO's outcomes system, or (b) wish to establish their own system of outcomes assessment independent of that required by managed care. Generally, the MBHOs that are serious about establishing and maintaining an ongoing outcomes system will consult with its provider panel about many of the matters discussed in these two chapters. Knowing the issues involved will enable the provider to speak more intelligently about them, provide educated input into the process, and increase their perceived value to the MBHO.

WHAT ARE OUTCOMES?

Before discussing the assessment and reporting of treatment outcomes, it is important to have a clear understanding of what is meant by the term. Experience has shown that its meaning varies depending on the source.

Donabedian (1985) has identified outcomes, along with structure and process, as the three dimensions of quality of care (see chapter 2). As for the relationship between Donabedian's three facets of quality of care, Brook, McGlynn, and Cleary (1996) have noted that

If quality-of-care criteria based on structural or process data are to be credible, it must be demonstrated that variations in the attribute they measure lead to differences in outcome. If outcome criteria are to be credible, it must be demonstrated that differences in outcome will result if the processes of care under the control of health professionals are altered. (p. 966)

Bobbitt et al. (1998) have proposed a six-component model of quality of care that also includes *outcomes*. The other five components are *access, satisfaction, defined interventions, efficiency,* and a *formal quality improvement program*. The first three components are important from the patient's perspective while the last three are important from the perspective of the service delivery system. As Table 6.1 illustrates, the quality indicators for each component will vary according to the way the service delivery is organized, whether that be a solo practice, group practice, MBHO, or health plan. In essence, Bobbitt et al. offer a model that mirrors Donabedian's, but with much more detail and specificity.

The outcomes, or results, of treatment should not imply a change in only a single aspect of functioning. Thus, the term is generally used in the plural (i.e., outcomes) to convey that interventions typically affect or result in changes in multiple domains of the patient's life (Berman, Rosen, Hurt, & Kolarz, 1998). Stewart and Ware (1992) have identified five broad aspects of general health status: physical health, mental health, social functioning, role functioning, and general health perception. Treatment may affect each of these aspects of health in different ways, depending on the disease or disorder being treated and the effectiveness of the treatment.

There are various definitions of the term "outcomes." Generally, it refers to the results of the specific treatment that was rendered. Berman, Hurt, and Heiss (1996) define outcomes as the change in the clinical, functional or subjective state of a patient, or in his utilization of services over a specific time period. Bieber, Wroblewski, and Barber (1999) have identified commonalties of existing definitions of outcomes, such that (a) outcomes are results that may be favorable or unfavorable to the individual, (b) can be applied to individuals, subpopulations or populations, and (c) can cover various lengths of time.

In considering the types of outcomes that might be assessed in behavioral health care settings, a substantial number of clinicians probably would identify symptomatic change in psychological status as being the most important. However important change in symptom status may have been in the past, there has been a realization that change in many other aspects of functioning, such as those identified by identified by Stewart and Ware (1992), are equally important indicators of treatment effectiveness. As Sederer et al. (1996) have noted,

Outcome for patients, families, employers, and payers is not simply confined to symptomatic change. Equally important to those affected by the care rendered is the patient's capacity to function within a family, community, or work environment or to exist independently, without undue burden to the family and social welfare system. Also important is the patient's ability to show improvement in any concurrent medical and psychi-

TABLE 6.1
Components of Quality Behavioral Health Care by Level of Delivery System Organization

Components	Solo Practitioner	Practice Group	MBHO	Health Plan
Access	Ability to take on new patients; range of services offered; hours worked; consumer "friendliness" of office staff and procedures	Range of services made available—crisis, intensive outpatient, day treatment, specialities; customer "friendliness"	Geographic distribution of providers; credentialed providers with range of specialities; access times defined by time of contact of first appointment; phone access statistics; system-wide customer friendliness	Similar to MBHO
Satisfaction	Retention of current patients; word of mouth; individually administered surveys; complaints not formally addressed unless made to regulatory boards	More formalized surveys; possible measurement of individual differences in provider performance; complaints may be formally addressed by practice administration	Performance targets set for random sample within defined population; survey across large populations of individuals; complaints about service and outcome formally tracked and evaluated	See MBHO
Outcomes	Impression of success; comments by patients; review of records; possible use of specific instruments	Adoption of short outcome measures	Large scale use of outcomes instruments; structural and process measures, e.g., HEDIS 3.0, PERMS 1.0; hospitalization and rehospitalization rate; inappropriate use of higher levels of care, e.g., ER visits for care that could be provided in an outpatient setting	Broad and extensive measures similar to those used for MBHO

(Continued)

TABLE 6.1
(Continued)

Components	Solo Practitioner	Practice Group	MBHO	Health Plan
Defined Interventions	Primarily provided in training	Beginning use of practice guidelines and specific treatment techniques; greater likelihood that some staff will use such guidelines; this practice based on training of individuals and ability of group to provide training on guidelines and techniques	Adoption of formal practice guidelines and best practices; level of care guidelines	Best practices and medical care guidelines
Efficiency	Ability to take on new patients; ability to retain patients and use time wisely	Ability to offer range of services; direct service hours meet financial targets; clear treatment termination criteria, average length of treatment for different types of cases, ability to divert hospitalizations	Based on managing administrative overhead and insuring that appropriate utilization is maintained (preventing overutilization of inappropriate higher levels of care and promoting access to appropriate levels of care—primarily outpatient); appropriate per-unit pricing	Same as MBHO, except cuts across all medical conditions
Formal QI Program	Rarely evident—quality improvement occurs through continuing education and review of own case load—case consultation	Review of cases in group; case staffings; review of critical incidents; continuous quality improvement (CQI) processes and projects are operational	Formal program as defined by NCQA—quality improvement efforts are operational in all levels of system	Same as MBHO as defined by NCQA

Note. From "Managed Behavioral Health Care: Current Status, Recent Trends, and the Role of Psychology," Table 1, by B. L. Bobbitt, C. C. Marques, & D. L. Trout, 1998. *Clinical Psychology: Science and Practice, 5,* p. 60. Copyright 1998 by the American Psychological Association. Reprinted with permission.

atric disorder. . . . Finally, not only do patients seek symptomatic improvement, but also they want to experience a subjective sense of health and well being. (p. 2)

Thus, "outcomes" holds a different meaning for each of the different parties who have a stake in behavioral health care delivery. As will be shown next, what is measured generally depends on the purpose(s) for which outcomes assessment is undertaken.

INTEREST IN BEHAVIORAL HEALTH CARE OUTCOMES

The tremendous interest in the assessment of outcomes that has developed in MBHOs and other behavioral health care settings over the past decade is somewhat of a phenomenon. Those who were in the behavioral health care field prior to the 1990s can recall a time when the term "outcomes," at least as it pertained to the treatment of mental health and substance abuse patients, was rarely mentioned. Now, it is even more rare to *not* hear the term in workshops, conference presentations, and published articles and newsletters having to do with psychological or behavioral interventions. What has led to the interest in this particular aspect of intervention? How do the different stakeholders in a patient's care vary in their interests in treatment outcomes? How do individual providers and organizations such as MBHOs use outcomes information? Answers to these questions will provide the foundation necessary for considering the more "nuts and bolts" issues that must be addressed in developing a systematic approach to assessing and managing outcomes.

Impetus for Outcomes Assessment Initiatives

The movement to initiate programs to measure, monitor, and manage behavioral health care outcomes has undergone a period of dramatic growth. What accounts for this? It appears to be born out of a number of separate but interrelated circumstances that have emerged with some prominence at approximately the same time. Alone, each does not present itself as an overpowering force in physical or behavioral health care; together, however, these forces have acted as a formidable impetus to change in the way health care is provided.

Need to Control Costs. The costs of mental health problems and the need for behavioral health care services in the United States have risen over the past several years and are particularly disconcerting. In 1995, approximately $1 trillion, or 14.9% of the gross domestic product, was spent on health care, and a 20% increase was expected by the year 2000 ("Future Targets," 1996). A Substance Abuse and Mental Health Services Administration (SAMHSA) summary of various findings in the literature indicated that America's bill for direct health care costs for mental health and substance abuse treatment in 1990 was $81 billion (Rouse, 1995). In 1997, spending for behavioral health care was estimated to be $85 billion (Coffey, Mark, King, Harwood, McKusick, Genuardi, Dilonardo, & Buck, 2000). These figures compare to the 1983 direct *and* indirect mental health costs of $73 billion reported by Harwood, Napolitano, and Kristiansen (cited in Kiesler & Morton, 1988). As reported by

Ceridian Benefits Services (cited in "Monthly change in average health insurance premiums," 2000) at the time of this writing, single coverage monthly medical premiums for HMOs and non-HMO were $194 and $213, respectively, while HMO and non-HMO monthly family premiums were $536 and $580, respectively.

What accounts for the changes in behavioral health care costs over the past 2 decades? Lyons, Howard, O'Mahoney, and Lish (1997) point to the early 1980s as the beginning of the increasing demand for behavioral health services. At about this time, the stigmatization of those seeking behavioral health care services began to decrease as societal attitudes toward behavioral health problems and services became more accepting. Increasing acceptance of mental health and substance abuse services, along with increasing levels of stress in the lives of Americans that began to occur in the early 1980s led to increased behavioral health care utilization and accompanying costs to employers. As discussed in chapter 1, the establishment of behavioral health care "carve-out" organizations utilizing various utilization management strategies (e.g., precertification for treatment, employing a system of utilization review, establishing provider panels and "gatekeeper" models) was (and still is) successful in controlling costs. But MBHOs have since realized that some intervention practices may not be worthwhile or at least as cost-effective as others, and that identifying the "best practices" could lead to cost savings and increased quality and value of their services. Obviously, outcomes data is needed to make these determinations.

CQI Efforts to Manage Quality. In chapter 2, it was noted that the health care industry has embraced the CQI principles that have long been in place in the business and manufacturing industries. The key to the successful implementation of any CQI program is the gathering and analysis of data — outcomes data — on an ongoing basis (Berman et al., 1996). These data provide the feedback that is necessary to determine if efforts toward improving the quality of the provided services have had a positive impact; if not, further interventions would be warranted.

Accreditation and Regulatory Requirements. Berman et al. (1998) indicated that possibly the greatest impetus for the assessment of outcomes on an ongoing basis has come from accreditation bodies such as JCAHO and NCQA. Accreditation from one or both of these bodies infers that the organization has passed fairly stringent structure, process, and outcomes measurement standards. Thus, it helps ensure that the health care consumer is receiving services that meet or exceed at least a minimally acceptable level of quality. Accreditation by one or both of these organizations commonly is required for a health care organization to compete in the marketplace.

Both JCAHO and NCQA have been involved in the accreditation of health care organizations for a number of years. In the past, MBHOs were subject to the same requirements as nonbehavioral managed care organizations, either as an independent organization or a delegate of another organization that was responsible for all the consumer's health care needs. It has not been until recently that JCAHO and NCQA have each established a separate set of requirements, review processes, and expectations for the accreditation of MBHOs. Within each of these sets of requirements are standards that require the MBHO to be involved in some form of outcomes assessment activities. Because gaining and maintaining accreditation status from either of these organizations is essential for most MBHOs to be competitive, it is imperative for these organizations to have an ongoing program of outcomes assessment in some form or another.

Accreditation from JCAHO or NCQA is not necessarily a requirement for an MBHO to offer services to the public. There are, however, regulatory bodies that do make outcomes assessment a requirement. The QISMC standards for Medicare patients discussed in chapter 2 are a good example. It is likely that other regulatory bodies—state and federal—will make similar demands in the future.

Pressures for Accountability.   The push toward accountability with regard to the quality and value of health care services has been noted numerous times in the literature (e.g., Andrews, 1995; Schlosser, 1996). Lyons et al. (1997) point out the particular importance of accountability in the behavioral health field, given that this field has had greater price elasticity (i.e., its cost impacts its consumption), has favored an open-ended (unlimited) approach to treatment, and has a history of more unpredictable service utilization than what might have been found in the general health care arena previously. As they have indicated,

> "The task of making the mental health delivery system more accountable involves: (a) making use of the best scientific evidence from the mental health services literature on effectiveness and efficacy, (b) creating best-practice protocols, and (c) developing benchmark and feedback mechanisms that allow practitioners to improve their practice" (p. 13)

This, of course, necessitates the use of outcomes assessment information.

Advances in Technology.   Any useful outcomes management system requires that data be gathered and analyzed easily, and the resulting information be fed back to consumers of that information in a timely manner. Only within the past decade or so has this been possible. The availability of inexpensive, efficient microcomputers and networking capabilities has made this possible. The burgeoning of the Internet and intranet systems have made available additional resources for establishing workable systems of outcomes assessment and management. Now, it is relatively easy to obtain, process, and disseminate outcomes and other quality improvement data. Patient and collateral questionnaires can be administered online, and the resulting data automatically entered into a database; alternately, data can be gathered via paper-and-pencil questionnaires and subsequently scanned, key-entered or faxed into the database. In addition, other data can be useful for outcomes management purposes, and these are commonly accessible from claims databases. Available software allows for regular generation of generic or customized reports of outcomes information, scheduled to meet the needs of the organization (e.g., monthly, quarterly). Upon their generation, these reports can be automatically sent to other relevant stakeholders in the patient's care via e-mail, fax, or post.

Beyond the electronic technology, one must also consider the development of assessment tools that fit well into outcomes assessment programs. This is no small consideration. As Schlosser (1996) had noted:

> Instruments designed from the earlier era of pure psychotherapy research are nowadays being called into service for clinical "outcomes assessment" purposes, the appropriateness of which is a matter of debate. One problem with using older instruments for outcomes assessment is that they may not be well suited to the task. Most of these instruments were designed and normed years before the advent of managed care and the

widespread adoption of brief psychotherapy. They are typically too lengthy or focused
on variables of little salience to modern behavioral healthcare. (p. 285)

Schlosser's (1996) view is consistent with the instruments that were selected for
presentation in chapter 5. Thus, the development of instruments such as the SF-
36/SF-12, OQ-45, BASIS-32, and other instruments that are brief and measure domains that are important to the various stakeholders in the patient's treatment surely
must be considered another technological advance.

Other Reasons.   Other reasons for the push toward assessing outcomes have
been observed over the years. For example, in addition to developments related to requirements for accountability, Schlosser (1996) attributed the interest in outcomes assessment to (a) the development of measurement tools required for research in
health-producing factors and health care interventions; (b) advancement in the ac-
quisition and understanding of psychotherapy-related data; and (c) outcomes assessment filling the void left by the demise of routine administration of test batteries.
Questions about medical decision-making that arose from regional variations in behavioral health care practice patterns, as well as the need for MBHOs to decrease
their provider panel size were noted by Berman et al. (1996). Lyons et al. (1997)
pointed to the growing movements by consumer groups such as the National Alliance for the Mentally Ill (NAMI) and their concern about choice, quality, and value in
mental health as yet another factor in the increasing interest in outcomes.

Stakeholders' Recognition of the Importance
of Outcomes Measurement in MBHOs

The implementation of any type of outcomes assessment initiative does not come
without effort from and cost to the MBHO. However, if implemented properly, all interested parties should find the yield from the outlay of time and money to be substantial. But just who is interested in the behavioral health care outcomes, and what
specifically are they interested in?

Strupp & Hadley (1977; Strupp, 1996) have formulated what they refer to as the *tripartite model* of mental health and therapeutic outcomes. This model basically states
that the judgment of the mental health of an individual and the degree to which
change in mental health is brought to bear by therapeutic intervention must be considered from the vantage points of the patient, the treating professional, and society.
Table 6.2 presents an overview of the possible mixtures and implications of the types
of tripartite judgments that may be made about an individual's mental health or the
outcomes of therapeutic intervention with him/her.

Based on this model, Strupp and Hadley (1977; Strupp, 1996) concluded that (a) a
given individual's level of mental health or therapeutic change may be judged differently, depending on the which of the three vantage points are taken: (b) the differences in judgment result from each party's individual interests; (c) one must recognize the limited utility of judgments made from a single perspective; (d) a
comprehensive description of the patient's mental health can come only from assessing and integrating the affect, psychological structure, and behavior of the patient,
which represent the three facets of the tripartite model; and (e) judgment of treatment
outcomes ultimately becomes an issue of human values and public policy rather than
a research issue.

TABLE 6.2
The Tripartite View of Mental Health and Therapy Outcomes

| Category | Configuration[1] | | | Mental Health Status |
	B	W	S	
1	+	+	+	Well-functioning, adjusted individual; optimal mental health.
2	+	−	+	Basically healthy person; troubled by dysphoric mood, perhaps due to minor trauma affecting self-esteem, temporary reverses, discouragement, loss, grief reaction.
3	+	+	−	May have fragile ego (borderline condition, schizoid personality, etc.) but functions well in society and feels content. Underlying psychotic process may be present, but defenses may be reasonably effective.
4	+	−	−	Similar to Category 3, but affect may be labile or dysphoric. Has basic ego weakness but functions adequately in society.
5	−	+	+	Society judges person's behavior as maladaptive (e.g., unconventional lifestyle), but his or her sense of well-being and personality structure are sound.
6	−	−	+	Similar to Category 2, except that social performance is considered maladaptive (e.g., as part of a grief reaction, person may withdraw, give up job, etc.).
7	−	+	−	Person with ego defects, psychopaths, character disorders, conversion reactions (la belle indifference), and individuals who have poor reality testing and poor insight.
8	−	−	−	Clearly mentally ill.

[1]B = adaptive behavior (society); W = sense of well-being (individual); S = personality structure (professional).

Note. From "The Tripartite Model and the *Consumer Reports* Study," Table 1, by H. H. Strupp, 1996. *American Psychologist, 51*, p. 1020. Copyright 1996 by the American Psychological Association. Reprinted with permission.

The importance of Strupp and Hadley's model here is that brings to the forefront the fact that there is no single perspective from which to judge outcomes, because that judgment will reflect only the judging stakeholder's specific vested interest in the patient's status. *Stakeholders* can be defined as "those individuals and groups for whom the results of these [outcomes] data will potentially have an impact, including consumers/patients, family members, clinicians, administrators, employers, politicians, and insurance and managed care companies" (Berman et al., 1998). Thus, the interest in, importance, and benefit of any particular type of treatment outcome will vary from one stakeholder to another.

Patients' Interests. Strupp (1996) and Oss and Sloves (2000) see the patient's outcomes interest as achieving happiness and contentment, thus experiencing highly subjective feelings of well-being. But patients' interests extend beyond just feeling good. Cagney and Woods (1994) identify several benefits to patients, including enhanced health and quality of life, improved health care quality, and effective use of the dollars paid into benefits plans. Outcomes information can also help patients identify preferred providers, track their treatment progress, and discuss treatment options with their providers (Berman et al., 1998; Bieber et al., 1999).

Providers' Interests. For providers, the outcomes data can result in improved clinical skills, important information related to the quality of care and local practice standards, increased profitability, and decreased concerns over possible litigation

(Cagney & Woods, 1994). Bieber et al. (1999) note that outcomes information can help the provider support treatment decisions, track patient progress, and assess the effectiveness of his methods. This information can also help identify areas of service requiring change, and to develop strategies for increasing the quality of care. For Strupp (1996), outcomes information affords insights into patients' personality structure relative to the intervention provided.

Care Managers' Interests.   Outcomes information can assist care managers in assessing the progress of individual patients during an episode of care. It can also be helpful in making decisions about the need for additional services beyond those that were initially authorized. In aggregate, this information can provide a means of determining the effectiveness of individual providers for the various types of problems. This, in turn, can help ensure that the care manager is referring patients to those providers who are best suited for treating the presenting problem.

MBHOs' Interests.   Like their care managers, MBHOs can use outcomes information to monitor outcomes and quality of care across providers (Bieber et al., 1999). The benefits derived from its use include increased profits, retention of accreditation status, information that can shape the practice patterns of their providers, and a decision-making process based on delivering quality care (Cagney & Woods, 1994).

Payers' Interests.   Cagney and Woods (1994) see the potential payer benefits as including healthier workers, improved health care quality, increased worker productivity, and reduced or contained health care costs. Berman et al. (1998) and McLellan and Durell (1996) see outcomes information as important in decreasing or controlling utilization and reducing costs. This information can also be used by payers to select individual providers or to evaluate entire MBHO systems (Bieber et al., 1999).

Other Third-Party Interests.   There are numerous other parties that potentially could be considered stakeholders and thus have an interests in the outcomes of a given patient. The patient's family, for example, may want to be sure that the patient is progressing toward his premorbid level of role functioning. Employers also are interested in the patient's return to a level of functioning necessary to perform his job and increased productivity. They also are interested in decreasing absenteeism, on-the-job accidents, and turnover rates (Lyons et al., 1997). Other important stakeholders may include groups such as researchers and government agencies, all of which will have their own specific agenda and will view outcomes data accordingly.

The interests of all stakeholders for a given outcomes initiative are extremely important. They should provide the context in which outcomes assessment takes place. As Berman et al. (1998) put it, "it is the starting point which should frame all other aspects of the evaluation" (p. 121).

Common Reasons for Implementing Outcomes Systems

There are numerous reasons why an MBHO might wish to establish and maintain a system for assessing and managing treatment outcomes. In a survey of 73 behavioral health care organizations, the top five reasons identified by the participants as to why they had conducted an outcomes program were (in descending order): evaluation of patients with specific disorders, evaluation of provider effectiveness, evaluation of integrated treatment programs, management of individual patients, and support of sales and marketing efforts (Pallak, 1994). All are very legitimate reasons for expending the time, effort, and resources necessary for establishing and maintaining an outcomes assessment system. But there are also many other reasons.

Assistance in Real-time Clinical Decision-making. It is not uncommon for one to view an outcomes system as something that provides information at the back end of treatment. But as the Pallak (1994) survey has shown, many value information that is gathered as part of an outcomes management system for what it can contribute to the ongoing management of patients. In that survey, 44% of the respondents indicated that they conducted outcomes studies to "manage individual patients," and 31% said that it was used for "settings triage/level of care decisions."

Going beyond these two rather broad categorizations, there is any number of real-time uses for the type of information that one might gather in support of an outcomes initiative. For example, data obtained at the time of treatment initiation can be used for *problem identification* and, concomitantly, *support for treatment authorization, treatment planning,* and *application of treatment recovery curves.* Ongoing *tracking of patient progress* through re-administration of outcomes instruments can assist in determining whether adjustment in the treatment plan is required, and in the *determination of the need for additional treatment.* However, it is important to note that none of this is possible unless the outcomes system in place provides a means of feeding back to the provider the information on a timely basis. This information must be made available at a time when it can make difference, *not* only after the patient's episode of care has been completed. Providing this type of real-time information can be a key factor or incentive to getting clinicians to "buy in" to an outcomes program and thus, can be a key factor to the success of all outcomes programs.

Determination of Treatment Outcomes. Clinicians can employ outcomes assessment to obtain a direct measure of how much patient improvement has occurred as the result of a completed course of treatment intervention. Here, the findings are more beneficial to the clinician than to the patient because a pre- and posttreatment approach to the assessment is utilized. The information will not lead to any change in the patient being assessed, but the feedback it provides to the clinician could assist him or her in the treatment of other patients in the future.

Development of "Best Practices" and Treatment Guidelines. Andrews (1995) has indicated that the aggregation of the outcomes research results provides "the underpinnings for practice guidelines" (p. 19). The Committee on Quality Assurance and Accreditation Guidelines stated that "outcomes research is vitally important to improve the base of evidence related to treatment effectiveness. Outcomes research is needed to provide explicit direction in identifying performance indicators associated with good outcomes for different patient characteristics, types of treatment programs, and types of managed care organizations" (Institute of Medicine, 1997, p. 5). Indeed, it is only with outcomes data that a professional organization (e.g., American Psychological Association, American Psychiatric Association), governmental agency (e.g., HCFA), or specific MBHOs can begin to answer questions related to what type of treatment works best for whom, what type of patients receive the most benefit from the organization/provider, and other questions related to improving the quality and effectiveness of care.

At this time, the use of guidelines in MBHOs appears limited. Thirty-one percent of Pallak's (1994) survey respondents reported their use of outcomes information to evaluate the effectiveness of different treatments, and 32% to evaluate or compare treatment guidelines. Berman et al.'s (1998) observation of newsletter and trade paper reports suggested that only about 20% of health care organizations used guidelines and only 12% planned to do so. This will change, but not as a matter of choice. Accreditation through NCQA and JCAHO now requires the measurement of an MBHO's compliance with treatment guidelines.

Development of Predictive Models and Treatment Recovery Curves.   The value of predictive models and treatment recovery curves was discussed at length in chapter 2. Recall that development of these tools for planning and monitoring treatment requires outcomes data. It is unlikely that an MBHO would implement an outcomes assessment system solely for these purposes. On the other hand, being able to use outcomes data for predictive modeling and generating treatment recovery curves can provide added value to the MBHO beyond whatever the primary purpose of the system might be. This can increase the payback to the MBHO and thus help justify the cost of implementing an outcomes system.

Development of an Objectively Based Provider Profiling System.   Provider profiling is process by which service providers (psychiatrist, psychologists, social workers, nurses, etc.) are evaluated and usually ranked based on some objective criteria (Berman et al., 1996). Pallak (1994) found that 57% of his sample used outcomes data to evaluate or compare provider effectiveness. In addition to improvement in symptomatology, functioning, and well-being and other outcomes data, profiling can be based on any number of clinical and nonclinical variables, such as data related patient demographics and treatment satisfaction, claims, average length of treatment, transition of patients to higher levels of care, recidivism, and compliance with contractual obligations. Of course, the accuracy and utility of the profiling will depend on the case-mix adjustment procedures that are implemented to "level the playing field" and permit valid comparisons of providers (see later; also see Sperry et al., 1996).

Indeed, provider profiling can be another extremely useful tool for MBHOs in their efforts to improve the quality of the care they offer to plan members. Through profiling, areas of strength, training needs, and problematic support processes can be identified and appropriate interventions designed. On the other hand, profiling can be quite threatening to providers if it is used to determine rewards (e.g., bonuses, promotions) or punishments (e.g., lower rates of referral, termination from provider panels; Berman et al., 1998). Thus, the success of any profiling system will be dependent on the degree to which it is used to increase provider abilities and enhance processes, and its purpose is perceived as such by the providers.

Support for CQI Efforts.   The importance of CQI programs in MBHOs, and the importance of outcomes assessment information to those programs, are addressed in chapter 2 and other chapters of this book. Suffice it to say here that treatment outcomes information powers the engine of the CQI process by providing the fuel for the evaluation of current performance, the determination of means of improving that performance, evaluation of those improvement efforts, and so on. In addition, the more an outcomes initiative is consistent with other CQI initiatives within the MBHO, the more it is likely to be "bought into" and supported by the MBHO.

One specific type of CQI effort that has appeared in literature is that of *treatment redesign*. Treatment redesign "refers to changes in the specific interventions and treatment techniques that comprise the client's full episode of care: the initial interview, the therapy and the medications" (Bologna & Feldman, 1995, p. 60; see also Bologna & Feldman, 1994). Bologna, Barlow, Hollon, Mitchell, and Huppert (1998) identified the growing interest in treatment redesign as one of the responses to the challenges that MBHOs and other health care organizations must face in this "era of accountability." Here, Bologna and her colleagues refer to changes in the provision of treatment that begin at the level of a specific intervention for a specific patient during a specific episode of care, and proceed to wider coverage within a system of care. The initiation of programmatic changes for specific diagnostic groups is given as an example. As with any other CQI effort, this approach requires the use of outcomes information to drive the redesign efforts.

Fulfillment of Regulatory and Accreditation Requirements. This is yet another area that has been covered in chapter 2 and elsewhere in this book. The reader is referred to these discussions for further information.

Generation of a Report Card of Organization/Provider Performance. Another result of the move toward accountability in health care delivery has been the development of *report cards*. For many, the term may conjure up memories of an earlier time in a person's life when a report card was a vehicle for reporting a student's school performance to a third party, such as the student's parents. In the context of health care — behavioral or otherwise — the report is usually of the performance an organization's system of health care delivery against pre-defined measures. The audience is the purchasers of health care services and other stakeholders. In some cases, the report card is oriented only to reporting the results of a single organization on any number of variables. Data may be trended allow a display of the results of the organization's quality improvement efforts across two or more points in time. Internal or external benchmark data might also accompany the organization's trended data. Because this information does not allow a comparison of the publishing organization's results to those of other organizations, this type of report card is limited in its utility to health care purchasers.

In other cases, the report card presents the results of several participating organizations (usually competitors) on a set of mutually agreed upon measures using specific "scoring" and reporting methodologies. This enables purchasers of health care services to compare each organization's performance against other organizations and/or a benchmark, thus permitting more informed conclusions about the value they are getting for their health care dollar. Probably the best known report card is the annual report of data for NCQA's Health Plan Employer Data and Information Set (HEDIS; NCQA, 2000a). Most of the HEDIS measures are oriented to reporting the performance of medical health care delivery systems. The HEDIS measures do include some behavioral health care performance measures, such as average length of inpatient stay and percent of depressed patients on antidepressant medication who had three or more follow-up visits within 12 weeks of the intital diagnosis. Much more relevant sets of report card measures are contained in the Consumer-Oriented Mental Health Report Card developed by the Center for Mental Health Statistics Improvement Program (MHSIP; 1996) Task Force, and the Performance Measures for Managed Behavioral Healthcare Programs 1.0 (PERMS 1.0) and PERMS 2.0, developed by the American Managed Behavioral Healthcare Association (AMBHA; 1995, 1998).

Generation of a Score Card of MBHO Performance.   Unlike report cards, score cards are intended for internal use by the MBHO. As Bieber et al. (1999) indicated, they

> provide information at the systems level and key processes within the system, determined by a leadership group within a health care organization. A key feature of such measures is that they provide critical, real-time information to management, which supports action-oriented decision-making. These decision-support tools provide performance rankings for overall health care systems or specific processes or outcomes, such as patient access, clinical processes, and customer satisfaction. . . . [They] are put in place to help identify and manage variation in the system. . . . (p. 178)

It is not uncommon for some types of performance measures and monitors to be reported in both report cards *and* score cards. Examples here could be change in symptom severity level from intake to discharge, and patient satisfaction with the quality of care for all inpatients hospitalized during a reporting period. However, data related to 30-day (recidivism) rates, hospitalization rates per 1,000 covered lives, average length of stay, access rates to emergent, urgent and routine care, and so forth are likely to be of greater interest and utility to the MBHO than to its customers. They therefore are more likely to be reported in a score card than in a report card.

Other Support of Marketing Efforts.   Report cards can serve as a powerful marketing tool for MBHOs. They can succinctly convey to their existing and prospective customers information about the structure, processes, and outcomes of the care that they offer. What may not be offered (at least in regularly reported results) is information related to the *value* of their services. In this context, value can be broadly defined as the amount of improvement per dollar spent. Value estimates answer the customer's question, "How much bang am I getting for my buck?" Improvement could be expressed in many ways, such as average changes in scores on outcomes measures (e.g., average decrease in SA-45 GSI T scores during an episode of care), movement from one level of functioning to another (e.g., number of patients that displayed clinically significant improvement on the OQ-45, number of patients unemployed at the time of treatment initiation who secured gainful employment), or substantial decrease in negative behaviors (e.g., number of patients that maintained sobriety for 1 month). Value here might be determined by calculating the cost of attaining the criteria for improvement on the specified variable(s) for a single patient or group of patients over a period of time.

Another means of determining value has received quite a bit of attention over the past several years. This has to do with *cost offset*. Cost-offset studies seek to determine to what extent (if any) savings in other areas of his functioning can offset the cost of a patient's treatment. These studies commonly focus on cost savings in one of two areas. The first is medical expenditures. Medical cost-offset studies look at the savings in nonpsychiatric medical expenses (inpatient treatment, outpatient and emergency room visits, medication, lab work, etc.) that result from the treatment of a behavioral health problem or disorder. The literature is replete with studies demonstrating that individuals with behavioral health problems utilize more nonpsychiatric medical resources that those with no such disorders (see Friedman, Sobel, Myers, Caudill, & Benson, 1995). Medical cost-offset information is particularly useful in systems that provide or manage both the medical *and* behavioral health care benefits of a health plan since the savings will be reflected in the organization's bottom line and lowered health care premiums. One complication in pursuing this type of investigation is that medical cost-offset effects usually appear after an extended period of time; consequently, they are not likely to be demonstrated when patients switch to other plans before the offset effect can take place.

The other area of cost offset, and a major focus of related studies, is that related to employment. According to the American Psychological Association (1996), the health conditions most limiting the ability to work are mental disorders. For example, major depression resulted in $23 billion in lost workdays in 1990; and in 1985, behavioral health problems resulted in over $77 billion in lost income. Also, the National Depressive and Manic-Depressive Association (as cited in "Depression Still Undertreated Despite Efforts to Redress," 1997) reported that depression costs employers $4,200 per depressed worker, or $250 per employee, with only 28% of these costs going toward actual treatment. Here, the financial effects of improvement in such areas as rates of productivity and absenteeism can be easily calculated and compared against the cost of providing behavioral health care to employees. Obviously, data on work productivity cost offset is of particular interest when the purchaser of the behavioral health care benefits is an employer or employer group.

There may be many other, idiosyncratic reasons why an MBHO wishes to initiate an outcomes system. Because of the range of questions and needs that the outcomes system might be asked to address, there is no one system or approach to the assessment of treatment outcomes that is appropriate for all MBHOs. Because of the various types of outcomes one may be interested in, the reasons for assessing them and the manner in which they may impact decisions, any successful and useful outcomes assessment approach must be customized. Customization should reflect the needs of the primary benefactor of the assessment information (e.g., patient, payer, provider), with consideration to the secondary stakeholders in the therapeutic endeavor. Ideally, the identified primary benefactor would be the patient. After all, as Andrews (1995) noted, "Outcomes measurement is the cornerstone of good clinical care" (p. 21). Although this is not always the case, it appears that only rarely would the patient not benefit from involvement in the outcomes assessment process. And as Docherty and Dewan (1995) have pointed out,

Although survival is and should be the key motivating factor for an organization's involvement in outcomes measurement, there are even stronger reasons for this involvement. A healthcare network that chooses to respond solely to the immediate demands of regulatory agencies or the perceived marketplace, without regard to the medical necessity and theoretical justification for this work, does so at its own social and economic peril.

Such a superficial system would miss the main benefit to be derived from outcomes assessment and measurement; namely, the ability to address the major problems that now affect our field and undermine its credibility and, hence, its fundability. A sophisticated, comprehensive outcomes measurement system will allow us to effectively remedy the root causes of those problems and thus move our entire system of care to a new and more effective mode of functioning. We would not think of trying to conduct a business enterprise without a careful financial accounting system. "Guesstimates" of costs and profitability are unacceptable. It makes quite as little sense not to demand the same kind of careful accounting and accountability with regard to the *quality* of healthcare. Just as we have quantitative financial management, we require quantitative clinical management. (p. 2)

WHAT TO MEASURE

Deciding to assess outcomes in a systematic fashion, and then committing to that decision is the first hurdle that must be passed in the development of an outcomes initiative. This can be a difficult process. Once it is passed, the MBHO must make another difficult decision, that is, which outcomes to measure. As discussed earlier, probably the most frequently measured variable is that of symptomatology or psychological/mental health status since disruption in this dimension is probably the most common reason why people seek behavioral health care services in the first place. However, there are other reasons for seeking help. Common examples include difficulties in coping with various types of life transitions (e.g., a new job, a recent marriage or divorce, other changes in the work or home environment), an inability to deal with the behavior of others (e.g., spouse, children), or general dissatisfaction with life. Thus, one may find that for some patients, improved functioning on the job, at school or with family or friends is much more relevant and important than symptom reduction. For other patients, improvement in their quality of life or sense of well-being may be more meaningful.

What do many of the various stakeholders say are important domains to measure? Berman et al. (1996) indicated that most MBHOs are interested in measuring symptomatology and functioning, as well as either cost or utilization. Participants of the 1999 Santa Fe Summit for the American College of Mental Health Administration were asked to rank the importance of 15 behavioral health indicators from three major areas: access, process, and outcomes ("Outcomes indicators less prevalent atop Summit list," 1999). Participants included representatives from major accreditation bodies, such as NCQA, JCAHO, and CARF, funding groups, MBHOs, consumers, both APAs, and performance measurement companies. The top-ranked indicator was the rate at which persons served are better, worse or unchanged as the result of treatment. The Pallak (1994) survey found that 65% of the respondents reported outcomes studies involving measurement of symptom severity. This was second only to patient satisfaction (71%) which, as stated before, it not a true outcome domain. This same survey also revealed that 58% reported measuring level of functioning and 49% reported measurement of social functioning. Daniels, Kramer, and Mahesh (1995) found that 50% of those members of Council of Group Practices surveyed indicated that they used pre- and posttreatment clinical functioning as a quality indicator.

Thus, there instances in which changes in psychological distress or disturbance either (a) provide only a partial indication of the degree to which therapeutic intervention has been successful; (b) are not of interest to the patient or a third-party payer; (c) are unrelated to the reason why the patient sought services in the first place; or (d) are otherwise inadequate or unacceptable as measures of improvement in the patient's condition. In these cases, measurement of related variables may be necessary, or may even take precedence over the assessment of symptoms.

Considerations for Selecting Outcomes Variables

The specific aspects or dimensions of patient functioning that are selected to become part of the outcomes assessment program will depend on the purpose for which the assessment is being conducted. It is not a simple matter to determine exactly what should be measured. The issue is complicated by a desire to meet the needs of each individual patient as well as those of the MBHO patient population as a whole. Careful consideration of the following questions should greatly facilitate the decision.

Why Do the Patients Seek Services?   People pursue treatment for many reasons. The patient's stated reason for seeking therapeutic assistance may be the first clue in determining what is important to measure. Measures selected for use for all patients serviced by MBHOs should reflect the most common reasons reported by the patient population.

What Does the Patient Hope to Gain From Treatment?   The patient's stated goals for the treatment that he is about to receive may be a primary consideration in the selection of which outcomes to measure. MBHOs again will want to meet the frequently reported goals for the patients they serve.

What Are the Patient's Criteria for Successful Treatment?   The patient's goals for treatment may provide only a broad target for the therapeutic intervention. Having the patient identify exactly what would have to happen to consider treatment successful, would help further specify the most important constructs and/or behaviors to measure. As before, MBHOs will need to determine what criteria their patients generally see as being important for treatment success.

What Are the MBHO's Criteria for the Successful Completion of the Current Therapeutic Episode?   What the patient identifies as being important to accomplish during treatment might reflect a lack of insight into his or her problems, or it might be inconsistent with what an impartial observer would consider indicative of meaningful improvement. In individual cases such as these, it probably would be appropriate for the clinician to determine what constitutes therapeutic success and the associated outcomes variables, and include these with those identified by the patient. At the same time, the establishment of one or more measureable criteria for treatment success that are applicable across the MBHO's patient population would also be desirable.

What Effects Can One Expect From the Intervention That Is Offered During the Therapeutic Episode?   One may select one or more variables that meet several of the previous needs, but they may not necessarily appropriate for a given patient or patient population. Lyons et al. (1997) give the example of how one might wish to measure changes in social or role functioning as a result of inpatient treatment. This level of care is intended to stabilize symptoms or manage the risk to self or others, *not* to improve their marital relationship or ability to function on the job. Thus, assessing functioning at the beginning and end of treatment is fruitless. In another situation, one might wish to use decrease in alcohol or other substance use as an outcomes variable. This is a commonly used variable but it is not likely to yield any useful information in populations that have a low incidence of such problems or for whom specific substance abuse treatment was not provided.

Will the Measurement of the Selected Variables Lead to Actionable Information? An MBHO could probably identify any number of outcomes variables that would provide information related to the degree to which their patients have benefited from the treatment they received. But one will likely find that only a relative few provide actionable information. For example, suppose an MBHO frequently provides services to health plan members who experience work-related difficulties. Any number of behaviors could contribute to these problems. A detailed assessment of various aspects of these patients' work lives can uncover specific reasons why they are experiencing impairment in on-the-job functioning. Thus, one would routinely want to assess variables such as relationships with peers, relationships with supervisors, productivity, tardiness, and absences with these types of patients. The results will provide clues as to where to focus the intervention efforts and increase the probability of improved work functioning.

What Are the Criteria for the Successful Completion of the Current Therapeutic Episode by Significant Third Parties? From a strict therapeutic perspective, this should be given the least amount of consideration. From a more realistic perspective, one cannot overlook the expectations and limitations that one or more third parties have for the treatment that is rendered. The expectations and limitations set by the patient's parents/guardian, significant other, health plan, employer, third-party payer, guidelines of the organization in which the clinician practices, and possibly other external forces may significantly play into the decision about what is considered successful treatment or when to terminate treatment.

What, if Any, Are the Outcomes Initiatives Within the Provider Organization? One cannot ignore any other outcomes or quality improvement programs that have already been initiated by the MBHO. Consistency with existing CQI or other outcomes programs will be important for obtaining buy-in from the MBHO's senior management. And as discussed in chapter 7, this type of buy-in is critical to the success of any outcomes initiative.

Are the Outcomes Variables Meaningful or Useful Across the Levels of Care? MBHOs would be well-advised to ensure that the selected measures allow for tracking of desired outcomes domains across the continuum of care. This would allow for a more accurate determination of improvement regardless of whether the patient is seen at only one level of care (e.g., outpatient) or transitions from one level of care to one or more other levels (e.g., inpatient to partial hospitalization to outpatient). For example, the symptom domains assessed by instruments such as the SA-45 or BSI might be better selections as outcomes measures than those domains assessed by the BPRS in MBHOs where there is a relatively high percentage of patients that begin an episode of care through inpatient treatment but later transition to outpatient treatment. Unlike that assessed by the BPRS, the symptomatology measured by the SA-45 and BSI is much more relevant across the continuum of care and thus lends itself better to tracking a greater percent of patients during an episode of care.

Do the Outcomes Variables Allow Meaningful Comparisons Across MBHOs? One of the factors that Eisen (2000) identified as being important for enhancing the utility of outcomes data is standardization of the indicators that are measured. Citing the work of Lambert, Ogles and Masters, she indicated that more than 1,430 different outcomes measures were used in 348 outcomes studies published between 1983 and

1988. Obviously, differences in the outcomes variables selected for use by one MBHO limit their usefulness in determining how it compares to other MBHOs. As a related issue, Eisen also noted that lack of standardization of the operational definitions of those selected measures across organizations poses an additional problem. These issues should not be a major concern for those few MBHOs who have no need or desire to make industry comparisons. However, for those that anticipate making such comparisons, it will be important to determine what are the more frequently measured, clearly defined outcomes variables that are employed by either competing MBHOs or organizations that are viewed leaders in setting standards for the managed care industry. In this regard, participation in performance measurement systems such as the HEDIS and PERMS systems mentioned earlier has clear and significant benefits.

What Is the Burden of Measuring the Selected Variables? The task of gathering outcomes data should not become too burdensome in terms of the financial and labor resources that would be required. As a general rule, the more outcomes data one attempts to gather from a given patient or collateral, the less likely he will obtain any data at all. The key is to identify the point where the amount of data that can be obtained from a patient and/or collaterals and the ease at which it can be gathered, are optimized.

But the issue here not only has to do with the number of variables; there also is the matter of the difficulty one might experience in obtaining data for a single variable. For example, an MBHO might choose to use data from structured clinical interview conducted at both the beginning and end of a treatment episode. This type of data might provide excellent, useful outcomes information and meet the needs of several stakeholders. At the same time, the fact that obtaining this data would require a total of two hours of unreimbursed clinical staff time would make it prohibitive. In addition to the cost and availability of labor, burden might also present itself in other forms, such as the training that would be needed to obtain the desired data, getting patients to complete outcomes at treatment termination or follow-up, or the need to develop customized instrumentation to measure the desired outcomes variable(s) in the MBHO's patient population. The issue here is one of practicality given the MBHO's resources and capabilities.

HOW TO MEASURE

Once the decision of *what* to measure has been made, one must then decide *how* it should be measured. Much of what has just been presented will play into the decision of the "how." In some cases, the "what" will dictate the how. In others, there will be multiple options for the how of the measurement.

Sources of Information

One of the most important considerations related to how outcomes data are obtained is where or whom this data should come from. Certain types of outcomes data will necessitate the use of specific sources of information while other types can be validly obtained from more than one source. In addition, the type of setting and population will also have a bearing on the selection of the best source of data (Berman et al., 1996).

Patient Self-Report.   In many cases, the most important data will be that obtained directly from the patient using self-report instruments. Underlying this assertion is the assumption that valid and reliable instrumentation, appropriate to the needs of the patient, is available; the patient can read at the level required by the instrument(s); and the patient is motivated to respond honestly to the questions asked. Barring one or more of these conditions, other options should be considered. Pallak's (1994) survey revealed that 82% of the respondents used patient self-report outcomes data.

Using patient self-report data may be viewed with suspicion by some (Strupp, 1996). These suspicions may be based on the potential problems just mentioned (see Bieber et al., 1999) or others. This author has personally witnessed the rejection of outcomes information that contradicted staff impressions, just because it was based on patient self-report data. The implication was that such data is not valid. Generally, such concerns are not justified. As Strupp has noted,

> Patients may exaggerate benefits [of treatment] or distort their recollections in other ways, but unless they are considered delusional, there seems to be no reason for questioning their reports. To be sure, one would like to obtain collateral information from therapists, clinical evaluators, significant others, as well as standardized tests, but the information from collateral sources is intrinsically no more valid than the patients' self-reports. None the less, society is biased in favor of "objective" data and skeptical of "subjective data." (p. 1022)

Collateral Sources.   Other types of data gathering tools may be substituted for self-report measures. Rating scales completed by the clinician or other members of the treatment staff may provide information that is as useful as that elicited directly from the patient. Use of observer ratings for outcomes data was reported by 39% of Pallak's (1994) survey respondents. In those cases in which the patient is severely disturbed, unable to give valid and reliable answers (e.g., younger children), unable to read or is an otherwise inappropriate candidate for a self-report measure, clinical rating scales can serve as a valuable substitute for gathering information about the patient. Related to these clinical rating instruments are parent-completed inventories for child and adolescent patients. These are particularly useful in obtaining information about the behavior of children or adolescents that might not otherwise be known. Information might also be obtained from other patient collaterals, such as siblings, spouses, teachers, coworkers, employers, and (in some cases) the justice system, all of which can be valuable by itself or in combination with other information.

Administrative Data.   Another potential source of outcomes information is administrative data. In many of the larger organizations, this information can easily be retrieved through the organization's claims and authorization databases, data repositories and warehouses, and other databases that make up the MBHO's management information system (MIS). Data related to the patient's diagnosis, dose and regimen of medication, physical findings, course of treatment, resource utilization, rehospitalization during a specific period of time, treatment costs, and other types of data typically stored in these systems can be useful in evaluating the outcomes of therapeutic intervention. Thirty-nine percent of those responding to Pallak's (1994) survey reported the use of medical record reviews.

Multiple Sources. Many would agree that the ideal approach for gathering outcomes data would be to use multiple sources (Berman et al., 1998; Bieber et al., 1999; Lambert & Lambert, 1999; Strupp, 1996). Indeed, outcomes information based on data obtained from patients, collaterals, and administrative sources can provide enhanced insights into the effectiveness of the services offered by MBHOs. They also may facilitate the identification of root causes of problems within the treatment system. Inherent in this approach, however, are increased costs and the potential for contradictory information and concomitant questions about how to proceed when contradictions occur. As Lambert and Lambert point out, "The data generated from these viewpoints are always subject to the limitations inherent in the methodology; none is 'objective' or most authoritative" (p. 116). Berman et al. (1998) have suggested that the potential for this type of problem can be reduced by specifying at the outset which outcomes measure(s) will be given the most consideration. Yet, this tact is not likely to completely eliminate issues that may arise from conflicting data. One therefore must be prepared with other approaches to resolving contradictory information that make sense from the perspective of the MBHO.

Who to Measure

Among the many issues related to how one might assess outcomes is the matter of which patients to assess. On the surface, this appears to be another "no-brainer." One would want include all patients receiving services through the MBHO to ensure an accurate presentation of the outcomes of those services. In most instances this is idealistic but not very practical.

Who to Include. Including all patient groups receiving services can present a number of problems. First and foremost is determining which outcomes indicators should be followed and which measures to use for the patient population in question. For example, imagine trying to design and implement an outcomes program that includes change in level of symptomatology as an outcomes measure for all patients groups—children, adolescents, adults, and geriatric patients. The "appropriate" types of symptomatology that would be measured and the instrumentation that would be used for this purpose would be different for each of these age populations. Thus, it would be necessary to acquire and train staff in the use of several age-appropriate measures and implementation procedures. This would increase the burden placed on the system and lessen the probability of establishing and maintaining a successful outcomes system.

Depending on the MBHO or provider setting, similar problems might be encountered as a result of ignoring other potentially complicating or confounding subpopulations based on other demographic or clinical variables (e.g., including all diagnostic groups). This is not to say that an outcomes system should not try to address the needs of all of the types of patients served by the MBHO. Rather, as will be discussed further in chapter 7, trying to measure the outcomes of all services to all patients at the same time will be difficult, and in at least the earlier stages of implementation, it will decrease the chances of establishing and maintaining a successful outcomes assessment system. Accomplishing such a goal would not be impossible, but it would be easier to begin small and measure only one or a few subpopulations on a limited number of outcomes variables. As success is achieved, the system can be expanded to include other subpopulations.

How Many to Include. Once a decision is made about whom to measure, the next question becomes how many of the targeted patient groups should be assessed during any given measurement cycle. Ideally, one would want to assess every patient (Docherty & Streeter, 1996; McLellan & Durell, 1996), but this becomes increasingly problematic from the standpoints of costs, labor, and logistics as the number of patients within an MBHO increases. This is particularly the case when one or more posttreatment follow-up assessments are included in the methodology. The alternative here is to use a sample of the each selected group of patients. In fact, using a sample may be preferable, assuming the sample is representative of the target group. It allows for more intensive efforts at obtaining follow-up data, thus reducing the chances of patient self-selection. Moreover, it provides as same information that would be obtained from all patients in the group under investigation.

Berman and Hurt (1996) provide some general guidelines for how many patients should be assessed:

> The number of cases you need to study depends on how you will be using the outcomes data. For provider profiling, one needs at least 20 diagnostically homogeneous patients per clinican to get stable change data. In heterogeneous populations, another order of magnitude is indicated. In facility benchmarking, a random sampling of at least 300 cases per facility is minimum. If quality improvement is the intent, then 12 to 20 cases per predictor variable (or per category) within each setting is a minimum number. If disease management is the goal, 100 percent of the target cases is optimmal, unless there is a very large sample. (p. 41)

One should consult with a statistician to determine the minimum acceptable sample size for his particular setting and needs.

Berman and Hurt (1996) go on to suggest several target goals for data collection. For instance, within 6 months of implementation, one should be obtaining data from 90% of the patient population at baseline and, for those still in treatment, 70% at later points in time. For clinician-reported data, one should strive for 100% at baseline and 95% at later points during the episode of care. Completion rates for posttreatment follow-up assessments should be around 50% during the first year of the outcomes system's implementation, and in the 50% to 70% range thereafter.

WHEN TO MEASURE

There are no hard and fast rules or widely accepted conventions related to when outcomes should be measured. The common practice is to assess the patient at least at treatment initiation, and then again at termination/discharge. Obviously, at the beginning of treatment, the clinician should obtain a baseline measure of whatever variables will be measured at termination of treatment. The problem with relying solely on this approach is that sometimes the time at which treatment ends is unpredictable (Lyons et al., 1997). Patients may end treatment abruptly with no warning, or treatment may run indefinite lengths of time. Either circumstance can make self-report data difficult to obtain. However, there are solutions to this problem.

Measurement can take place at other points in time, that is, during treatment and upon postdischarge follow-up. Sperry et al. (1996) recommend what they refer to as *concurrent outcomes measurement*. This is similar to what this author previously referred to as "outcomes monitoring" in chapter 2. Here, outcomes are measured at various points during the course of the treatment. This has the advantage of not only gathering outcomes information, but also providing feedback to the clinician regarding the effect of the treatment. As Sperry et al. point out, the common pre–post treatment assessment methodology provides feedback only after treatment has been completed. This approach provides no information that can be of use for particular patient currently undergoing treatment.

This still raises the issue of when to assess outcomes. Should it be done based on the number of sessions that have been completed (e.g., every third session), or at specific points in times from the date of treatment initiation (e.g., every fourth week)? And how many times should a patient be asked to complete an outcomes protocol? With regard to the first issue, Berman et al. (1996) argue for the "time-from-initial-contact model" over the "session model." This permits the gathering of meaningful data in MBHOs that treat patients at multiple levels of care. It eliminates issues relating to equating such things as number of outpatient sessions to number of inpatient or partial hospitalization days, for example, in terms of likely benefit to the patient. The time-from-initial-contact method also allows for meaningful data gathering posttreatment, since there is no session that can be used to gauge the next time of measurement once treatment has been terminated.

Many would argue that postdischarge/posttermination follow-up assessment provides the best or most important indication of the outcomes of therapeutic intervention. Two types of comparisons may be made on follow-up. The first is a comparison of the patient's status on the variables of interest—either at the time of treatment initiation or at the time of discharge or termination—to that of the patient at the time of follow-up assessment. Either way, this follow-up data will provide an indication of the more *lasting* effects of the intervention. Generally, the variables of interest for this type of comparison include symptom presence and intensity, feelings of well-being, frequency of substance use, and social or role functioning. The question here has to do with how long after discharge should follow-up assessment take place. There are varying thoughts on this matter. Berman et al. (1996) point out that there is no specific time frame for outcomes measurement. Rather, it will depend on the population being measured and the type, modality, and goals of the treatment. Consistent with this line of thinking, McLellan and Durell (1996) suggest that follow-up for inpatients should take place 2 to 4 weeks after discharge while outpatient follow-up should take place at either 3, 6, or 12 months posttermination. In general, this author recommends that postdischarge outcomes assessment probably should take place no sooner than one month after treatment has ended, regardless of the patient's last level of care. When feasible, waiting three to six months to assess the variables of interest is preferred when the last level of care was outpatient treatment.

The second type of posttreatment investigation involves comparing the frequency or severity of some aspect(s) of the patient's life circumstances, behavior or functioning which occurred during an interval of time prior to treatment, to that which occurred during an equivalent interval of time immediately following following termination. This methodology is commonly used in determining the medical cost-offset benefits of treatment and requires a different approach to the timing of follow-up assessments. Assessments being conducted to determine the frequency at which some behavior or event occurs (as may be needed to determine cost-offset benefits) should be administered no sooner than the reference time interval used in the baseline assessment. For example, suppose that the patient reports 10 emergency room visits during the 3-month period prior to treatment. If one wants to know if the patient's emergency room visits have decreased after treatment, the assessment cannot take place any earlier or later than 3 months after treatment termination. Not only can this provide an indication of the degree to which treatment has helped the patient deal with his problems, it also can demonstrate how much medical expenses have been reduced through the patient's decreased use of costly emergency room services.

A final issue related to the "when" of measurement has to do with the number of times one imposes upon the patient to complete the outcomes instruments. As Lyons et al. (1997) have astutely observed:

> Measurement at multiple time points is desirable in theory; however, in practice, each additional assessment further burdens respondents, potentially jeopardizes compliance, and complicates data management. Therefore, the coordinator of the outcomes measurement must successfully balance the information needs with the respondent's capacity to complete the assessment accurately and reliably. (p. 41)

One solution they offer is to incorporate the outcomes protocol into the routine assessment activities that normally take place during the course of treatment. This will have the effect of being perceived as the MBHO's standard practice, not as something extra the patient is asked to do.

HOW TO ANALYZE OUTCOMES DATA

An often overlooked consideration, or one that is commonly assigned secondary importance in the up-front planning for an outcomes assessment program is how to analyze the outcomes data. It is easy to view this as a back-end task that can be dealt with later. The fact is, decisions about how one plans to analyze outcomes data can have a significant impact on many of the considerations discussed earlier. Using an air travel analogy, this author has heard one statistical consultant say many times, "If you want me there for the landing, I need to be there for the takeoff." Not having a decision about how data are going to be analyzed before implementation of the outcomes system can have disastrous consequences later on.

The questions that the gathered data are intended to answer will drive the types of analyses to be performed. These analyses can be nothing more than a simple presentation of mean scores or percentages that are trended over time, to the calculation inferential statistics which examine the significance of changes in the data from one measurement period to the next. It may also involve more sophisticated statistical procedures, such as risk or case-mix adjustment of the data for provider rankings or predictive modeling for identifying at-risk patients. Again, the analyses should be appropriate to the questions that the system is designed to answer. Knowing what types of analyses need to be conducted may have a huge bearing on what data is collected, how it is collected, and when it is collected.

Comparison to a Standard

Generally, there are two common approaches to analyzing outcomes data. The first is to compare the results to some standard. Falling short of the standard would indicate the need for some form of intervention. In a CQI model, this would be followed by remeasurement after the intervention has had ample time to cause an effect. Meeting or surpassing the chosen standard presents a couple of options. One is continue with the standard processes of care (i.e., "If it's not broken, don't fix it"). The other option embraces the spirit of CQI by working toward surpassing the current standard. Again, efforts toward improvement are implemented and the results are re-evaluated later.

Taking the route of comparing against some standard or set of standards begs the question of which standard to employ. But even before that, one must decide which *type* of standard best meets the needs of their outcomes system. There are a few options here, each with its own set of advantages and drawbacks.

Industry Standards and Benchmarks. The HEDIS, PERMS, and other published data sets can provide valuable information about the success other MBHOs have achieved on standard performance measures. Use of this information in this way is referred to as *benchmarking*, "an ongoing process of comparing [an] organization's performance on services, practices, and outcomes with some identified standard, such as . . . competitors' performance" (Christner, 1977, p. 2). Benchmarking allows the MBHO and other stakeholders to see how the MBHO compares to similar organizations. Use of benchmarks can serve as a powerful marketing tool, particularly when the organization is outperforming its competitors. More importantly, positive findings can show the organization that it is on track for providing the highest quality of care available. Of course, performing below the industry standard may have negative effects on growing the MBHO's business; on the other hand, it can also identify areas in which improvement is needed.

The downside here is that performance measures on which industry-wide data is available are not always what the MBHO or its stakeholder feel are most important or relevant to the care of their patients. For example, NCQA's HEDIS measures include the following:

- Mental health utilization—inpatient discharges and average length of stay
- Chemical dependency utilization—inpatient discharges and average length of stay
- Antidepressant medication management

Among the AMBHA's PERMS 2.0 measures are the following:

- 30-, 90-, and 365-day readmission rates for mental health
- 30-, 90-, and 365-day readmission rates for substance abuse
- Availability of psychotherapy and/or medication management for patients with schizophrenia
- Family visits for children undergoing mental health treatment

Note that for the most part, these data sets (and others like them) actually report performance on structure and process measures, not outcomes measures. However, this does not limit their utility in an outcomes management program. As Aday, Begley, Lairson, Slater, Richard, and Montoya (1999) have pointed out, "structure elements of healthcare influence what is and is not done in the process, in addition to how well it is done. This process in turn influences the outcome . . . that people experience as a result of their encounters with the process" (p. SP32).

Organizational Performance Goals.   In many MBHOs, the standard that is used is set by the organization itself. To some degree, it probably will be based on a combination of what the industry standard is and what the MBHO sees as being realistic given the people it serves, the resources available, expectations from stakeholders, accreditation and regulatory requirements, and whatever other demands it must meet to remain successful and solvent. It is not unusual for MBHOs to set a performance goal which, based on baseline data, is well within reach of the organization. Once reached and maintained for a reasonable period, the goal is raised and the organization is once again challenged to improve its performance, and so on. This has the effect of rewarding staff with a sense of accomplishment and success, thus reinforcing continued efforts toward quality improvement and moving the organization toward the ultimate goal for the measure in question.

Normative and Risk-Adjusted Data.   Population-specific data can serve as yet another standard against which to compare performance. This approach is somewhat similar to a comparison to benchmark or industry standards. The major difference is that it relies on data that are more specific to different types of patient populations and the characteristics that distinguish them from other populations. Standardized normative data that typically accompanies published psychological tests is a good example. These data permit a fair comparison of groups of patients with like groups of patients, thus eliminating some of the potential effects of confounding variables. Many of these measures also have nonpatient normative data that also can be a useful (perhaps the most useful) source of comparison information since they provide a means of tracking patients' progress toward recovery on the variable(s) of interest.

Frequently, appropriate standardized, population-specific comparison data are not available for the outcomes variables that are important to the MBHO. In these situations, *risk adjustment* procedures are frequently used to allow fair comparisons among different groups of patients. Simply put, risk adjustment generally refers to a statistical process that "corrects results for differences in a population with respect to patient mix, allowing for more valid comparisons across groups" (Bieber et al., 1999, p. 174). Adjustment of outcomes measures based on differences on nontreatment variables that have an effect on outcomes of treatment, has the effect of "leveling the playing field" and thus helps ensure that any differences that do exist between groups are related to the quality of care they receive. Berman at al. (1996, 1998) have identified several general domains that should be included as variables in risk adjustment procedures. These include patient demographic characteristics (e.g. age, sex), clinical characteristics (e.g., symptom severity at the initiation of treatment, dual diagnosis of mental health and substance abuse disorders), and the psychosocial context of the disorder (e.g., social support, employment). The reporting of risk-adjusted data is rapidly becoming the standard for conveying outcomes data.

Determination of Amount and Type of Change

The other common approach is to determine if a patient or a group of patients have changed on one or more outcomes variables from one point in time to another as a result of therapeutic intervention. If there has been change, one also wants to know how much. This represents an approach that is probably more in line with the training of behavioral scientists and thus is likely to be much more appealing than making comparisons to some standard.

Changes in Individual Patients.   There are two general approaches to the analysis of treatment of individual patient outcomes data. The first is by determining whether changes in patient scores on outcomes measures are *statistically significant*. The other is by establishing whether these changes are *clinically significant*. The issue of clinical significance has received a great deal of attention in psychotherapy research during the past several years. This is at least partially due to the work of Jacobson and his colleagues (Jacobson, Follette, & Revenstorf, 1984, 1986; Jacobson & Truax, 1991) and others (e.g., Christensen & Mendoza, 1986; Speer, 1992; Wampold & Jenson, 1986). Their work came at a time when researchers began to recognize that traditional statistical comparisons do not reveal a great deal about the efficacy of therapy.

Jacobson and Truax (1991) broadly define the clinical significance of treatment as "its ability to meet standards of efficacy set by consumers, clinicians, and researchers" (p. 12). Further, they noted that:

> While there is little consensus in the field regarding what these standards should be, various criteria have been suggested: a high percentage of clients improving . . . ; a level of change that is recognizable by peers and significant others . . . ; an elimination of the presenting problem . . . ; normative levels of functioning at the end of therapy . . . ; high end-state functioning at the end of therapy . . . ; or changes that significantly reduce one's risk for various health problems. (p. 12)

From their perspective, Jacobson and his colleagues (Jacobson & Truax, 1991; Jacobson et al., 1984) felt that clinically significant change could be conceptualized in one of three ways. Thus, for clinically significant change to have occurred, the measured level of functioning following the therapeutic episode would have to either (a) fall outside the range of the dysfunctional population by at least two standard deviations from the mean of that population, in the direction of functionality; (b) fall within two standard deviations of the mean for the normal or functional population; or (c) be closer to the mean of the functional population than to that of the dysfunctional population. Jacobson and Truax viewed the third option (c) as being the least arbitrary, and they provided different recommendations for determining cutoffs for clinically significant change, depending upon the availability of normative data.

At the same time, these same investigators noted the importance of considering the change in the measured variables of interest from pre- to posttreatment *in addition to* the patient's functional status at the end of therapy. To this end, Jacobson et al. (1984) proposed the concomitant use of a reliable change index (RCI) to determine whether change is clinically significant. This index, modified on the recommendation of Christensen and Mendoza (1986), is nothing more than the pretest score minus the posttest score divided by the standard error of the difference of the two scores.

There are other approaches to analyzing individual patient data for clinically significant change. Excellent discussions of the RCI and some of these methods can be found in Hsu (1996, 1999), Jacobson, Roberts, Berns, and McGlinchey (1999), Kazdin (1999), Saunders, Howard, and Newman (1988), and Speer and Greenbaum (1995). Interested readers are encouraged to review these and other articles on the topic before deciding which approach to determining clinically significant change is best suited for their particular outcomes assessment system.

Changes in Groups of Patients.   Changes in groups of patients from one point in time to the next has typically been examined through the use of any of a number of tests of statistical differences in mean scores. This is generally quite appropriate and not likely to draw much criticism (assuming the most appropriate test for the data has been employed). Although it may be important to know that a real change in a sample or population has taken place, these types of tests do not provide any indication of the magnitude of that change. For example, one cannot infer that a difference at the .001 level is of a greater magnitude than one at the .005 level; all that can be said is that the chances that a real difference occurs are much greater when the .001 significance level is reached than they are when the significance level is .005.

To answer questions related to the magnitude of change, behavioral (and medical) health care researchers are turning more to employing statistics to measure *effect size*. Effect size can be defined as a "standardized measure of change in a group or a difference in changes between two groups" (Kazis, Anderson, & Meenan, 1989). It is typically computed by dividing the difference between the pre- and posttreatment means by the pretreatment standard deviation (of $ES = [m_1 - m_2 / s_1]$). Cohen (1988) interprets ES values of less than 0.1 as indicating a trivial or no effect; 0.1–0.3 as indicating a small effect; 0.3–0.5, a moderate effect; and greater than 0.5, a large effect. Note that others advocate for other magnitude cutoffs (for example, see Hopkins, 1997). Regardless, as Kazis et al. point out, effect sizes provide for a more interpretable measure of change and allow for comparison of differences on different measures within or between outcomes systems.

Another approach would be to analyze the data using both effect size and significance test methods. This is being seen more frequently in the published literature. Doing so would not require significantly more effort beyond that for one or the other method, and it would satisfy the needs of all stakeholders and other interested parties.

REPORTING OF OUTCOMES DATA

Another often overlooked or neglected aspect of an outcomes system is how the outcomes findings and related data will be reported. Reporting is an important part of any outcomes assessment program. It is the vehicle by which feedback about CQI and other improvement interventions is conveyed and on which judgments about "next steps" are made. It is critical for ensuring that effort toward improving the quality of health care—behavioral or otherwise—is having an effect, and therefore warrants due consideration.

Intent of the Report

The first issue to consider in making decisions about outcomes reporting is what is the intent of the report. This should be a relatively easy decision if one has taken the time to define the purpose of the outcomes system and what questions it is supposed to answer. Of course, there may be multiple reasons for initiating the system and multiple questions that need to be answered, and trying to address all questions and matters of interest may be problematic from a reporting standpoint. The amount of available information also may be problematic. Too much information may be burdensome to the reader and detract from the conveyance of what is really important. The issue then becomes one of determining which information is considered primary, which is secondary, and so forth, and how much information can really be showcased and remain meaningful.

Intended Audience

Just as important as the intent of the report is who the report will be directed to. Often, these two factors go hand in hand. The stakeholders will most certainly have had say in defining the purpose of the outcomes system, and they will be the primary recipients of the outcomes information. Problems may arise when the needs of more than one stakeholder must be met. One solution to this problem is to develop different reports for the different stakeholders. A good example of this is the development of both a score card and a report card to distribute the outcomes information. The score card would be used to convey information that is most important to the MBHO's senior management, while the report card would be distributed to patients, payers, providers, and/or other third parties with a vested interest in the MBHO's quality improvement program.

How to Report the Data

How outcomes information is reported depends largely on the intended audience. Different audiences will have different levels of comprehension and different preferences for how they would like to see the information presented. For instance, for MBHO administrative or other internal uses, tabular reporting of outcomes data may be preferable to reporting via the use of pie charts, histograms, cumulative frequency curves, or other graphic forms of data presentation. Conversely, stakeholders such as patients, payers, and employers may find it easier to interpret the data if they are graphically presented. The use of color and other eye-catching graphics would certainly be the choice in sales presentations or when the data is presented for other marketing purposes.

When to Report

The frequency at which outcome data is reported may depend on several variables. The first has to do with the time intervals for which aspects of the selected outcomes variables are considered. For example, the outcomes instrumentation may contain items or entire scales that ask the patient to report how frequently he has been bothered by certain symptoms, engaged in specific behaviors or cognitions, or felt a certain way *during a specific time period*. With these types of measures, it does not make sense to gather, much less report data any more frequently than the interval of time that the patient must consider in responding to the questions. Doing so results in overlapping reporting periods for the measured outcomes variables. If an intervention has been initiated during the period of overlap, the meaning of the results of *both* periods becomes muddied to the point of uselessness.

Related to this issue is the minimum amount of time one would expect an intervention must have in order to begin to have an effect on the variable of interest. For example, reporting outcomes data on patients receiving outpatient substance abuse treatment on a weekly basis may not allow enough time to plan and implement an intervention, and allow that intervention to have an effect and show results during the next reporting period. Similarly, efforts to bring down 30-day readmission rates for psychiatric inpatients (a frequently reported outcomes measure) would not be served by monthly outcomes reporting. Instead, quarterly or semi-annual reporting would allow the MBHO or clinician enough time to receive and evaluate outcomes data from the previous reporting period, develop and implement a plan of intervention (e.g., ensure the patient has an ambulatory follow-up appointment scheduled to occur within 7 days of the discharge date; see Nelson, Maruish, & Axler, 2000), and then determine the effects of that intervention on the re-admission rate for the current reporting period.

One or more stakeholders or other third parties may dictate the reporting cycle. For example, payers may wish to see data on their covered lives on a monthly basis, regardless of the whether this presents any meaningful information. Accreditation organizations such a JCAHO and NCQA may request data on an annual basis, even though more frequent reporting would be much more useful to the MBHO or its providers. This latter situation is less problematic because more frequent reporting can take place in addition to the required interval of reporting.

Finally, measuring, processing, analyzing, and reporting outcomes all have a cost in terms of the materials, equipment, and manpower that are required for these tasks. Thus, the resources that are available to the MBHO will limit the frequency of reporting. In some settings, adequate resources may be allocated for quarterly measurement and reporting; in others, the resources may permit only annual measurement and reporting. Other things being equal, the amount of resources that are dedicated to these activities generally is a good indication of the organization's commitment to the outcomes initiative.

What to Do With the Information

It is important to specify how the outcomes results can be or will be used to improve the quality of the MBHO's services. After all, this is where the rubber meets the road. One needs to have at least some general ideas of what actions should be taken when the need for service-related improvements is indicated. Information related to the clinical and/or nonclinical aspects of the MBHO's services is nice to know, but it becomes meaningless and a waste of time, effort, and money if nothing is done with it. This means a willingness to make changes, including changes in treatment, based on findings from the data. Whether this involves the integration of disorder-specific guidelines or something more generally applicable, the challenge may frequently be to get care providers to do things differently from the way they usually do them. The MBHO should have an idea of what will need to be done—and have a commitment to act on it—before getting started.

HOW TO USE OUTCOMES INFORMATION

Having outcomes information is one thing; doing something with it is another. One can dedicate a large amount of money and other expensive resources to build an elaborate outcomes assessment system that yields important and useful information. But if this information is not used, or not used to its fullest potential, the system may quickly become a white elephant on its way to an untimely death.

Common reasons for developing and implementing an outcomes system within an MBHO were discussed earlier in this chapter. Any one of these could be a primary, or an important secondary reason why a particular MBHO is interested in and therefore seeks to obtain outcomes information. The question here has to do with what must be done with the information that is produced by the outcomes system in order to fulfill the purpose(s) for which the system was created. Table 6.3 presents examples

TABLE 6.3
Examples of Ways to Use Outcomes Information
to Achieve the Purpose of the Outcomes System

Reason for Assessing Outcomes	What to Do With Outcomes Information
Determine outcomes of treatment	• Determine quality of services provided to MBHO's clientele • Determine what works best for whom
Assist in clinical decision-making	• Provide information to clinicians on a timely basis for treatment planning and monitoring
Develop guidelines for treatment	• Determine what aspects of care have the most impact on producing positive outcomes
Develop predictive models	• Develop algorithms for predicting length of treatment, most appropriate treatment, amount of recovery • Use predictive models for monitoring patients along the projected path of recovery
Develop a provider profiling system	• Identify the most effective providers and reward their performance • Identify the least effective providers and provide remediation • Identify types of patients with whom providers are most effective and make referrals accordingly
Support CQI efforts	• Identify opportunities for improvement within the MBHO • Provide feedback about current status of an aspect of care targeted for performance improvement • Provide feedback about the effects of interventions made to improve performance
Fulfill regulatory and accreditation requirements	• Use the data to support NCQA/JCAHO quality improvement studies that are required for accreditation or reaccreditation • Use data to fulfill state and federal regulatory requirements
Generate score cards	• Use trended data on important performance measures to demonstrate to the MBHO upper management the effectiveness of services provided to health plan members over time
Generate report cards	• Compare the MBHO's data for standard performance measures with those of other MBHOs
Support other marketing efforts	• Combine with financial information to determine cost savings and cost offset of behavioral health care services

of ways in which the information can be use to support each of the previously identified common reasons for conducting a program of ongoing outcomes assessment.

The list presented in Table 6.3 is by no means exhaustive. It does help to under-
score the need to decide exactly how the resulting information can provide the support for and justify the time, effort, and money that is needed to maintain the outcomes system. It also should lead one to question whether the amount and type of
data that the planned outcomes system would yield, would indeed serve the intended purpose(s) of the system. If not, one would need to reconsider and perhaps
modify previous decisions related to the who, what, when, and how of the planned
measurement activity.

SUMMARY

Increasingly, MBHOs are responding to demands for the measurement of treatment
outcomes being voiced by stakeholders in patients' care. This has been reinforced by
other factors that are driving all types of businesses in this new millenium. MBHOs
are using outcomes information to support clinical and nonclinical aspects of their
operations and to answer specific questions related to how to improve the quality of
the services they offer.

Designing a system to obtain and report outcomes information in any MBHO is
not a simple task. Those responsible for their organization's outcomes assessment
system have a number of issues that should be decided upon before detailed plans
for actual implementation are made. Questions related to who, what, how, and when
to measure, as well as how to analyze and report the data are all important. Equally
important are the questions of if and how the outcomes information can support the
intended purpose of the system. Answers to these questions will bear directly upon
the success of the system. Leaving any of these questions without a well thought out
answer will have negative if not disastrous effects, possibly to the point of making
the system effectively worthless.

7

Implementing Test-Based Outcomes Assessment Systems

As chapter 6 showed, developing a useful outcomes assessment system requires careful consideration of many basic but often overlooked issues that are critical to its success. Arriving at the final look and feel of the system can be a long, arduous and frequently stressful undertaking. If done properly, however, it can yield a great pay-off in terms of the information it will yield and the savings from the wasted effort that otherwise would result from poor planning. But deciding on who, what, when and how to measure, as well as how to use the resulting information, is only half the battle. The program must be implemented. One must now begin the task of developing the structure and processes for gathering, transmitting, storing, processing, analyzing, and reporting outcomes data and information. Issues related to the implementation of the system into the MBHO's daily operations warrant at least the same careful consideration that is afforded to the design of the system. Whereas design flaws limit the amount of useful information, flaws and oversights in the implementation plan can cause the system to crash, yielding *no* useful information. Instead, time, effort, and resources are wasted, and the credibility of the responsible party may be lessened or lost.

Along with addressing these issues, many MBHOs have yet another major challenge to face: implementation of the outcomes initiative across multiple systems of providers and facilities. Anyone who has been involved in the implementation of even *small*, ongoing data gathering efforts knows that this can be a tremendous undertaking. Now consider doing this in a large system—on a scale possibly involving tens of thousands of providers from several provider networks scattered throughout the United States! Needless to say, a carefully thought-out plan for implementing an outcomes program across the MBHO provider system must be developed if the system is to become fully operational and provide useful information.

This chapter will focus on the most important issues related to the implementation of outcomes systems within MBHO systems. Attention is given to matters that will bear directly upon the success of the implementation process, which in turn will directly bear on the probability that the outcomes assessment system will be successful.

Because of this, the approach here will be more directive than that taken in the previous chapter.

EVALUATE THE MBHO'S READINESS TO MOVE FORWARD

Prior to actually beginning to work on a plan to implement an outcomes system, it is important to make sure MBHO is ready to proceed with what can be a long, challenging process that will undoubtedly involve a series of obstacles that must be overcome. This is the reality of this type of endeavor—one that cannot be escaped. At the same time, there are many things that can be done to make the implementation of the system proceed on as smooth and steady a course as is possible. The first step is to determine how prepared the MBHO is to proceed in the process. Information obtained at this point can help the MBHO move through each of the stages of preparation for launching the system that are discussed below.

Evaluate the Basic Design of the System

Chapter 6 presented many issues related to the basic design of the system. It is important that at least tentative decisions regarding these few but very important matters have been reached by those leading the effort toward establishing an outcomes system in the MBHO. Thus, there should be at least a general idea of, and consensus among those spearheading the outcomes effort on:

- What questions will be answered by the outcomes data.
- What will be measured (e.g., symptomatology, functionality).
- Who will be measured (e.g., all patients, specific diagnostic groups).
- How it will be measured (e.g., claims data, patient-self-report data, staff rating).
- When it will be measured (e.g., termination, 6 months posttermination).
- How the data will be analyzed (e.g., comparison against benchmarks, tests of significance).
- How the results of the analyses will be presented to answer the questions being asked (e.g., comparison against a benchmark, case-mix adjustment results)
- How the information will be used (e.g., feedback to staff for CQI projects, development and application of predictive modeling).

Verifying that these issues are indeed resolved to the satisfaction of all stakeholders in outcomes initiative and to others who have been involved up to this point is an important step that should take place before proceding further. Uncertainty or confusion over any of these matters can have deleterious consequences later on. Thus, it is worthwhile to take the time to take one last look at the decisions related to them.

Evaluate Organizational Readiness for the System

Initiating an outcomes assessment program in any MBHO or other behavioral health care setting can be a tremendous undertaking from many perspectives. At the very least, it necessitates change. This, in turn, can (and frequently does) evoke a variety of reactions, ranging from curiosity and doubt, to feelings of anxiety and fear, to subtle or overt oppositional behavior. It therefore becomes important to take stock of the MBHO as a whole, as well as those aspects that are particularly relevant to the ability to successfully implement an outcomes program, in preparation of actually putting together the nuts and bolts of the system.

Wetzler (1994) has identified five broad factors that health care organizations should consider when assessing itself in preparation of the initiation of an outcomes management system. The first factor to consider is the *institutional environment*. This refers to the size and type of the organization, how its governance is structured, and relevant external factors, such as the penetration of managed care in the community it serves. The second factor is the organization's *leadership*. Third, assessment of the organization's *information and analysis capacities* is extremely important as one considers the implementation of a highly data- and information-dependent initiative such as an outcomes assessment program. The fourth factor is the *resources* that are or will be available to support the program. The last factor is the current activities that can serve as *leverage* in the implementation and ongoing maintenance of the outcomes program. Wetzler also has identified several aspects within each of these five factors that deserve particular attention. Table 7.1 presents the five factors and each of their associated aspects. Also presented are representative questions that might be asked in assessing each one. Many of the organizational aspects listed in Table 7.1 are considered especially important by this author and will be given due attention in the sections that follow.

Determine How to Evaluate the Success of the System

As has been previously stated, there are many aspects of an outcomes assessment system that can be neglected in its planning stages. An easily overlooked but extremely important facet of any outcomes program is the method by which the program will be evaluated. In other words, how can the MBHO tell if the program is successful? Perhaps the issue is even more basic than "how." The idea of conducting an

TABLE 7.1
Factors to Consider in Evaluating Organizational Readiness
to Implement an Outcomes Assessment Program

General Factor	Aspects of the General Factor	Representative Question to Ask
Institutional environment	Commitment to quality	Is a commitment to quality evident throughout the MBHO?
	Appreciation of health care as a science and an art	Is the application of scientific principles evident in the MBHO?
	Willingness to entertain new ideas	Is the MBHO open to new opportunities and trying new ideas?
	Willingness to take risks	Are the MBHO and its employees willing to take risks?
	Level of fear	Does fear of reprisal for mistakes impede learning and seeking alternate solutions?
	Appreciation of the consumer's perspective	Does the MBHO listen to and educate its customers?
	Degree to which learning is fostered	Does the MBHO learn from its staff and its patients?

(Continued)

TABLE 7.1
(Continued)

General Factor	Aspects of the General Factor	Representative Question to Ask
Leadership	One respected person willing to lead	Is there a respected person who is willing to lead the outcomes program?
	Organizational goal of outcomes management	Is the MBHO willing to adopt outcomes management as an organizational goal?
	Others willing to participate in the program	Is there other staff willing to participate in the program?
	Commitment of senior management	Is senior management 100% behind the outcomes program?
Information and analysis capacities	Availability of measurement instruments	Are appropriate outcomes measurement instruments available, or do they have to be developed?
	Ability to develop and implement data collection methodology	Can the MBHO adapt existing procedures to meet the demands of collecting outcomes data?
	Availability of statistical expertise	Is a statistical consultant available?
	Decision makers comfortable using quantitative analyses	Will clinicians use the information provided by the outcomes system?
Resources	Management time	Does the outcomes manager have enough time to manage the system?
	Decision-makers' time	Do the MBHO's high-level decision-makers have enough time to make well thought out decisions about the outcomes program?
	Staff time	Does the MBHO's staff have the time and motivation needed to make the outcomes program a success?
	Hardware and software	Are adequate hardware and software available?
	Database development and data management	Are adequate database resources available?
	Statistical analysis	Is someone dedicated to perform the needed statistical analyses?
Leverage	Coordination with other quality initiatives	Are there other MBHO quality initiatives with which outcomes assessment can achieve synergy?
	Coordination with other research activities	Are there other MBHO research activities with which outcomes assessment can achieve synergy?
	Sharing of personnel and other resources	Can other MBHO resources be devoted to the outcomes program on a part-time basis?
	Participation in a multi-organizational consortium	Is there an opportunity for the MBHO to work cooperatively with other organizations on outcomes projects?

Note.   General factors and aspects of general factors are from Wetzler (1994).

evaluation of the system itself may not even be considered. But unless the MBHO's leaders are uninformed, it is highly unlikely that the issue will not be raised at some point. It therefore is important from the standpoints of practicality, accountability, and continuous quality improvement that a plan for evaluating the impact of the system on the MBHO be developed.

The success of an MBHO-based outcomes system can be determined in several different ways. One measure of the success would be its impact on the MBHO's bottom line. For example, outcomes information might result in savings by assisting in quickly determining the most appropriate level of care for a given patient; identifying the best type of treatment, thus eliminating wasteful, ineffective interventions; or determining the need for additional services beyond those initially authorized. Unfortunate as it might be, the degree to which the outcomes system financially impacts the MBHO may be what the organization views as the primary measure of the success of the system.

Of course, there are other (and to many, more meaningful) ways to evaluate the success of an outcomes assessment program. Each MBHO will have at least one, and probably multiple reasons for initiating an outcomes assessment system. Thus, evaluating the program against criteria directly related to the reason(s) for initiating a system of outcomes assessment in the first place is a logical way to proceed in determining the system's success. It speaks directly to providing justification for the system's existence and associated benefits as initially conceptualized. Taking this approach, the criteria selected to judge the success of the program would be specific to each MBHO. Table 7.2 presents some examples of criteria that might be used to evaluate outcomes systems, developed for each of the previously identified common reasons for initiating an outcomes program (see chapter 6). In the end, the set of criteria that is formally adopted may be that which the MBHO's management team dictates. However, this should not deter those spearheading the outcomes initiative from including additional criteria that would be useful from a CQI perspective.

Seek Feedback from Key MBHO Staff

At this point, those championing the outcomes initiative should be comfortable with the general plan for the proposed system. Now it would be beneficial to ask for feedback about the envisioned system from some of the key people in the organization. This might include the medical director, the quality improvement manager, one or more care managers, and even a few providers. Ideally, one would have sought input from these people during the project formulation phase, so there should be no major surprises now. But having a final round of input may prevent embarrassing moments when the plan is presented to the organization's decision-makers for approval.

SECURE SUPPORT AND COMMITMENT FOR THE OUTCOMES SYSTEM

Implementation of outcomes systems in any health care delivery system — regardless of its size and complexity — is not an easy task. Once the purpose or goal of the outcomes system is decided on, one of the biggest challenges facing the MBHO is getting all involved parties — from the organization's leadership to providers and their support staff — "on board" with the program. This can be quite difficult, and it will probably take a good deal of selling to get the type of commitment necessary to make the program work. All levels of the organization must be convinced that the outcomes system is going to result in changes that will somehow benefit patients and them-

TABLE 7.2
Examples of Criteria for Evaluating Outcomes Assessment Systems

Reason for Assessing Outcomes	Examples of Relevant Evaluation Criteria
Determine outcomes of treatment	• Level of psychological and social role functioning measured six months posttreatment termination • Amount of symptomatic change from the time of treatment initiation to treatment termination that can be considered statistically significant.
Assist in clinical decision-making	• Patient progress reports sent to providers within one day of patient's completion of outcomes instruments • Care managers use patient progress reports for treatment authorization and level of care decisions • Providers and/or care managers report patient progress reports facilitate the clinical decision-making process
Develop guidelines for treatment	• Outcomes-based treatment guidelines developed for one or more diagnostic groups • Existing treatment guidelines evaluated using outcomes information
Develop predictive models	• Statistical model for the prediction of length of stay/episode of care, developed from outcomes data, found to be accurate 85% of the time • Providers report usefulness of recovery curves in monitoring treatment over time
Develop a provider profiling system	• Generation of annual provider rankings based on risk-adjusted outcomes data • Provider rankings used to award "Preferred Provider" status to network clinicians
Support CQI efforts	• Outcomes information used in root cause analysis of poor patient satisfaction findings • Outcomes information used to identify specific areas of clinical care that present opportunities for improvement
Fulfill regulatory/accreditation requirements	• NCQA/JCAHO quality improvement standards met using outcomes data • QISMC Quality Assessment and Performance Improvement (QAPI) program (Domain 1) standards met
Generate score cards	• Quarterly outcomes score cards distributed to senior management • Outcomes score card information used to determine provider network training needs
Generate report cards	• Organization data presented with data from other MBHO outcomes consortium members on standard measures • Outcomes report card included in marketing and sales materials provided to potential customers
Support other marketing efforts	• Increased revenues attributable to outcomes information • Outcomes data included as part of the MBHO's annual report to shareholders

selves, either directly in their individual work or indirectly through the benefits that will accrue to the organization.

Support from the MBHO's Leadership

Perhaps the biggest challenge is "selling" the idea of a system for the measurement and management of treatment outcomes to the MBHO's leadership. Obtaining the support at this level is consistently identified as a necessary step in the implementation process (Bengen-Seltzer, 1999; Docherty & Dewan, 1995; Kraus & Horan, 1998; Ofstead, Gobran, & Lum, 2000; Wetzler, 1994). The leadership must be convinced that the benefits that will accrue to their organization will far outweigh the cost and other burdens that usually accompany these types of endeavors. They need to be sure that in the long run, they are doing the right thing for the organization, themselves, their staff, and of course, their patients.

Selling the System.   What are the key selling points of an outcomes system? These will vary from one MBHO to another, but are some general guidelines for identifying those aspects of the system that will help to sell it to the leadership. First, one should be prepared to present a well-thought-out vision of what the system will look like, what it will likely require in terms of initial and ongoing resources, and what the benefits will be for the MBHO. One should also be able to convey that this vision has been shared with and is supported by key members within the organization.

Second, money will be an issue. Being able to demonstrate cost savings or offset from delivering more effective and efficient services, increased business, etc., that will result from the implementation of the system will go a long way in obtaining the leadership's approval. In lieu of this, one should be able to provide cost projections that can be justified by the tangible and intangible benefits that will accrue to organization from the system.

A third selling point is related to the second. The costs that will be incurred can be tied to the reasons for which the proposed plan for an outcomes assessment was developed in the first place. For example, if the system will provide information that will meet JCAHO or NCQA requirements for outcomes measurement—requirements necessary for an accreditation status that is required in order to stay competitive in the marketplace—then this might be used to justify reasonable costs. Similarly, the score cards that can be generated from the outcomes data can provide the MBHO management with the opportunity to make more informed decisions about the organization.

Fourth, each MBHO is likely to have "hot buttons" that can serve as idiosyncratic selling points for the system. The key is to know what those buttons are and tie them into the system.

Selling the proposed outcomes system may not present much of a problem if the MBHO's leadership initiated the idea for its development (or exploration thereof) in the first place. Although in this instance one would be "preaching to the choir," it is likely that the proposed system will still be subject to scrutiny. Thus, use of one or more of the earlier selling points may be required.

Expressed Commitment to the Endeavor.   Being successful in obtaining the leadership's buy-in to the proposed system should involve more than just getting an "OK" to proceed with its development and implementation. One should also seek the leadership's commitment to the system and all that its implementation entails. A clear demonstration of this commitment is upper management's involvement in the project. As Bengen-Seltzer (1999) indicated,

> Leadership needs to demonstrate its commitment to the new outcomes system or measures in a tangible, proactive way that is hands-on and visible to the staff that will be using the system. It's not enough to make rhetorical statements or just provide fiscal sup-

port; leadership needs to be present at regular meetings and be part of the team that develops and refines the system. (p. 7)

The degree of involvement advocated by Bengen-Seltzer might be considered unrealistic in some MBHOs. However, there are other ways in which management can show its commitment. The first is through the funding that it is willing to budget for the program, both in the present fiscal year and the years that follow. Approval for hiring new employees to meet the staffing needs of the program, budgeting for the necessary computer equipment and software, and joining an MBHO consortium for pooling outcomes data can be very important signs of the leadership's commitment. It is also important to communicate this commitment to all levels of the organization. This should occur not only through the usual intraorganizational corporate channels but also through the leadership's acknowledgment of the program's importance to the MBHO in meetings with middle- and lower-level managers, in public forums, and during other appropriate opportunities.

Support from the Staff

Commitment from the leadership of the organization is critical to securing commitment from providers and other front line staff. However, it does not guarantee such commitment at the lower levels of the MBHO. Efforts must directed to all levels of staff to ensure that they too are committed to having a successful outcomes program.

Selling the System.   Provider, administrative, and support staff are likely to view the outcomes system as an added burden (Eisen, Leff, & Schaefer, 1999; Kraus & Horan, 1998; Wetzler, 1994). Thus, one should not be surprised by their resistance to the implementaion of an outcomes assessment system. Selling of the system should therefore begin by communicating to the staff the purpose of the system and potential benefits that can accrue to the MBHO and those who are involved in the system's implementation (Bieber et al., 1999). Also, inviting representatives of both the clinical and administrative staffs to become part of the decision-making process (e.g., as members of an implementation team) will get them involved in project, promote ownership of the system among them, and help sell the program to their peers.

In addition, several experts have provided suggestions as to how to bring the clinical provider staff on board and become supportive of the program. For example, Berman and Hurt (1996) recommend that the system be designed to study processes, and not people. That is, providers must know that the information obtained from the system will not be used by the MBHO to make personnel decisions. Also, ensuring that the system will provide immediate feedback about their patients and thus be useful in clinical decision-making, will increase the value of the system in their eyes. (This topic is discussed further in a later section of this chapter.) Bengen-Seltzer (1999) stresses the importance of making the system and its measures relevant to the clinician's daily practice, including measures of daily functioning as outcomes variables, having benchmark data available for comparison to external providers, and allowing the provider the opportunity to learn more about what works and what does not work through the outcomes data.

Selling the nonclinical administrative and support staff on how the system may benefit them may be a bit more difficult than selling the clinical provider staff. Here, the best one may be able to do is to actively seek their input at all points in the development and implementation process, minimize the burden placed on them by the system, and provide incentives or a means of showing appreciation for their efforts. Other strategies for selling the system to staff are presented later in a separate section below.

Expressed Commitment to the Endeavor. Unlike at the upper management and leadership levels, there is only a limited number of things the MBHO care provider and administrative/support staff can do to directly express their commitment to the implementation of an outcomes assessment system. Probably the most important show of commitment would be their involvement in the planning and feedback process for the system, particularly among those staff members who are respected by their peers, open to new ideas, and influential in generating excitement for new projects within the MBHO.

FORM AN OUTCOMES ASSESSMENT SYSTEM TEAM

The discussion and recommendations made thus far in this and the previous chapter have not been directed to anyone in particular in the MBHO or provider network. That is, they are intended for anyone who either is directed by the MBHO's leadership to investigate the possibility of establishing an outcomes assessment system, or has taken this initiative on their own, either alone or as part of a task force or work group. The efforts to this point may have been informal and the group (if more than one person) loosely organized. With the leadership's buy-in and commitment to a system of outcomes assessment, it is now important that a formal, empowered committee or team be assembled to the tackle the work that must be accomplished to launch the system and maintain it on an ongoing basis. Formation of such a team should be the first step that follows approval for the system.

The question of who or what functional positions should be on the team is relatively straightforward. It should include representatives of each functional unit of the MBHO or provider organization that will be impacted by the system. At the minimum, one would expect this to include a representative of the providers, administrative staff, receptionists, information system staff, statisticians, leadership, and, ideally, other stakeholders in the outcomes system, such patients, payers, and employers. The team should be large enough to ensure input from all involved parties, but not so large as to be unwieldy and slow to accomplish the work that needs to be done.

Initially, the team should be focused on implementing the system. After the system is up and running, the team's primary task should be shifted to the evaluation of the system's utility, making decisions that will help improve it, and ensuring that it meets the needs of the MBHO. Consequently, the makeup of the team may change from time to time to reflect the team's change in focus. Regardless of the functional makeup, individuals selected to serve on the team should be those who are openly supportive of the system and want to make it work, or at least are open to the idea and are willing to contribute their best efforts to making the program a success.

ANALYZE THE DAILY WORKFLOW
OF THE ORGANIZATION

Needless to say, no single implementation plan is going to be successful across *all* MBHO and provider settings. The general approach to gathering outcomes data will need to be customized to ensure full integration into each particular provider's and organization's daily workflow. The importance the integration of data gathering into the daily office routine to the success of any outcomes measurement system cannot be stressed enough. Overcoming the integration and implementation beast starts with doing a thorough analysis of the MBHO's day-to-day workflow.

Conducting a workflow analysis in any setting requires a complete and thorough understanding of what goes on in all aspects of the setting in which the outcomes measurement tasks will take place. In MBHOs, as in any other setting, this includes: knowing how services are requested and how those requests are processed; how referrals are made; what obligations the patient, provider, and MBHO have to each other; what is reasonable to expect from each party as far as outcomes-related tasks are concerned; and what are the likely structural and process barriers to successfully incorporating this added work into the provider's and MBHO's routine way of doing things.

The best way to conduct the workflow analysis is through a combination of descriptions of daily processes from the parties involved and through direct observation by someone external to these processes. For example, one should be speaking with intake coordinators, care managers, medical records personnel, care providers, clinical directors, and anyone else involved in the authorization, provision, and management of treatment in a network provider MBHO. Receptionists and appointment schedulers working at service delivery sites would also be included. Each of these people will have the best perspective on what they do and how they do it. They will also be able to help identify potential barriers to the integration of a test-based outcomes system into the MBHO's or psychologist's daily workflow.

In addition to speaking with the staff, it is important for a member of the implementation team who is not actually involved in the daily flow of business to actually observe the process. This has two benefits. First, it allows for a confirmation of what has been reported as being the "standard operating procedures" for the organization. Second, it also affords an opportunity to identify important aspects of the daily workflow that those who are closely involved with it may overlook or consider irrelevant to outcomes assessment process.

On completion of the workflow analysis, it is always helpful to construct a flow chart of the process into which data gathering and outcomes reporting activities will need to be incorporated. An accurate flow chart will facilitate decisions about how and where to best integrate the required outcomes system activities into the daily flow of business. Thus, having relevant staff verify the accuracy with which the current workflow is portrayed in the chart is critical to avoiding misconceptions about what actually goes on "down in the trenches."

Once there is a clear understanding of what the daily processes are, it is time to develop a plan for integrating the envisioned outcomes system into those processes. This will involve careful thought about what needs to be done, what there is to work with, what additional resources are necessary, and how to put it all together.

IDENTIFY AND SOLVE BARRIERS
TO IMPLEMENTATION

It is through the workflow analysis that one is able to identify most, if not all, potential barriers to the successful implementation of the system. These barriers can range from the physical facilities themselves, to processes that have been in place for years, to the personnel and their defined roles within the organization. From there, one can begin to develop ways to overcome these barriers. Lyons et al. (1997) have identified three general categories for the types of barriers that can be encountered in implementing an outcomes system. These include *ethical considerations, psychological factors, and organizational and operational factors.*

Ethical Considerations

Lyons et al. (1997) equate ethical considerations with "care for the rights of consumers" (p. 129). They break this down to concerns about *informed consent, minimization of risk of harm, choice,* and *confidentiality.* These, of course, are the same considerations that must be addressed in any type of psychological research involving human subjects.

Informed Consent. Generally, informed consent is required when the gathering and use of outcomes data is done in the context of a specific research project that is not part of the MBHO's business process. In instances in which the outcomes assessment system is implemented to be part of the organization's service delivery routine, informed consent is probably no more required than it would be if a primary care provider asked for an analysis of a blood sample. It might be useful, however, to include a notice in the health plan member's certificate of coverage that informs them of the outcomes program, what may be required of them related to this program, and how the data obtained as part of the program might be used. Moreover, Eisen et al. (1999) reported an approach whereby the clinician informs the patient at intake that (a) the outcomes assessment will be used to help identify symptoms and problems; (b) it will serve as a baseline for comparison with data obtained at a later date; and (c) he will not be denied services if he does not complete the assessment. This information could then be repeated each time that the patient is asked to provide data for the outcomes program.

Minimization of Any Risk of Harm. As Lyons et al, (1997) point out, the chances of there being any risk of harm from participation in an outcomes program are minimal. Some providers might raise concern about asking questions pertaining to suicide and other psychopathology, but the evidence does not suggest that this should be a matter for concern.

Choice. Like risk of harm, the ability to choose to participate or not participate in outcomes data collection is seldom an issue. As Lyons et al. (1997) point out, "consumers feel free to answer or to ignore surveys, depending on their wishes" (p. 131). But there may be exceptions, such as when an MBHO requires the completion of certain paperwork that includes outcomes-related questions, in order to receive benefits. Lyons et al. indicate that one way to meet the MBHO's requirements while still offering the patient a choice to participate might be to include a response option on the outcomes measure where the patient indicates that they do not wish to respond. This approach would enable the patient to meet the requirements of the MBHO while maintaining their right to choose to participate.

Confidentiality.   These issues apply to data that are obtained as part of an outcomes assessment program, particularly as it relates to the storage and reporting of individual patient data. Reporting of outcomes data in aggregate form (e.g., score cards, report cards) is much less of a concern. Regardless, the MBHO can take measures to ensure the confidentiality of outcomes data. For instance, both Lyons et al. (1997) and Kraus and Horan (1998) recommend the use of unique numeric patient identifiers that are not tied to social security numbers, birth dates, or anything else that could be used to identify an individual patient's data. Lyons et al. also recommend the formation of a committee to oversee the fair information practices identified by Gellman and Frawley (1996).

These and other ethical issues are discussed in detail in chapter 9. Regardless, it behooves those responsible for the design and implementaion of an outcomes system to seek both legal and professional (ethical) counsel about this matter early in the process.

Psychological Factors

This set of potential barriers has to do with issues that those who are asked to supply the data may have. This includes both staff members (clinical and nonclinical) and patients.

Staff Resistance.   One of the most difficult barriers to pass is that having to do with eliciting the necessary cooperation of the MBHO's providers and administrative staff. Lyons et al. (1997), drawing upon Rosen and Weil's (1996) work related to the implementation of computer technology, talk about three types of staff participants in the implementation process. *Eager adopters* are open to the new system and actively welcome its implementation. *Hesitant prove its worthers* are receptive to the idea, but put off giving acceptance until the eager adopters demonstrate that it is important or useful to their jobs. They tend to use both support-seeking and problem-solving coping strategies. Thus, placing this type of person in a position where success or benefits can be experienced early, as well as showing them that the outcomes system makes sense, is useful and can be mastered, will help overcome their lack of confidence in and hesitancies about the system. *Resisters* generally view the initiative as not being worthwhile and will be resistant to attempts to convince them otherwise. Their resistance may be displayed in concerns about confidentiality and the potential negative impact on the therapeutic relationship. According to Lyons et al., "Resisters tend to use avoidance as their primary coping strategy. Quite likely, the only workable strategy for engaging resisters . . . is to have consistent oversight and announce consequences for noncompliance" (p. 136).

Providers tend to be extremely busy and already have a number of hoops to jump through in order to receive reimbursement for their work. As discussed earlier, one way of eliciting the cooperation of providers is to make sure that they get something useful for their troubles. Data gathered in support of any outcomes initiative can become most useful to providers when they are able to reap some *immediate* benefit from their efforts. Here, the challenge becomes one of providing information about their patients quickly enough to assist in daily clinical decision-making.

Patient Resistance.   Patient resistance may stem from many sources. Two common reasons for resistance are a lack of understanding of the purpose (and therefore, the consequences) of the outcomes assessment, and a failure to see any personal benefit from their participation (Lyons et al., 1997). Playing into this are the demands that are being made on the patient's time, particularly if what is being required is the completion of a lengthy outcomes measure on multiple occasions (Eisen et al., 1999). Lyons et al. suggest that completion of patient self-report measures should be limited to 20 minutes or less. This author's experience, however, suggests that a patient-completed measure should not exceed a completion time of 10 minutes.

In cases of patient resistance, it would be helpful to explain how the information will be used to their benefit. Of course, this approach will best be served if the psychologist himself is convinced of the utility of the data to the individual patient. Berman and Hurt (1996) note that "if clinicians view the data as clinically valuable, this attitude will be conveyed to the patient" (p. 40).

Organizational and Operational Factors

Although identified as separate factors, the type of organizational factors referred to by Lyons et al. (1997) are essentially those that were discussed in the preceding sections.

DEVELOP A SYSTEM FOR MANAGING OUTCOMES DATA

By their nature, outcomes assessment systems are data-driven systems. Thus, the implementation of a system that allows for the necessary gathering, storing, analyzing, and reporting outcomes data is critical to the success of the system. Knowledge of the MBHO's daily workflow is important to ensure that the data management system designed for any given MBHO is efficient, economical, and generally acceptable to the staff who are involved in the system's daily operations.

Identify the Instrumentation to Measure the Selected Outcomes Variables

Chapter 6 addressed the issue of the selection of what outcomes variables to measure. With these having been determined, one must then decide which instrument(s) can provide the best measure of those variables for the MBHO. Generally, selection of outcomes instrumentation can be facilitated by the application of the selection criteria presented in chapter 4. However, other factors may need to be taken into consideration.

It is possible that some MBHOs will not be able to find any commercially available or public domain instruments that meet their desired outcomes system requirements. In these cases, there are two options. One is to modify the requirements to be consistent with what *is* available. This involves some compromise which, in the beginning year or two of the project, may be quite acceptable. The alternative is for the MBHO to develop its own instrumentation. This will ensure that the organization will get exactly what it wants. However, such an approach is costly in terms of both development expenses and the delay in implementing the outcomes system that will result from having to await the completion of the instrument development process, especially if one employs the industry standards set by American Educational Research Association et al. (1999). In cases such as these, this author recommends going with the first option.

Identify Processes for Maximizing Patient Participation Rate

Before considering the best means of managing data, thought should first be given to ways in which to obtain the greatest amount of valuable and useful data for the outcomes system. Part of this issue was addressed in the previous discussion on overcoming patient barriers. In addition to those recommendations, specific data collection processes can be implemented that can help achieve maximum participation from patients during data collection. Based on Eisen et al.'s (1999) recommendations, this author recommends the following procedures for obtaining baseline measures from patients:

- Have the patient arrive early enough for their first appointment (e.g., 30 minutes early) to complete the initial measurement without running into the time scheduled with the provider.
- Inform the patient that this and subsequent measurements are part of the provider's or the MBHO's routine intake procedures, and that the obtained information will assist them in providing the highest quality of care. Consider developing a brief script to assist the support staff in enlisting the cooperation of the patient (see Radosevich et al., 1994).
- As appropriate to the instrumentation that is selected, patients who cannot complete the outcomes instrumentation unassisted (e.g., due to poor reading ability, visual impairment) should have them administered to them via a structured interview format by a trained clinical or nonclinical staff member.
- Postpone the completion of outcomes measures by severely disturbed patients until they are able to provide valid responses to the instrumentation's questions.
- As appropriate, use incentives (e.g., coffee, pastries) to increase participation.
- Inform the patient that the provider will review the results of the measurement with them.

Eisen et al. (1999) also provide recommendations for maximizing participation in subsequent outcomes assessments. Based on these, the following are recommended for postbaseline measurements taken during treatment, at the time of treatment termination, and posttreatment termination:

- Appoint a support staff member to be responsible for tracking and notifying patients when it is time for the next measurement.
- Coordinate patients' outcomes monitoring to occur with scheduled appointments with their providers, and inform the providers of the schedule for remeasuring their patients.

- Use a combination of mail-out forms and telephone follow-up, along with the opportunity to complete a patient satisfaction survey, to increase responses to posttreatment follow-up measurements.

With experience, the MBHO will arrive at additional ways to increase the participation of the health plan members that they serve.

Identify Means of Entering and Transmitting Data

There are several options for entering outcomes data. These include direct online entry via personal computer, Internet, or intranet software by the person providing the information; key entry of respondent data into these same systems by an administrative staff member; scanning of scannable or faxable forms; or IVR technology. Selection of the best system for the MBHO should be based on consideration of cost, the availability of the desired entry format for the instrumentation being used, and compatibility with the MBHO's business flow. Compatibility with the reporting needs of the MBHO also must be taken into consideration. Note that in some cases, a particular data entry and reporting system may be found to be optimal from a cost and implementation standpoint, consequently, it may actually dictate the selection of instrumentation to be used for data gathering.

In considering the available technologies, one should keep in mind that providers should have access to means of quickly and effortlessly transmitting data and receiving information back. The availability of fax in most service delivery offices makes this medium a very practical and inexpensive means of sending and receiving information. The Internet also provides a quick and inexpensive means of transmitting data. However, many practitioners still do not have access to the Internet, thus posing a significant problem to system-wide implementation. The reader is referred to chapter 4 for a discussion of the advantages and limitations of Internet, fax, and IVR technologies.

Identify a Means of Storing and Retrieving Data

Of course, once transmitted, the data need to be stored for immediate and later use. Databases need to have the capacity to store large amounts of data, permit data entry via the mode selected for use with the outcomes system, and allow easy access to data for both regular, planned analyses and reporting as well as for special projects and investigations.

Radosevich, McPherson, and Werni (1994) have identified a set considerations that should be taken into account in choosing or designing a database. They include the following:

- *Import and export capabilities.* The database should be able to receive input from and send output to other software required for the system (e.g., spreadsheets, statistical packages, report generators).
- *Openness of the database structure.* The ability to modify the database's structure would be necessary in order to handle the inevitable changes that will be required after piloting or initial implementation.

- *Ease in linking from other systems.* The database should be able to import data from other databases that it will have to interface with (e.g., claims database).
- *Querying capability.* One should be able to view, change, and ask questions of the data, and to use the answers for report generation.
- *Methods for handling missing data.* The database should be able to handle missing data in whatever manner would be appropriate for the system.
- *Exporting capabilities that permit trended data analysis.* Any outcomes system must be able to make comparisons of data obtained at different points in time.
- *Capacity to support a "tickler" system.* The database should have the ability to identify patients requiring follow-up measurement (either during or after the episode of care) at designated points in time and, preferably, to generate letters to these individuals notifying them of the need for re-assessment.

In addition, Ofstead, Gobran, and Lum (2000) provide an extensive set of questions to consider when selecting a data management system. These are presented in Table 7.3.

TABLE 7.3
Questions to Consider When Selecting a Data Management Product

Issues important to clinicians:

1. Does the system support the instruments you want to use?
2. Can your existing staff handle the data management and report generation tasks without much hassle?
3. Does the system provide meaningful output (reports) in a timely fashion?
4. Does the system allow the addition of questions or customization?
5. Can the system support longitudinal patient records, so that the clinician can assess change over time?
6. Will patients find the assessment tools and processes "user-friendly"?

Issues important to staff:

1. Is the technology simple and reliable to use?
2. Are manuals and adequate technical support readily available?
3. Is there a training program, or are people expected to learn the system on their own?
4. How much time does it take to enter data for each patient?
5. How are errors corrected?
6. How are reports generated?
7. What type of assistance will most patients require?
8. How flexible is the data collection for patients with special needs (e.g., those with vision problems, motor control problems, computer phobia, language/literacy issues, etc.)?

Additional issues important to administration:

1. Does the vendor have a good track record in *this line of business?*
2. Does the system require the user to perform extensive setup or design?
3. What are the hardware and space requirements needed to run the system?
4. Will the system be integrated with other programs or used on a network?
5. Does staff need special training?
6. Is continuing oversight by an MIS professional required?
7. Who has control of and ownership of the data?
8. How much does it *really* cost to make it work in your practice for the volume of patients needing assessment (including software, hardware, forms, per-patient charges, telephone/fax fees, technical support, training, data analysis, and customization)?

Note.   From "Integrating Behavioral Health Assessment with Primary Care Services" (p. 172), by C. L. Ofstead, D. S. Gobran, and D. L. Lum, in M. E. Maruish (Ed.), *Handbook of psychological assessment in primary care settings*, 2000b, Mahwah, NJ: Lawrence Erlbaum Associates. Copyright 2000 by Lawrence Erlbaum Associates. Reprinted with permission.

Identify Means of Making Outcomes-Derived Information Immediately Available for Clinical Decision-Making

The capability of real-time processing of outcomes data collected at intake or during the course of treatment via the Internet, a faxback system, or an in-office PC system makes it possible for the system to support important decisions related to need for treatment. It can also assist in determining the most appropriate LOC for the individual patient. For these reasons, every effort should be made to build into the outcomes assessment system the ability to provide immediate feedback to the MBHO's providers and care managers (Berman & Hurt, 1996; Lyons et al., 1997). This information will be viewed as being valuable and, as indicated previously, having access to it when it is most beneficial can be a major selling point for providers, care managers, and other MBHO staff members who may be involved in the clinical decision-making process (e.g., clinical directors, peer reviewers).

In planning for the provision of feedback, it is important to elicit from the clinical decision-makers input about the outcomes information they would like to receive and the form in which it should be presented. One way of doing this is to develop several mock reports using various combinations of tables, graphs and text for conveying the information, and then present the mock-ups to a sample of the clinical decision-makers who will be using these reports. Based on their feedback, a final report can be constructed and programmed for use with the outcomes system. Failure to elicit this type of input may result in the provision of information that will be of little or no value to the intended audience and, consequently, decreased motivation for decision-makers to be active participants and supporters of the outcomes system.

DEVELOP A PLAN TO INTEGRATE THE GATHERING AND PROCESSING OF OUTCOMES DATA INTO THE DAILY WORKFLOW

Armed with the decisions about what the outcomes system is intended to do and how that will be accomplished, and with knowledge of the daily workflow, one must now develop a plan for integrating the proposed outcomes system into the daily business operations of the MBHO and its providers. The trick is to accomplish this task while creating a minimum of disruption and burden for the staff who have to administer the system on an ongoing basis. This is not always an easy task. However, there are a few things that the outcomes team can do to facilitate this.

One may find that it is useful first to examine the outcomes assessment systems of other MBHOs to find out what has and has not worked in both the gathering of data and the reporting outcomes information (Bieber et al., 1999). Also, it is helpful to list all elements of the data gathering and reporting process (e.g., determination of which patients to engage, transmission of the data to central processing, faxing the patient report to the provider), and then insert these elements on the MBHO's current work flow chart. This will result in the development of a revised workflow chart with the outcomes assessment processes incorporated. And as before, one should elicit feedback from all involved parties to determine whether the proposed plan for integrating the outcomes system into the daily workflow is realistic and will actually work.

Figure 7.1 is a workflow chart presented by Bieber et al. (1999) for integrating an outcomes assessment system into a large, multifacility provider of inpatient psychi-

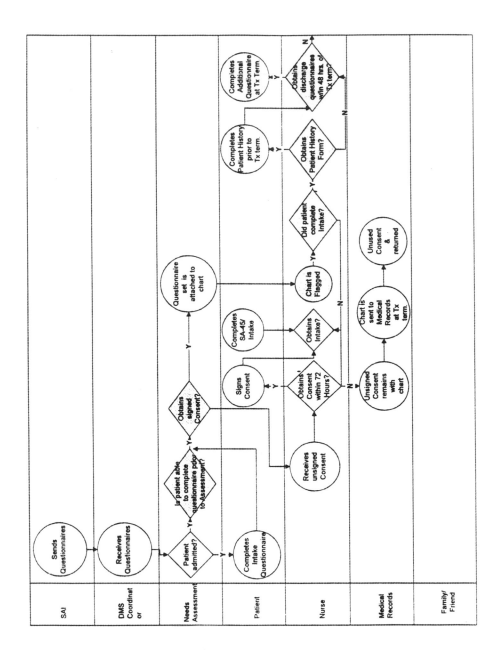

224

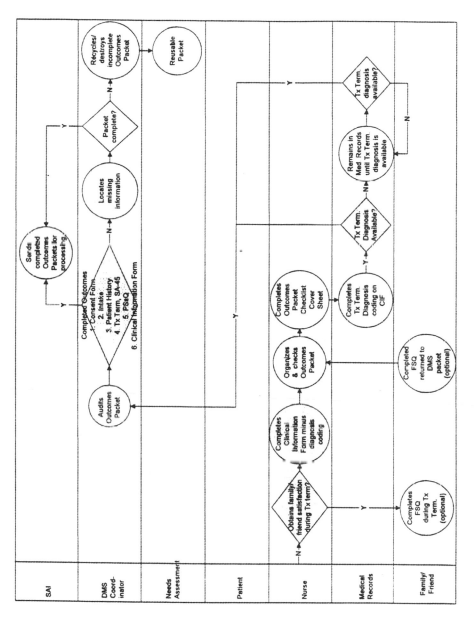

FIG. 7.1. Outcomes assessment workflow for an adult psychiatric inpatient facility. From "Design and Implementation of an Outcomes Management System within Inpatient and Outpatient Behavioral Health Settings" (pp. 202–203). In M. E. Maruish (Ed.), *The use of psychological testing for treatment planning and outcomes assessment* (2nd ed.), 1999b, Mahwah, NJ: Lawrence Erlbaum Associates. Copyright 1999 by Lawrence Erlbaum Associates. Reprinted with permission.

atric and substance abuse services. Note how the role of each of the key clinical and nonclinical staff members and collaterals in the outcomes data gathering process is detailed as the patient moves through the episode of inpatient care.

Feedback from the staff may reveal that the proposed workflow is unrealistic or not doable for one reason or another. Consequently, changes can be made to help ensure the success of the program. These changes may necessitate modifications pertaining to decisions that were made much earlier in the project planning and development process. These, in turn, may necessitate changes to related procedures. Thus, it is important to approach this part of the process with openness and flexibility, realizing that what is thought to be a well thought out plan may require some alteration.

PILOT-TEST THE SYSTEM

No outcomes assessment system should be fully implemented without first piloting it. In spite of all the thought and revisions that have been put into the system up to this point, one can be sure that even on a small scale, problems will emerge. Identifying problems before rolling out the system throughout the entire organization can ultimately help reduce resistance to the initiative, alleviate unrealistic fears, avoid embarrassment (by the outcomes team), and prevent a lot of wasted time and money.

In planning the pilot study, the following are recommended:

- Select only a few of the MBHO's organizational or provider sites to participate.
- Make sure that both supporters of the outcomes initiative and resisters participate in the project (Bieber et al., 1999; Lyons et al., 1997). Having resistant staff involved will ensure that the shortcomings of the implementation plan are quickly revealed.
- Ensure that all aspects of the outcomes assessment system are tested. One might even consider having some aspects of the system tested at one site, others at another site, and still others at a third site.
- Allow the pilot to run for as long as it may take to test all aspects of the system. In some cases, only a few weeks of time may be necessary; in other instances, the pilot may need to run for several months. The latter will more likely be the case in large, multisite MBHOs or with more comprehensive or complicated systems.
- Obtain feedback from all staff—clinical and nonclinical—who participated in the pilot test. Everyone's experience and opinions are important.
- Use of the staff's feedback to fine-tune the system to correct the identified problems. If it was a problem during the pilot, it probably will be a problem during the implementation phase.

TRAIN STAFF IN THE IMPLEMENTATION PROCESS

An integral part of ramping up for the implementation of a new outcomes system is the training of *all* organization staff who will be involved in the running of program on a daily basis. Those who are involved in the gathering, processing, or use of the outcomes data—from the office receptionist to the clinical director—can make or break the system. Thus, training of the involved parties in the implementation of the onsite processes and procedures should be included in the implementation plan. This step should not be an afterthought or be otherwise treated lightly. It is also a step that should be taken only after the "bugs" identified during the pilot phase have been worked out.

Bieber et al. (1999) provide some general recommendations with regard to training:

> When conducting training, it is important to identify the learners' current level of knowledge and begin teaching from that point forward. Consider what three to five things learners must know to be motivated and able to collect high quality data. Include all employees responsible for providing clinical data, implementing patient surveys, or managing medical records. Design training materials so that current staff can use them to train new staff when needed. Depending on the work environment, it might be possible to train in half-day sessions, via teleconferencing, or via telephone conferencing. The training should be timed so that data collection will begin within a week of the training. It is also important to have a support line in place to answer questions once the actual implementation begins.
>
> Employees will probably resist changes if they feel threatened. . . . One approach [to countering this reaction] is to identify informal leaders who support the move to outcomes measurement and arrange to have them participate in training sessions. (p. 207)

There are a number of other things that can be done to help maximize the impact of the training. Things like scheduling multiple training sessions at different times to meet different work schedules, and developing useful and comprehensive training and reference materials will help increase the chances of the meeting the criteria for success for the outcomes system. Lyons et al. (1997) suggest the use of case vignettes to assess the reliability of the data collection procedures. To assist in getting buy-in into the program, Bengen-Seltzer (1999) recommends having the clinical staff train other clinical staff using a "train the trainers" approach. Wetzler (1994) advocates for training senior managers first, the theory being that they can help guide the effort. He also recommends that during training, "outcomes" and their role in the organization be defined, their limitations be identified, and the scope of the system be clarified.

At this point in the process, one would hope that the implementation team has figured everything out—considered all the things that must be done, identified all that can go wrong, and have solutions to all of these problems. This is certainly hoped for, but it probably won't happen. Questions that were not considered even in passing will be raised. This is good, for it is better for it to happen now than after implementation has begun. If one does not know the answer immediately, the response should not be faked nor the question treated lightly. Thank the staff for raising the issue and let them know that it hadn't been considered. Let them know that the matter will be brought before the outcomes team and they get back to all of them with the answer.

An important part of the training process is the designation of someone to be the primary overseer of the day-to-day implementation of the outcomes system. This should be someone onsite who is knowledgeable of all aspects of the implementation procedures and in contact with all of the principals of the system's implementation. As suggested by Bieber et al. (1999), it should be someone who can spot-check the adequacy of all aspects of implementation, answer any questions about the system that may arise, and train any new staff who come on board after the system is implemented. Someone like an office manager or possibly a receptionist (depending on the person's particular capabilities) might be considered, or a full- or part-time position might be created for this purpose. In MBHO systems with multiple sites, it may be wise to appoint an individual at each site to oversee that site's implementation.

IMPLEMENT THE OUTCOMES SYSTEM

Once the preceding steps have been completed, it's time to begin the implementation of the system. As part of the implementation plan, it's best to begin on a small scale. For example, consider limiting efforts to gathering data on just adult outpatients instead of trying to cover the entire patient population. One may want to focus on measuring just the outcomes of treatment on reduction of symptomatology rather than also looking at increases in social or work functioning. One might also decide that it would be better to wait to be sure that the data gathering and transmission process is working smoothly before adding the clinician feedback piece. As all of the kinks in "Version 1" are worked out, the team may then begin adding one or more other facets of the outcomes system to the process. And as these become stable processes, additional pieces can be added on until the system is fully operational.

In the beginning, frequent, regular (i.e., weekly) meetings of the outcomes team and the onsite outcomes coordinator(s) are recommended. This will provide an opportunity for the team to find out about any problems that may occur, and to provide the onsite coordinator with suggestions for solutions. It is also an opportunity to hear about the successful aspects of the implementation plan. Knowing what works well can provide keys to solving problematic situations. Based on this information, the outcomes team may wish to make changes in one or more of the processes. In some cases, these changes must be made immediately. The team may decide to make relatively minor tweakings or add new components or features at regularly scheduled times (i.e., the first week of each month), or wait until enough of these desired minor changes have amassed to make the disruption that will accompany the changes worthwhile.

During the initial phase of implementation, it also is important to provide all staff in the process with some form of positive reinforcement for their efforts. This might come in any number of cost-free or inexpensive forms, such as having the leadership personally visit them or send e-mails conveying congratulations and gratitude for their work, or buying doughnuts and bagels for the nonclinical staff, or allowing an additional casual day during the week. At the very least, all staff should be provided with feedback about how successful they have been in implementing the system. For example, a weekly report of the MBHO's performance on relevant implementation variables (e.g., how many eligible patients were asked to complete the baseline survey, how many of these patients agreed to participate, how many actually completed the baseline survey, reasons given for declining participation) might be sent to the staff or posted in a common area in the MBHO's and/or providers' offices.

EVALUATE THE SYSTEM AGAINST PREVIOUSLY ESTABLISHED CRITERIA AND MODIFY AS NECESSARY

Once it is up and running, it is time to begin evaluating the system against the criteria for success that were established earlier. Here, the outcomes team must determine which criteria are being met as well as those that are not. As for the latter, an analysis of what's been going on with processes, procedures, instrumentation or whatever, is called for. Identification of the likely source(s) of the problem(s) and modification of the system to overcome these problems follow. Once changes to the system are implemented, the criteria for success are again applied to determine if the changes suggested by the previous analysis have indeed impacted the program in the expected manner. If they have not, other solutions will have to be implemented to eliminate the identified problems. These, in turn, are evaluated later, and so on, in a manner that is consistent with a CQI system for dealing with problems and improving quality.

Sometimes, one might find a problem area insurmountable, no matter how times changes are made. As a result, it might be appropriate to lower or eliminate the success criteria that are not being met, and/or have other criteria take their place. Or, one or more aspects of the outcomes system might have to be modified so that the system becomes a more realistic possibility for the MBHO, given the particular set of circumstances. Facing the reality of the situation should not be viewed as a form of failure or otherwise negatively; at the same time, spinning one's wheels over a problem that just is not going away should not be viewed in a positive light.

SUMMARY

Arriving at a good, consensual idea of what an MBHO's outcomes assessment system should look like, how it should perform, and what questions or needs it should address can be a slow-moving and sometimes painful procedure. However, it is just the first step in a long process that will result in having a useful outcomes assessment system up and running. Champions of the system must then sell it, first to the leadership and then to all other levels of the organization. With the support of the MBHO in hand, the task of working out the plan for implementing the system should begin. Development of a well thought out implementation plan is key to the success of any outcomes system. Unfortunately, this sometimes does not occur and as a result, the likelihood of having a useful and successful system is jeopardized from the beginning.

First, an outcomes assessment team should be formed to manage the process of developing, implementing, and later, maintaining the system on an ongoing basis. Then, a thorough analysis of the daily work flow of the MBHO's service delivery system should be conducted. This will allow for the identification of potential barriers to implementation that must be overcome, and may even suggest solutions to these problems. This information also will be useful in arriving at the decisions that must be made related to how to efficiently collect, store, manage, and maintain the confidentiality of outcomes data from patients and clinical staff. With information in hand, a tentative plan for integrating the data gathering and reporting aspects of the program should be developed and passed on to all of those who will be involved in any aspect of the data management process for review. Based on their feedback, the proposed workflow should be revised to take into account any staff-identified barriers that may remain. Next, all aspects of the data gathering and reporting processes should be pilot-tested. This will allow for the identification of previously unforeseen barriers to the implementation process and final tweaking of the implementation processes.

Training all staff members on the operation of the system in general, along with their particular responsibilities, should then take place. This system can then go "live," starting out on a small scale and gradually increasing the scope of the activities as success is achieved. During the initial phases of the implementation, regular meetings of the outcomes team are recommended, as is provision reinforcement for and feedback about the fruits of their efforts. As necessary, modifications in the system can be made.

8

Applications and Opportunities in Primary and Integrated Care Settings

Strosahl (1996) stated that managed behavioral health care is shifting its focus from cost containment and supply-side strategies to three other areas: evidence-based clinical services, a population-based care philosophy, and integration of service delivery systems that previously were independent. Regarding the latter, Lipsitt (1997) has noted, "Those who govern managed care companies and administer large industries have discovered that health plans that fragment delivery of services are more costly and less likely to be given high 'satisfaction' ratings by patients than those that provide 'one-stop shopping' " (pp. 10–11).

As Groth-Marnat and Edkins (1996) point out, the past 3 decades has produced a significant increase the number of psychologists who work in general health care settings. They attribute this phenomenon to several factors, including the realization that psychologists can improve a patient's physical health by helping to reduce overutilization of medical services and prevent stress-related disorders; offering alternatives to traditional medical interventions; and enhancing the outcomes of patient care. The recognition of the financial and patient-care benefits that can accrue from the integration of primary medical care and behavioral health care has resulted not only in professional and academic-level discussions and investigations, but also in actual implementation of integrated behavioral health programs in primary care settings. In fact, in the Surgeon General's report on mental health, Satcher (2000) identified the increased reliance on primary health care as one of the defining trends in the mental health field during the past 25 years. The degree to which integrated service delivery is present in participating primary care practices varies as a function of a number of factors (e.g., funding, third-party reimbursement criteria, staff interest and commitment to such programs, availability of resources, office space limitations). Regardless of the extent to which these services are merged, efforts toward attaining this goal attest to the belief that any steps toward integrating behavioral health care services — including psychological testing — in primary care settings represents an improvement over the more traditional model of segregated service delivery.

This chapter focuses on the significant contributions that psychological testing can make to the delivery of services in primary care settings — particularly those with integrated behavioral health care services — as well as specific tools that can aid in this endeavor. However, before proceeding with this discussion, it is important for the reader to first understand the reasons why psychological testing specifically and behavioral health care services in general can be important to primary care service delivery. Thus, the following section provides an overview of the impetus for, current interest in, and efforts toward the integration of behavioral health care in primary medical care settings. The intent is not to present a comprehensive exposition of efforts in this area; rather, it is hoped that the information contained herein will create a context that facilitates an understanding of the detailed information presented in the remaining sections of this chapter.

BEHAVIORAL HEALTH DISORDERS IN PRIMARY CARE SETTINGS: CURRENT STATUS OF IDENTIFICATION AND TREATMENT

The re-emergence of interest in the integration of primary and behavioral health care services has made it the focus of much discussion. Frequently, discussion of this topic takes place without clarifying what is meant by the term "primary care." The Institute of Medicine (IOM; Donaldson, Yordy, Lohr, & Vanselow, 1996) has offered a definition of primary care that is comprehensive and cuts to the core focus of this area of medical practice specialties. Thus,

> Primary care is the provision of integrated, accessible health care services by clinicians that are accountable for addressing a large majority of personal health care needs, developing a sustained partnership with patients, and practicing in the context of family and community. (p. 32)

The IOM (Edmunds et al., 1997) further explains that:

> *integrated care* refers to comprehensive, coordinated, and continuous services whose processes are seamless across different levels of care. *Accountability* refers to the responsibility for quality of care, patient satisfaction, efficient use of resources, and ethical behavior. The *context of the family and community* refers to an understanding of the importance of living conditions, cultural background, and the impact of family dynamics on health status and also recognizes the caregiving role of families [italics added]. (p. 87)

Who are considered primary care providers, or PCPs? The answer probably will vary depending on who is asked. This author has adopted the inclusion criteria used in mid-1970s legislation that mandated training a larger number of primary care physicians. According to Borus (1985), PCPs include physicians with the medical specialties of "family medicine, family practice, general internal medicine, and general pediatrics, seeing these physicians as most likely to meet patients' ongoing primary care needs" (p. 1302). Some would also include OB/GYNs in this category. In addition, there are the "nonmedical" primary care providers "nurse practitioners, physicians' assistants, health aids, health ombudsmen, and care managers . . . who work with primary care physicians to provide ongoing care and coordination of patients' care needs over time" (p. 1302). Note, however, that references to "primary care providers" in publications reported below may not always be as inclusive as the definition just presented.

Prevalence of Behavioral Health Disorders in Primary Care Settings

Health care consumers present themselves to medical health care providers for any number of reasons. Lipsitt (as cited in Locke & Larsson, 1997) reported that over 80 million physician visits accounted for eight common complaints: fatigue, back pain, headaches, dizziness, chest pain, dyspnea, abdominal pain, and anxiety. Locke and Larsson's review of the literature suggested that the most common of the somatic complaints addressed by physicians could be placed into one of five symptom groupings—gastrointestinal, neurological, autonomic, cardiovascular, and musculoskeletal—and that many of these are commonly seen in anxious and depressed patients. Based on observations reported in the literature, Katon and Walker (1998) summarized what they consider important ideas about the nature of physical symptoms in primary care patients:

1. The majority of physical symptoms in primary care patients are not associated with an organic disease process.
2. The presence of psychological distress or a psychiatric disorder increases health care utilization and disability, whether or not a physical disease is present.
3. Factors such as early family environment, prior illness, and specific personality traits can predispose an individual to develop medically unexplained symptoms.
4. There is an association between the number of medically unexplained physical symptoms and the lifetime risk of psychological distress and psychiatric disorder, and the strength of this relationship increases as patients move into more specialized care settings.
5. Medically unexplained symptoms account for a significant percentage of total medical care costs.
6. Medically unexplained symptoms have a major impact on the quality of the doctor–patient relationship. (pp. 15–16)

That physical complaints often belie the presence of an underlying behavioral health problem is most clearly illustrated in a 1991 national study of the prevalence of depressive symptoms reported by Zung, Broadhead, and Roth (1993). In this study, 765 family physicians from across the United States provided data from the Zung SDS on nearly 76,000 adult patients, along with information related to the reason for their medical visit. The five most frequently reported reasons for seeing these physicians were checkups, upper respiratory infections, hypertension, throat symptoms, and problems with skin/nails/hair. Among the top 25 most common reasons for seeing their physician, depression ranked 24th (1.2% of the sample) and anxiety ranked 25th (1.1% of the sample). At the same time, using a pre-established cutoff of the Zung score (SDS ≥ 55), 21% of the total sample were found to be experiencing clinically significant depressive symptoms.

Klinkman (1999) notes that psychiatric problems in primary care settings are characterized or defined by the five "C's:" Common, Chronic, Comorbid, Concealed, and Costly. The literature is replete with data that attests to the high prevalence of patients that are seen in primary care settings with clinically significant behavioral health problems. Table 8.1 presents only a small sample of the data that demonstrate the frequency with which primary care providers encounter these individuals. Supporting data can be found in Barsky and Borus (1995); Dreher (1996); Hankin and Otkay (1979); Katon and Roy-Byrne (1989); Kessler, Burns, Shapiro, Tischler, George, Hough, Bodison, and Miller (1987); Sato and Takeichi (1993); Skinner (1990); Smith (1994); Smith, Rost, and Kashner (1995); Spitzer, Kroenke, Linzer, Hahn, Williams, deGruy, Brody, and Davies (1995); Spitzer, Williams, et al. (1994); Tiemens, Ormel, and Simon (1996), and Von Korff, Shapiro, Burke, Teitelbaum, Skinner, German, Turner, Klein, and Burns (1987).

Data on the prevalence of the comorbidity of behavioral health disorders and other illnesses, diseases, or disorders commonly seen in primary care settings provide an even clearer picture of the situation. For example, Ciarcia (1997) reported significant comorbidity rates of depression with cancer (18–39%), myocardial infarction (15–19%) rheumatoid arthritis (13%), Parkinson's disease (10–37%), stroke (22–50%), and diabetes (5–11%), with overall medical outpatient and inpatient rates of 2–15% and 12%, respectively. In a 1988 study of a community sample of over 2,500 people, Wells, Golding, and Burnam (cited in Academy of Psychosomatic Medicine, 1997) found that the 6-month, risk-adjusted prevalence rates of mental disorder were 24.7% and 17.5% for those with and without a chronic medical condition, respectively. The lifetime mental disorder prevalence rates were 42.2% and 33%, respectively. As for specific disorders, Wells and his colleagues found prevalence rates of comorbid mental disorders to be 37.5% for neurologic disorders, 34.5% for heart disease, 30.9 % for chronic lung disease, 30.3% for cancer, 25.3% for arthritis, 22.7% for diabetes, and 22.3% for hypertension.

TABLE 8.1
A Sample of Reported Prevalences for Behavioral
Health Disorders in Primary Care Settings

Study/Source	Disorder	Prevalence
Perez-Stable et al. (1990)	Major depression	6–16%
	Anxiety	10%
	Any	10–30%
Schulberg & Burns (1988)	Any	25%
Jenkins (1997)	Psychosocial problems (UK)	Approximately 33%
Johnson et al. (1995)	Alcohol abuse and dependence	5%
	Mood disorder	26%
	Anxiety disorder	18%
	Eating disorder	3%
	Somatoform disorder	14%
Ciarcia (1997, September)	Major depression	6%
Katon & Schulberg (1992)	Depression (outpatient)	5–10%
	Depression (inpatient)	6–14%
Locke & Larsson (1997)	Somatization	50%+
Institute for International Research (1997)	Anxiety disorders	20%

Note. Some listed prevalence rate data were extracted from secondary sources. From "Introduction," by M. E. Maruish, in *Handbook of Psychological Assessment in Primary Care Settings* (p. 7), by M. E. Maruish (Ed.), 2000, Mahwah, NJ: Lawrence Erlbaum Associates. Copyright 2000 by Lawrence Erlbaum Associates. Reproduced with permission.

It is especially important to be aware of the extent to which comorbidity of behavioral health disorders with one another can occur in primary care settings. Johnson, Spitzer, Williams, Kroenke, Linzer, Brody, deGruy, and Hahn (1995) found that among the 5% of the 1,000 primary care patients identified with alcohol abuse and dependence (AAD) using the PRIME-MD, 47% met the criteria for one or more *other* mental disorders. Thus, among those identified with AAD, 33% were also diagnosed with a mood disorder, 22% with an anxiety disorder, 6% with an eating disorder, and 14% with a somatoform disorder. Among the non-AAD patients, 35% were found to have one or more PRIME-MD-identified disorders. The rate of comorbidity of these disorders with one or more other PRIME-MD-identified disorders was 65% for mood disorders, 82% for anxiety disorders, 84% for eating disorders, and 73% for somatoform disorders.

All in all, Strosahl's (1996) summary of and conclusions about the situation are not surprising:

> The primary health care system is the de facto mental health system in the United States. General physicians provide fully half of all formal mental health care in the United States. They account for roughly 70 percent of all psychotropic prescriptions and fully 80 percent of antidepressants. Most studies suggest that somewhere between 50 and 70 percent of primary care medical visits have a psychosocial basis. Further, studies have suggested that as many as 50 percent of primary care patients have clinically elevated anxiety and/or depression. (p. 96)

THE COST OF BEHAVIORAL HEALTH DISORDERS

The costs attributed to behavioral health care disorders tend to vary, depending on the source of information. Table 8.2 presents just a sample of direct, indirect, and total costs that have cited for various disorders or groups of disorders. One will note some discrepancies in identified costs associated with a given disorder or group of disorders (e.g., anxiety). Regardless, the costs are high, with the annual total exceeding $300 billion. A more detailed report of costs—financial and other—can be found in SAMHSA's *Substance Abuse and Mental Health Statistics Handbook* (Rouse, 1995).

One aspect of costs that may not have been completely accounted for in the data presented in Table 8.2 but bears mentioning, is medical health care utilization. For instance, Zung, Broadhead, and Roth (1993), citing a 1988 article by Regier et al., indicated that the number of outpatient visits for patients with depressive disorders is three times that of the average patient. As part of Katzelnick, Kobak, Greist, Jefferson, and Henk's (1997) investigation, almost 30% of high utilizers of inpatient and outpatient medical services during a 2-year period at one HMO screened positive for depression; however, they were less likely to have a serious medical condition than those high utilizers without depression. Moreover, high utilizers were almost four times more likely to be formally diagnosed as depressed by their primary care physicians. Katon and his colleagues (as cited in Academy of Psychosomatic Medicine, 1996) found that half of the high utilizers of health care in their HMO sample were psychologically distressed. The top 10% of health care utilizers ($n = 767$) accounted for 29% of all primary care visits and 52% of all specialty visits. Moreover, Smith and his colleagues (also cited in Academy of Psychosomatic Medicine, 1996) found that the medical costs for depressed patients were twice as high as those for non-

TABLE 8.2
A Sample of Annual Cost Estimates for Behavioral Health Disorders

Study/Source	Disorder	Total Costs	Direct Costs[a]	Indirect Costs[b]
"Directions: Anxiety Costs Big Bucks" (1997)	Anxiety disorders	$65 billion	$15 billion	$50 billion
"NIMH Official Cites High Cost of Schizo-phrenia" (1996)	Schizophrenia	$65 billion	$19 billion	$46 billion
Burns (1997)	Depression	$44 billion	$12 billion	$32 billion
Rouse (1995)	Mental health dis-orders	$147.9 billion	$67 billion	$80.9 billion
	Alcohol disorders	$98.7 billion	$10.6 billion	$88.1 billion
	Drug abuse disor-ders	$66.9 billion	$3.2 billion	$63.7 billion
Rice & Miller (1996, Au-gust)	Anxiety disorders	$46.5 billion	$10.7 billion	$35.8 billion
	Schizophrenia	$32.5 billion	$17.3 billion	$15.2 billion
	Affective disor-ders	$30.4 billion	$19.2 billion	$11.2 billion
	Other disorders	$38.4 billion	$19.7 billion	$18.7 billion
"Nearly 40 Percent of Older Suicide Vic-tims. . . ." (1997)	Depression in the elderly (65+)	c	$800 million	c
Stoudemire et al. (1986)	Major depression	$16 billion	c	c

Note.   Some of the listed prevalence rate data were extracted from secondary sources. Differences in costs associated with specific disorders reported by different sources may reflect differences in the years surveyed. From "Introduction," by M. E. Maruish, in *Handbook of Psychological Assessment in Primary Care Settings* (p. 9), by M. E. Maruish (Ed.), 2000, Mahwah, NJ: Lawrence Erlbaum Associates. Copyright 2000 by Lawrence Erlbaum Associates. Reproduced with permission.
[a]Includes costs related to treatment (e.g., medical, administrative, support services, etc.).
[b]Includes costs incurred indirectly (e.g., loss of wages and productivity, incarceration, death, etc.).
[c]Not reported.

depressed patients were. These considerations are important because the comparison of inpatient and outpatient medical care utilized *before* behavioral health treatment to that utilized *after* treatment is often used as an outcomes measure. Also, it is frequently used as the basis for assertions of medical cost offset resulting from that treatment.

Treatment of Behavioral Health Care Problems by Primary Care Providers

As has been shown, the situation that exists in the United States today is one in which (a) behavioral health problems of various degrees of severity exist in significant number; (b) approximately half of the people with these problems seek treatment from their family physician or other primary care provider; and (c) a significant proportion of these same people are among the highest utilizers of medical resources. The question one must ask is: How is the primary care medical system performing as the de facto behavioral health care system (Regier, Narrow, Rae, Manderscheid, Locke, & Goodwin, 1993)? The answer is clear: Not well. The inadequacy of primary care providers in dealing effectively with patients with behavioral health problems has been recognized numerous times in the literature. This inadequacy can be seen in two general areas of service delivery: detection of the problem and appropriate treatment.

Inadequate Detection and Treatment of Behavioral Health Disorders. Detection of mental health and substance abuse/dependence symptoms and disorders are problematic for the primary care provider. Selden's (1997) and Burns' (1997) reviews of the literature suggests that anywhere between one third to one half of patients with behavioral health disorders seen in primary care settings go undetected. Higgins' review (1994) found the rate of unrecognized mental illness in primary care settings to be 33%–79% for adults and 44%–83% for children, based on the studies employing DSM-III/DSM-III-R-based structured interviews.

Perhaps more important is the fact that the rates for the detection of specific disorders appear to vary considerably. The Academy of Psychosomatic Medicine's (1996) review of literature findings suggest that with inpatient populations, the rate of accurate diagnosis is 14%–50% for depression, 14%–37% for delirium and dementia, and 5%–50% for alcohol-related disorders, with only 11% of patients with a mental disorder having a discharge diagnosis reflecting these disorders. A study conducted in the Netherlands by Tiemens, Ormel, and Simon (as reported in "Detection of Psychological Disorders Unrelated to Outcomes," 1996) also found variability in detection accuracy with a sample of 340 primary care patients. The detection rates for patients receiving ICD-10-based diagnoses were approximately 60% for those with current depression, 54% for dysthymia, 59% for generalized anxiety disorder, 79% for agoraphobia, and 92% for panic disorder, with approximately 54% of those with any definite disorder being detected. Moreover, Sturm and Wells (1996) found that in the RAND Medical Outcomes Study, detection rates in prepaid and fee-for-service general medical practices differed, with detection of the latter being higher.

The seriousness of these problems is highlighted by Barraclough, Bunch, Nelson, et al. (as cited in Cole, Raju, & Barrett, 1997), who indicated that approximately 15% of patients with severe depression lasting 1 month or longer commit suicide, and that half of these patients see their physicians sometime during the month before their death. The problem seems to be particularly serious in geriatric populations. An NIH Consensus Development Panel on Depression in Late Life (also cited in Cole et al., 1997) indicated that among elderly patients, 75% of those committing suicide had seen their primary care providers within a short period of time prior to their demise. Even more disconcerting is a report in *Decade of the Brain* (as cited in "Nearly 40 Percent of Older Suicide Victims Visit Doctor during Week before Killing Themselves," 1997) indicating that almost 40% of older persons who commit suicide visit primary care providers within one week of killing themselves.

Why is detection of mental illness a problem? A special issue of the *American Journal of Managed Care* (1999) identified several reasons for the problems encountered by providers in detecting depression. These included patients' unwillingness to reveal their mental health histories, somatic manifestations of the disorder, the brief amount of time providers have to spend with patients during office visits, separation of health care for mental health and medical problems, and the demands for the provider's attention. Intuitively, one would expect that some of these same factors, as well as others, also affect the primary care provider's ability to detect many other types of behavioral health problems. Klinkman (1999) echoed many of these same potential explanations. In addition, drawing on findings from a 12-year prospective study of the weekly course of major depression by Judd, Akiskal, Maser, Zeller,

Endicott, Coryell, Paulus, Kunovac, Leon, Mueller, Rice, and Keller (1998), he suggested that one problem is that "in primary care, physicians must deal [with patients] with varying degrees of dysfunction at different times and who may not always need treatment" (p. S784).

Even if behavioral health problems are detected, the treatment that is provided to these patients frequently may be inadequate. For instance, Tiemens et al.'s Netherlands study (as reported in "Detection of Psychological Disorders Unrelated to Outcomes," 1996) indicated that there was no link between detection of a mental disorder and either improved outcome scores on the Comprehensive International Diagnosis Interview—Primary Care Version or in improved occupational functioning. In addition, at 1 year postdetection, only a third of patients initially assigned a diagnosis recovered and half still met the criteria for a diagnosis. However, most reported data are related to the treatment of depressed patients. For instance, the National Depressive and Manic-Depressive Association (cited in "Depression Still Undetected Despite Efforts at Redress," 1997) reported that "up to half of depressed patients treated by primary care physicians receive no antidepressants, and only 10.7% of those who do receive medication are given adequate dosages over sufficient lengths of time" (p. 1). Rome (as cited in Burns, 1997) indicated that studies show that about 50% of those depressed patients who are accurately identified receive appropriate treatment. In addition, Wells' review of three large health policy studies of treatment of depression in the general medical sector (as cited in Academy of Psychosomatic Medicine, 1996) indicated that antidepressant treatment was prescribed 20% of the time and at suboptimal dosages; for 40% of these cases, the dosage was subtherapeutic. These are important considerations. As Wells, Sherbourne, Schoenbaum, Duan, Meredith, Unutzer, Miranda, Carney, and Rubenstein (2000) have noted, depression is expected to be the second leading cause of disability throughout the world during the 21st century. Adequate treatment of this disorder can have a positive impact on the productivity and quality of life of patients being treated in primary care settings.

Solutions to the Problem.   Approximately half of the behavioral health care services in the United States today are delivered in primary care settings by professionals limited in their ability to accurately identify and appropriately treat individuals suffering from mental health or substance abuse problems. The fact is, patients with behavioral health care problems will continue to turn to their primary care provider rather than a behavioral health care specialist for treatment, in spite of these well-intentioned professionals' inability to consistently provide the highest possible quality of service.

Given this state of affairs, there are a number of steps that could be taken to improve the chances that patients needing behavioral health care services will receive appropriate, high quality care. One remedy for the current state of affairs is to improve the primary care provider's level of knowledge and skills in the area of behavioral health care. Lipkin (1996) identified the following areas in which primary care providers should become knowledgeable: diagnostic criteria; diagnostic tools; epidemiology; adaptations of their practice to the cultural beliefs of the patient population; and brief approaches to treatment, including relaxation and those treatments that are psychopharmacological, cognitive, and supportive in nature. Consistent with the recommendations of Higgins (1994), Lipkin also indicated that providers should develop interviewing skills that enable them to relate effectively to the patient, elicit the information necessary for the assignment of an appropriate diagnosis, and engage the patient in a plan of treatment.

Sperry et al. (1996) have suggested that the implementation of more regular screening procedures would be beneficial, given the fact that less than half of patients with behavioral health problems in primary care settings are identified. In short,

> psychiatric illness is to medicine today what hypertension was 20 years ago: a major source of morbidity, disability, and mortality that could be prevented by earlier detection of disease, accomplished via mass screening by primary care providers. (p. 201)

Higgins (1994), however, does not support widespread screening; rather, he advocates the development of tools that will assist the primary care provider in identifying those patients who can benefit from behavioral health interventions. Consistent with Higgins' and Lipkin's (1996) assertions,

> Primary care physician recognition appears to be a necessary but not sufficient step to improve the outcome of psychiatric and psychological disorders in primary care settings. . . . To enhance outcomes, programs to improve screening for behavioral and psychiatric disorders in primary care must be accompanied by interventions that increase the knowledge and skill of providers in treating these disorders ("Detection of Psychological Disorders Unrelated to Outcomes," 1996, p. 9 [Editor's Note]).

There are two other ways in which changes can come about through the provider. The first is by ensuring that only *appropriate* referrals are made to mental health specialists. Jenkins (1997) indicates that in order to ensure specialist services are well targeted, criteria for referrals need to be developed. These criteria should be based on epidemiological factors such as diagnosis, symptom severity, risk of danger to self or others, and the extent to which the care of the patient can be shared between the two providers.

Another means of improving care is through the implementation of guidelines for treatment of specific disorders. Both the Agency for Healthcare Research and Quality, or AHRQ (formerly called the Agency for Health Care Policy and Research, or AHCPR), and the American Psychiatric Association have developed guidelines for the treatment of depression in primary care settings (as cited in "Depression Still Undertreated Despite Efforts at Redress," 1997). According to Sturm and Wells (1996), cost savings would be realized if the quality of care provided to depressed patients were improved through the use of such tools. They indicate that:

> Spending the additional 20 to 30 percent for care that follows practice guidelines could quadruple the value of mental health care: The return on each dollar spent on care improves patients' ability to function on the job and around the house. The potential to improve the cost-effectiveness of care is especially great for depressed patients who visit general medical providers such as internists or family doctors. (p. 65)

Educational efforts also should be directed to the primary care patients. Certainly, making materials about the nature and treatment of behavioral health disorders available to patients, family members, and other significant people in the patients' lives (e.g., employers, friends) can help remove the stigma that perpetuates misunderstanding and impedes the delivery of needed treatment to those afflicted with behavioral health problems. In addition, one could support efforts such as the National

Mental Illness Awareness Week or the National Depression Screening Day ("Depression Still Undertreated Despite Efforts to Redress," 1997). Patient education should also be geared toward helping those who need behavioral health care services make informed choices about the provider they choose and the treatment they receive (Del Vecchio, 1996). This knowledge leads to empowerment, which in turn can lead to increased care quality and decreased costs.

Possibly equal in importance to the provider- and patient-related changes toward improving primary-care–delivered behavioral health care services are changes in the financial/incentive arrangements that play into the provider's day-to-day practice. Mitchell and Haber (1997) indicate that revision of the financial incentive structure to improve the recognition and treatment of mental health disorders will result in improvement in the patient's quality of life and possibly lowered overall medical costs. Certainly, the move to create parity in benefits structures for medical and behavioral health services is a step in the right direction. Indeed, Haley, McDaniel, Bray, Frank, Heldring, Johnson, Lu, Reed, and Wiggins (1998) felt that over time, capitated reimbursement systems will provide primary care providers more incentives to collaborate with generalist psychologists offering services such as testing and evaluation, psychotherapy, crisis intervention, and follow-up care.

Implementation of any or all of these potential solutions should improve the quality of services that primary care providers offer to their patients with mental health or substance abuse problems. However, as Edmunds et al. (1997) point out,

> the challenges in monitoring behavioral health care in primary care settings are magnified by the increased scope and complexity of the health conditions that are expected to be treated in the primary care settings, the wide variability in the extent of psychiatric training received by family physicians and other primary care practitioners, and the rapid development of new treatments that makes it increasingly difficult for practitioners to stay current. (p. 89)

Given this, Edmunds et al.'s recommendations for maximizing the quality and benefits of treatment that patients with behavioral health problems can receive in the primary care setting are models of collaborative care between primary and behavioral health care professionals. Of particular interest among today's more forward thinkers are those models of *integrated primary behavioral health care*.

Integration of Primary and Behavioral Health Care Services

The integration of primary medical care and behavioral health care has existed in various forms for many years, going under labels such as "primary care psychology," "primary care health psychology," and "family systems medicine" (Pingitore, 1999). However, only recently has it gained the attention and prominence of both the medical and behavioral health care professional communities as an effective and efficient means of attending to a significant portion of those primary care patients suffering from mental health and substance abuse problems. The reasons for the growing interest in integrated primary and behavioral health care are as varied as the qualities that define it and the various options by which it can be provided. These include financial factors, external pressures, and practical considerations, which are discussed at length by Maruish (2000b).

Strosahl (1996) indicates that effective integration of primary medical care and behavioral health care requires behavioral health care to adopt a general model of service delivery "that is consistent with the goals, strategies, and culture of primary care" (p. 93). Accordingly,

> The *primary mental healthcare* [italics added] model involves providing direct consultative services to primary care providers and, where appropriate, highly condensed treatment services for patients that are tailored to the primary care culture. The guiding philosophy of this model is to provide behavioral health services to a population of primary care patients. Like primary medical care, consultative and/or condensed treatment services are delivered as a first-line intervention. If a patient fails to respond to this level of intervention (or is obviously in need of highly specialized services), a transfer of care to the mental health specialty system occurs. (p. 93)

A number of approaches to or models of primary mental health care have been developed and implemented. A discussion of some of the various models for an integrated system of primary medical care and behavioral health care and the options for service delivery within each can be found elsewhere (e.g., Katon, 1999; Mori, LoCastro, Grace, & Costello, 1999; Peek, 1997; Peek & Heinrich, 1995; Pruitt, Klapow, Epping-Jordan, & Dresselhaus, 1998; Strosahl, 1996). In particular, the reader is referred to Doherty, McDaniel, and Baird (1996) for the presentation of a model that, in this author's opinion, provides a fairly comprehensive and detailed means of conceptualizing the broad range of possibilities for integration. Table 8.3 reveals the hierarchical nature of this model, this hierarchy depending on both the physical proximity of behavioral health care and other health care providers, and the degree to which collaboration, communication, and a shared sense of vision and treatment paradigms exist. The higher the level of a given service delivery organization or program, the more integrated are the cultures and services of its medical and behavioral health care providers and, consequently, the better equipped it is to handle more demanding cases. A detailed description of each of these levels, where they generally can be found, and the types of cases which they are best and least suited to handle also are presented in Table 8.3.

In many cases, the type of collaborative approach that is taken will be limited by the type of managed care that is being provided to the health plan's covered lives. Thus, one would expect staff model HMOs to be more capable of developing a higher level collaborative model than a network model HMO or one that offers a behavioral health carve-out benefit (see Kanapaux [1998] for a discussion of problems of developing an integrated system within network model HMOs). Regardless of the type of approach that is taken, Haley et al. (1998) offer 10 "tips" for increasing the likelihood of developing psychological services in primary care settings (pp. 237–243). These are:

- *Don't wait for your patients to come to you.* The psychologist should be visible to and accessible to both the primary care provider and his patients. One might even consider seeing patients in their homes.
- *Many of your patients are really sick.* Effort should be made to find out as much about the patient's physical problems and their impact on the patient's psychosocial functioning.
- *No more Lone Ranger — join the posse.* The psychologist should work to develop alliances and collaborate with other health care professionals. He needs to be a team player who is flexible in order to work effectively with other specialists.

TABLE 8.3

Levels of Systematic Collaboration Between Therapists and Other Health Professionals

Level	Description	Where Practiced	Handles Adequately	Handles Inadequately
I. Minimal collaboration	Mental health and other health care professionals work in separate facilities, have separate systems, and rarely communicate about cases.	Most private practices and agencies.	Cases with routine medical or psychological problems that have little biopsychosocial interplay and few management difficulties.	Cases that are refractory to treatment or have significant biopsychosocial interplay.
II. Basic collaboration from a distance	Providers have separate systems at separate sites, but engage in periodic communication about shared patients, mostly by telephone and letter. Communication is driven by specific patient issues. Mental health professionals view each other as resources, but operate on their own, with little sharing of responsibility and little understanding of each other's cultures. There is little sharing of power and responsibility.	Settings with active referral linkages across facilities.	Cases with moderate biopsychosocial interplay, for example, a patient has diabetes and depression, and management of both problems proceeds reasonably well.	Cases that have significant biopsychosocial interplay, especially when the medical or mental health management is not satisfactory to one of the parties.
III. Basic collaboration on site	Mental health and other health care professionals have separate systems but share the same facility. They engage in regular communication about shared patients, mostly by phone or letter, but occasionally meet face to face because of close proximity. They appreciate the importance of each other's roles, may have a sense of being part of a larger, though	HMO settings and rehabilitation centers where collaboration is facilitated by proximity, but there is no systemic approach to collaboration and misunderstandings are common. Also, medical clinics that employ therapists but engage primarily in	Cases with moderate biopsychosocial interplay that require occasional face-to-face interactions between providers to manage and coordinate complex treatment plans.	Cases with significant biopsychosocial interplay, especially those with ongoing and challenging management problems.

somewhat ill-defined team, but do not share a common language or an in-depth understanding of each other's worlds. As in Levels I and II, medical physicians have considerably more power and influence over case management decisions than the other professionals, who may resent this.

| IV. Close collaboration in a partly integrated system | Mental health and other health care professionals share the same sites and have some systems in common, such as scheduling and charting. There are regular face-to-face interactions about patients, mutual consultation, coordinated treatment plans for difficult cases, and a basic understanding and appreciation for each other's role and culture. There is a shared allegiance to a biopsychosocial systems paradigm. However, the routines are still sometimes difficult, team-building meetings are held only occasionally, and there may be operational discrepancies such as copays for mental health but not for medical services. There are likely to be unresolved but manageable tensions over medical physicians' greater power and influence on the collaborative team. | referral-oriented collaboration rather than systemic mutual consultation and team building.

Some HMOs, rehabilitation centers, and hospice centers that systematically build teams. Also some family practice training programs. | Cases with significant biopsychosocial interplay and management complications. | Complex cases with multiple providers and multiple large systems involvement, especially when there is the potential for tension and conflicting agendas among providers or triangling on the part of the patient or family. |

TABLE 8.3
(Continued)

Level	Description	Where Practiced	Handles Adequately	Handles Inadequately
V. Close collaboration in a fully integrated system	Mental health and other health care professionals share the same sites, the same vision, and the same systems in a seamless web of biopsychosocial services. Providers and patients have the same expectations of a team offering prevention and treatment. All professionals are committed to a biopsychosocial systems paradigm and have developed an in-depth understanding of each other's roles and cultures. Regular collaborative team meetings are held to discuss patient issues and team issues. There are conscious efforts to balance power and influence among the professionals according to their roles and areas of expertise.	Some hospice centers and other special training and clinical settings.	The most difficult and complex biopsychosocial cases with challenging management problems.	Cases when the resources of the health care team are insufficient or when breakdowns occur in the collaboration with larger service systems.

Note. From "Five Levels of Primary Care/Behavioral Healthcare Collaboration," by W. J. Doherty, S. H. McDaniel, and M. A. Baird, *Behavioral Healthcare Tomorrow*, October 1, 1996, Vol. 5, No. 5, pp. 26–27. Copyright 1996. Reprinted with permission from Manisses Communications Group, Inc. (1-800-333-7771).

- *Psychotherapy ain't enough.* The psychologist must expand his range of services beyond the more traditional psychotherapeutic and testing activities to related activities, such as psychoeducational services, crisis intervention, outcomes and other research-related programs, community outreach, and program development.
- *Patients don't know why they are seeing you unless you tell them.* The psychologist needs to be aware of the context in which the referral was made and ensure the patient is clear about why the referral was made.
- *Hurry up.* The psychologist must change from a traditional style of practice to one that is consistent with the fast-paced environment of the primary care office. Assessments must be quickly completed and the findings and recommendations quickly conveyed to the referring physician.
- *Don't give any tests that you can't carry in your briefcase.* Any test instruments used should be brief, face valid, and acceptable to both patients and referring providers.
- *Stand up for what you know, and ask about what you don't know.* The psychologist must demonstrate his psychological expertise to other health care providers. At the same time, he needs to acknowledge his limited knowledge in other fields and be willing to seek out others in order to eliminate his deficiencies in these areas.
- *No specialists allowed — be prepared for anything and everything.* Psychologists need to be "generalists" who are capable of dealing with a wide range of medical and psychosocial disorders. Training and experience in medical settings is a must.
- *Refer out when necessary.* Not all patients with behavioral health problems can be effectively assessed or treated in the primary care setting. The psychologist must be able to quickly determine when a patient needs to be referred out to another psychological practitioner.

Stout and Cook (1999) echo some of these same recommendations.

POTENTIAL CONTRIBUTIONS OF PSYCHOLOGICAL TESTING IN PRIMARY CARE SETTINGS

As discussed in earlier chapters of this book, psychological testing has come to be recognized by MBHOs for more than just its usefulness at the beginning of treatment. Its utility has been extended beyond being a mere tool for describing an individual's current state, to a means of facilitating the understanding and treatment of behavioral health care problems throughout and beyond the episode of care. As discussed in chapter 2, several commercial and public-domain psychological tests that are available can be employed as tools (a) to assist in *clinical decision-making* activities, including screening, treatment planning, and treatment monitoring; (b) for measuring and monitoring the *outcomes* of treatment; and (c) more directly, used as *treatment techniques* in and of themselves. These instruments are useful not only in mental health and substance abuse treatment settings, but also in other settings in which the need to identify and provide services for behavioral health problems exists. One such setting is the primary care setting.

Following is an overview of considerations related to psychological test instruments and the potential roles that psychological testing can play in primary care settings. Note that how and for what purpose psychological testing is applied in primary care settings is not necessarily dependent on the type or degree of behavioral health care integration that exists therein. Nor is its use necessarily dependent on who among the provider team administers the test or applies the results. With proper training or under the supervision of a psychologist or other qualified professional formally trained and experienced in the use of these instruments, primary care providers can appropriately administer most psychological test instruments and employ the results in their offices and facilities. And indeed, one important contribution psychologists can make in the primary care setting is ensuring the proper use of psychological tests by nonpsychological personnel (Maruish, 2000b).

General Considerations

The introduction of psychological testing in primary care settings, either alone or as part of a package of managed behavioral health care services, can greatly enhance the diagnostic and treatment options offered by primary care providers. However, there are a few very important considerations to be mindful of if testing is to be fully accepted as a part of the services offered by primary care providers or provider organizations.

One consideration is related to the reimbursement issue that was previously discussed. Testing must be able to pay for itself. Like this author, Ficken (1995) commented on how the managed care has limited the reimbursement for (and therefore the use of) psychological testing. In general, he sees the primary reason for this as being a financial one. In an era of capitated health care coverage, the amount of money available for behavioral health care treatment is limited. Managed care organizations therefore require a demonstration that the amount of money spent for testing will result in a greater amount of treatment cost savings. Again, this author is unaware of any published or unpublished research to date that can provide this demonstration. In addition, Ficken notes that much of the information currently provided by psychological testing is not relevant to the treatment of patients within a managed care environment. Understandably, managed care organizations are reluctant to pay for gathering such information.

The issue of reimbursement for psychological testing takes on another dimension in primary care settings which are not fully integrated with behavioral health care. This is the matter of who pays for the testing: the patient's health plan or the MBHO. This of course is an arrangement that should be specified in the written agreement between the primary care practice and the MBHO or individual psychologist prior to initiating the service.

Another consideration relates to general concerns that primary care providers have expressed regarding the use of self-administered psychological tests. One concern is their belief that patients do not want providers to ask questions related to psychosocial problems. Sperry et al. (1996), however, believe that the literature does not bear this out and suggest that part of the problem may be the provider's own discomfort in asking about these matters. Sperry and Brill (1997) indicated that the use of screening tools can actually reduce the provider's and the patient's discomfort in obtaining information of this nature, particularly if these tools are viewed as "lab tests." Moreover, Sperry and Brill note that patients are more comfortable revealing problems on self-administered tests than to providers. Patients are even more apt to disclose pertinent information if the screening tools are presented to them as lab tests. For those still concerned with this matter, Haber and Mitchell (1997) suggest that a behavioral health questionnaire may be combined with a physical examination and presented as an annual "personal health evaluation" to help reduce any stigma that the patient may feel about responding to questions pertaining to their mental health and substance use.

Lastly, a significant consideration related to the use of psychological tests for screening or monitoring patients has to do with how the results are used. As alluded to earlier, recognition of the presence of a disorder "appears to be a necessary but not sufficient step to improve the outcome of psychiatric and psychological disorders in primary care settings" ("Detection of Psychological Disorders Unrelated to Outcomes," 1996, p. 8). Particularly in screening, the practitioner must be able to provide appropriate intervention for whatever disease or disorder that is being assessed by the instrument. Moreover, Callahan (1997) noted that widespread screening for depression may result not only in an increase in prescription medications (if current treatment guidelines are followed) but also in pharmacological interventions for populations for whom their efficacy has not been proven (e.g., patients with milder forms of depression). Although this observation was limited to depressive symptomatology, it also likely applies to other forms of psychological symptomatology, such as anxiety.

Screening in Primary Settings

Among the most significant ways in which behavioral health care services can contribute to an effective primary care delivery system is by quickly identifying individuals in need of behavioral health or substance abuse treatment. In the field of psychology, the most efficient and thoroughly investigated screening procedures involve the use of self-report psychological test instruments. The power or utility of a psychological screening test lies in its ability to determine, with a high level of confidence, whether or not the respondent likely has a particular disorder or condition and the degree of its severity, and/or whether or not he likely is a member of a population with clearly defined characteristics. The most commonly used psychological screeners in daily clinical practice are those designed to help identify the presence of some specific type of psychological disturbance (e.g., depression) or some specific aspect of psychological dysfunction (e.g., psychotic ideation), or to provide a broad overview of the respondent's point-in-time mental status or level of distress.

Implementation of Screening Into the Daily Flow of Service Delivery. The utility of a screening instrument is only as good as the degree to which it can be integrated into a primary care setting's daily regimen of service delivery. This, in turn, depends on a number of factors. The first and most important consideration is the primary care physician. Findings from Shedler's (2000) interviews and focus groups with primary care physicians revealed a general reluctance to incorporate psychological screening into their offices' daily routine. This reluctance reflected concerns about discomfort in exploring their patients' emotional matters, feeling inadequate in the area of psychiatry, feeling that tests they used in the past (e.g., BDI, Zung SDS) did not meet their needs, and most of all, the time required for screening. From their standpoint, the ideal test would (a) require no special training, time from the physician or their staff, or paper work; (b) not interfere with the daily work flow; (c) provide a DSM-IV diagnosis of the full range of disorders commonly seen in primary care settings; and (d) be accepted by patients. Obviously, no such test exists. But then this is where the value of the psychologist lies. Thus, successful implementation of any screening process must begins with "selling" the primary care physician (whom many would view as the primary customer for the service) on the services that psychologist can provide, as well as enlisting his cooperation in implementing the service.

The second consideration is staff acceptance and commitment to the screening process. This comes only with a clear understanding of the importance of the screening, the usefulness of the obtained information, and how the screening process is to be incorporated into the organization's daily business flow.

The third consideration is the ease and speed of administering and scoring of the screener, and the amount of time required to train the provider's staff to successfully incorporate the screener into their daily workflow. Depending on the particular primary care setting, either the psychologist or the primary care staff will assume frontline responsibility for the administering and/or scoring the scoring instrument. Consequently, these tasks must be as quick and simple as possible.

The fourth factor relates to the instrument's use. Generally, screeners are developed to assist in determining the likelihood that the patient does or does not have the specific condition or characteristic that the instrument is designed to identify. Use for any other purpose (e.g., assigning a diagnosis based solely on screener results, determining the likelihood of the presence of other characteristics) only serves to undermine the integrity of the instrument in the eyes of staff, payers, and other parties with a vested interest in the screening process.

The fifth factor has to do with the ability of the provider to act on the information obtained from the screener. It must be clear how the clinician should proceed based on the information available.

Ficken (1995) provides an example of how screeners can be integrated into an assessment system designed to assist primary care physicians in identifying patients with psychiatric disorders. This system (which also allows for the incorporation of practice guidelines) appears to take into account the first three utility-related factors mentioned above. It begins with the administration of a screener that is highly sensitive and specific to DSM- or ICD-related disorders. These screeners should require no more than 10 minutes to complete and should identify frequently seen, treatable conditions that are associated with significant disability. Also, "[the screeners'] administration must be integrated seamlessly into the standard clinical routine" (p. 13). Somewhat similar to the sequence described by Derogatis and Lynn (1999), positive findings would lead to a second level of testing. Here, another screener that meets the same requirements as those for the first screener and that affirms or rules out a diagnosis would be administered. Positive findings would lead to additional assessment for treatment planning purposes. Consistent with standard practice, Ficken recommends confirmation of screener findings by a qualified psychologist or physician.

Mori et al. (1999) present another screening process that has the psychologist take a more proactive part in the referral aspect of the process. In their *direct contact model*, patients complete a two-part questionnaire—the PRIMECARE Questionnaire (LoCastro, Mori, Grace, & Costello, 1996; Mori, LoCastro, Grace, Costello, & Gibeau, 1997)—during their visit to the primary care provider's office. This first part of the questionnaire contains 19 items measuring psychological and health-related symptoms. The second part lists 13 behavioral medicine services (e.g., pain management, depression, smoking cessation) to which patients can indicate an interest in learning about. Based on responses to the second set of questions, the psychologist initiates phone contact with the patient, assesses his needs, and offers services appropriate to those needs. This proactive approach enables

> clinicians [to] address patients' desire for treatment; educate these patients about the nature and extent of services provided; clarify myths about psychological and behavioral services; address pragmatic issues, such as travel and time constraints; and, most important, initiate a positive relationship with the patient. In the context of this positive and supportive interaction, clinicians guide patients into appropriate treatment or help patients address and work through their treatment reluctance (p. 144).

Who to Screen. There are several approaches to screening that can be taken in primary care settings. One is to screen all patients new to the primary care practice. Here, the approach would be to conduct a high-level screening for the presence of significant levels of distress or psychological disturbance. Everyone gets screened, regardless of his or her presenting problem. This information is gathered routinely, just like medical and other pertinent historical information. This has the advantage of not only helping to identify the presence of hidden or unspoken psychological problems, but also of providing a baseline measure of psychological functioning that may be useful in the future. And just like other recommended aspects of medical care, screening for psychological distress might be scheduled on a regular basis—for example, annually—for the same reason that heart rate, blood pressure, cholesterol, weight, and other health indicators are measured regularly.

Conversely, and much more commonly, screening procedures might be applied only when problems are suspected. Here, one might want to consider using a disorder- or symptom-specific instrument, such as a brief measure of depression, instead of a general nonspecific psychological screener. To some, this might seem to be a much more cost-effective and efficient use of screeners. However, the literature consistently attests to the fact that the real expense will probably come in the utilization of costly resources by those suffering from behavioral health problems that go undetected in the primary care setting. Thus, a general distress screener might be a better choice.

Another good use of psychological screeners in primary care settings is to assist in formal and informal disease management programs. Routinely screening patients with serious and chronic medical problems for common comorbid psychological problems can have more than just financial payoffs. For instance, there is a large body of literature (e.g., Frasure-Smith, Lesperance, & Talajic, 1993, 1995a, 1995b; Lesperance, Frasure-Smith, & Talajic, 1996; Silverstone, 1987) that indicates that post-myocardial infarction (MI) patients with depression have much higher morbidity and mortality rates than do post-MI patients without depression. Here, early detection of depression not only improves the quality of life—it may actually help to prolong the patient's life.

There are many other medical diseases and disorders with frequently co-occurring psychological disorders. Congestive heart failure, diabetes, COPD, asthma, lupus, and postpartum depression are just a few examples. The point here is that there may be a big payoff from any of a number of standpoints—financial, quality of life, and recovery—that may accrue from being able to identify and treat comorbid psychological problems. The trick is to do it quickly and inexpensively, something for which psychological screeners are, by their nature, designed.

Other Considerations for Psychological Screening. Ficken's (1995) screening scenario includes the use of disorder-specific instruments. This certainly seems to be an acceptable approach in settings where screening instruments are administered only to those who are suspected of having a specific disorder, or if effort is being made to identify only those with one or only a few types of disorders. However, in both these and other situations, there are others that recommend a different approach. As Sperry et al. (1996) point out,

> A serious limitation of all of these [disorder-specific] scales is their focus on only one type of pathology. Studies have demonstrated high comorbidity among psychiatric disorders, and this also suggests that a focus on any single disorder is inappropriately narrow. Screening programs for psychiatric disorders in primary care settings should be broad-based, and not limited to any single disorder. (p. 206)

Similarly, in addressing the issue of screening for depression in primary care settings, Zimmerman, Lish, Farber, Hartung, Lush, Kuzma, and Plescia (1994) note that

> Coexistence of depression with other forms of pathology seems to be the rule, not the exception. We would predict the same to be true of other disorders as well . . . Consequently, even if the clinical evaluation that follows the screening questionnaire is limited to disorders that are positive on the questionnaire, it will nevertheless often need to cover multiple psychiatric disorders. Proper case finding in primary care . . . requires attention to a range of illnesses. . . . (p. 394)

Another important consideration related to the use of psychological screeners is their level of sensitivity, or the degree to which those taking the test are identified as having the behavioral problem(s) the instrument was designed to detect. As discussed in chapter 2, the more sensitive the instrument is, the greater the number of test-takers that will be mistakenly identified as having the assessed problem. These *false positives* can lead to unnecessary work and costs for the provider (Locke & Larsson, 1997). At the same time, instruments with lower sensitivity (and thus, higher specificity) will yield more *false negatives* that can result in the type of increased work and medical costs that some of the literature has associated with undetected behavioral health problems. Thus, unless one incorporates something like the two-staged screening described earlier, one must decide which type of identification error is more acceptable, and then carefully evaluate potential screening instruments and associated cutoff scores for the psychometric characteristics.

Treatment Planning, Monitoring, and Outcomes Assessment in Primary Care Settings

The discussion about the general aspects and issues of the use of psychological testing for treatment planning, monitoring, and outcomes assessment that was presented in chapter 2 generally applies to these same activities when they are performed in primary care settings. However, perhaps with the exception of disease management programs, the chances that these types of activities would be carried out in a given primary care setting will likely be related to the degree to which psychological services are integrated into that particular practice. If psychological interventions and related services are not provided by a health care delivery team member as part of the his or her regular duties, it is unlikely that the practice will be interested in using the services of a behavioral health care professional for any of these tasks. These tasks will not be necessary since patients will be referred out for behavioral health treatment.

PSYCHOLOGICAL MEASURES USEFUL FOR ASSESSMENT IN PRIMARY CARE SETTINGS

Many of the tests and other measures described in chapter 5 are appropriate for use in primary care settings. Included among these are the SA-45, the Zung anxiety and depression scales, the CES-D, D-ARK, CAGE-AID, SF-36/SF-12, and the GHAA session-specific satisfaction survey (VSQ). All of these instruments have demonstrated utility for various purposes in primary care practices. But there are also a number of other low- or no-cost psychological measures that have been designed specifically for use in primary care or other medical settings. As in chapter 5, this section presents an overview of instruments that this author finds promising in terms of their potential to assist in the various types of assessment that might be conducted in primary care settings. As was recommended in chapter 5, an attempt has been made to present some basic findings that have been reported in either original sources or published reviews of the literature. Those considering any of the instruments discussed in this chapter are urged to conduct a more thorough review of the literature on these instruments for themselves.

Primary Care Evaluation of Mental Disorders (PRIME-MD)

Probably the best known of the instruments designed specifically for use in primary care settings is the Primary Care Evaluation of Mental Disorders, or PRIME-MD (Hahn et al., 1999; Spitzer et al., 1994). The PRIME-MD actually consists of two different instruments that are used for two-staged screening and diagnosis. The first instrument administered, the Patient Questionnaire (PQ), is a patient self-report screener consisting of 26 items that assess for symptoms of mental disorders or problems that are commonly seen in primary care settings (see Figure 8.1). The general areas screened for include: *somatization, depression, anxiety, alcoholism, eating disorder,* and *health status.*

The PQ essentially is a case-finding tool. On completion of the PQ, the physician scans the answer sheet to determine if the patient's responses suggest the patient may have a specific DSM-IV diagnosis in one of these five targeted areas. If so, the PCP administers relevant modules from the second part of the PRIME-MD, the Clinical Evaluation Guide (CEG), to the patient during the visit. For example, if the patient responds to either of the two depression screening questions from the PQ in a manner suggestive of the possible presence of a depressive disorder, the PCP would administer the mood module from the CEG to the patient while in the examining room. The mood module, like the other four disorder-specific modules, is a structured interview consisting of yes/no branching questions that assess for the presence of each of the criteria for major depressive disorder, partial remission of major depressive

PATIENT QUESTIONNAIRE

Updated for DSM-IV™

NAME: _____   AGE: _____

SEX: ☐ Male ☐ Female   TODAY'S DATE: _____

INSTRUCTIONS: This questionnaire will help in understanding problems that you may have. It may be necessary to ask you more questions about some of these items. Please make sure to check a box for <u>every</u> item.

*During the **PAST MONTH**, have you been bothered A LOT by...*							*During the **PAST MONTH**...*		
	YES	**No**			**YES**	**No**		**YES**	**No**
1. stomach pain	☐	☐	12.	constipation, loose bowels, or diarrhea	☐	☐	21. have you had an anxiety attack (suddenly feeling fear or panic)	☐	☐
2. back pain	☐	☐							
3. pain in your arms, legs, or joints (knees, hips, etc)	☐	☐	13.	nausea, gas, or indigestion	☐	☐	22. have you thought you should cut down on your drinking of alcohol	☐	☐
			14.	feeling tired or having low energy	☐	☐			
4. menstrual pain or problems	☐	☐	15.	trouble sleeping	☐	☐	23. has anyone complained about your drinking	☐	☐
5. pain or problems during sexual intercourse	☐	☐	16.	your eating being out of control	☐	☐	24. have you felt guilty or upset about your drinking	☐	☐
6. headaches	☐	☐							
7. chest pain	☐	☐	17.	little interest or pleasure in doing things	☐	☐	25. was there ever a single day in which you had five or more drinks of beer, wine, or liquor	☐	☐
8. dizziness	☐	☐							
9. fainting spells	☐	☐	18.	feeling down, depressed, or hopeless	☐	☐			
10. feeling your heart pound or race	☐	☐					Overall, would you say your health is:		
11. shortness of breath	☐	☐	19.	"nerves" or feeling anxious or on edge	☐	☐	Excellent ☐ Very good ☐ Good ☐ Fair ☐ Poor ☐		
			20.	worrying about a lot of different things	☐	☐			

FIG. 8.1. PRIME-MD Patient Questionnaire. Copyright © 1992 Pfizer Inc. All rights reserved. Reproduced with permission. PRIME-MD® is a trademark of Pfizer Inc.

disorder, dysthymia, and minor depressive disorder, with rule-outs for bipolar disorder and depressive disorder due to physical disorder, medication, or other drug. (The first page of the CEG mood module is presented in Fig. 8.2.) If other responses to the questions on the PQ suggest the possibility of the presence of DSM-IV diagnoses in any of the other four broad diagnostic areas, the modules related to the areas in questioned are also administered by the PCP.

The major findings from the published research supports the use of the PRIME-MD in primary care settings. Among them are the following:

- The overall rate of agreement between PRIME-MD diagnoses made by PCPs and diagnoses made within 48 hours of the PRIME-MD visit by mental health professionals using semistructured, blinded telephone interviews was relatively good for any psychiatric diagnosis in general ($\kappa = .71$), as well any mood, anxiety, alcohol, and eating disorder ($\kappa = .55-.73$; Spitzer et al., 1994). Kappa coefficients for specific disorders ranged from .15 to .71. The diagnoses made by mental health professionals are considered the standard against which PCP PRIME-MD diagnoses are assessed. Because of the lack of medical training on the part of the mental health professionals, somatoform disorders were not considered in these or similar analyses.

- For specific diagnoses, sensitivities ranged from .22 for minor depressive disorder to .81 for probable alcohol abuse/dependence (Spitzer et al., 1994). Specificities ranged from .91 for anxiety disorder NOS to .98 for major depressive disorder and probable alcohol abuse/dependence. The high specificities obtained across the CEG modules indicates that PCPs using the PRIME-MD rarely make false positive diagnoses. Positive predictive values ranged from .19 for minor depressive disorder to .80 for major depressive disorder.

- The prevalence of threshold mental disorders diagnosed by the PRIME-MD were quite similar to those obtained from the mental health professionals' telephone interviews (Spitzer et al., 1994).

- Using diagnoses made by mental health providers as the criteria, the PQ was found to have sensitivities ranging from 69% for the mood module to 94% for the anxiety module; specificities ranging from 53% for the anxiety module to 91% for the alcohol module; PPPs ranging from 27% for the alcohol module to 62% for the mood module; and overall accuracy rates ranging from 60% for the anxiety module to 91% for the alcohol module (Spitzer et al., 1994).

- The sensitivity and specificity for the PQ two-item depression screen to major depression was essentially identical to that of the Zung SDS, which was also administered to the same sample (Spitzer et al., 1994).

- Using the Short Form General Health Survey (SF-20; Stewart, Hays, & Ware, 1988), Spitzer et al., (1994) and Spitzer et al. (1995) also found that health-related quality of life (HRQL) was related to severity of PRIME-MD-identified psychopathology. Thus, patients with threshold disorders had significantly more HRQL-related impairment than patients who were symptom-screen negative, those who had symptoms but no diagnosis, and those with subthreshold diagnoses.

- Johnson et al.'s (1995) findings supported those of Spitzer et al., (1994) and Spitzer et al. (1995). Johnson et al. found that patients from the same PRIME-MD 1000 Study with CEG-diagnosed alcohol abuse and dependence (AAD) with a

MOOD MODULE

MAJOR DEPRESSION

For the last 2 weeks, have you had any of the following problems <u>nearly every day</u>?

1.	Trouble falling or staying asleep, or sleeping too much?	**Yes**	**No**
2.	Feeling tired or having little energy?	**Yes**	**No**
3.	Poor appetite or overeating?	**Yes**	**No**
4.	Little interest or pleasure in doing things?	**Yes**	**No**
5.	Feeling down, depressed, or hopeless?	**Yes**	**No**
6.	Feeling bad about yourself — or that you are a failure or have let yourself or your family down?	**Yes**	**No**
7.	Trouble concentrating on things, such as reading the newspaper or watching television?	**Yes**	**No**
8.	Being so fidgety or restless that you were moving around a lot more than usual? **If No:** What about the opposite — moving or speaking so slowly that other people could have noticed? **Count as Yes if Yes to either question, or if psycho-motor agitation or retardation observed during interview.**	**Yes**	**No**
9.	In the last 2 weeks, have you had thoughts that you would be better off dead or of hurting yourself in some way? **If Yes:** Tell me about it.	**Yes**	**No**
10.	Are answers to five or more of #1 to #9 Yes (one of which is #4 or #5)?	**Yes**— *Major Depressive Disorder* Go to #12	**No**

FIG. 8.2. *(Continued)*

PARTIAL REMISSION OF MAJOR DEPRESSION

11. Have you ever had a time when you were either much
    more down or depressed, or had even less interest or
    pleasure in doing things?
    If Yes: At that time, did you have many of the problems
             that I just asked you about, like trouble sleeping,
             concentrating, feeling tired, poor appetite, little
             interest in things?
    Count as Yes only if, in the past, patient probably had
    five of symptoms #1 to #9 and acknowledges some
    current depressed mood or little interest or pleasure.

DYSTHYMIA

12. Over the last 2 years, have you often felt down or
    depressed, or had little interest or pleasure in doing things?
    Count as Yes only if also Yes to: Was that on more than
    half the days over the last 2 years?

13. In the last 2 years, has that often made it hard for you to do
    your work, take care of things at home, or get along with
    other people?

MINOR DEPRESSION

14. Was Major Depression (including partial remission)
    diagnosed at #10 or #11?

15. Are answers to two or more of #1 to #9 Yes (one of which
    is #4 or #5)?

BIPOLAR

16. Did a doctor ever say you were manic-depressive or give
    you lithium?
    If Yes: When was that? Do you know why?

DEPRESSION DUE TO PHYSICAL DISORDER,
MEDICATION, OR OTHER DRUG

17. Are current depressed symptoms
    probably due to the biological
    effects of a physical disorder,
    medication, or other drug?

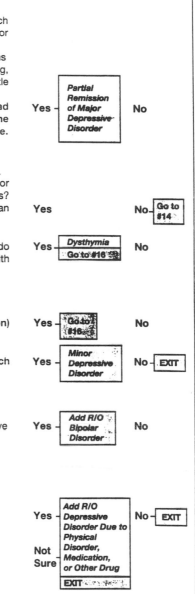

-2-

FIG. 8.2. PRIME-MD Clinical Evaluation Guide Mood Module. Copyright © 1992 Pfizer
Inc. All rights reserved. Reproduced with permission. PRIME-MD® is a trademark of
Pfizer Inc.

comorbid psychiatric disorder reported worse HRQL impairment than those with ADD and no co-occurring psychiatric diagnosis on five of the six SF-20 scales. When compared to patients with no ADD or psychiatric diagnosis, their reported HRQL was worse on all six SF-20 scales.

The reader is referred to Hahn et al. (1999) for an excellent detailed overview of the major PRIME-MD development and validation research that has been conducted to this point. As a summary of these and other research findings, Hahn et al. indicated that

> the PRIME-MD might play a useful role in the routine care of primary care patients. When the PRIME-MD is administered to an unselected group of primary care patients, 80% will trigger at least one module of the Clinical Evaluation Guide. In half of those evaluations, the physician will be rewarded by the confirmation of a mental disorder. Two thirds of these disorders will meet criteria for a *DSM-IV* diagnosis and the remaining third will have a minor or "subthreshold" disorder. If the physician is familiar with the patient, the yield of new diagnoses will still double the number of patients whose psychopathology is detected. Finally, there is strong evidence that even previously detected disorders will be more specifically and precisely identified. (pp. 898–899)

There may be other uses of the PRIME-MD that have not yet been empirically investigated but which should also benefit other types of medical patients. This might include those being seen by medical specialists or being followed in disease management programs. Also, one might consider administering only portions of the instrument. For example, the PQ might be used as a routine screener, to be followed by a nonstructured clinical interview regardless of the results. Similarly, a practice interested in increasing its providers' detection of mood disorders may wish to forgo the administration of the PQ and administer the CEG mood module to all patients.

Overall, research on the PRIME-MD to date indicates its utility as a means for busy PCPs to greatly improve their ability to screen/case-find and diagnose patients with behavioral health disorders that commonly present themselves in primary care settings. With the exception of diagnosing somatoform disorders, this same instrument can be used by behavioral health care professionals seeing patients in this type of setting. Case finding and diagnosing somatoform disorders according PRIME-MD results require medical knowledge that nonphysician behavioral health care professionals typically do not have.

Instruments Derived from the PRIME-MD

Although quite efficient, problems in implementation of the PRIME-MD into daily primary care practices can be problematic. One problem has to do with the amount of time the busy PCP must spend administering the CEG portion of the instrument. Data from the PRIME-MD 1000 Study indicated that the overall average CEG administration time was 8.4 minutes, with an average of 5.6 minutes for those with no PRIME-MD diagnoses and 11.4 minutes for those patients with a diagnosis (Hahn et al., 1999). Considering the fact that 75% of PCP visits usually last no more than 15 minutes (Schappert, 1992), the seemingly short period of time it takes to administer the CEG can be enough to discourage its use. Consequently, Spitzer and his colleagues have begun to explore the development of other versions of the instrument requiring much less time on the part of the PCP.

Because the PRIME-MD was developed to detect only the most commonly seen behavioral health disorders in primary care practices, one must be mindful that it (and the derivative instruments described later) will not be sensitive to all disorders. Other instrumentation will be required if PCP or psychologist wishes to perform a more comprehensive screening for behavioral health disorders.

Patient Health Questionnaire (PHQ).   In response to complaints about the time that it takes to administer the CEG portion of the PRIME-MD, Spitzer and his colleagues developed the Patient Problem Questionnaire (PPQ; Spitzer, Williams, & Kroenke, 1997). The PPQ was essentially a completely self-report version of the PRIME-MD, where all of the CEG questions were presented in a paper-and-pencil format. This instrument has evolved into what is now known as the Patient Health Questionnaire (PHQ; Spitzer et al., 1997).

There are two versions of the PHQ. The "long" version of the PHQ is a four-page patient self-report instrument, with the first three pages presenting diagnostic questions that correspond to the questions from the mood, anxiety, alcohol abuse/dependence, and eating disorder modules of the CEG. The fourth page contains optional questions inquiring about menstruation, pregnancy and childbirth, and recent psychosocial stressors (see Fig. 8.3). The "short" version (the Brief PHQ) presents only the mood and panic disorder questions, along with the same questions found on the fourth page of the longer PHQ. The following discussion pertains to findings regarding the long version of the PHQ.

Unlike the PRIME-MD, the PHQ assesses only eight disorders: four threshold disorders meeting DSM-IV Criteria (major depressive disorder, panic disorder, other anxiety disorder, bulimia nervosa) and four subthreshold disorders that do not meet DSM-IV criteria (other depressive disorder, probable alcohol abuse/dependence, somatoform disorder, binge eating disorder). In addition, the response choices for the depressive and somatoform disorder items were changed from the original PRIME-MD "yes/no" presence format to a multiple-choice frequency format. This allows the depression items to yield a symptom severity level that can be useful in treatment planning, monitoring, and outcomes assessment. For the somatization items, this helps to identify only the clinically significant symptoms. Moreover, the developers added one additional question for those indicating problems in any of the diagnostic sections: "How difficult have these problems made it for you to do your work, take care of things at home, or get along with other people?"

To validate the PHQ, 3,000 primary care (family practice and general internal medicine) patients were administered the PHQ, along with the SF-20 and questions pertaining physician visits and disability days (Spitzer, Kroenke, Williams, et al., 1999). Their physicians were asked questions about their familiarity with the patient, knowledge of current mental and physical disorders, and current mental health treatment or referrals for such treatment being made that day. As during the PRIME-MD study, behavioral health professionals conducted 48-hour structured, follow-up interviews with 585 of the patients. The diagnoses made by mental health professionals were again considered the standard against which PCP PRIME-MD were assessed. Because of their lack of medical training, somatoform disorders were not considered in these or similar analyses.

Spitzer et al.'s (1999) analyses of the data supported the validity and utility of the PHQ, in that:

- The sensitivities, specificities, overall accuracy rates, and kappa coefficients for the PHQ were quite comparable to those found for the original PRIME-MD. The

PATIENT HEALTH QUESTIONNAIRE (PHQ)

This questionnaire is an important part of providing you with the best health care possible. Your answers will help in understanding problems that you may have. Please answer every question to the best of your ability unless you are requested to skip a question.

Name _____ Age_____ Sex: ☐ Female ☐ Male Today's Date_____

1. During the <u>last 4 weeks</u>, how much have you been bothered by any of the following problems?

	Not bothered	Bothered a little	Bothered a lot
a. Stomach pain	☐	☐	☐
b. Back pain	☐	☐	☐
c. Pain in your arms, legs, or joints (knees, hips, etc.)	☐	☐	☐
d. Menstrual cramps or other problems with your periods	☐	☐	☐
e. Pain or problems during sexual intercourse	☐	☐	☐
f. Headaches	☐	☐	☐
g. Chest pain	☐	☐	☐
h. Dizziness	☐	☐	☐
i. Fainting spells	☐	☐	☐
j. Feeling your heart pound or race	☐	☐	☐
k. Shortness of breath	☐	☐	☐
l. Constipation, loose bowels, or diarrhea	☐	☐	☐
m. Nausea, gas, or indigestion	☐	☐	☐

2. Over the <u>last 2 weeks</u>, how often have you been bothered by any of the following problems?

	Not at all	Several days	More than half the days	Nearly every day
a. Little interest or pleasure in doing things	☐	☐	☐	☐
b. Feeling down, depressed, or hopeless	☐	☐	☐	☐
c. Trouble falling or staying asleep, or sleeping too much	☐	☐	☐	☐
d. Feeling tired or having little energy	☐	☐	☐	☐
e. Poor appetite or overeating	☐	☐	☐	☐
f. Feeling bad about yourself, or that you are a failure, or have let yourself or your family down	☐	☐	☐	☐
g. Trouble concentrating on things, such as reading the newspaper or watching television	☐	☐	☐	☐
h. Moving or speaking so slowly that other people could have noticed. Or the opposite—being so fidgety or restless that you have been moving around a lot more than usual	☐	☐	☐	☐
i. Thoughts that you would be better off dead, or of hurting yourself in some way	☐	☐	☐	☐

FOR OFFICE CODING: Som Dis if at least three of #1a–m are "Bothered a lot" and lack an adequate biol explanation. Maj Dep Syn if answer to #2a or b and five or more of #2a–i are at least "More than half the days" (count #2i if present at all). Other Dep Syn if #2a or b and two, three, or four of #2a–i are at least "More than half the days" (count #2i if present at all)   1

FIG. 8.3.   *(Continued)*

3. Questions about anxiety.

		NO	YES
a.	In the <u>last 4 weeks</u>, have you had an anxiety attack—suddenly feeling fear or panic?	☐	☐

If you checked "NO," go to question 5.

		NO	YES
b.	Has this ever happened before?	☐	☐
c.	Do some of these attacks come <u>suddenly out of the blue</u>—that is, in situations where you don't expect to be nervous or uncomfortable?	☐	☐
d.	Do these attacks bother you a lot or are you worried about having another attack?	☐	☐

4. Think about your last bad anxiety attack.

		NO	YES
a.	Were you short of breath?	☐	☐
b.	Did your heart race, pound, or skip?	☐	☐
c.	Did you have chest pain or pressure?	☐	☐
d.	Did you sweat?	☐	☐
e.	Did you feel as if you were choking?	☐	☐
f.	Did you have hot flashes or chills?	☐	☐
g.	Did you have nausea or an upset stomach, or the feeling that you were going to have diarrhea?	☐	☐
h.	Did you feel dizzy, unsteady, or faint?	☐	☐
i.	Did you have tingling or numbness in parts of your body?	☐	☐
j.	Did you tremble or shake?	☐	☐
k.	Were you afraid you were dying?	☐	☐

5. Over the <u>last 4 weeks</u>, how often have you been bothered by the following problems?

		Not at all	Several days	More than half the days
a.	Feeling nervous, anxious, on edge, or worrying a lot about different things	☐	☐	☐

If you checked "Not at all," go to question 6.

		Not at all	Several days	More than half the days
b.	Feeling restless so that it is hard to sit still	☐	☐	☐
c.	Getting tired very easily	☐	☐	☐
d.	Muscle tension, aches, or soreness	☐	☐	☐
e.	Trouble falling asleep or staying asleep	☐	☐	☐
f.	Trouble concentrating on things, such as reading a book or watching television	☐	☐	☐
g.	Becoming easily annoyed or irritated	☐	☐	☐

FOR OFFICE CODING: Pan Syn if all of #3a–d are "YES" and four or more of #4a–k are "YES." Other Anx Syn if #5a and answers to three or more of #5b–g are "More than half the days."

2

FIG. 8.3. *(Continued)*

6. Questions about eating.

		NO	YES
a.	Do you often feel that you can't control <u>what</u> or <u>how much</u> you eat?	☐	☐
b.	Do you often eat, <u>within any 2-hour period</u>, what most people would regard as an unusually <u>large</u> amount of food?	☐	☐

If you checked "NO" to either a or b, go to question 9.

		NO	YES
c.	Has this been as often, on average, as twice a week for the last 3 months?	☐	☐

7. In the last 3 months have you <u>often</u> done any of the following in order to avoid gaining weight?

		NO	YES
a.	Made yourself vomit	☐	☐
b.	Taken more than twice the recommended dose of laxatives	☐	☐
c.	Fasted (not eaten anything at all for at least 24 hours)	☐	☐
d.	Exercised for more than an hour, specifically to avoid gaining weight after binge eating	☐	☐

8. If you checked "YES" to any of these ways of avoiding gaining weight, were any as often, on average, as twice a week?   NO ☐   YES ☐

9. Do you ever drink alcohol (including beer or wine)?   NO ☐   YES ☐

If you checked "NO," go to question 11.

10. Have any of the following happened to you <u>more than once in the last 6 months</u>?

		NO	YES
a.	You drank alcohol even though a doctor suggested that you stop drinking because of a problem with your health	☐	☐
b.	You drank alcohol, were high from alcohol, or were hung over while you were working, going to school, or taking care of children or other responsibilities	☐	☐
c.	You missed or were late for work, school, or other activities because you were drinking or hung over	☐	☐
d.	You had a problem getting along with other people while you were drinking	☐	☐
e.	You drove a car after having several drinks or after drinking too much	☐	☐

11. If you checked off <u>any</u> problems on this questionnaire so far, how <u>difficult</u> have these problems made it for you to do your work, take care of things at home, or get along with other people?

☐ **Not difficult at all**   ☐ **Somewhat difficult**   ☐ **Very difficult**   ☐ **Extremely difficult**

FOR OFFICE CODING: Bul Ner if #6a-c and #8 are all "YES"; Bin Eat Dis the same but #8 is either "NO" or left blank; Alc Abu if any of #10a–e is "YES."   3

FIG. 8.3. *(Continued)*

12. In the last 4 weeks, how much have you been bothered by any of the following problems?

	Not bothered	Bothered a little	Bothered a lot
a. Worrying about your health	☐	☐	☐
b. Your weight or how you look	☐	☐	☐
c. Little or no sexual desire or pleasure during sex	☐	☐	☐
d. Difficulties with husband/wife, partner/lover, or boyfriend/girlfriend	☐	☐	☐
e. The stress of taking care of children, parents, or other family members	☐	☐	☐
f. Stress at work outside of the home or at school	☐	☐	☐
g. Financial problems or worries	☐	☐	☐
h. Having no one to turn to when you have a problem	☐	☐	☐
i. Something bad that happened recently	☐	☐	☐
j. Thinking or dreaming about something terrible that happened to you in the past—like your house being destroyed, a severe accident, being hit or assaulted, or being forced to commit a sexual act	☐	☐	☐

13. In the last year, have you been hit, slapped, kicked, or otherwise physically hurt by someone, or has anyone forced you to have an unwanted sexual act?

NO ☐   YES ☐

14. What is the most stressful thing in your life right now? _____

_____

15. Are you taking any medication for anxiety, depression, or stress?

NO ☐   YES ☐

16. FOR WOMEN ONLY: Questions about menstruation, pregnancy, and childbirth.

a. Which best describes your menstrual periods?

☐ Periods are unchanged	☐ No periods because pregnant or recently gave birth	☐ Periods have become irregular or changed in frequency, duration, or amount	☐ No periods for at least a year	☐ Having periods because taking hormone replacement (estrogen) therapy or oral contraceptives

	NO (or does not apply)	YES
b. During the week before your period starts, do you have a serious problem with your mood—like depression, anxiety, irritability, anger, or mood swings?	☐	☐
c. If YES, do these problems go away by the end of your period?	☐	☐
d. Have you given birth within the last 6 months?	☐	☐
e. Have you had a miscarriage within the last 6 months?	☐	☐
f. Are you having difficulty getting pregnant?	☐	☐

Developed by Drs Robert L. Spitzer, Janet B.W. Williams, Kurt Kroenke, and colleagues, with an educational grant from Pfizer Inc. For research information, contact Dr Spitzer at ris8@columbia.edu. The names PRIME-MD® and PRIME MD TODAY™ are trademarks of Pfizer Inc.

TX221Y99A © 1999, Pfizer Inc

Printed in USA/August 1999

4

FIG. 8.3.   Patient Health Questionnaire. Copyright © 1992 Pfizer Inc. All rights reserved. Reproduced with permission. PRIME-MD® is a trademark of Pfizer Inc.

only significant differences found in these operating characteristics were that the PHQ obtained a lower specificity for any eating disorder, a higher specificity for any anxiety disorder, and a higher kappa for panic disorder.

- Although the PHQ overall prevalence for any diagnosis was less that that obtained in the original PRIME-MD study (Spitzer et al., 1994), the PHQ-derived and behavioral health professional-derived diagnostic prevalences were quite comparable. Also, the score on an depression severity index (the sum of scores on the nine depressive symptoms) derived from the PHQ administration correlated .84 with that obtained from the telephone interview.

- While 85% of the PCPs could review the PHQ results in less than 3 minutes, only 16% of the physicians in the original PRIME-MD could administer the CEG in the same amount of time.

- As in the Spitzer et al. (1995) study with the PRIME-MD, HRQL was related to severity of PRIME-MD identified psychopathology. Patients with threshold disorders had more HRQL-related impairment than patients with subthreshold disorders, whose impairment was worse than those who had symptoms but no diagnosis, whose HRQL impairment was greater than those whose symptom screen was negative. With one exception, the differences between each group on each of the six SF-20 scales was significant at $p < .05$. These same groups also differed significantly ($p < .001$) from each other in both the number of visits to a physician during the previous 3 months (with one exception) and days kept from usual activities (again, with one exception).

- The percent of patients with any psychiatric disorder which went unrecognized by the PCP prior to seeing PHQ results was comparable to that found with the PRIME-MD 1000 Study patients (46% vs. 48%). This rate was lower than the PRIME-MD for any mood and any anxiety disorder, but higher for probable alcohol abuse/dependence and any eating disorder.

- The last PHQ question ("How difficult have these problems made it for you . . .") was found to be associated with the probability that the patient had a threshold or subthreshold diagnosis. Also, correlation of this question with the 6 SF-20 scores ranged from .27 to .53, indicating a relationship with functional impairment.

The PHQ can provide an excellent solution for those PCPs who want to be more thorough in screening their patients for behavioral health problems but simply do not have enough time to do so. In addition, since DSM-IV diagnostic criteria apply in all settings, the instrument should be appropriate and valid for use in other medical and behavioral health settings. For this same reason and because of the modular design (i.e., disorder-specific items being grouped together), it would appear quite appropriate to "pull out" and administer an individual section of the PHQ (e.g., the depression questions) for screening for one type of disorder (e.g., major depression).

IVR-Administered PRIME-MD (IVR-PRIME-MD).   Recognizing how CEG administration time and other factors (e.g., training issues) impede the implementation of the PRIME-MD in busy primary care offices, Kobak, Taylor, Dottl, Greist, Jefferson, Burroughs, Mantle, et al. (1997) turned to the use of interactive voice response (IVR) technology as a platform on which a patient self-administered version of the instrument could be administered. This technology would allow patients toll-free access to a computerized administration of the PRIME-MD 24 hours a day, 7 days a week. As with the PHQ, the time to review the results would be minimal.

Kobak, Taylor, Dottl, Greist, Jefferson, Burroughs, Mantle, et al. (1997) sought to validate the IVR version of the PRIME-MD (hereafter referred to as the IVR-PRIME-MD) using 170 outpatients from various primary care and behavioral health settings, as well as 30 nonpatients. The IVR-PRIME-MD differs from the original PRIME-MD in two ways. First, it does not include PQ and CEG somatization questions because of the need for medical expertise to correctly score these questions. Second, it includes obsessive–compulsive and social phobia questions and diagnostic criteria. All 200 participants were administered the IVR-PRIME-MD and the SCID (mood, anxiety, eating disorders, and psychoactive substance use modules) within 72 hours of each other. One hundred five of the participants were also administered a modified version of the PRIME-MD which, like the IVR-PRIME-MD, excludes the PQ and CEG somatization questions but included the obsessive–compulsive and social phobia questions and diagnostic criteria. The SCID-derived diagnoses served as the standard against which both the IVR-PRIME-MD and PRIME-MD results were compared.

Results from the Kobak, Taylor, Dottl, Greist, Jefferson, Burroughs, Mantle, et al. (1997) supported the IVR-PRIME-MD as both an alternative to the standard form of the PRIME-MD and as a valid diagnostic instrument. The percent of subjects who screened positive on the PQ portion of the IVR and standard forms were 81% and 80%, respectively. Comparison with SCID results indicated that rates for the identification of any psychiatric disorder were comparable (60% vs. 59%, respectively). Comparable results were also found for the identification of individual diagnoses except for dysthymia, with the IVR version identifying 23% and the SCID 9%. Analyses of the results of the subsample of 105 participants completing the IVR-PRIME-MD, PRIME-MD, and SCID revealed comparable identification rates for any psychiatric disorder (62%, 57%, and 61%, respectively) and, with the exception of dysthymia, for all individual diagnoses. Again, the IVR-PRIME-MD tended to identify more participants as having dysthymia. In addition, the rate at which the IVR-PRIME-MD assigned diagnoses to the nonpatient community (37%) was lower than that for the patients from specialty care clinics (90%) and drug study patients (86%).

Looking at only those patients who were seen in primary care settings (n = 80), Kobak, Taylor, Dottl, Greist, Jefferson, Burroughs, Mantle, et al. (1997) found no significant differences between prevalence rates of individual diagnoses obtained by the IVR-PRIME-MD, PRIME-MD, and SCID. However, the IVR-PRIME-MD diagnostic rate for alcohol abuse/dependence was double that of the SCID, while the SCID's diagnostic rate of any anxiety disorder was double that of the IVR-PRIME-MD. Moreover, with the exception of the alcohol abuse diagnosis, the prevalence rates for Kobak et al.'s primary care subsample did not differ significantly from Spitzer et al.'s (1994) PRIME-MD Study 1000 primary care sample.

The IVR-PRIME-MD and PRIME-MD diagnostic rates were compared using the SCID diagnoses as the standard of accuracy (Kobak, Taylor, Dottl, Greist, Jefferson, Burroughs, Mantle, et al., 1997). Overall, the diagnostic efficiency statistics both were quite good. For the "any diagnosis," the respective IVR-PRIME-MD and PRIME-MD sensitivities, specificities, and positive predictive values were 88% and 88%, 79% and 83%, and 85% and 89%. Kappa coefficients for the two instruments were .66 and .70, respectively, indicating that both instruments showed significant agreement with the SCID for the presence of any diagnosis. For individual diagnoses, the rates were comparable between instruments, with the PRIME-MD rates tending to be slightly better than those for the IVR-PRIME-MD. Kappa coefficients for individual diagnoses ranged from .03 to .77 for the IVR-PRIME-MD and −.04 to .83 for the PRIME-MD, with all but one being significant for the IVR-PRIME-MD and all but three being signficant for the PRIME-MD. With one exception ("any anxiety disorder"), there were no significant differences in the proportion of times that each of the two instruments differed on a SCID diagnosis when differences did occur.

The average time for all participants to complete the IVR-PRIME-MD was 11.5 minutes; for the primary care subsample, it was 9.5 minutes (Kobak, Taylor, Dottl, Greist, Jefferson, Burroughs, Mantle, et al., 1997). Note that this does not involve any clinician time as compared to the average 8.4 minutes of clinician time that Spitzer et al.'s (1994) physicians required for completion of the PRIME-MD CEG. Also notable is the fact that 10% of the diagnoses assigned by primary care physicians in the Kobak et al. were incorrect because of scoring errors.

In another investigation, Kobak and his colleagues (Kobak, Taylor, Dottl, Greist, Jefferson, Burroughs, Katzelnick, & Mandell, 1997) explored the comparability of findings from the both the IVR-PRIME-MD and a computerized desktop version of the PRIME-MD to each other and those from a live, telephone administration of the SCID-IV for a group 51 outpatient psychiatric patients. Again, the PRIME-MD somatization module was not included while obsessive-compulsive and social phobia modules were added. In summary,

> the [desktop and IVR] versions of the PRIME-MD worked well. Prevalence rates for any diagnosis, for any affective disorder, and for any anxiety disorder obtained by the [two] computer interviews were similar to those obtained by the SCID-IV. Prevalence rates for individual diagnoses were also similar, with the exception of dysthymia and obsessive–compulsive disorder. . . . Diagnostic accuracy using the SCID-IV as the "gold standard" was high for both the IVR and desktop versions of the PRIME-MD. Sensitivity, specificity, positive predictive value, and overall accuracy rates were high for most diagnoses, and accuracy rates were similar to those obtained by clinician-administered primary care screening interviews, such as . . . the clinician-administered PRIME-MD. Problems with poor positive predictive value . . . that have plagued past screeners have been largely overcome with the computer PRIME-MD. (pp 1055–1056)

Preliminary investigations of the IVR-PRIME-MD show that it yields results that are generally consistent with those that would be obtained from the administration of the PQ and CEG of the PRIME-MD, the desktop PRIME-MD, and, more importantly, the SCID. In addition to the clinician administration time savings advantage that it has over the PRIME-MD, use of the IVR-PRIME-MD version has other advantages. These include no required clinician training to use the instrument properly, the ability of the patient to complete the administration outside of the clinician's office, and the tendency of patients to be more open to responding to certain types of questions. The drawbacks of this instrument are the same as those that can be found for the PHQ, and for any instrument that is administered via an IVR format. Issues regarding the latter were discussed in detail in chapter 4.

Major Depression Screener.   In some primary care settings, the greatest interest will be in screening patients only for depression. There are a number of excellent, well-validated screeners with proven validity and reliability that are available. Another option for the psychologist is a screening procedure that can be derived from the PQ and CEG portions of the PRIME-MD.

Whooley, Avins, Miranda, and Browner (1997) found that the two-item PQ screener was highly sensitive to major depression; however, specificity was only modest. Expanding on this work, Brody, Hahn, Spitzer, Kroenke, Linzer, deGruy, & Williams (1998) found that for the primary care outpatients from the PRIME-MD 1000 study, 97% of those with diagnosed major depression and 94% of those with no major depression were accurately identified if (a) they answered yes to either of the two depression questions on the PQ, and (b) they indicated the presence of at least two of four core depressive symptoms "nearly every day for the past 2 weeks." These core symptoms are *Sleep disturbance, Anhedonia, Low Self-esteem*, and *Appetite change*, which are easily remembered with the acronym "SALSA." In regression analyses, these were found to account for almost all of the variance in well-being and functional status (as measured by the SF-20) that can be explained by the nine depression symptoms queried in the PRIME-MD CEG. They correspond to Items 1, 3, 4, and 6 of the PRIME-MD CEG mood module, and to Items 2a, 2c, 2e, and 2f of the PHQ. The items and scoring criteria for the major depression screener are presented in Fig. 8.4.

In addition, Brody et al. (1998) found that regardless of the presence of major depression, the degree of symptomatic and functional impairment tend to increase with an increase in the endorsement of the four SALSA symptoms. Also, the authors pointed out that suicide ideation will be found in almost 25% of the patients who endorse three or four of the symptoms. The results from the study led the authors to conclude that

> Using the 2-item PRIME-MD depression screening questionnaire followed by an evaluation of the core subset of depressive symptoms of sleep disturbance, anhedonia, low self-esteem, and appetite changes is an efficient and effective way of identifying and classifying primary care patients with depression who are in need of clinical attention. (p. 2474)

The PRIME-MD, along with its alternate versions and derivatives, represent the products of efforts to help solve the problem of the identification of mental health and substance abuse problems in primary care settings. Neither the original instrument nor its variations enjoy the long history of psychometric research that accompanies the more commonly used psychological assessment instruments. The initial research is quite encouraging and supportive of their use as screening tools. But, as with any of the newer, less researched instruments, caution should be exercised in their use pending additional empirical findings.

Mini-International Neuropsychiatric Interview (M.I.N.I.)

Another instrument that is similar to the PRIME-MD is the Mini-International Neuropsychiatric Interview (M.I.N.I.). Sheehan et al. (1998) developed the M.I.N.I. to fulfill a need that they saw as not being met by instruments such as the PRIME-MD, that is, "a need for a structured interview that would bridge the gap between the detailed, academic, research-oriented interview and the ultrashort screening tests designed for primary care" (p. 23). The instrument was designed to assess 17 DSM-IV Axis I diagnoses as well as Axis II antisocial personality disorder and suicidality. These disorders were thought to be the most common, based on findings from the NIMH Epidemiologic Catchment Area Program (Regier, Myers, Kramer, et al., 1984) and the National Comorbidity Survey (Kessler, McGonagle, Zhao, et al., 1994). Reliability and validity data for this instrument is presented in Sheehan, Lecrubier, Sheehan, Janavs, Weiller, Keskiner, Schinka, Knapp, Sheehan, and Dunbar (1997) and Lecrubier, Sheehan, Weiller, Amorim, Bonora, Sheehan, Janavs, and Dunbar (1997).

PRIME-MD Major Depression Screener

1) During the past month, have you often been bothered by
   a) Little interest or pleasure in doing things?
   b) Feeling down, depressed, or hopeless?

(If "yes" to 1a or 1b, proceed to #2)

2) For the last 2 weeks, have you had any of the following problems *nearly every day?*
   a) Trouble falling or staying asleep, or sleeping too much?
   b) Little interest or pleasure in doing things?
   c) Feeling bad about yourself, or feeling that you are a failure or have let yourself or your family down?
   d) Poor appetite or overeating?

Interpretation: "Yes" to 2 or more of 2a–2d is a strong indicator of major depression.

FIG. 8.4.   PRIME-MD major depression screener and scoring criteria. From "Identifying Patients with Depression in the Primary Care Setting," by D. S. Brody, S. R. Hahn, R. L. Spitzer, K. Kroenke, M. Linzer, F. V. deGruy, & J. B. Williams, 1998, *Archives of Internal Medicine, 158,* 2469–2475. Copyright © 1992 Pfizer Inc. All rights reserved. Reproduced with permission. PRIME-MD® is a trademark of Pfizer Inc.

The M.I.N.I. actually is a family of five instruments: the M.I.N.I. as described above (see Fig. 8.5 for the major depression module from the M.I.N.I.); the M.I.N.I.-Plus, which assesses for 23 disorders and is geared toward research applications; the M.I.N.I.-Screen, designed for use in primary care settings; the M.I.N.I. Patient Health Survey, also designed for use in primary care settings; and the M.I.N.I.-Kid, a structure instrument for use with children and adolescents. Although the M.I.N.I. was primarily developed for use primary care settings, it also has been employed in studies investigating impulse-control disorders (Lejoyeux, Feuche, Loi, Solomon, & Ades (1999), compulsive buying (Lejoyeux, Haberman, Solomon, & Ades, 1999), and phobic symptoms (Berlin, Sachon, Bisserbe, Bosquet, Eiber, Grimaldi, & Balssa, 1997).

The focus of this discussion will be on the M.I.N.I.-Screen and the M.I.N.I. Patient Health Survey. The reader is referred to Sheehan, Lecrubier, et al. (1997) and Sheehan, Lecrubier, et al. (1998) for discussions concerning the other instruments in the M.I.N.I. suite.

M.I.N.I.-Screen.   For primary care settings, Sheehan and his colleagues (Sheehan et al. 1998) idntifed a need to ask about more than the six types of disorders that are covered in the PRIME-MD. This led to the development of the *M.I.N.I.-Screen,* a yes/no checklist that asks the respondent about the presence of 25 psychiatric symptoms and associated behaviors that have occurred during the past month or past year (see Fig. 8.6). The assumption is that the results would be used to guide decisions about the need to administer all or portions of the lengthier M.I.N.I. instruments.

M.I.N.I. Patient Health Survey.   The M.I.N.I. Patient Health Survey (PHS) is another version of the M.I.N.I. intended for use in primary care settings (see Fig. 8.7). It is distributed in conjunction with the SmithKline Beecham MindSet program materials that were developed for use in training primary care physicians in the detection

A. MAJOR DEPRESSIVE EPISODE

(➡ MEANS : GO TO THE DIAGNOSTIC BOXES, CIRCLE NO IN ALL DIAGNOSTIC BOXES, AND MOVE TO THE NEXT MODULE)

A1	Have you been consistently depressed or down, most of the day, nearly every day, for the past two weeks?	NO	YES	1
A2	In the past two weeks, have you been less interested in most things or less able to enjoy the things you used to enjoy most of the time?	NO	YES *	2
	IS A1 OR A2 CODED YES?	➡ NO	YES	

A3   **Over the past two weeks, when you felt depressed or uninterested:**

a	Was your appetite decreased or increased nearly every day? Did your weight decrease or increase without trying intentionally (i.e., by ±5% of body weight or ±8 lbs. or ±3.5 kgs., for a 160 lb./70 kg. person in a month)? IF YES TO EITHER, CODE YES.	NO	YES *	3
b	Did you have trouble sleeping nearly every night (difficulty falling asleep, waking up in the middle of the night, early morning wakening or sleeping excessively)?	NO	YES	4
c	Did you talk or move more slowly than normal or were you fidgety, restless or having trouble sitting still almost every day?	NO	YES *	5
d	Did you feel tired or without energy almost every day?	NO	YES	6
e	Did you feel worthless or guilty almost every day?	NO	YES	7
f	Did you have difficulty concentrating or making decisions almost every day?	NO	YES	8
g	Did you repeatedly consider hurting yourself, feel suicidal, or wish that you were dead?	NO	YES	9

ARE 5 OR MORE ANSWERS (A1-A3) CODED YES?

```
┌─────────────────────────────────┐
│ NO              YES *           │
│                                 │
│ MAJOR DEPRESSIVE                │
│ EPISODE  CURRENT                │
└─────────────────────────────────┘
```

IF PATIENT HAS CURRENT MAJOR DEPRESSIVE EPISODE CONTINUE TO A4,
OTHERWISE MOVE TO MODULE B:

A4 a	During your lifetime, did you have other periods of two weeks or more when you felt depressed or uninterested in most things, and had most of the problems we just talked about?	➡ NO	YES	10
b	Did you ever have an interval of at least 2 months without any depression and any loss of interest between 2 episodes of depression?			

```
┌─────────────────────────────────┐
│ NO              YES      11      │
│                                 │
│ MAJOR DEPRESSIVE                │
│ EPISODE  PAST                   │
└─────────────────────────────────┘
```

* If patient has Major Depressive Episode, Current, code YES in corresponding questions on page 5

FIG. 8.5.   M.I.N.I. Major Depression Module. Copyright © 1996 D. V. Sheehan et al. All rights reserved. Reproduced with permission.

and treatment of behavioral health disorders. The PHS contains patient-completed modules to assess for the presence of four disorders: major depressive disorder, alcohol dependence, panic disorder, and social anxiety disorder. Sheehan et al. (1997) administered the patient-completed M.I.N.I. and the patient-completed version of the Structured Clinical Interview for DSM-III-R Patients (SCID-P; Spitzer et al., 1990) as a diagnostic standard, to a group of 370 adults, 62 of whom were nonpatient controls. In investigating the patient-completed M.I.N.I.'s diagnostic efficiency, the following respective kappa coefficient statistics and sensitivity, specificity, PPP, NPP, and overall efficiency percentages were obtained for the modules covered by the PHS: .55, 77%, 79%, 75%, 81%, and 78% for major depressive disorder; .59, 70%, 89%, 69%, 90%, and 84% for current panic disorder; .31, 76%, 75%, 30%, 96%, and 75% for current social phobia; and .60, 89%, 90%, 52%, 99%, and 90% for alcohol dependence.

M.I.N.I. PATIENT SCREEN

IN THE PAST MONTH, have you suffered from:

1.	depression	❏ NO	❏ YES
2.	sadness	❏ NO	❏ YES
3.	unhappiness	❏ NO	❏ YES
4.	loss of interest or pleasure	❏ NO	❏ YES
5.	despair or gloom	❏ NO	❏ YES
6.	feeling suicidal or wishing you were dead	❏ NO	❏ YES
7.	elated mood or unusual energy	❏ NO	❏ YES
8.	persistent irritability	❏ NO	❏ YES
9.	panic attacks	❏ NO	❏ YES
10.	unexpected anxiety symptoms	❏ NO	❏ YES
11.	fear of crowds, traveling or being away from home alone	❏ NO	❏ YES
12.	fear of being the focus of attention	❏ NO	❏ YES
13.	fear of situations, places or things	❏ NO	❏ YES
14.	recurrent, unwanted impulses, thoughts, or images	❏ NO	❏ YES
15.	excessive worry	❏ NO	❏ YES
16.	hearing voices when there was no one around	❏ NO	❏ YES
17.	believing that others were plotting against you	❏ NO	❏ YES
18.	fear of gaining weight or becoming fat	❏ NO	❏ YES
19.	eating binges	❏ NO	❏ YES
20.	reexperiencing a traumatic event	❏ NO	❏ YES

IN THE PAST 12 MONTHS did you:

21.	drink more than 3 drinks in a 3 hour period	❏ NO	❏ YES
22.	have a problem with drugs	❏ NO	❏ YES
23.	feel no guilt after doing something wrong	❏ NO	❏ YES
24.	behave irresponsibly	❏ NO	❏ YES
25.	How many times have you seen a physician in the last year?	_____	

FIG. 8.6.   M.I.N.I.-Screen. Copyright © 1996 D. V. Sheehan et al. All rights reserved. Reproduced with permission.

MINI Patient Health Survey

Patient name: .... Date: ....

NO	YES	
☐	☐	1. Have you been consistently depressed or down, most of the day, nearly every day, for the past two weeks?
☐	☐	2. In the past two weeks, have you been less interested in most things or less able to enjoy the things you used to enjoy most of the time?

> **If your answer to both questions above is "NO", please proceed to Section II without answering question 3 below.**

3. Over the past two weeks, when you felt depressed or uninterested:

NO	YES	
☐	☐	a Was your appetite decreased or increased nearly every day? Did your weight decrease or increase without trying intentionally (i.e. by ±5% of body weight or ±8 lbs or ±3.5kg for a 160 lb/70kg person in a month)? (If yes to either, please check "YES".)
☐	☐	b Did you have trouble sleeping nearly every night (difficulty falling asleep, waking up in the middle of the night, early morning wakening or sleeping excessively)?
☐	☐	c Did you talk or move more slowly than normal or were you fidgety, restless or having trouble sitting still almost every day?
☐	☐	d Did you feel tired or without energy almost every day?
☐	☐	e Did you feel worthless or guilty almost every day?
☐	☐	f Did you have difficulty concentrating or making decisions almost every day?
☐	☐	g Did you repeatedly consider hurting yourself, feel suicidal, or wish that you were dead?

NO	YES	
☐	☐	1. In the past 12 months, have you had 3 or more alcoholic drinks within a 3 hour period on 3 or more occasions?

> **If your answer to this question is "NO", you have completed section II – please do not answer the questions below. Please proceed to Section III.**

2. In the past 12 months:

NO	YES	
☐	☐	a Did you need to drink more in order to get the same effect that you got when you first started drinking?
☐	☐	b When you cut down on drinking did your hands shake, did you sweat or feel agitated? Did you drink to avoid these symptoms? (If yes to either, please check "YES".)
☐	☐	c During the times when you drank alcohol, did you end up drinking more than you planned when you started?
☐	☐	d Have you tried to reduce or stop drinking alcohol but failed?
☐	☐	e On the days that you drank, did you spend substantial time in obtaining alcohol, drinking, or in recovering from the effects of alcohol?
☐	☐	f Did you spend less time working, enjoying hobbies, or being with others because of your drinking?
☐	☐	g Have you continued to drink even though you knew that it caused you problems?

FIG. 8.7. (Continued)

MINI Patient Health Survey

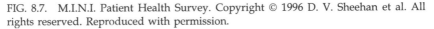

	NO	YES
1. Have you, on more than one occasion, had spells or attacks when you suddenly felt anxious, frightened, uncomfortable or uneasy, even in situations where most people would not feel that way? Did the spells peak within 10 minutes? (If yes to either please check "YES".)	☐	☐
2. At any time in the past, did any of those spells or attacks come on unexpectedly or occur in an unpredictable or unprovoked manner?	☐	☐

If your answer to both questions above is "NO", please proceed to Section IV without answering any other questions below in Section III.

	NO	YES
3. Have you ever had one such attack followed by a month or more of persistent fear of having another attack, or worries about the consequences of the attack?	☐	☐
4. During the worst spell that you can remember:		
a Did you have skipping, racing or pounding of your heart?	☐	☐
b Did you have sweating or clammy hands?	☐	☐
c Were you trembling or shaking?	☐	☐
d Did you have shortness of breath or difficulty breathing?	☐	☐
e Did you have a choking sensation or a lump in your throat?	☐	☐
f Did you have chest pain, pressure or discomfort?	☐	☐
g Did you have nausea, stomach problems or sudden diarrhea?	☐	☐
h Did you feel dizzy, unsteady, lightheaded or faint?	☐	☐
i Did things around you feel strange, unreal, detached or unfamiliar, or did you feel outside of or detached from, part or all of your body?	☐	☐
j Did you fear that you were losing control or going crazy?	☐	☐
k Did you fear that you were dying?	☐	☐
l Did you have tingling or numbness in parts of your body?	☐	☐
m Did you have hot flushes or chills?	☐	☐
5. In the past month, did you have such attacks repeatedly (2 or more) followed by persistent fear of having another attack?	☐	☐

	NO	YES
1. In the past month, were you fearful of or embarrassed by being watched or being the focus of attention, or fearful of being humiliated? This includes things like speaking in public, eating in public alone or with others, writing while someone watches, or being in social situations?	☐	☐
2. Is this fear excessive or unreasonable?	☐	☐
3. Do you fear these situations so much that you avoid them or suffer through them?	☐	☐
4. Does this fear disrupt your normal work or social functioning or cause you significant distress?	☐	☐

FIG. 8.7. M.I.N.I. Patient Health Survey. Copyright © 1996 D. V. Sheehan et al. All rights reserved. Reproduced with permission.

Sheehan et al. (1997) looked at the concordance between diagnoses assigned by the clinician-rated and patient-completed versions of the M.I.N.I. Specific κ values were not reported, but were described as being "high" (> 0.75) for current panic disorder and current alcohol dependence, "good" (0.60–0.74) for major depressive disorder, and "low" (< 0.50) for current social phobia.

Perhaps with the exception of social phobia, the PHS appears to be another quick and easy screening instrument that can be useful in primary care settings. In addition, Sheehan et al. (1998) indicate the availability of computerized, IVR, and foreign translation versions of the M.I.N.I. It would be important to see further research on the PHS, but the design of the instrument (as a straightforward query of DSM-IV criteria) and the available data suggests that the PHS is an appropriate and useful screen for the presence of some disorders commonly seen in primary care settings.

Duke Anxiety-Depression Scale (DUKE-AD)

A relatively unknown depression screener that may meet the needs of many primary care settings is the Duke Anxiety–Depression Scale, or DUKE-AD (Parkerson, 1999; Parkerson & Broadhead, 1997; Parkerson, Broadhead, & Tse, 1996). The DUKE-AD is a 7-item instrument developed by Parkerson and his colleagues at the Duke University Medical Center as a derivative of the Duke Health Profile (DUKE; Parkerson, 1999; Parkerson, Broadhead, & Tse, 1990, 1991). The DUKE is a 17-item self-report measure of functional health status designed for use in primary care settings. It contains 6 scales that measure function and 5 scales that measure dysfunction. One of the dyfunction scales is the DUKE-AD, which is actually a hybrid combination of the DUKE's separate Anxiety and Depression scales. The DUKE-AD consists of items that assess for giving up too easily, concentration problems, feeling comfortable around people, and problems related to sleep, tiring easily, feeling depressed, and nervousness (see Fig. 8.8). Each item is responded to using a 3-point (0–2) Likert scale, with possible total raw scores ranging from 0–14. A score of 5 or greater indicates that symptoms of anxiety and/or depression are "excessive."

The DUKE-AD development work was carried out by Parkerson et al. (1996) during a study that involved the analyses of the response of 413 adult primary care patients to the DUKE, the CES-D, and the State Anxiety Inventory (SAI; Spielberger, 1983). Parkerson et al. obtained many forms of psychometric support for the use of the measure from these data. First, the DUKE-AD achieved an alpha coefficient of 0.69. This is relatively high, given that the instrument contains only 7 items. Patients with high scores on the SAI (raw score $\geq$ 46) and the CES-D (raw score $\geq$ 16) were found to to have significantly higher scores on the DUKE-AD, and an ROC AUC of 82% was obtained for symptoms of both depression and anxiety.

Using the SAI cutoff score as the criterion for the presence of anxiety and a DUKE-AD raw score of 5 or greater for classification of patients as anxious, the DUKE-AD achieved a sensitivity, specificity, PPP, and NPP of 79%, 75%, 63%, and 87% (Parkerson et al., 1996). Using the CES-D cutoff score and a DUKE-AD cutoff score to classify patients as depressed, the sensitivity, specificity, PPP, and NPP of 73%, 78%, 73%, and 79%, respectively. Moreover, the baseline DUKE-AD scores were significantly higher ($p < .05$) for, or more predictive of, patients who had worse 18-month outcomes on five variables: having at least one follow-up visit, number of follow-up visits, number of referrals and/or hospitalizations, follow-up illness severity, and follow-up charges.

Parkerson et al. (1996) split the sample into high-risk (DUKE-AD raw score of 5 or greater) and low-risk subsamples and found that the high-risk group had significantly higher SAI and CES-D scores than the low-risk group. The high-risk group also had significantly lower quality of life and social support scores, and significantly higher severity of illness and social stress scores than the low-risk group as measured by other study instruments. They also presented with significantly more health problems at baseline and were more likely than the low-risk subsample to have at least

Duke Anxiety-Depression Scale (DUKE-AD)

INSTRUCTIONS: Here are some questions about your health and feelings. Please read each question carefully and check (√) your best answer. You should answer the questions in your own way. There are no right or wrong answers.

	Yes, describes me exactly	Somewhat describes me	No, doesn't describe me at all
1. I give up too easily	2	1	0
2. I have difficulty concentrating	2	1	0
3. I am comfortable being around people	0	1	2

*DURING THE **PAST WEEK**:*
 How much trouble have you had with:

	None	Some	A Lot
4. Sleeping	0	1	2
5. Getting tired easily	0	1	2
6. Feeling depressed or sad	0	1	2
7. Nervousness	0	1	2

HOW TO SCORE

1. Add the scores next to each of the blanks you checked.
2. If your total score is 5 or greater, then your symptoms of anxiety and/or depression may be excessive.

(For exact scoring, multiply the total score by 7.143 to obtain the DUKE-AD score on a scale of 0 for lowest to 100 for highest symptom level.)

FIG. 8.8.   Duke Anxiety-Depression Scale (DUKE-AD). Copyright © 1994–1999 by the Department of Community and Family Medicine, Duke University Medical Center, Durham, NC, USA. All rights reserved. Reproduced with permission.

one return visit. The high-risk group was more frequently (p = .003) diagnosed by their care providers as being anxious or depressed without the benefit of knowing the DUKE-AD scores.

In another study, Parkerson and Broadhead (1997) extended their investigation of the validity of the DUKE-AD using a sample of 481 ambulatory primary care patients. Two hundred eighty-two of these patients screened positive for depressive symptoms on the CES-D. These and the other 199 patients also were administered the DUKE (from which the DUKE-AD scores were extracted), the Diagnostic Interview Schedule (DIS; Robins et al. (1981), a measure of symptom severity, and a measure of social support. The alpha coefficient for this group was 0.61. Patients with a DIS-assigned DSM-III-R major anxiety (panic, agoraphobia, and/or generalized anxiety) had a significantly higher DUKE-AD mean score than those without (p < .0001). These results were also found in comparisons of patients with and without a major depression or dysthymia diagnosis, and for those with and without either a major anxiety or depression diagnosis. In addition, the ROC AUCs derived from these 3 comparisons were supportive of the DUKE-AD as screener, with findings of 72% for a major anxiety disorder, 78% for major depression/dysthymia, and 76% for the presence of either type of anxiety or depressive disorder.

Using a DUKE-AD raw score cutoff of 5 or greater for classification, Parkerson and Broadhead (1997) divided their sample into high-risk ($n = 220$) and low-risk ($n = 261$) groups for further comparisons. First, they found the following respective sensitivity, specificity, PPP, NPP, and total correct classification percentages: 71%, 59%, 25%, 92%, and 61% for those with a DIS-assigned major anxiety disorder; 82%, 64%, 37%, 93%, and 67% for those with major depression/dysthymia; and 74%, 66%, 48%, 86%, and 68% for those with any anxiety or depressive disorder. Second, similar to the previous study, they found the high-risk group to have a significantly higher severity of illness and significantly lower social support and perceived health status.

Research to date indicates that the DUKE-AD may be an excellent option for rapidly screening primary care patients for symptoms of anxiety and/or depression that require further evaluation. It is easy to administer and score, and requires very little in terms of patient and staff time.

Outcome Questionnaire Short Form (OQS-10)

Recognizing the need for a brief and unobtrusive instrument for screening primary care patients for psychological distress, Lambert, Finch, Okiishi, Burlingame, McKelvey, and Reisinger (1997) developed the Outcome Questionnaire Short Form (OQS-10) from the original OQ-45 (see chapter 5). In doing so, they selected the 10 items that best discriminated a community sample from a sample of patients with DSM Axis I disorders (see Fig. 8.9). Responses to these items were given on a 5-point Likert scale (scored 0–4), which could yield a maximum total score of 40. Lambert et al. found that with a cutoff score of 19, the OQS-10 correctly identified 76% of the mental health patient group and 84% of the community sample. Preliminary data do not suggest gender or age differences, but some racial differences have been noted. More data is needed to determine if separate, demographically based norms are required.

The psychometric properties of the OQS-10 are quite impressive for such a brief instrument (Lambert et al., 1997). Data from a large community sample ($n = 180$) revealed an alpha coefficient of .82 and a 3-week test–retest reliability of .62. An alpha coefficient of .92 was obtained from the results of a sample of 403 patients from a variety of mental health settings, and the test–retest reliability for a sample of 292 medical patients was found to be significant ($p < .01$). Correlations with other instruments provided evidence of concurrent validity for the OQS-10. Significant correlations ($p < .01$) were found with the SCL-90-R GSI (.75), the BDI (.58), the Inventory for Interpersonal Problems (.68), and the Social Adjustment Rating Scale (.71).

Additional support for the psychometric integrity of the OQS-10 was presented by Seelert, Hill, Rigdon, and Schwenzfeler (1999). They administered the OQS-10, the DUKE, a demographic and health questionnaire, and the SF-36's general health questionnaire to 292 adult family practice patients. The DUKE-AD was scored from the responses to the DUKE. Seelert et al. found the OQS-10 to correlate with the DUKE-AD at .72 ($p < .001$). The data resulted in an alpha coefficient finding of .88, and factor analysis yielded two factors: the positively worded "psychological well-being" and the negatively worded "psychological distress." These factors correlated ($p < .01$) with the DUKE-AD at .51 and .53, respectively. Using the a DUKE-AD score of 5 or greater as the criterion for classifying clinically significant anxiety or depression, di-

MINI-OQ®

A Brief Outcome Questionnaire (OQ®-10.2)

YOUR NAME:		TODAY'S DATE: / / .
YOUR AGE: _____ YEARS OLD.	MALE: FEMALE	ID #:

INSTRUCTIONS: Looking back over the last week, including today, help us understand how you have been feeling. Please read each item carefully and mark the circle under the category which best describes your current situation. For this questionnaire, work is defined as employment, school, housework, volunteer work, etc.

		Never	Rarely	Sometimes	Frequently	Almost Always	DO NOT MARK IN THIS COLUMN
1	I am a happy person.	□	□	□	□	□	
2	I am satisfied with my life.	□	□	□	□	□	
3	I am satisfied with my relationships with others.	□	□	□	□	□	
4	I feel loved and wanted.	□	□	□	□	□	
5	I feel my love relationships are full and complete.	□	□	□	□	□	
6	I feel fearful.	□	□	□	□	□	
7	I feel something is wrong with my mind.	□	□	□	,□	□	
8	I feel blue.	□	□	□	□	□	
9	I feel lonely.	□	□	□	□	□	
10	I feel stressed at work/school.	□	□	□	□	□	

Examination Copy

Developed by Michael J. Lambert, Ph.D., Art E. Fintch, John Okishi & Curtis W. Reisinger, Ph.D.
© 1998 American Professional Credentialing Services, LLC. All Rights Reserved. Licensure Required For All Uses.
Telephone: 1-888-MH-SCORE (1-888-647-2673)   E-Mail: apcs@erols.com   Web: http://www.oqfamily.com

TOTAL:

NOTE: SCORING TEMPLATE AND SCORE VALUES ARE NOT SHOWN ON THIS EXAMINATION COPY.

FIG. 8.9. Outcome Questionnaire Short Form (OQS-10). Copyright © 1998 American Professional Credentialing Services, LLC. All rights reserved. Licensure required for all uses: e-mail: apcs@erols.com; web site: www.oqfamily.com. Reproduced with permission.

agnostic efficiency statistics were computed for a range of OQS-10 raw scores (10–17). The authors indicated a preference for a score *range* rather than a fixed cutoff point. However, the data suggest that the optimum OQS-10 cutoff score for this sample was 12. This classified 50% of the sample as distressed and yielded a sensitivity of 72%, a specificity of 78%, a PPP of 81%, and an overall hit rate of 73%. Schwenzfeier, Anderson, Hill, Rigdon, and Seelert (2000) used this same data to investigate the ability of each of the psychological distress and psychological well-being factors to predict the number of prescription medications reported by the 214 patients in the study who did not have a psychiatric diagnosis.

Aside from the brevity, it also has the advantage of assessing both symptomatology and patient's functioning in the world (Lambert et al., 1997). Not only was the well-being factor significantly correlated with number of prescription medications ($p < .01$), hierarchical regression analysis indicated that low well-being scores were significantly related to a greater number of prescription medications ($p < .01$). These relationships were not found for the distress factor. Overall, research to date suggests that the OQS-10 provides yet another option for the psychologist involved in the screening of primary care patients.

Beck Depression Inventory–FastScreen (BDI–FastScreen)

Recently, the publisher of the BDI has made available an abbreviated version of the instrument developed specifically for use in primary care settings. The Beck Depression Inventory–FastScreen (BDI–FastScreen) and associated research have actually appeared in the published literature for a number of years under the pre-publication title of the Beck Depression Inventory for Primary Care, or BDI-PC. BDI–FastScreen, as it is now marketed, was developed to meet the need for a depression screening instrument that does not contain items that are sensitive to symptoms of medical illnesses. In a medical population, these can yield a relatively high number of false positives. It contains BDI-II items that reflects DSM-IV diagnostic criteria for major depressive disorder and focuses on cognitive and affective symptoms of the disorder, including sadness, pessimism, past failure, loss of pleasure, self-dislike, self-criticalness, and suicidal thoughts or wishes.

The studies that have been published on the BDI–FastScreen have investigated the psychometric and diagnostic properties of the instrument on various types of primary and other medical care populations. These include adult medical inpatients (Beck, Guth, Steer, & Ball, 1997), adult primary care outpatients (Beck, Steer, Ball, Ciervo, & Kabat, 1997), adult outpatients being seen by general internal medicine specialists (Steer, Cavalieri, Leonard, & Beck, 1999), and adolescent outpatients (Winter, Steer, Jones-Hicks, & Beck, 1999). The findings reported thus far support the use of the BDI–FastScreen for screening of depression in primary care patients. The major results can be summarized as follows:

- Internal consistency is quite acceptable, with obtained alpha coefficients ranging from 0.85 to 0.88.
- Using a raw score cutoff of 4 or more for classification and results from the PRIME-MD CEG Mood Module as the criterion, the obtained BDI–FastScreen sensitivities for major depressive disorder were found to range from 82% to 97%. Specificities ranged from 82% to 99% as overall efficiencies ranged from 91% to 98%.
- Area under the ROC curve was 98% or greater.
- On average, the raw scores of patients with major depression were 4 to 9 times higher than those without major depression. Effect sizes for the differences between those with and without major depression ranged from approximately 3.5 to 4.5.
- BDI–FastScreen raw scores were not related to age, gender, ethnicity, or medical status.
- Raw scores were significantly correlated ($p < .001$) with a DSM-IV mood disorder $r = .69$), the Beck Anxiety Inventory for Primary Care (BAI-PC; $r = .86$), and the Depression subscale of the Hospital Anxiety and Depression Scale ($r = .62$). Item–scale correlations ranged from .47 for the past failure item to .78 for the suicidal thought and wishes item.

The BDI–FastScreen can serve as a quick and reasonably economical means of screening for major depresssion in primary care settings. As noted in the BDI–FastScreen *Manual*, "a cutoff score from 3 to 5 and above is recommended for yielding maximum clinical efficiency in screening for [major depressive disorder] in medical polulations in which the underlying prevalence of [major depressive disorder] ranges from 5% to 40%" (Beck, Steer, & Brown, 2000). A published version of the BAI-PC that screens for severity of seven subjective symptoms of anxiety will likely be released in the near future. Given that the preliminary findings indicate a high correlation with the BDI–FastScreen, it will be interesting to note the degree to which the BAI-PC will be able to discriminate between affective and anxiety disorders.

SUMMARY

The U.S. health care industry has undergone dramatic changes during the past 2 decades. What once was a loosely monitored system of care with skyrocketing costs has been changed to one with tight controls providing only limited services and choice of providers. These and other efforts to keep costs down (e.g., carve-out behavioral health benefits, lack of parity between medical and behavioral health benefits) have been particularly limiting to those seeking help for mental health and substance abuse problems. For these and other reasons (e.g., stigma associated with mental illness), a considerable number of individuals with behavioral health problems have turned to their PCPs for help — help that is often not provided or does not adequately meet the patient's needs.

Fortunately, the winds of change are now blowing in the favor of behavioral health care proponents. The enactment of the Mental Health Parity Act of 1996, the industry's realization of the benefits of one-stop health care, NCQA and JCAHO accreditation standards, and the growing belief that potential long-term health care cost savings can result from the appropriate treatment of behavioral disorders — these and other circumstances bode well for greater access to more and/or better behavioral health care services. They also serve as the impetus for a more pervasive integration of primary and behavioral health care services throughout the United States. Goldstein et al. (2000) summarized the current state of these affairs by noting that

1. A large portion of patients who seek services from primary care providers experience significant psychological distress or symptomatology.
2. Primary care providers, in general, are not sufficiently skilled to identify or provide appropriate treatment to these patients.
3. Consequently, patients with behavioral health problems consume a large portion of the available primary care resources.
4. Identifying and adequately treating the behavioral health problems of primary care patients in the primary care setting has been shown to result in significant cost savings.
5. Consultation, liaison, and educational services offered by behavioral health professionals can be instrumental in ensuring the success of these intervention efforts in the primary care setting. (p. 735)

The alliance of primary and behavioral health care providers is not a new phenomenon; it has existed in one form or another for decades. And the literature provides evidence of cost savings related to long-term medical care, lost income, and lowered work productivity that can accrue as a result of this alliance. Yet, other data do not support the medical cost-offset conclusions. The reality of the situation most likely lies somewhere in between. Regardless, the value the behavioral health care professional brings to the primary care setting — either as an off-site consultant or as an on-site collaborative member of the primary care team — is attested to daily in primary care practices throughout the country. Moreover, there is every indication that the picture of interdisciplinary cooperation in the primary care setting will become more commonplace as the move to integrate behavioral and primary care gains momentum. The extent to which these two services will become integrated will, of course, depend on any number of factors (e.g., reimbursement structures, funding, available office space, staff interest, and motivation) that will vary from setting to setting.

Psychologists and other trained behavioral health care professionals can uniquely contribute to efforts to fully integrate their services in primary care settings through the establishment and use of psychological testing services. Information obtained from psychometrically sound self-report tests and other-report instruments (e.g., clinician rating scales, parent-completed instruments) can assist the primary care provider in several types of clinical decision-making activities, including screening for the presence of mental health or substance abuse problems, planning a course of treatment, and monitoring patient progress. Testing can also be used to measure the outcome of treatment that has been provided to patients with mental health or substance abuse problems, thus assisting in determining what works for whom.

There are a number of psychological test instruments that are appropriate for use in primary care settings. Some were originally developed for use in behavioral health settings but have been found useful in primary and other medical care practices; other were designed specifically for use in primary care settings. In all, the psychologist has a large array of tools that are psychometrically sound, efficient, economical, easy to use, and provide the type of information needed to help complete the various measurement tasks that may be required in a busy primary care practice.

The degree to which psychological testing services become part of the package of primary behavioral health care services will depend on the value they bring to the integrated service delivery system. The key to the success of this endeavor will be in the psychologist's ability to educate and demonstrate to primary care providers how psychological testing can be a cost-effective means of helping to serve the needs of a significant portion of their patient population.

9

Ethical and Professional Issues

Working with or for an MBHO can present many challenges to clinicians, especially those who began practicing prior to the last decade. These challenges can include such things as lower rates of compensation, having to get assessment or treatment sessions authorized prior to seeing a patient, having someone else determine the best or most acceptable type of treatment or assessment instrument for one's patient, being available for an appointment within days or hours of a request for treatment or evaluation, or any of a number of other requirements. But for some, one of the most difficult aspects of working for or with an MBHO involves situations that are likely to elicit questions about the MBHO's or their own behavior. That is, "Am I (or the MBHO) acting in a manner that is consistent with the ethics of my profession?" Such questions can be quite troubling. And at times, one may struggle to arrive at a personally and professionally acceptable answer or resolution to such real or perceived ethical conflicts. For many, dealing with ethical issues can be the most difficult and distasteful aspect of working for an MBHO.

This final chapter focuses on ethical and other professional issues relevant to psychological assessment that may arise during the provision of this service within an MBHO context. The basis for the ethical issues that are discussed in the sections that follow are the American Psychological Association's *Ethical Principles of Psychologists and Code of Conduct* (*Ethical Principles*; 1992) and one of its companion documents, *General Guidelines for Providers of Psychological Services* (*Guidelines*; APA, 1987). For some, each of these documents might be perceived as a cause of additional burden or anxiety that makes practicing the profession of psychology in MBHOs that much more difficult. At the same time, each can serve as a source of guidance and reassurance when navigating through situations that challenge one's sense of what is right and wrong, what one should or should not do, in clinical settings. The PAWG's report on problems in the use of psychological assessment in the current health care environment that was made to APA's Board of Professional Affairs (Eisman et al., 1998) will serve the basis of discussion for other professional issues related to the use of psychological testing in MBHO settings.

GENERAL CONSIDERATIONS

Before discussing ethical and professional issues that are either directly or indirectly related to the applications of psychological testing in MBHOs, it first is important to establish a context for these discussions with more general issues related to appropriate test usage in contemporary health care settings. This will facilitate the discussions that follow.

Ethics and Morality

Before launching into an investigation of a given topic, it is always important to make sure that one has a clear understanding of what is being discussed. One point of clarification that has been raised by several authors (e.g., Acuff, Bennett, Bricklin, Canter, Knapp, Moldawsky, & Phelps, 1999; Cummings, 1998a; Shore, 1998) is the distinction between *morality* and *ethics*. Shore indicates that "Morality has to do with how we treat other people. Ethics, the philosophy of morality, provides guideposts for 'doing the right thing' " (p. 67). As Cummings has stated, "Whereas moral responsibility is a vision of what the profession can ideally be, a code of ethics is the lowest common denominator of acceptable behavior" (p. 54).

For the purpose of this chapter, perhaps Acuff et al. (1999) offer the most informative and relevant explanation of the distinction between the two concepts:

> The terms *ethics* and *ethical* can have various connotations depending on the context in which they are used. For example, the term *ethical* may refer to overarching moral principles, such as autonomy, beneficence (doing good for others), nonmalficence (doing no harm), fidelity, and justice.
>
> In a more narrow sense, the term ethical may refer to the "APA Ethical Principles of Psychologists and Code of Conduct" . . . or to codes of ethics adopted by state boards of psychology. These codes of conduct mandate or prohibit specific actions and they may have the force of law. [MBHOs'] actions often seem to offend the "ethics" of many practitioners and the public in the first sense of the term: that is, they are seen as morally outrageous. (p. 565)

Given the less than positive attitude that organizations such as the American Psychological Association and the psychologists they represent have toward managed care in general, charges of unethical and immoral behavior that have been leveled against the industry are not surprising. For example, Miller (1998) listed 11 different managed care practices that he views as unethical. These include a disregard for personal and medical privacy, false advertising, deceptive language in their corporation names (e.g., "Choice Health"), violation of scientific ethics, practicing outside of one's competency areas, creating conflicts of interest, keeping secrets about such conflicts, informed consent violations, kickbacks for referrals, squandering money on nonmedical-related activities (e.g., high executive salaries), and not reporting information related to potential harm from its services.

Shore (1998), on the other hand, charges managed care's use of "irrational" exercises of authority as being immoral from several standpoints. First, managed care is alleged to remove patients' personal power through the removal of their rights to privacy, choice, and the ability to make decisions about their treatment. This is said to be accompanied by their clinicians' fear of speaking out against the company or advocating for their patients. Second, Shore indicates that managed care companies foster dependency on them by determining what is considered "medical necessity," and by limiting patients as to whom they can see and what treatment they can undergo. Third, she claims that the utilization review process results in an intrusion into the patient's privacy which can "retraumatize" the patient. Fourth, managed care is said to prey on a vulnerable population. That is, mental health patients are viewed by Shore as often being unable to fight for treatment. Finally, managed care companies are viewed as putting their interest in profits before the care of the consumers.

The blanket allegations of the types of behavior that Miller, Shore, and others have made against managed care — and managed behavioral health care in particular — are not totally without merit. However, whether these types of behavior should be considered unethical or immoral is a judgment that should be made on a case-by-case basis. In this author's opinion, such a determination should be made using criteria other than what is dictated to psychologists by the APA's *Ethical Principles*, for what really is at issue here is the managed care company's actions relative to its own set of standards of ethical and moral behavior. And as discussed next, it is this discrepancy between what psychologists feel is the "right thing to do" and that which the managed care companies feel is right for them and their shareholders that is the source of a lot of the animosity that can exist between the psychological profession and MBHOs.

General Source of Ethical Concerns

The inclusion of this chapter in this book is not serendipitous. Whether the focus is on treatment or testing, psychologists working for or with MBHOs will likely have to deal with issues that that involve the application of APA's *Ethical Principles* at some point in time. Recall that 42% of the almost 16,000 respondents to the CAPP survey (reported in chapter 1) indicated that "ethical dilemmas created by managed care" was a concern (Phelps et al., 1998), and 54 to 58% of the 556 psychologists in the New Jersey managed care survey (Rothbaum et al., 1998) "felt pressure to compromise ethics." In addition, 25% of the respondents to Murphy et al.'s (1998) survey of Division 42 (Independent Practice) members reported "persistent" difficulties with managed care-related ethical dilemmas, while another 45% indicated "more concerns than is consistent with general practice" (p. 47).

Part of the reason for these reports is that ethical issues arising during the provision of services to MBHO patients are the same types of issues that one is likely to face with self-pay or indemnity insurance patients. The other part is more directly related to the structure and function of MBHOs, as well as the highly charged emotions that both providers and patients have toward managed care. These latter points and the negative press that managed care has been receiving seem to have sensitized the public and the profession to managed care practices that are not consistent with the way they think they should be done. The perception often is one of managed care acting in an unethical or immoral manner when, in fact, this certainly is not always the case.

There are two important factors related to the questions raised about MBHOs' ethics or morality and concerns about providing services through them. These have to do with the nature of the professional relationship and the inadequacy of APA's ethical code for dealing with the types of issues that are raised in MBHOs.

Multiple Relationships.   Several writers have pointed to the change in the therapeutic relationship that has come about as the result of managed care. Petrila (1998) reports that a number of changes in the organization of health care services have arisen from or were reinforced by the introduction of managed care. Changes such as practitioners moving from small practices to larger entities, mergers of provider organizations, and competition among MBHOs on the issue of pricing have changed the therapeutic relationship from being a two-party relationship (clinician and patient) to three-party relationship, which now includes the managed care company. Cooper and Gottlieb (2000) and Bilynsky and Vernaglia (1998) have made similar observations.

Citing Blum, Bilynsky and Vernaglia (1998) note that "Under managed care, the mental health services dyad has become a triad" (Blum, 1992, p. 251). As suggested by this citation, adding the MBHO into the treatment services mix not only creates individual relationships between the MBHO and both the clinician and the patient, but it also can affect the therapeutic relationship between patient and clinician. Specifically, they point to the potential for altering the patient's rapport with the clinician, limiting the patient's ability to make decisions about their own treatment, and influencing the transference and/or countertranference between patient and clinician. As for the relationship between the clinician and the MBHO, Bilynsky and Vernaglia note that

> For years, as third parties took the place of patient payment for psychotherapy [and psychological testing services], psychologists have had to negotiate the balance between client needs and insurance coverage. While this equilibrium required attention to both the patient and insurer, loyalty and ethical responsibilities were still assured to the client. In this new era of managed care, however, the psychologist may feel forced between the dual demands of patient care and managed-care policies, a position that may compromise the unilateral dedication of psychologists to their clients. (p. 55)

As will become evident later in this chapter, the demands of their patients and the demands of MBHOs with whom they contract can be a major source of ethical conflicts which psychologists may experience in their professional lives. In some instances, these types of conflicts can be avoided; in other cases, the psychologist must seek to resolve them using the professional standards and through the help and guidance of colleagues.

Adequacy of the Current Code of Ethics.   When it comes to discussions of the ethical conflicts that arise as part of doing business with managed care, there is one issue which always seems to be raised. This has to do with the adequacy of APA *Ethical Principles* for providing guidance on ethical issues that are sometimes considered unique to the provision of services in MBHO settings. Some would conclude that the ethical issues that arise during the course of treating MBHO patients are not unique (e.g., Austad, Hunter, & Morgan, 1998; Austad & Morgan, 1998; Berman, 1992; Haas & Cummings, 1991). Thus, it would be natural to assume that the code of ethics that has served the profession well before the dawn of managed care is adequate for the situations that arise in MBHO settings. Indeed, this was the conclusion of members of an APA task force on ethical practice in organized systems of care (Acuff et al., 1998), who also seemed to imply that the frequency and intensity at which these issues occur in MBHO settings seem to draw attention to and lead one to question the adequacy of the ethical principles in these settings.

However, many would argue this point. For example, Cooper and Gottlieb (2000) point out that the current version of the *Ethical Principles* was released (in 1992) prior to the realization of what the full impact of managed care would be. In addition, they note that the rapidly changing nature of managed behavioral health care and the complexity of the issues that arise therein make it difficult to develop a useful, comprehensive set of guidelines. Pollack (1998) points out that the current version of the *Ethical Principles* for psychologists has no direct reference to activities of those employed by MBHOs as utilization reviewers. In this role, psychologists are still viewed as being subject to these principles. Pollack's interviews with MBHO peer reviewers revealed a number of ethical issues that they had to deal with, including issues or conflicts pertaining to competence, confidentiality, conflict of interest, dual relationships, competence of providers with whom they had to deal, and the demands of the MBHO. Even Haas and Cummings (1991) indicated that "psychologists need support systems to help them navigate these environments" (p. 50). Newman and Bricklin (1991) observed that APA's *Guidelines* (APA, 1987) do not fully address concerns about managed care's cost-containment approach to behavioral health care delivery. Moreover, Hanson and Sheridan (1997) feel that more could be done to assist psychologists and graduate students in dealing with the ethical issues that arise in managed care (e.g., development of an ethics casebook).

Austad et al.'s (1998) review of the ethical issues pertaining to the practice of psychology in managed care led them to conclude that "controversy regarding psychotherapy, ethics, and managed care has grown to be increasingly intense and acrimonious. Consensus surfaces on only one matter—the professional code of ethics for psychologists needs to be revised to make it more relevant for clinicians who must cope with a changing health care environment" (p. 71). Cummings (1998a) provides a clear summary of the current situation:

> An ethical code that represents consensus achieved essentially before the health-care revolution often does not directly address the dilemmas confronting practitioners in the current era. In achieving a new consensus that will lead to updating this ethical code, the profession must address issues of moral responsibility that are broader than codification of minimum acceptable conduct and that do not carry sanction. In essence, the practitioner must ask what is the very best that the profession can be in the new health-care environment—an ideal that in every era has preceded codifications. (p. 65)

It is clear to this author that the adequacy of the 1992 edition of APA's *Ethical Principles* for helping psychologists survive the multiple pressures and demands of managed behavioral health care falls short of what is needed and desired by those working in this type of environment. This is regardless of whether the psychologist is functioning as an MBHO clinician, care manager, utilization/peer reviewer, or administrator. The *Ethical Principles* need to be revised to reflect the relationships and concomitant expectations that now exist in the patient-psychologist-MBHO triad and in the relationship between the MBHO and the psychologist care manager/utilization reviewer. Until that time, psychologists must continue to rely on the *Ethical Principles* and *Guidelines*, along with consultation with colleagues to deal with the ethical issues that confront them in the course of providing services to MBHO patients.

Within this context, the discussion now turns to some of the more common types of ethical issues and professional concerns that psychologists must confront in their work with MBHOs. The ethical issues that are discussed later most commonly arise with regard to the provision of psychotherapeutic services. This point is reflected in the discussion of these issues in the professional literature. These same issues, however, generally are pertinent to discussions of psychological testing in MBHOs. As necessary and appropriate, issues that are generally identified as arising from the provision of psychotherapy will be extrapolated to the provision of psychological testing and assessment services. General approaches to dealing with these issues also will be provided. Following this, other professional issues and concerns relevant to testing activities in MBHOs and identified by Eisman et al. (1998) in their PAWG report are discussed. Here also, proposed solutions to these matters are discussed.

ETHICAL ISSUES AND CONCERNS

There are a number of principles and standards in APA's *Ethical Principles* document that bear directly or indirectly upon appropriate and ethical use of psychological testing and assessment in MBHOs systems. The most obvious, of course, is Standard 2, Evaluation, Assessment, and Intervention. Also relevant, however, are those principles and standards that are related to conflict of interest, competence, integrity, confidentiality, informed consent, welfare of the consumer, and social responsibility. Acuff et al. (1999) contend that the ethical dilemmas that are most likely to occur in organized systems of care involve informed consent, confidentiality, abandonment, and utilization management/review. Although these (and other) principles and standards are pertinent to other types of services offered through MBHOs, the content of the professional literature suggests that these issues may be of greater concern with regard to the delivery of psychotherapy and other forms of treatment.

Following are presentations and brief discussions of those ethical principles and standards that are felt to be most relevant to the applications of psychological testing and assessment in MBHOs. The information presented is not intended to be a comprehensive or exhaustive discussion of these very important topics. Rather, the intent is to alert the psychologist who either contracts with or is an employee of an MBHO to potential problems related to the authorization of psychological testing or the use of test results that may arise, and to provide guidance related to the resolution of these issues.

The Basic Issue: Conflicts between Psychology's Ethics and MBHOs' Requirements

A discussion of ethical issues essentially is a discussion of a conflict between one set of ethics and another set of ethics, requirements, or demands that are opposing or inconsistent with each other. In this discussion, the conflict of concern is that involving APA's *Ethical Principles* and the business ethics, requirements, or demands of MBHOs.

There are many perspectives on this conflict. It is this author's opinion that much of the hostility and claims of unethical/immoral behavior leveled against MBHOs and other managed health care companies by behavioral health practitioners, patients, and advocates is related to unrealistic expectations about what managed care should or should not be doing for the those receiving services under these types of health care programs. There appears to be a belief that managed care companies should have the same altruistic intentions as the practitioners who are employed by or contract with them. This is not the case. Make no mistake about it: managed care companies exist primarily to make money. They have a fiduciary responsibility to their owners or shareholders to be profitable and remain financially solvent (Barnhill & Small, 1998), and there is nothing wrong with that. That is *not* to say that they do not care about the lives of the patients they serve — it is just that they will not be able to serve anyone if they are not profitable. They also have a responsibility to the purchaser (e.g., employer) of the behavioral health care services offered by the MBHO (Cummings, 1998a). At the same time, the practitioner has a fiduciary responsibility to the patient (Austad et al., 1998; Haas & Cummings, 1991).

As mentioned earlier, ethical issues emerge are from differences in psychology and business ethics. As Shueman (1997) points out, "Health care is a business, and it is the tools and values of business that will continually be brought to bear in health care to create more efficient, more effective delivery systems" (p. 556). As a business, an MBHO's goals generally are to eliminate unnecessary services, reduce costs, and maintain or increase treatment effectiveness (Bilynsky & Vernaglia, 1998). Working directly for or contracting with an MBHO, the psychologist is expected to subscribe to these same goals. As Cummings (1998a) summarizes,

> One of the greatest reasons for a misunderstanding between practitioners and managed care companies is the different source of responsibility each has. The managed care company is responsible to the buyer (i.e., the entity contracting with the carve-out). It has a clear-cut contract with a health plan, insurer, purchasing alliance, or some other form of *intermediate consumer*. The therapist, on the other had, has a therapeutic contract with the patient, defined as the *end consumer*. Intermediate consumers (buyers) clearly have different requirements from the end consumers (patients). . . . (p. 54)

Another aspect of the health care mix that must be considered is the relationship between the MBHO and the patient. It is a relationship that takes on a dimension that has not been the case in the past. Murphy (1998) points out that

> Under indemnity insurance, psychologist and patient, within the context of the therapeutic relationship, determined the care that would best address a patient's need. Under managed care, treatment is affected by the decisions patients make about the coverage they purchase well before they enter the therapeutic relationship. . . . The psychologist must attend to issues arising from the contractual relationship between the patient and payer that is also reflected in the contract between the psychologist and the payer rather than an exclusive focus on quality of care. The contractual relationships that patients and psychologists have with managed care companies reflect a fundamental change in the relationship between the patient and psychologist, and it is at the core of the ethical and values issues psychologists face. (p. 44)

Under the principle of *fidelity* (Beauchamp & Childress, 1988; Haas & Cummings, 1991), when a psychologist works within an MBHO system, he assumes *two* sets of responsibilities. First, as a therapist, he is obliged to advocate for the rights and interests of the patient, which includes quality care. At the same time, he should support the goals of the MBHO. When the goals of the MBHO are inconsistent the patient's best interests or with the psychologist's ability to provide quality care to the patient, a conflict of interest arises (Cooper & Gottlieb, 2000).

Because the profit motive and pressures for cost containment that are found in MBHO settings are likely to compete with quality of care decisions (Acuff et al., 1999), it is quite likely that psychologists employed as care managers, peer reviewers, and utilization management/review staff must deal with more instances of conflict of interest than practitioners are likely to experience. And if the volume itself were not enough, APA's CAPP Task Force on Ethical Practice (Committee for the Advancement of Professional Practice, 1998) has recommended that psychologists functioning as utilization reviewers be held accountable as psychologists making treatment decisions (Cooper & Gottlieb, 2000). Pollack's (1998) informal survey of utilization reviewers suggested that these individuals are generally able to deal with various types of conflicts, but the survey also revealed dilemmas that had caused them to struggle to come to an resolution.

As previously suggested, the ethical issues that psychologists will confront in their dealings with MBHO will arise from a conflict between their obligations to the patient and those to the MBHO. Thus, the foregoing discussion of conflict of interest is an important one for this section of this chapter. It should provide a context for and a better understanding of the nature of the psychological testing and assessment issues that follow, all of which involve some type of conflict between the psychologist's professional ethics and the ethics, responsibilities or demands of the MBHO.

Issues Specific to Testing and Assessment

There are many principles and standards from APA's *Ethical Principles* that apply to conflicts surrounding testing and assessment needs and activities in MBHO settings. Some are specific and bear directly on these issues (see Standard 2: Evaluation, Assessment, and Intervention; APA, 1992); others have more general application to a wide variety of clinical services offered by psychologists (e.g., Principle A: Competence; APA, 1992). The discussion begins with the testing-specific issues, and then proceeds to the issues are more general in nature. Discussion of principles and standards that are related both directly and more generally to testing and assessment issues is deferred to the general discussions in the subsections that follow.

Feedback of Test Results to Patients.   A standard that was introduced with the publication of the 1992 version of the *Ethical Principles* document is Standard 2.09 (APA, 1992). It states that "psychologists ensure that an explanation of the results is provided using language that is reasonably understandable to the person being assessed or to another legally authorized person on behalf of the client" (p. 1604). This essentially codifies what many psychologists had already incorporated into their assessment activities for a number of years. In fact, some psychologists use a specific approach to providing test results feedback as a therapeutic technique (see the discussion of Finn's [1996a, 1996b] *therapeutic assessment* in chapter 4). Although few would argue about benefits of providing this type of feedback to patients, there is no guarantee that MBHOs will authorize one or more sessions specifically for this purpose. Here, an MBHO may authorize a specified number of sessions for testing and leave it up to the psychologist to decide how best to use those sessions. However, there is clearly a greater likelihood that the demands of the psychologist's professional ethics will conflict with an MBHO's policies and procedures for authorizing this type of psychological testing activity.

There are several possible means by which conflict over the provision of feedback can be resolved. Here, the psychologist can point to the empirical support for the benefits of therapeutic assessment or variants thereof (see chapter 2). Barring agreement from the MBHO to pay for this type of activity, one may still be able to use a portion of an authorized treatment session to review the test results with the patient. Although it may not produce the same benefits as the type of approach espoused by Finn and his colleagues, the MBHO is much more likely to accept this approach as one which will benefit the patient and help the psychologist satisfy his professional code of ethics. Another avenue is to discuss other options for the psychological testing and/or feedback session, including self-pay or referral to other clinicians or organizations that can provide the services along with the testing (Bilynsky & Vernaglia, 1998).

Another option is for the psychologist to offer to provide the therapeutic feedback services at no cost to the patient. Although it is likely to be the least desirable solution, it does show responsiveness to Principle F of the *Ethical Standards,* which encourages psychologists to dedicate a portion of their time to pro bono work. With some MBHOs, these sorts of activities may be looked upon quite favorably and may result in unexpected benefits to the psychologist (e.g., increased referrals, special consideration when requesting authorization for other patients). At the same time, other MBHOs might react to this same solution in just the opposite manner.

Potential Misuse of Tests, Test Data, and Test Reports.   Standard 2.02 (APA, 1992) states that

(a) Psychologists who . . . use psychological assessment techniques, interviews, tests, or instruments do so in a manner and for purposes that are appropriate in light of the research on and evidence for the usefulness and proper application of the techniques.

(b) Psychologists refrain from misuse of assessment techniques, interventions, results, and interpretations and take reasonable steps to prevent others from misusing the information these techniques provide. This includes refraining from releasing raw test results or raw data to persons, other than to patients or clients as appropriate, who are not qualified to use such information. (p. 1603)

There are a several problem areas that may arise from this standard. The most obvious has to do with the release of test results. Surrounding this are issues related to confidentiality and informed consent, which are discussed later in this section. In addition, it is not uncommon to hear allegations that decisions related to psychological testing in MBHO systems are made by nonpsychologists with no formal training in the development and use of psychological test instruments (another issue that will be discuss later in this chapter). Moreover, there also may be legitimate concerns about who in the MBHO reviews the results of authorized testing. Here, the psychologist could express his concerns about releasing information to someone who may not understand how to interpret or use psychological test data. One could also propose sending all psychological test data and reports to a psychologist or another appropriately trained professional who can ensure that the findings are understood and properly used within the MBHO system.

A separate but related issue addressed in Standard 2.02(a) has to do with the appropriate use of testing itself. The issue here involves the request for testing that is not appropriate for the patient, the question to be answered, or both; or an authorization for testing that specifies the instrumentation to be used. Steere (1984) discussed the importance of the psychologist ensuring that the goal of assessment is clearly understood by himself and the referring agent (in this case, the MBHO). He must then determine whether his assistance in achieving this goal is "concerned with the well being of the [patient] and does not constitute a danger to the [patient]" (p. 56). This should be accompanied by an attempt to "ameliorate the indirect negative effects of both the assessment procedures themselves and their consequence" (p. 58). This may involve informing the MBHO that the type of testing or the specific test requested is inappropriate for the goal that the MBHO is trying to achieve through the testing. This would be accompanied by an assessment of the attainability of the goal and if appropriate, a recommendation of how to achieve it. This, in turn, may involve a recommendation to do no testing, to use instrumentation other than that specified by the MBHO, or to refer the patient for another type of assessment.

For example, suppose a psychiatrist suspects that a patient he has just evaluated has been experiencing seizures. At the psychiatrist's request, the MBHO refers a patient to the psychologist (who is competent in neuropsychological testing) for a neuropsychological evaluation to determine if there is indeed some form of brain dysfunction. The MBHO authorizes an assessment using the WAIS-III, Bender–Gestalt, and MMPI-2. Although the goal is clear, neither the referral for neuropsychological assessment or the specified instrumentation are appropriate to address the issue. Here, the psychologist should recommend that the patient first be seen for a neurological evaluation. Neuropsychological testing using more appropriate instrumentation (e.g., subtests from the Halstead–Reitan or Luria–Nebraska batteries) can then follow should there be positive or equivocal neurological findings.

Use of Tests by Unqualified Professionals. Standard 2.06 (APA, 1992) states that "Psychologists do not promote the use of psychological assessment techniques by unqualified persons" (p. 1603). Related to this standard is the issue of releasing test data and reports to unqualified individuals that was just discussed. However, there is another and more obvious area of potential conflict that is related to this standard. This has to do with the use of psychological tests by nonpsychologists. In this regard, Standard 2.02 (b) (APA, 1992) also is relevant. It indicates that "Psychologists . . . take reasonable steps to prevent others from misusing the information [assessment] techniques provide" (p. 1603). It is unclear whether this standard is meant to include attempts to prevent unqualified professionals from *conducting* psychological testing. If so, an ethical issue may arise when tests are used by either other psychologists or nonpsychologists who are not qualified to use them, due to lack of appropriate training or legal limitations.

Many psychologists would argue that only trained, licensed psychologists should be administering, scoring, and interpreting psychological test instrumentation, and that psychologists should do all that they can to discourage the use of tests by nonpsychologists. This author does not agree with this position and feels that in many cases, protests against test usage by nonpsychologists reflect nothing more than guild issues. The fact is that many psychiatrists, social workers, counselors, and members of other behavioral health professions have been adequately trained in the use of psychological tests in general or in the use of specific tests, and that in many cases, they are legally permitted to conduct psychological testing. And some nonpsychologists have even developed tests that are frequently found in psychologists' armamentariums of clinical instruments. For example, J. C. McKinley, coauthor of the original MMPI, was a psychiatrist. The Patient Health Questionnaire (PHQ; see chapter 9) was developed by Robert Spitzer, a psychiatrist; Janet Williams, a social worker; and Kurt Kroenke, an internist. Thus, use of tests by nonpsychologists is not an issue in all cases.

The *Ethical Principles* address cases where the psychologist becomes aware of testing that is being conducted by an unqualified professional who also is on the MBHO provider panel. Standards 8.04 and 8.05 (APA, 1992) indicate that:

When psychologists believe that there may have been an ethical violation by another psychologist, they attempt to resolve the issue by bringing it to the attention of that individual if an informal resolution appears appropriate and the intervention does not violate any confidentiality rights that may be involved.

If an apparent ethical violation is not appropriate for informal resolution . . . or is not resolved properly in that fashion, psychologists take further action appropriate to the situation, unless such action conflicts with confidentiality rights in ways that cannot be resolved. Such action might include referral to state or national committees on professional ethics or to state licensing boards. (p. 1611)

Generally, these two standards provide excellent guidance even in cases where the party in question is not a psychologist. However, proceeding to the point of lodging a complaint with the licensing board or ethics committee of that party's profession may be inappropriate or fruitless.

Dealing with issues related to the use of tests by unqualified professionals can be quite difficult, time-consuming, and frustrating. As suggested earlier, the situation can be even worse when the psychologist who identifies the problem is an MBHO employee working as a care manager or peer reviewer.

Use of Tests in Outcomes Assessment Programs. There is an increasing interest on the parts of MBHOs to establish outcomes assessment programs in MBHOs (see, in particular, chapters 2, 6, and 7). With the training that psychologists undergo during their graduate school and early postdoctoral years, one would assume that most clinical psychologists are quite capable of significantly contributing to in the development, implementation, and ongoing maintenance of outcomes programs in MBHOs. And on the surface, this does seem to be the case. However, Pratt, Berman, and Hurt (1998) raise issues related to the competencies that are required (e.g., research skills) and the informed consent that may be involved, particularly when the psychologist acts as an employee of or consultant to the MBHO involved in its outcomes assessment program. These matters are discussed in the general discussions of these topics that follow.

Competence

The assessment-specific and related standards address issues pertaining to the psychologist's competency in the area of psychological testing and assessment. On the matter of competency, Principle A (APA, 1992) states that

Psychologists strive to maintain high standards of competence in their work. They recognize the boundaries of their particular competencies and limitations of their expertise. They provide only those services and use only those techniques for which they are qualified by education, training, or experience. Psychologists are cognizant of the fact that the competencies required in serving, teaching, and/or studying groups of people vary with the distinctive characteristics of those groups. (p. 1599)

Related to this principle are two standards. The first is Standard 1.04 (a) (Boundaries of Competence; APA, 1992), which states that "Psychologists provide services . . . and conduct research only within the boundaries of their competence, based on their education, training, supervised experience, or appropriate professional experience" (p. 1600). Standard 1.05 (Maintaining Expertise; APA, 1992) states that "Psychologists who engage in assessment, . . . research, . . . or other professional activities maintain a reasonable level of awareness of the current scientific and professional information in their fields of activity, and undertake ongoing efforts to maintain competence in the skills they use" (p. 1600).

In MBHO settings, the issue of competency has been raised frequently with regard to the ability of psychologists to provide brief, goal-focused psychotherapy (see Cummings, 1998a; Petrila, 1998; Shuemen, 1997). Many psychologists obtained their training prior to the advent of managed care and thus must obtain some type of training in the models of short-term treatment in order to provide effective services in MBHO settings. Similar competency-related issues may arise with regard to testing. Psychologists may not have received training in the types of tests and other assessment procedures that MBHOs currently authorize. Those whose training has focused primarily on the use of lengthy, multiscale objective tests (e.g., the MMPI-2) or projective instruments (e.g., the Rorschach) that probably will not be authorized frequently, would be obliged to obtain some form of training on instruments for which they are likely to receive authorization (e.g., Beck Depression Inventory, Brief Screening Inventory) if they wish to continue to receive referrals or authorizations for testing.

There is another area of psychological testing in MBHOs that can result in competency-related issues. This is the area the of outcomes assessment. Depending on the degree to which the psychologist is involved in the development or management of an outcomes assessment program, there can be a number of skills that the psychologist must possess in order to competently perform his responsibilities. Pratt et al. (1998) suggest that such skills may require both clinical and research skills, pointing particularly to competence in conducting outcomes evaluation when it is part of daily clinical practice, presumably as opposed to outcomes evaluation as part of a well-controlled, time-limited study. Competency in psychometrics and test development also would be important if one's involvement in an outcomes assessment program includes the development of outcomes instruments. In addition, this author would argue that knowledge and/or skills in areas such as quality or performance improvement and management of outcomes information might be considered requisite skills for psychologists whose involvement in an outcomes program is extensive.

Integrity

Principle B (APA, 1992) states that "Psychologists seek to promote integrity in the science, teaching, and practice of psychology. In these activities psychologists are honest, fair, and respectful of others" (p. 1599). With the restrictions and qualifications for the authorization of services that one may encounter, it should not surprise anyone to hear that some behavioral health care providers may now and again engage in what is commonly referred to as "gaming the system" (Barnhill, 1998; Bilynski & Vernaglia, 1998; Cummings, 1998a; Lazarus & Sharfstein, 2000; Murphy, 1998). The term is used to describe various ways in which psychologists, psychiatrists, and other behavioral health care professionals may present false or inaccurate information to the MBHO in a manner that results in some financial benefit to the patient or the provider himself. Common means of gaming the system are the reporting of inaccurate (more severe) diagnoses or CPT procedural codes that enable the patient to receive authorization for initial or additional services, or to protect the patient's confidentiality. Although the provider certainly may engage in such behavior for his own benefit, the results of at least one small, informal survey (Barnhill, 1998) would suggest that this is mostly done for the patient's benefit.

Although gaming the system is usually discussed with regard to authorization or payment for treatment sessions, there certainly is opportunity to game the system to obtain authorization for or use the results of psychological testing for other gains. The psychologist could make false or inaccurate claims in order to justify or meet the criteria for the authorization of testing. For instance, a psychologist who feels that an assessment of any patient is not complete without the administering the MMPI-2, knows that the only way that the MBHO is going to authorized the testing is if he makes a strong case that there is a diagnostic question that cannot be resolved any other way than through MMPI-2 findings. Similarly, the results of the testing could be inaccurately reported or, more likely, misinterpreted to reach conclusions that support a request for additional treatment sessions or even more extensive (and costly) testing. An example might be a psychologist who exaggerates the findings from the MMPI-2 to indicate a level of symptom severity that he knows will result in the MBHO's authorizing additional outpatient therapy sessions.

Regardless of whether concern for the patient's welfare or concern for the psychologist's bank account is the motivating force, inappropriate or unnecessary use of psychological testing, false claims of the benefits that will ensue from such testing, and deliberate distortion of testing results are all dishonest behavior and constitute a violation of Principle B of the *Ethical Principles*. Moreover, one must remember that among other things, it is just this sort of behavior that has led to MBHOs instituting very narrow criteria for authorizing psychological testing. Thus, engaging in this type of behavior not only calls into question the individual psychologist's behavior, but also the integrity of the profession itself in the eyes of those who draft psychological testing policies for the MBHO.

Confidentiality

One of the greatest concerns about managed care that psychologists and patients have raised has to do with the issue of confidentiality. Acuff et al. (1999) define confidentiality as "the ethical and legal duty imposed on therapists to protect sensitive information obtained in the delivery of professional services from disclosure to third parties" (p. 569). They argue that the type and amount of sensitive information that are required by MBHOs are greater than had been the case prior to the introduction of managed care. Nevertheless, it is an issue that can present many problems, especially when one considers confidentiality is at the heart of the therapeutic relationship and may result in concerns about trust (Murphy, 1998). It is but one of the issues raised by managed care detractors to show what is wrong with MBHOs (e.g., Miller, 1998; Shore, 1998).

The *Ethical Principles* address the matter of confidentiality in several of its standards. Standard 5.02 (APA, 1992) states that "Psychologists have a primary obligation and take reasonable precautions to respect the confidentiality rights of those with whom they work or consult, recognizing that confidentiality may be established by law, institutional rules, or professional or scientific relationships" (p. 1606). Guidance as to how to help ensure confidentiality is offered through other standards. Standard 5.01 (APA, 1992) indicates that

(a) Psychologists discuss with persons and organizations with whom they establish a scientific or professional relationship . . . (1) the relevant limitations on confidentiality, including limitations where applicable in group, marital, and

> family therapy or in organizational consulting, and (2) the foreseeable uses of
> the information generated through their services.
>
> (b) Unless it is not feasible or is contraindicated, the discussion of confidentiality
> occurs at the outset of the relationship and thereafter as new circumstances
> may warrant. (p. 1606)

The matter of "foreseeable uses" may be a tricky one for the psychologist to address with the patient. Certainly, as the party that authorizes services, MBHOs have to right to know that testing has been performed and has been done so in an acceptable manner (Cummings, 1998a). More specifically, certain personnel (e.g., care managers) have a need to see patient information as part of their responsibility to authorize and monitor treatment. Information may also be used for other purposes, such as research (a significant consideration in organizations with outcomes assessment programs) or for review by regulatory or accrediting bodies during scheduled MBHO record audits. Moreover, once information is provided to MBHOs, there is no guarantee as to who will see it, what will be done with it, or the level of confidentiality at which it is treated (e.g., see O'Neill, 1998). Pollack (1998) reports instances where clerical personnel were assigned review responsibilities. Cooper and Gottlieb (2000) raise issues related to the possibility of information becoming part of a national data base, while Bilynski and Vernaglia (1998) encourage psychologists to investigate how records are stored and destroyed. One also must wonder the extent to which information provided through the Internet, such as when psychological tests and other outcomes instruments are administered online, can remain confidential. The use of the Internet becomes an even bigger issue as MBHOs move toward implementing Internet-based authorization request and other business processes.

Once the possible use of the information are discussed, Standard 5.05 (APA, 1992) becomes applicable. It states that "Psychologists . . . may disclose confidential information with the appropriate consent of the patient or the individual or organizational client (or of another legally authorized person on behalf of the patient or client), unless prohibited by law" (p. 1606). Although some would argue that patients generally do not understand the full extent to which a signed release of information allows information to be shared (Acuff et al., 1999), this author feels that if Standard 5.01 has been met, there should be little reason for concern from an ethical standpoint. In addition, Sweeney, Stutman, and Martin (1998) indicate that such consent should generally address legal issues that might arise from the release of confidential information.

A number of authors have recommended that psychologists should release only the minimal amount of information that is necessary to meet the demands of the MBHOs (see Barnett, 1998; Calfee, 1998; Cooper & Gottlieb, 2000; O'Neill, 1998). This is consistent with Standard 5.03(a) that states, "psychologists include in written and oral reports, consultations, and the like, only information germane to the purpose for which the communication is made" (APA, 1992, p. 1606). Also consistent with this standard is the recommendation from Nagy (1998) and Cooper and Gottlieb to not submit clinical notes (or in the case of testing, raw test data), but instead provide the MBHO with a summary of the treatment (or test results). O'Neill raises a related issue that pertains to whether the patient is aware of the level of detail in the information that is submitted to the MBHO. This and similar confidentiality matters bring one to the issue of informed consent.

Informed Consent

An issue that is consistently included in discussions of ethics in managed behavioral health care settings is that of informed consent. According to Standard 4.02(a) (APA, 1992) of the *Ethical Principles,*

> Psychologists obtain appropriate informed consent to therapy or related procedures [such as psychological testing], using language that is reasonably understandable to participants. . . . [I]nformed consent generally implies that the person (1) has the capacity to consent, (2) has been informed of significant information concerning the procedure, (3) has freely and without undue influence expressed consent, and (4) consent has been appropriately documented. (p. 1605)

The first three of APA's four qualifications for informed consent are generally consistent with Petrila's (1998) three elements for informed consent. That is, informed consent must be voluntary (i.e., not given under duress), knowledgeable (i.e., the patient must have adequate knowledge), and competent. Regarding competency, Petrila draws upon the work of Roth, Meisel, and Lidz (1977), who indicated that competency might be interpreted in one of five ways: the patient understood the choices and their consequences, the patient was able to express a choice, the decision is rational, the decision was not affected by a mental health or substance abuse problem, and the patient truly understood the information conveyed.

In the age of managed care, Murphy (1998) sees patients as needing to become more assertive about and responsible for the care that they receive. Consequently, it is important for patients to have all the information necessary to make informed decisions about their care. Part of the psychologist's role in providing this information includes ensuring that the patient is aware of several important considerations, including the limits of their mental health benefits (Acuff et al., 1999; Bilynski & Vernaglia, 1998; Cooper & Gottlieb, 2000; Petrila, 1998; see also Standard 1.25[e], APA, 1992); limits regarding confidentiality (Bilynski & Vernaglia, 1998; Cooper & Gottlieb, 2000; see also Standards 1.24 and 5.01, APA, 1992); and the psychologist's reimbursement and financial arrangements with the MBHO (Bilynski & Vernaglia, 1998; see also Standard 1.25, APA, 1992). Acuff et al. indicate that the information provided during discussions of informed consent with patients should also include type of service to be offered and anticipated number of treatment sessions (see Standard 1.07 and 4.01, APA, 1992) as well as the psychologist's role as both a provider of treatment and an agent of the MBHO (see Standards 1.17, 1.21, and 4.03, APA, 1992).

Informed consent as it pertains to actual treatment in MBHO settings has received appropriate attention. However, there is little in the professional literature that speaks specifically to the issue of informed consent as it pertains to psychological testing and assessment. Certainly, the qualifications referred to Standard 4.02(a) apply, and matters pertaining to confidentiality of test data and test reports, health plan coverage and payment for such services, and the role of the psychologist are all pertinent in obtaining informed consent for psychological testing procedures. In addition, psychologists working with or for MBHOs that have incorporated an outcomes assessment program into their care delivery system have an additional obligation of informing their patients of the consequences of their participating in this program (Pratt, Berman, & Hurt, 1998). Relevant here is information concerning the patient's right to refuse participation; the need for posttreatment contact for follow-up assessment; how the outcomes data might be used (e.g., clinical and/or research purposes); and all concomitant confidentiality issues. It is important to note that separate consent must be obtained when the outcomes assessment is part of a time-limited research project that is *not* a component of the MBHO's routine service delivery system.

In concluding this discussion, there are two important points that must be mentioned. First, beyond the obvious ethical considerations, the issue of informed consent is also a legal issue (Sweeney et al., 1998). Thus, not obtaining *informed* consent may increase the psychologist's liability for damages that may be incurred from lawsuits filed against him by the patient. Second, obtaining informed consent is a continuous process (Cooper & Gottlieb, 2000; Nagy, 1998). The patient must be kept informed of his options relative to the services that are offered to him throughout the episode of care. Unlike treatment itself, testing generally will be a one-time procedure that will not require ongoing solicitation of informed consent. As alluded to previously, it may be required for those patients participating in outcomes assessment programs involving multiple administrations of outcomes instrumentation.

Social Responsibility

There will be instances in which the psychologist feels strongly about the necessity of administering one or more psychological tests to a patient for whom authorization for testing has been denied. At these times, one should be mindful of Principle F (APA, 1992), which states that

> Psychologists are aware of their professional and scientific responsibilities to the community and the society in which they live and work.... They apply and make public their knowledge of psychology in order to contribute to human welfare.... They are encouraged to contribute a portion of their professional time for little or no personal advantage. (p. 1600)

For many psychologists, reimbursement for testing will never be a prime consideration. Concern for the patient and offering the highest quality of care within reason will always take precedence over issues surrounding compensation for professional time. But those who normally would not give their time without financial consideration should be aware of Principle F's recommendation to do what may amounts to *pro bono* work, or work offered at a significantly discounted rate.

Providing testing services at a reduced rate or free of charge can be made easier through the use of testing instruments that are available at no or low cost to the psychologists. There are a number of such instruments, many of which are presented in chapters 5 and 8. The instruments discussed in those chapters have been included because of their affordability and the availability of literature that supports their use. It is hoped that psychologists' awareness of these and similar instruments will lessen the resistance to testing at least some patients who could benefit from testing but who might not otherwise have access to this service.

Resolving Ethical Issues

Up to this point, a number of potential ethical points related to psychological testing have been identified. A number of potential conflicts also have been identified. How should psychologists proceed in resolving such conflicts? A number of issue-specific suggestions were provided earlier. However, there also are a number of general approaches to consider. The first of these approaches is Standard 8.02 (APA, 1992), which states that "When a psychologist is uncertain whether a particular situation or course of action would violate [the APA] Ethics Code, the psychologist ordinarily consults with other psychologists knowledgeable about ethical issues, with state or national ethics committees, or with other appropriate authorities in order to choose a proper response" (p. 1611). Further guidance that is more specific to conflicts with MBHOs can be found in Standard 8.03 (APA, 1992), which indicates that

> if the demands of an organization with which psychologists are affiliated conflict with [the APA] Ethics Code, psychologists clarify the nature of the conflict, make known their commitment to the Ethics Code, and to the extent feasible, seek to resolve the conflict in a way that permits the fullest adherence to the Ethics Code. (p. 1611)

Related to this, Standard 1.21 (Third-Party Requests for Service; APA, 1992) states that

> (a) When a psychologist agrees to provide services to a person or entity at the request of a third party, the psychologist clarifies to the extent feasible, at the outset of the service, the nature of the relationship with each party. This clarification includes the role of the psychologist. . . , the probable uses of the services provided or the information obtained, and the fact that there may be limits to confidentiality.
> (b) If there is a foreseeable risk of the psychologist's being called upon to perform conflicting roles because of the involvement of a third party, the psychologist clarifies the nature and direction of his or her responsibilities, keeps all parties appropriately informed as matters develop, and resolves the situation in accordance with the ethical code. (p. 1602)

Note that these Standards do not give specific directions as to how to deal with conflicts that arise (e.g., "obligations to the patient always take precedence over those to the organization"). They only provide guidance as to a general approach to employ to assist in resolving conflicts. One useful approach to ethical dilemmas that psychologists might face in dealing with MBHOs is a series of questions that is offered by Acuff et al. (1999, p. 568). Answers to the following questions may help the psychologist arrive at a resolution that will meet the needs of both the patient and the MBHO:

1. What are my personal ethics on similar issues?
2. What is my gut-level opinion on a possible course of action?
3. Is this truly an ethical dilemma, or is it a business, technical, or other problem?
4. Is this a dilemma that I cannot resolve? Does it require systems change and/or organizational advocacy, or legal or legislative action?
5. If it is an ethical dilemma, who are the persons who have a legitimate stake in the resolution of the dilemma?
6. What are the relevant ethical principles?
7. Is a psychological or legal consultation needed?
8. Are there compelling reasons to deviate from the ethical standard?
9. What are the overarching ethical principles involved (e.g., patient autonomy, doing good for others, doing no harm, justice, or fidelity)?

The answers to these questions, with consideration of Standards 1.21, 8.02 and 8.03, should lead to the psychologist to develop and then evaluate possible alternatives for action, selection of one course of action, and then determination of whether that solution is both ethical *and* implementable. Note that Acuff et al. also provide specific recommendations to resolving issues related to informed consent, confidentiality, and utilization management in this same article.

Cooper and Gottlieb (2000) suggest another approach that has been proposed by Haas and Malouf (1995) for resolving ethical dilemmas. As summarized by Cooper and Gottlieb, this approach recommends that the psychologist first gather pertinent information, such as the ethical issues that are involved, all parties that have an interest in the outcome of the dilemma, and preexisting standards. This is followed by a review of the literature and/or collegial consultation to further explore perspectives that are relevant to ethical, social, or legal standards. Next, relevant ethical principles are identified, followed by the generation of possible and ethically appropriate solutions to problem. After evaluating each potential solution using a cost-benefit analysis, the optimal solution is selected and implemented. Subsequently, the outcome of the action is reviewed and evaluated in consultation with colleagues.

In the end, conflict resolution will involve a clear understanding of all relevant elements, application of the appropriate principles or standards, and the psychologist's judgment of the how best to proceed, all things being considered. Thus, given the exact same circumstances and using the same approach to problem resolution just indicated, it may not be unusual for two psychologists to arrive at different outcomes to the conflict before them — with both feeling satisfied that they had acted in an ethical manner.

Avoiding Ethical Conflicts

The best way to deal with ethical conflicts with MBHOs is to avoid them in the first place. There are several steps that the psychologist may take to prevent the types of conflicts that have been identified earlier from occurring. Following are a few broad recommendations in this regard.

Determine One's Fit With Managed Behavioral Health Care: General Considerations. One way of avoiding ethical and other conflicts with MBHOs is not to become involved with them in the first place. Cummings (1998a) presents five possible psychologist characteristics that should be taken into consideration by anyone contemplating either joining a MBHO provider panel or becoming an MBHO employee. The first has to do with the psychologist's agreement with managed care's approach to health care. As Cummings is quick to point out, "Managed care can be defined as the partial subordination of clinical considerations to business principles in the interest of rendering healthcare delivery economically viable. . . . Practitioners who find strong philosophical disagreement with market-oriented solutions to health reform will not be happy in this system" (p. 63). Second, psychologists who feel that the only effective treatment is long-term therapy will not be a good match for a system that focuses on brief or time-sensitive treatment. Third, those not skilled or otherwise trained in brief psychotherapeutic techniques must be willing to train and become proficient in this mode of service delivery. Fourth, the psychologist must have the stamina to carry a large caseload with a high turnover rate. Fifth, following from the fourth point, those needing the gratitude of patients or other forms of patient-provided reinforcement need to know that they are unlikely to receive it from MBHO patients. The inability to work for or with an MBHO given any of these requisite personal characteristics should dissuade the psychologist from pursuing a relationship with an MBHO as a network provider or employee. As Shueman (1997) points out, the same holds true for those who believe that *absolute* confidentiality is necessary for effective treatment.

Evaluate the MBHO Before Becoming an Employee or Network Provider. Assuming that the psychologist is comfortable in working under the conditions just described, he should then undertake an evaluation of the specific MBHO(s) with whom he wishes to enter into a relationship. MBHOs are not all the same. The manner in which they conduct business and are sensitive to ethical issues vary. A psychologist may feel comfortable working with or for one MBHO but not another. Therefore, it is wise to take a close look at the individual MBHO and its practices, and avoid generalizing from one organization to another.

To assist in this task, Haas and Cummings (1991) developed a set of questions that the prospective provider panel member should ask prior to pursuing an arrangement with any given MBHO. They are as follows:

1. *Who takes the risks?* If risks are borne by the psychologist, he may be less likely to ensure that his patients receive all of the services his patients need.

2. *How much does the plan intrude into the patient-provider relationship?* Here the issue becomes one of how much the psychologist's responsibilities to the MBHO might conflict with his responsibilities to the patient.

3. *What provisions exist for exceptions to the rules?* Lack of flexibility in benefits in some health plans may lead the psychologist to look for ways to work around (e.g. "game") the system.

4. *Are there referral sources if patient needs should exceed plan benefits?* In other words, how can the psychologist ensure that there are viable options for treatment when his patients' benefits run out?

5. *Does the plan provide assistance or training in helping the provider to achieve treatment goals?* If required, will the MBHO provide the training needed for the psychologist to become proficient in the art of brief treatment?

6. *Does the plan minimize economic incentives to hospitalize patients?* If so, this can increase the probability that conflict between the psychologist and the MBHO will occur.

7. *Are there ways in which the plan is open to provider input?* Being open to provider input is one way in which MBHOs can show that the psychologist is valued for more than just the services he provides. This is less of a concern today than it was 10 years ago, due to the fact that MBHO accreditation bodies such as NCQA and JCAHO require input from their provider panels.

8. *Does the plan clearly inform their policy holders of the limits of benefits?* One will want to be sure that the MBHO does all that it can to educate health plan members about the limits to their benefits. This can make obtaining informed consent easier and prevent misunderstandings that the psychologist might otherwise have to deal with later on.

Calfee (1998) suggests obtaining other information about an MBHO before deciding whether to join its provider panel. Knowing some basic information (e.g., who owns the business, how long it has been operating, how many lives it is responsible for, how providers are selected for inclusion in the provider network) is always important. She also identifies other types of information that this author considers much more important from conflict prevention standpoint. This includes how medical necessity is determined, how quality is monitored, how utilization review is conducted, how open the MBHO is to psychologists' requests for additional benefits, what services the psychologist is expected to provide to health plan members, and how the MBHO will maintain the patient's confidentiality. Bilynsky and Vernaglia (1998) offer some of these same recommendations.

What information is important to have regarding the MBHO's testing and assessment policies and practices? For those who have a particular interest in providing testing services or who just feel that such services are an important part of quality behavioral health care, there are several things that one should find out about how an MBHO handles testing requests and issues before joining its provider network. The most important of these are the following:

- Under what circumstances is psychological testing authorized? Does the MBHO consider exceptions to the standard criteria for authorization?
- Does a doctoral level psychologist review and approve requests for psychological testing?
- Does the MBHO require copies of the raw test data?
- Can the psychologist use tests of his own choosing to answer the questions that initiated the testing, or is the psychologist limited to the use of only those tests that have been selected or approved by the MBHO?
- What is the rate of reimbursement per test? Per test battery?
- Can the psychologist be reimbursed for the tests administered by a trained psychological assistant, supervisee, or intern or other student under his supervision?
- Will the MBHO authorize a session to provide feedback about test results to the patient?
- What is the process that the patient or psychologist has for appealing a denial for authorization of testing services?

The answers to any one of these questions may bear strongly on the psychologist's decision to sign on with a given MBHO.

Engage in Risk Management.   Having the type of information suggested above will help lessen the probability that the psychologist will need to employ the conflict resolution techniques that were presented earlier. Once he becomes a member of the MBHO's provider panel, there are other ways the psychologist can minimize the risk of ethical conflict and legal exposure. This is commonly referred to as *risk management.* Calfee (1998) defines risk management as "the task of protecting a clinician's financial assets from a variety of potentially negative events" (p. 227). Essentially, it is a proactive approach to avoiding litigation. Although Calfee's discussion of risk management is directed to the avoidance of litigation and resulting financial loss, the term can also apply to the avoidance of ethical conflicts in which litigation is not involved.

Calfee (1998) presents a summary of the four-step approach to a risk management developed by Richards and Rathbun (1983). The first step is the identification of problematic situations that may arise during the course of providing services to MBHO patients. A review of relevant literature can be helpful in this regard. However, the psychologist would be better served by obtaining information related to patient satisfaction, appeals of medical necessity decisions, provider and patient complaints, current quality improvement activities, and findings from accreditation and regulatory site audits that are specific to the MBHO. MBHOs have this information, but their willingness to release it to members of their provider panels likely varies from one company to another.

The second step of the Richards and Rathbun (1983) process is to analyze the potential problems that were identified. For example, the psychologist may find that during the previous year, there had been many patient complaints related to the confidentiality of psychological test findings. Similarly, he may discover that a significant percentage of requests for authorization of psychological testing or for sessions to provide patients with feedback about their test results had been denied. Patient satisfaction survey results may suggest that there have been general issues related to patients receiving enough information to give truly informed consent for treatment and other procedures.

With the analyses of the potentially problematic areas, step three involves the psychologist developing means of minimizing the risk of the occurrence of these problematic issues arising using *risk-control* and/or *risk-transfer* techniques (Richards & Rathbun, 1983). Risk control essentially involves greatly lowering or totally eliminating the risk. In the case of matters pertaining to the use of psychological testing, the psychologist might decide to totally eliminate associated risks by refusing to accept referrals for testing. Securing liability insurance or ensuring that his contract includes language indemnifying him from legal responsibility are examples of risk transfer. Unfortunately or not, there is no way to transfer risk associated *ethical* issues and decisions associated with psychological testing.

The fourth and final step for the psychologist is simply monitoring the effectiveness of the risk control techniques that have been selected (Richards & Rathbun, 1983). Changes or modifications in these strategies are made as appropriate.

OTHER PROFESSIONAL ISSUES AND CONCERNS

In addition to the issues that arise as a result of clashes between the ethics of the psychologist and the business practices of MBHOs, there are other issues that have emerged with regard to MBHOs' stance toward psychological testing. In 1998, APA's Board of Professional Affairs, PAWG, released a two-volume report of its investigation into the benefits, problems, limitations, and costs of psychological testing and assessment in contemporary health care delivery (Eisman et al., 1998, also published as Eisman et. al., 2000; Meyer et al., 1998). This report brought to light many situations and conditions that frequently arise in dealings with MBHOs that most psychologist find particularly problematic. This section presents the major findings of the PAWG, followed by the PAWG's recommendations for dealing with these problems.

Problems Encountered by Psychologists

The PAWG's work unveiled several potential troublesome or problematic aspects of dealing with managed care companies about matters pertaining to psychological testing and assessment. This is not to say that conflicts always arise over these matters. Indeed, several of these reported areas of contention have not manifested themselves in settings that this author is aware of. There is, however, no doubt that these problems do exist in some MBHOs. Several problems identified by the PAWG that share a common theme have been grouped together for the purpose of this discussion.

Many MBHO Testing Practices Are in Conflict With the APA Ethical Principles. The PAWG identified policies and practices that are in conflict with APA's *Ethical Principles* (Eisman et al., 1998). These have to do with issues pertaining to matters such as confidentiality of test data, the provision of test feedback to patients, and appropriate use of test instruments (e.g., using outdated versions of tests, no change in reimbursement rates when the more costly, updated versions are used). These and other ethical issues are generally addressed in the previous section of this chapter and will not be discussed further here.

Authorization for Testing can be a Lengthy Process Involving Decisions Made by Nonpsychologists. Authorization can be a lengthy process, with some patients deteriorating or leaving treatment before an authorization decision is made (Eisman et al., 1998). There are reports that some MBHOs use nonclinical utilization management staff or nonpsychologists not proficient in psychological testing to make decisions and review appeals to noncertifications pertaining to the authorization of this type of service. In many MBHOs this is not the case. There also are reports that patients must get a referral from their primary care physicians (PCPs) in order to be seen for behavioral health care services. Aside from any other concerns about such procedures, many PCPs are not well informed about how psychological testing can benefit the patient's treatment.

Authorization May be Specific to a Certain Test, Types of Tests, or Assessment Procedures. As Eisman et al. (1998) point out, the use of only specific tests may be authorized, thus eliminating the flexibility in test selection that is necessary as new information becomes available during the course of testing. Moreover, entire classes of non-mental health instruments (e.g., vocational, educational, normal personality) may not be authorized for reimbursement. This is despite the fact that instruments that fall in these and other categories may provide information that can help determine most effective and efficient intervention for the patient. Reimbursement for assessment-related interviews (e.g., interviews with the teachers of child patients) and psychological report writing also can be problematic.

Added to this is the reluctance of MBHOs to authorize the administration of batteries of two tests of the same type (Eisman et al., 1998). According to the PAWG, MBHOs do not realize how batteries of tests can offer unique information about the patient; rather, the focus is on costs. As for the administration of two similar tests, MBHOs view this practice as rarely being indicated. From the psychologist's standpoint, however, it can permit confirmation of findings, information about unique aspects of the construct being measured, and lowering of liability exposure through cross-validation of findings.

Administration of Tests for Certain Purposes May Not be Approved. One area of concern has to do with the restriction or "banning" of the use of psychological testing for specific purposes. Use of testing for diagnostic and disposition purposes is a prime example. Eisman et al. (1998) observe that some payors feel that diagnostic interviews are sufficient to arrive at a diagnosis and to determine various aspects of care, such as appropriate LOC and modality of treatment, or readiness for termination of treatment. Some MBHOs encourage differential diagnosis via medication trials, such as prescribing Ritalin in cases where ADHD is suspected. Moreover, MBHOs that see themselves in the business of providing acute care are not interested in authorizing testing to aid in the identification of chronic conditions or characterological problems for which they do not intend to authorize treatment. Perhaps most concerning is the fact that MBHOs may not consistently authorize testing being conducted for risk management purposes, such as with cases of suspected or potential dangerousness to self or others or those with complicated diagnostic issues that may have a bearing on how restrictive care should be for the patient.

In responding to these limitations in testing, PAWG contends that it is often the case that psychological testing is the best way to get around examiner and situational effects—defensiveness, deception, lack of insight, and so forth—that may interfere with obtaining an accurate picture of a patient's diagnosis, problems, and concerns (Eisman et al., 1998). As for the issue of encouraging differential diagnoses through medication trials, the PAWG identified many dangers accompanying this approach, including delaying appropriate treatment, overlooking other problems, patient discouragement, ignoring potentially problematic side effects, and perhaps most importantly, impacting the diagnosis and treatment later on in life by assigning an ADHD label to the patient. Discouraging testing for the identification of long-term or characterological problems is viewed as creating a dilemma for the psychologist: The psychologist may feel strongly that withholding testing services is unethical while going ahead and performing the testing, even at low or no cost to the patient, may be viewed by the MBHO as being "managed care unfriendly." Not permitting testing for risk management purposes may weaken the provider's ability to defend himself should there be a malpractice claim related to misdiagnosis or adverse treatment decisions.

Testing Conducted by Supervised Postdoctoral Psychologists, Interns, Students, and Technicians May Not be Reimbursed. Some MBHOs refuse to reimburse for testing or entire assessment activities that is conducted by someone other than the authorized provider (Eisman et al., 1998). This would include technicians who may be used for nothing more than the administration and scoring of tests (as is common in neuropsychological assessments), as well as students, interns, and postdoctoral fellows whose professional development depends on gaining supervised testing experience. PAWG also raised a related issue, that is, the reimbursement for computer scoring of psychological tests. In this author's opinion, PAWG's justification for MBHOs paying for computerized scoring (e.g., increase accuracy) is not very strong, except with instruments that involve complicated or lengthy scoring procedures or are otherwise prone to human scoring error.

Psychological Testing Specialists May Not be in the MBHO's Provider Network. Eisman et al. (1998) report two problems that may be found with regard to the MBHO's ability to provide the best testing services to health plan members they are responsible for. Both have to do with the availability of testing specialists. First,

MBHO geographical restrictions may limit testing referrals to only those providers within the given geographical area, eliminating the possibility of referral to the more appropriate psychologist for the type of testing that patient requires. Second, ethnic or linguistic minorities may receive testing referrals to providers who *generally* are best suited to meet the behavioral health care needs of the minority patient. Just because a psychologist can speak a minority patient's language or is sensitive to his needs does not mean that he is qualified to test the patient. Here, the MBHO is setting unrealistic expectations for the psychologist while not providing the patient the type of service he needs. The problem may be compounded by the MBHO's not reimbursing out-of-network services with culturally competent psychologists.

Reimbursement Rates are Low.   As might be expected, the PAWG raised issues related to the reimbursement rates for testing (Eisman et al. 1998). These are not limited to issues related actual hourly rates. Also included are issues pertaining to the authorization of an adequate amount of time to complete the testing and other assessment activities, as well as not allowing reimbursement for collateral interviews and report writing. Additional problems are sometimes encountered when reimbursement is denied *after* the testing has been completed. The PAWG reported instances where post-testing reviews that determined the testing to have been unnecessary, were deemed unreimbursable. There also were reports of denial of reimbursement for testing conducted for differential diagnosis when the determined diagnosis was found to be one that was not covered by the MBHO.

Testing May be Limited to Once per Year.   The PAWG report indicates that some MBHOs may allow testing just once a year (Eisman et al., 1998). Consequently, some psychologists may be compelled to make sure that a comprehensive assessment is performed, even in cases where a brief screener would be most appropriate. Here, the thinking is to "do it all now" because money may not be available again for another year.

The PAWG members summed up their findings by stating that

> It is clear . . . that the field of psychological assessment faces enormous obstacles in the current health care delivery system: outright refusal to endorse assessment as a worthwhile clinical activity, difficulties in gaining pre-authorization for testing, substantial problems with reimbursement, and interference in assessment decisions that are appropriately the purview of the psychologist that provides this service. (Eisman et al., 1998, p. 16)

The PAWG Recommendations

The PAWG's extensive review of the state of psychological testing in the current health care delivery system led this group to conclude that MBHO policies were not the sole reason for the decline of psychological testing in the managed care system (Eisman et al., 1998). Numerous factors—the focus on short-term treatment, pressures to make interventions more efficient and cost-effective, use of medication for diagnostic purposes, and (perhaps most important) the lack of empirical studies demonstrating the value of testing for treatment planning and outcomes—all have contributed to the current status of psychological testing in MBHOs. Given this set of circumstances, PAWG arrived at a set of general recommendations for improving the testing's standing and future in the health care delivery system.

Working Within the Profession.   The PAWG recommended that psychologists work within their own profession to promote the use of psychological testing in the areas of practice, training, and research (Eisman et al., 1998). As far as practice is concerned, the PAWG members recommended the development of a set of criteria to help psychologists, the public, and decision makers identify situations in which psychological testing would be most appropriate and helpful. This information could made available through the Internet, and perhaps through APA's home page. Improvements in graduate and continuing education could be made in order to better improve psychologists' skills and make them more aware of the current standards of practice and relevant ethical requirements. Examples here might include giving close scrutiny to faculty qualifications and course content for testing courses; developing guidelines for training in psychological testing for graduate, internship, and postdoctoral clinical programs; and working with professional organizations (e.g., APA's Division 5, the Society for Personality Assessment) to establish proficiency criteria for use of various tests and assessment approaches. As for the research area, the group recommended efforts toward reducing the gap between research and practice and training. One of the best examples given is coordinating activities related to demonstrating the cost-effectiveness of psychological testing when used for treatment planning or outcomes assessment.

Working With Managed Care.   Two general approaches are recommended for working with MBHOs that can help promote the role of psychological testing in those settings (Eisman et al., 1998). The first is through the establishment of a nationwide network of psychologists who work with MBHOs and other health care systems, who would be willing to help disseminate findings relative to the benefits of psychological testing. This group of psychologists also would engage in other activities intended to enlighten MBHOs about testing and how to use it appropriately. The second approach in working with MBHOs is actually directed toward psychologists and teaching them to work more effectively with these organizations. Essentially, this would involve educating them as to how to work *within* the system as opposed to working *against* it.

Working With Other Mental Health Professionals.   The PAWG identified misunderstandings between psychologists and other mental health professions (e.g., psychiatrists, social workers, psychiatric nurses) over the value of psychological testing as one source of tension between the two factions (Eisman et al., 1998). Interprofessional communication regarding the uses and benefits of psychological testing was recommended as one means of improving its image of and the demand for it. Presentations and workshops about testing at the meetings and conventions of these other professions, as well as striving to have articles published in their professional literature (e.g., refereed journals, other trade publications) are examples of how this could be accomplished.

Working With Patients/Consumers.   Testing's image also could be improved through efforts to educate the nonprofessional public (Eisman et al., 1998). Working through APA's Public Education campaign was suggested with regard to this recommendation.

Working Through Political Action. Finally, the PAWG identified the need to make psychological testing more prominent on state and national legislative and regulatory agendas (Eisman et al., 1998). In this regard, it recommended such tactics as educating lobbyists about the benefits of testing and working toward achieving consistency of treatment and testing benefits.

Other Recommendations

Others also have offered recommendations for improving the lot of psychological testing in the future, particularly with regard to its use in MBHOs. Graham (2000a) provides four suggestions in the regard. Similar to one of Eisman et al.'s (1998) recommendations, the first is that psychologists adopt a strong advocacy role in the promotion of psychological testing and assessment. In fact, he points to the PAWG's efforts in gathering and publishing its findings on research that supports the use and benefits of psychological testing as a good example. These types of efforts would provide the needed information to counter the conclusions drawn by testing's critics and health care's gatekeepers. Second, there should be more research that focuses on developing new instruments or validating existing instruments for applications or activities that are viewed as important by practitioners and, for that matter, MBHOs. For example, an MBHO working with a health plan to integrate primary and behavioral health care might value psychological test instruments that would identify those primary care patients who likely will be noncompliant with treatment. Third, psychologists should make greater use of computer technology and its ability to aid in clinical decision making. Finally, like another of Eisman et al.'s (1998) recommendations, Graham advocates changes in the training that graduate students receive. This would include incorporating advanced training in areas such as psychometric theory and test construction with traditional training in the use of test instruments.

Based on the findings of their survey, Camara et al. (2000) suggest three strategies for overcoming the economic barriers that have resulted from the proliferation of managed care and that reduce the quality and extent of testing and assessment services. The first is for psychologists to find ways to make testing and assessment a central component of their treatment planning and interventions. The message to convey is that testing is a "medical necessity" rather than an optional service. Camara et al. also espouse the approach that has been mentioned several times earlier in this book, that is, presenting evidence of the efficacy of psychological testing. As they put it,

> [Psychologists] must be able to justify the benefits of . . . assessment services in terms of treatment focus, treatment duration, and cost-to-benefit ratio. . . . Evidence demonstrating that assessment services in diagnosis or treatment have been effective in reducing the duration of treatment or reducing the recidivism of mental health problems will be viewed as compelling by managed care because of its economic relevance. (p. 153)

Last, psychological testing services must move away from being considered an independent psychological service to one in which it is viewed as an integrated component. Camara et al. suggest that evidence of success in this effort would be indicated by the incorporation of assessment services into practice guidelines.

Ambrose (1997) lists several suggestions for justifying the use of psychological testing to MBHOs. One is to provide the MBHO with information about which types

of patients are best served with testing. In this regard, he encourages the use of anecdotal information from cases that the MBHO's care managers are familiar with. Similarly, the psychologist can educate the MBHO as to the situations in which testing
will likely prove to be most helpful. Examples might be the use of brief screening instruments to identify depressed patients in MBHO-sponsored behavioral medicine
projects. In addition, one can demonstrate how testing can provide even those patients who have been in treatment for long periods of time, with hitherto unknown
insight into themselves and their problems. Finally, one may be able to show how information obtained from testing one patient or group of patients can be used to the
benefit of other patients seen by other providers, possibly resulting in substantial
cost-offset.

SUMMARY

It is difficult if not impossible for many practicing psychologists to avoid involvement with MBHOs in one way or another. It has become the predominant form of behavioral health care delivery in the United States and is likely to remain so in the
foreseeable future. Psychologists report several complaints against this system of
health care, many of which have to do with ethical issues. Some feel that the issues
that arise in MBHO settings are unique; others say that these issues have always been
there under other forms of insurance (e.g., indemnity plans). The fact is that psychologists dealing with managed and nonmanaged health care delivery systems experience both similar ethical dilemmas as well as ones that are unique to each system.
This includes ethical issues related to psychological testing that is requested and/or
performed in those systems. Moreover, psychologists also must contend with other
issues related to testing that are not ethical in nature yet provide challenges to their
ability to engage in the distinguishing aspect of their professional duties. Again,
some of these issues are unique to managed care, some are not.

APA's *Ethical Principles* provide the psychologist working for or with an MBHO
excellent guidelines for dealing with many of the testing-related issues that he will
most likely have to face. At the same time, these same principles fall short in several
areas in which ethical dilemmas arise in this type of setting. This can probably be accounted for by the fact the current version of the *Ethical Principles* was developed at
the beginning of the 1990s, before managed behavioral health care became a powerful force in the delivery of mental health and substance abuse services. Many of the
ethical issues that are unique to MBHO settings probably were not as frequent or
troublesome as they are today and maybe as a result, additions or modifications of
the 1992 *Ethical Principles* to reflect managed care issues was not thought to be necessary. Regardless, the fact is that inclusion of additional principles and guidelines in
APA's core ethics document is called for. In the meantime, psychologists perceiving
ethical conflicts concerning testing issues (or any other practice issues) in MBHOs are
encouraged to follow whatever guidelines that are currently provided in the *Ethical
Principles* and to seek counsel from colleagues or the APA when these principles are
found to be inadequate.

Solutions to the unique, nonethical issues related to testing in MBHOs require a
different tact. These will involve concerted efforts to educating the managed behavioral health care industry as to the importance and value of psychological testing for

multiple clinical activities, including screening for specific disorders, diagnosis, treatment planning, treatment monitoring, and outcomes assessment (see chapter 2). This will not be an easy task; there will have to be empirical and other objective proof to support psychology's contentions of the benefits of testing to the MBHOs. The profession as a whole needs to begin working on developing ways of providing this proof, for without it, there will not be any significant progress in elevating psychological testing above its current status in the eyes of the managed behavioral health care industry.

References

Academy of Psychosomatic Medicine (1996). Mental disorders in general medical practice: An opportunity to add value to healthcare. *Behavioral Healthcare Tomorrow, 5,* 55–72.

Academy of Psychosomatic Medicine (1997). Mental disorders in general medical practice: Adding value to healthcare through consultation–liaison psychiatry. In J. D. Haber & G. E. Mitchell (Eds.), *Primary care meets mental health: Tools for the 21st century* (pp. 255–292). Tiburon, CA: CentraLink Publications.

Acuff, C., Bennett, B. E., Bricklin, P. M., Canter, M. B., Knapp, S. J., Moldawsky, S., & Phelps, R. (1999). Considerations for ethical practice in managed care. *Professional Psychology: Research and Practice, 30,* 563–575.

Aday, L. A., Begley, C. E., Lairson, D. R., Slater, C. H., Richard, A. J., & Montoya, I. D. (1999). A framework for assessing the effectiveness, efficiency, and equity of behavioral healthcare. *The American Journal of Managed Care, 5,* SP25–SP44.

Ambrose, P. A. (1997). Challenges for mental health service providers: The perspective of managed care organizations. In J. N. Butcher (Ed.), *Personality assessment in managed health care* (pp. 61–72). New York: Oxford University Press.

American Educational Research Association, American Psychological Association, & National Council on Measurement in Education (1999). *Standards for educational and psychological testing.* Washington, DC: American Educational Research Association.

American Journal of Managed Care. (1999). Introduction. *American Journal of Managed Care, 5*(13), S764–S766.

American Managed Behavioral Healthcare Association. (1995). *Performance measures for managed behavioral healthcare programs.* Washington, DC: AMBHA Quality Improvement and Clinical Services Committee.

American Managed Behavioral Healthcare Association (1998). *Performance measures for managed behavioral healthcare programs 2.0 (PERMS 2.0).* Washington, DC: Author.

American Psychiatric Association. (1994). *Diagnostic and statistical manual of mental disorders* (4th ed.). Washington, DC: Author.

American Psychological Association. (1987). *General guidelines for providers of psychological services.* Washington, DC: Author.

American Psychological Association. (1992). Ethical principles of psychologists and code of conduct. *American Psychologist, 47,* 1597–1611.

American Psychological Association. (1995). *Finding information about psychological tests: A guide for locating and using both published and unpublished tests.* Washington, DC: Author.

American Psychological Association. (1996). *The costs of failing to provide appropriate mental health care.* Washington, DC: Author.

Andreasen, N. C., & Olsen, S. A. (1982). Negative versus positive schizophrenia: Definition and validation. *Archives of General Psychiatry, 39,* 789–794.

306

Andrews, G. (1995). Best practices for implementing outcomes management: More science, more art, worldwide. *Behaviioral Healthcare Tomorrow, 4*, 19–21, 74–75.

Andrews, G., Peters, L., & Teesson, M. (1994). *The measurement of consumer outcomes in mental health*. Canberra, Australia: Australian Government Publishing Service.

Appelbaum, S. A. (1990). The relationship between assessment and psychotherapy. *Journal of Personality Assessment, 54*, 791–801.

Appleby, L., Dyson, V., Altman, E., & Luchins, D. J. (1997). Assessing substance use in multiproblem patients: Reliability and validity of the Addiction Severity Index in a mental hospital population. *The Journal of Nervous and Mental Disease, 185*, 159–165.

Attkisson, C. C., & Greenfield, T. K. (1996). The Client Satisfaction Questionnaire (CSQ) scales and the Service Satisfaction Scale-30 (SSS-30). In L. I. Sederer & B. Dockey (Eds.), *Outcomes assessment in clinical practice* (pp. 120–127). Baltimore, MD: Williams & Wilkins.

Attkisson, C. C., & Greenfield, T. K. (1999). The UCSF client satisfaction scales: I. The Client Satisfaction Questionaire-8. In M. E. Maruish (Ed.), *The use of psychological testing for treatment planning and outcomes assessment* (2nd ed., pp. 1333–1346). Mahwah, NJ: Lawrence Erlbaum Associates.

Attkisson, C. C., & Pascoe, G. C. (Eds.). (1983). *Patient satisfaction in health and mental health services*. A special issue of *Evaluation and Program Planning, 6*, 185–418.

Attkisson, C. C., & Zwick, R. (1982). The Client Satisfaction Questionnaire: Psychometric properties and correlations with service utilization and psychotherapy outcome. *Evaluation and Program Planning, 6*, 233–237.

Austad, C. S., Hunter, R. D., & Morgan, T. C. (1998). Managed health care, ethics, and psychotherapy. *Clinical Psychology: Science and practice, 5*, 67–76.

Austad, C. S., & Morgan, T. C. (1998). Toward a social ethic of mental health care: Long-term therapy, short-term therapy, and managed health care. In R. F. Small & L. R. Barnhill (Eds.), *Practicing in the new mental health marketplace: Ethical, legal, and moral issues* (pp. 103–120). Washington, DC: American Psychological Association.

Baer, L., Jacobs, D. G., Meszler-Reizes, J., Blais, M., Fava, M., Kessler, R., Magruder, K., Murphy, J., Kopans, B., Cukor, P., Leahy, L., & O'Laughlen, J. (2000). Development of a brief screening instrument: The HANDS. *Psychotherapy and Psychosomatics, 69*, 35–41.

Baldessarini, R. J., Finkelstein, S., & Arana, G. W. (1983). The predictive power of diagnostic tests and the effect of prevalence of illness. *Archives of General Psychiatry, 40*, 569–573.

Barnett, J. E. (1998). Confidentiality in the age of managed care. *The Clinical Psychologist, 51*, 30–31.

Barnhill, L. R. (1998). Defining the issues: Survey research in ethics and managed care. In R. F. Small & L. R. Barnhill (Eds.), *Practicing in the new mental health marketplace: Ethical, legal, and moral issues* (pp. 11–35). Washington, DC: American Psychological Association.

Barnhill, L. R., & Small, R. F. (1998). Introduction. In R. F. Small & L. R. Barnhill (Eds.), *Practicing in the new mental health marketplace: Ethical, legal, and moral issues* (pp. 3–8). Washington, DC: American Psychological Association.

Barsky, A. J., & Borus, J. F. (1995). Somatization and medicalization in the era of managed care. *Journal of the American Medical Association, 274*, 1931.

Beauchamp, T., & Childress, W. (1988). *Principles of biomedical ethics* (3rd ed.). Baltimore, MD: Johns Hopkins University Press.

Beck, A. T., Epstein, N., Brown, G., & Steer, R. A. (1988). An inventory for measuring anxiety: Psychometric properties. *Journal of Consulting and Clinical Psychology, 56*, 893–897.

Beck, A. T., Guth, D., Steer, R. A., & Ball, R. (1997). Screening for major depression disorders in medical inpatients with the Beck Depression Inventory for Primary Care. *Behavior Research & Therapy, 35*, 785–791.

Beck, A. T., & Steer, R. A. (1990). *Beck Anxiety Inventory manual*. San Antonio, TX: Psychological Corporation.

Beck, A. T., Steer, R. A., Ball, R., Ciervo, C. A., & Kabat, M. (1997). Use of the Beck Anxiety and Depression Inventories for Primary Care with medical outpatients. *Assessment, 4*, 211–219.

Beck, A. T., Steer, R. A., & Brown, G. K. (1996). *Manual for the Beck Depression Inventory-II*. San Antonio, TX: The Psychological Corporation.

Beck, A. T., Steer, R. A., & Brown, G. K. (2000). *BDI-FastScreen for medical patients*. San Antonio, TX: The Psychological Corporation.

Bedell, J. R., Hunter, R. H., & Corrigan, P. W. (1997). Current approaches to assessment and treatment of persons with serious mental illness. *Professional Psychology: Research and Practice, 28*, 217–228.

Belar, C. D. (1997). Psychological assessment in capitated care. In J. N. Butcher (Ed.), *Personality assessment in managed health care: Using the MMPI-2 in treatment planning* (pp. 73–80). New York: Oxford University Press.

Benedict, J. G., & Phelps, R. (1998). Introduction: Psychology's view of managed care. *Professional Psychology: Research and Practice, 29,* 29–30.

Ben-Porath, Y. S. (1997). Use of personality assessment instruments in empirically guided treatment planning. *Psychological Assessment, 9,* 361–367.

Bengen-Seltzer, B. (1999, May). Nine tips for improving staff buy-in on outcomes. *Data: The Brown University Digest of Addicition Theory and Application, 17*(5), 7–9.

Berlin, I., Sachon, C., Bisserbe, J. C., Bosquet, F., Eiber, R., Grimaldi, A., & Balssa, N. (1997). Phobic symptoms, particularly fear of blood and injury, are associated with poor glycemic control in Type I diabetic adults. *Diabetes Care, 20,* 176–178.

Berman, W. H. (1992). The practice of psychotherapy in managed mental health care. *Psychotherapy in Private Practice, 11,* 39–45.

Berman, W. H., Darling, H., Hurt, S. W., & Hunkeler, E. M. (1994). Culture shock and symergy: Academic/managed care/corporate alliances in outcomes management. *Behavioral Healthcare Tomorrow, 3,* 23–29.

Berman, W. H., & Hurt, S. W. (1996). Talking the talk, walking the walk: Implementing an outcomes information system. *Behavioral Healthcare Tomorrow, 5,* 39–43.

Berman, W. H., Hurt, S. W., & Heiss, G. E. (1996). Outcomes assessment in behavioral healthcare. In C. E. Stout, G. A. Theis, & J. Oher (Eds.), *The complete guide to managed behavioral care.* New York: Wiley.

Berman, W. H., Rosen, C. S., Hurt, S. W., & Kolarz, C. M. (1998). Toto, we're not in Kansas anymore: Measuring and using outcomes in behavioral health care. *Clinical Psychology: Science and Practice, 5,* 115–133.

Beutler, L. E. (2000). David and Goliath: When empirical and clinical standards of practice meet. *American Psychologist, 55,* 997–1007.

Beutler, L. E., & Clarkin, J. (1990). *Systematic treatment selection: Toward targeted therapeutic interventions.* New York: Brunner/Mazel.

Beutler, L. E., Goodrich, G., Fisher, D., & Williams, O. B. (1999). Use of psychological tests/instruments for treatment planning. In M. E. Maruish (Ed.), *The use of psychological testing for treatment planning and outcomes assessment* (2nd ed., pp. 81–113). Mahwah, NJ: Lawrence Erlbaum Associates.

Beutler, L. E., Wakefield, P., & Williams, R. E. (1994). Use of psychological tests/instruments for treatment planning. In M. E. Maruish (Ed.), *The use of psychological testing for treatment planning and outcome assessment* (pp. 55–74). Hillsdale, NJ: Lawrence Erlbaum Associates.

Beutler, L. E., & Williams, O. B. (1995). Computer applications for the selection of optimal psychosocial therapeutic interventions. *Behavioral Healthcare Tomorrow, 4,* 66–68.

Bieber, J., Wroblewski, J. M., & Barber, C. A. (1999). Design and implementation of an outcomes management system within inpatient and outpatient behavioral health settings. In M. E. Maruish (Ed.), *The use of psychological testing for treatment planning and outcomes assessment* (2nd ed., pp. 171–210). Mahwah, NJ: Lawrence Erlbaum Associates.

Bilynsky, A. S., & Vernaglia, E. R. (1998). The ethical practice of psychology in a managed-care framework. *Psychotherapy, 35,* 54–68.

Blankertz, L., Cook, J., Rogers, S., & Hughes, R. (1997). The five Cs of choice: Outcomes measures for individuals with severe and persistent mental illness. *Behavioral Healthcare Tomorrow, 6,* 62–67.

Blum, S. (1992). Ethical issues in managed mental health. In S. Feldman (Ed.), *Managed mental health services* (pp. 245–265). Springfield, IL: Charles C Thomas.

Bobbitt, B. L., Marques, C. C., & Trout, D. L. (1998). Managed behavioral health care: Current status, recent trends, and the role of psychology. *Clinical Psychology: Science and Practice, 5,* 53–66.

Bologna, N. C., Barlow, D. H., Hollon, S. D., Mitchell, J. E., & Huppert, J. D. (1998). Behavioral health treatment redesign in managed care settings. *Clinical Psychology: Science and Practice, 5,* 94–114.

Bologna, N. C., & Feldman, M. J. (1994). Outcomes, clinical models and the redesign of behavioral healthcare. *Behavioral Healthcare Tomorrow, 3,* 31–36.

Bologna, N. C., & Feldman, M. J. (1995). Using outcomes data and clinical process redesign: Improving clinical services. *Behavioral Healthcare Tomorrow, 4,* 59–65.

Borus, J. F. (1985). Psychiatry and the primary care physician. In H. I. Kaplan & B. J. Sadock (Eds.), *Comprehensive textbook of psychiatry/IV* (4th ed.; pp. 1302–1308). Baltimore, MD: Williams & Wilkins.

Boulet, J., & Boss, M. W. (1991). Reliability and validity of the Brief Symptom Inventory. *Psychological Assessment: A Journal of Consulting and Clinical Psychology, 3,* 433–437.

Brantley, P. J., Mehan, D. J., & Thomas, J. L. (2000). The Beck Depression Inventory (BDI) and the Center for Epidemiologic Studies Depression Scale (CES-D). In M. E. Maruish (Ed.), *Handbook of psychological testing in primary care settings* (pp. 391–421). Mahwah, NJ: Lawrence Erlbaum Associates.

Brazier, J. E., Harper, R., Jones, N. M., O'Cathain, A., Thomas, K. J., Usherwood, T., & Westlake, L. (1992). Validating the SF-36 Health Survey questionnaire: New outcome measure for primary care. *British Medical Journal, 305,* 160–164.

Brink, T. L., Yesavage, J. A., Lum, O., Heersema, P. H., Adey, M., & Rose, T. L. (1982). Screening tests for geriatric depression. *Clinical Gerontologist, 1,* 37–43.

Brody, D. S., Hahn, S. R., Spitzer, R. L., Kroenke, K., Linzer, M., deGruy, F. V., & Williams, J. B. (1998). Identifying patients with depression in the primary care setting. *Archives of Internal Medicine, 158,* 2469–2475.

Brook, R. H., McGlynn, E. A., & Cleary, P. D. (1996). Quality of health care. Part 2: Measuring quality of care. *The New England Journal of Medicine, 335,* 966–970.

Brown, R. L. (1992). Identification and office management of alcohol and drug disorders. In M. F. Fleming & K. L. Barry (Eds.), *Addictive disorders* (pp. 25–43). St. Louis, MO: Mosby Year Book.

Brown, R. L., & Rounds, L. A. (1995). Conjoint screening questionnaires for alcohol and other drug abuse: Criterion validity in a primary care practice. *Wisconsin Medical Journal, 94,* 135–140.

Budman, S. H. (1999). Whither medical cost offset? Comments on Chiles et al. *Clinical Psychology: Science and Practice, 6,* 228–230.

Burlingame, G. M., Lambert, M. J., Reisinger, C. W., Neff, W. M., & Mosier, J. (1995). Pragmatics of tracking mental health outcomes in a managed care setting. *Journal of Mental Health Administration, 22,* 226–236.

Burnam, M. A., Wells, K. B., Leake, B., & Landsverk, J. (1988). Development of a brief screening instrument for detecting depressive disorders. *Medical Care, 26,* 775–789.

Burns, J. (1997). Providing care for the mind, body and soul. *Managed Healthcare,* 20–24.

Butcher, J. N. (1990). *The MMPI-2 in psychological treatment.* New York: Oxford University Press.

Butcher, J. N. (1997). Introduction to the special section of assessment in psychological treatment: A necessary step for effective intervention. *Psychological Assessment, 9,* 331–333.

Butcher, J. N., Dahlstrom, W. G., Graham, J. R., Tellegen, A. M., & Kaemmer, B. (1989). *MMPI-2: Manual for administration and scoring.* Minneapolis, MN: University of Minnesota Press.

Bystritsky, A., Linn, L. S., & Ware, J. E. (1990). Development of a multidimensional scale of anxiety. *Journal of Anxiety Disorders, 4,* 99–115.

Bystritsky, A., Stoessel, P., & Yager, J. (1993). Psychometric discrimination between anxiety and depression. *Journal of Nervous and Mental Disease, 181,* 265–267.

Cagney, T., & Woods, D. R. (1994). Why focus on outcomes data? *Behavioral Healthcare Tomorrow, 3,* 65–67.

Calfee, B. E. (1998). Risk management realities surface in new practice environment. In R. F. Small & L. R. Barnhill (Eds.), *Practicing in the new mental health marketplace: Ethical, legal, and moral issues* (pp. 227–238). Washington, DC: American Psychological Association.

Callahan, E. J. (1997). The future of psychology in family medicine. *Journal of Clinical Psychology in Medical Settings, 4,* 155–166.

Camara, W., Nathan, J., & Puente, A. (1998). *Psychological test usage in professional psychology: Report to the APA Practice and Science Directorates.* Washington, DC: American Psychological Association.

Camara, W. J., Nathan, J. S., & Puente, A. E. (2000). *Psychological test usage: Implications in professional psychology, 31,* 141–154.

Cates, J. A. (1999). The art of assessment in psychology: Ethics, expertise, and validity. *Journal of Clinical Psychology, 55,* 631–641.

Chambless, D. L., Renneberg, B., Goldstein, A., & Gracely, E. J. (1992). MCMI-diagnosed personality disorders among agoraphobic outpatients: Prevalence and relationship to severity and treatment outcome. *Journal of Anxiety Disorders, 6,* 193–211.

Chiles, J. A., Lambert, M. J., & Hatch, A. L. (1999). The impact of psychological interventions on medical cost offset: A meta-analytic review. *Clinical Psychology: Science and Practice, 6,* 204–220.

Chisholm, S. M., Crowther, J. H., & Ben-Porath, Y. S. (1997). Selected MMPI-2 scales' ability to predict premature termination and outcome from psychotherapy. *Journal of Personality Assessment, 69,* 127–144.

Christner, A. M. (1997, January). Using baselines and benchmarks can sharpen your outcomes evaluation. *Behavioral Health Outcomes, 2*(1), 1–3.

Christensen, L., & Mendoza, J. L. (1986). A method of assessing change in a single subject: An alteration of the RC index [Letter to the editor]. *Behavior Therapy, 17,* 305–308.

Ciarcia, J. J. (1997, September). *Major depressive disorder: The burdens and promise.* Paper presented at the annual retreat of the Council for Behavioral Group Practices, Washington, DC.

Ciarlo, J. A., Brown, T. R., Edwards, D. W., Kiresuk, T. J., & Newman, F. L. (1986). *Assessing mental health treatment outcomes measurement techniques.* DHHS Pub. No. (ADM)86-1301. Washington, DC: U.S. Government Printing Office.

Cicchetti, D. V. (1994). Guidelines, criteria, and rules of thumb for evaluating normed and standardized assessment instruments in psychology. *Psychological Assessment, 6,* 284–290.

CIGNA Behavioral Health. (1999). *Level of care guidelines for mental health and substance abuse treatment.* Eden Prairie, MN: Author.

Clair, D., & Prendergast, D. (1994). Brief psychotherapy and psychological assessments: Entering a relationship, establishing a focus, and providing feedback. *Professional Psychology: Research and Practice, 25,* 46–49.

Clark, M. E. (1996). MMPI-2 Negative Treatment Indicators content and content component scales: Clinical correlates and outcome prediction for men with chronic pain. *Psychological Assessment, 8,* 32–38.

Coffey, R. M., Mark, T., King, E., Harwood, H., McKusick, D., Genuardi, J., Dilonardo, J., & Buck, J. A. (2000). *National estimates of expenditures for mental health and substance abuse treatment, 1997* (SAMSHA Publication No. SMA-00-3499). Rockville, MD: Center for Substance Abuse Treatment and Center Mental Health Services, Substance Abuse and Mental Health Services Adminsitration.

Cohen, J. (1988). *Statistical power analysis for the behavioral sciences* (2nd ed.). Hillsdale, NJ: Lawrence Erlbaum Associates.

Cole, S., Raju, M., & Barrett, J. (1997). Depression in primary care: Assessment and management. In J. D. Haber & G. E. Mitchell (Eds.), *Primary care meets mental health: Tools for the 21st century* (pp. 139–153). Tiburon, CA: CentraLink Publications.

Commission on Chronic Illness (1957). *Chronic illness in the United States.* Vol. I. Cambridge, MA: Commonwealth Fund, Harvard University.

Committee for the Advancement of Professional Practice (CAPP) Task Force on Ethical Practice (1998). *Final report of the CAPP Task Force on ethical practice in organized systems of care.* Washington, DC: American Psychological Association.

Cooper, C. C., & Gottlieb, M. C. (2000). Ethical issues with managed care: Challenges facing counseling psychology. *The Counseling Psychologist, 28,* 179–236.

Copeland, J. R., Dewey, M. E., & Griffiths-Jones, H. M. (1986). A computerized psychiatric diagnostic system and case nomenclature for elderly subjects: GMS and AGECAT. *Psychological Medicine, 16,* 89–99.

Coughlin, K. M. (Ed.). (1997). *The 1997 behavioral outcomes & guidelines sourcebook.* New York: Faulkner & Gray.

Cummings, N. A. (1995). Impact of managed care on employment and training: A primer for survival. *Professional Psychology: Research and Practice, 26,* 10–15.

Cummings, N. A. (1998a). Moral issues in managed mental health care. In R. F. Small & L. R. Barnhill (Eds.), *Practicing in the new mental health marketplace: Ethical, legal, and moral issues* (pp. 53–66). Washington, DC: American Psychological Association.

Cummings, N. A. (1998b). Spectacular accomplishments and disappointing mistakes: The first decade of managed behavioral care. *Behavioral Healthcare Tomorrow, 7,* 61–63.

Cummings, N. A. (1999). Medical cost offset, meta-analysis, and implications for future research and practice. *Clinical Psychology: Science and Practice, 6,* 221–224.

Cummings, N. A. (2000). A psychologist's proactive guide to managed care: New roles and opportunities. In A. J. Kent & M. Hersen (Eds.), *A psychologist's proactive guide to managed mental health care* (pp. 141–161). Mahwah, NJ: Lawrence Erlbaum Associates.

Cummings, N. A., Budman, S. H., & Thomas, J. L. (1998). Efficient psycholotherapy as a viable response to scarce resources and rationing of treatment. *Professional Psychology: Research and Practice, 29,* 460–469.

Cushman, P., & Gilford, P. (2000). Will managed care change our way of being? *American Psychologist, 55,* 985–996.

Daniels, A., Kramer, T. L., & Mahesh, N. M. (1995). Quality indicators measured by behavioral group practices. *Behavioral Healthcare Tomorrow, 4,* 55–56.

D'Ath, P., Katona, P., Mullan, E., Evans, S., & Katona, C. (1994). Screening, detection and management of depression in elderly primary care attenders. I: The acceptability and performance of the 15 item Geriatric Depression Scale (GDS15) and the development of short versions. *Family Practice, 11,* 260–266.

Davies, A. R., & Ware, J. E. (1991). *GHAA's Consumer Satsifaction Survey and user's manual.* Wahsington, DC: Group Health Association of America.

Davison, M. L., Bershadsky, B., Bieber, J., Silversmith, D., Maruish, M. E., & Kane, R. L. (1997). Development of a brief, multidimensional, self-report instrument for treatment outcomes assessment in psychiatric settings: Preliminary findings. *Assessment, 4,* 259–276.

DeForge, B. R., & Sobal, J. (1988). Self-report depression scales in the elderly: The relationship between the CES-D and Zung. *International Journal of Psychiatry in Medicine, 18,* 325–338.

DeJonghe, J. F., & Baneke, J. J. (1989). The Zung Self-Rating Depression Scale: A replication study on reliability, validity and prediction. *Psychological Reports, 64,* 833–834.

Del Vecchio, P. (1996). Dialogue: How should primary care address the problem of psychiatric disorders? Demand-side analysis of mental health services in primary care. *Behavioral Healthcare Tomorrow, 5,* 48, 51, 54.

Depression Guideline Panel. (1993a). *Depression in primary care. Volume 1. Detection and diagnosis. Clinical practice guideline, Number 5* (AHCPR Publication No. 93-0550). Rockville, MD: U.S. Department of Health and Human Services, Public Health Service, Agency for Health Care Policy and Research.

Depression Guideline Panel. (1993b). *Depression in primary care. Volume 2. Treatment of major depression. Clinical practice guideline, Number 5* (AHCPR Publication No. 93-0551). Rockville, MD: U.S. Department of Health and Human Services, Public Health Service, Agency for Health Care Policy and Research.

Depression still undertreated despite efforts to redress. (1997, June). *Behavior Health Outcomes, 2,* 1–11.

Derogatis, L. R. (1983). *SCL-90-R: Administration, scoring and procedures manual-II.* Baltimore, MD: Clinical Psychometric Research.

Derogatis, L. R. (1992). *BSI: Administration, scoring and procedures manual-II.* Baltimore, MD: Clinical Psychometric Research.

Derogatis, L. R. (1993). *Brief Symptom Inventory (BSI) administration, scoring and procedures manual* (3rd ed.). Minneapolis, MN: National Computer Systems.

Derogatis, L. R., Lipman, R. S., & Covi, L. (1973). SCL-90: An outpatient psychiatric rating scale — preliminary report. *Psychopharmacology Bulletin, 9,* 13–27.

Derogatis, L. R., & Lynn, L. L. (1999). Psychological tests in screening for psychiatric disorder. In M. E. Maruish (Ed.), *The use of psychological testing for treatment planning and outcomes assessment* (2nd ed., pp. 41–79). Mahwah, NJ: Lawrence Erlbaum Associates.

Detection of psychological disorders unrelated to outcomes. (1996, September). *Behavioral Healthcare Outcomes, 1,* 7–9.

Dickey, B., & Wagenaar, H. (1996). Evaluating health status. In L. I. Sederer & B. Dickey (Eds.), *Outcomes assessment in clinical practice* (pp. 55–60). Baltimore, MD: Williams & Wilkins.

Diener, E. (2000). Subjective well-being: The science of happiness and a proposal for a national index. *American Psychologist, 34,* 34–43.

Directions: Anxiety costs big bucks. (1997, May). *Practice Strategies,* p. 10.

Docherty, J. P., & Dewan, N. A. (1995). *National Association of Psychiatric Health Systems guide to outcomes management.* Washington, DC: National Association of Psychiatric Health Systems.

Docherty, J. P., & Streeter, M. J. (1996). Measuring outcomes. In L. I. Sederer & B. Dickey (Eds.), *Outcomes assessment in clinical practice* (pp. 8–18). Baltimore, MD: Williams & Wilkins.

Doherty, W. J., McDaniel, S. H., & Baird, M. A. (1996). Five levels of primary care/behavioral healthcare collaboration. *Behavioral Healthcare Tomorrow, 5,* 25–27.

Donabedian, A. (1980). *Explorations in quality assessment and monitoring: The definition of quality and approaches to its assessment* (Vol. I). Ann Arbor, MI: Health Administration Press.

Donabedian, A. (1982). *Explorations in quality assessment and monitoring: The criteria and standards of quality* (Vol. II). Ann Arbor, MI: Health Administration Press.

Donabedian, A. (1985). *Explorations in quality assessment and monitoring: The methods and findings in quality assessment: An illustrated analysis* (Vol. III). Ann Arbor, MI: Health Administration Press.

Donaldson, M. S., Yordy, K. D., Lohr, K. N., & Vanselow, N. A. (Eds.). (1996). *Primary care: America's health in a new era.* Washington, DC: National Academy Press.

Dorfman, W. I. (2000). Psychological assessment and testing under managed care. In A. J. Kent & M. Hersen (Eds.), *A psychologist's proactive guide to managed mental health care* (pp. 23–39). Mahwah, NJ: Lawrence Erlbaum Associates.

Dorwart, R. A. (1996). Outcomes management strategies in mental health: Applications and implications for clinical practice. In L. I. Sederer & B. Dickey (Eds.), *Outcomes assessment in clinical practice* (pp. 45–54). Baltimore, MD: Williams & Wilkins.

Dreher, H. (1996). Is there a systematic way to diagnose and treat somatization disorder? *Advances: The Journal of Mind-Body Health, 12,* 50.

Dyson, V., Appleby, L., Altman, E., Doot, M., Luchins, D., & Delehant, M. (1998). Efficiency and validity of commonly used substance abuse screening instruments in public psychiatric patients. *Journal of Addictive Diseases, 17,* 57–76.

Eaton, W. W., Muntaner, C., & Smith, C. (1998). *Revision of the Center for Epidemiologic Studies Depression (CESD) Scale.* [On-line]. Available: http://mh.jhsph.edu/hrcesd/.

Edmunds, M., Frank, R., Hogan, M., McCarty, D., Robinson-Blake, R., & Weisner, C. (Eds.). (1997). *Managing managed care: Quality improvement in behavioral health.* Washington, DC: National Academy Press.

Eisen, S. V. (1996a). Behavior and Symptom Identification Scale (BASIS-32). In L. I. Sederer & B. Dickey (Eds.), *Outcomes assessment in clinical practice* (pp. 65–69). Baltimore, MD: Williams & Wilkins.

Eisen, S. V. (1996b). Client satisfaction and clinical outcomes: Do we need both. *Behavioral Healthcare Tomorrow, 5,* 71–73.

Eisen, S. V. (2000). Charting for outcomes in behavioral health. *The Psychiatric Clinics of North America, 23,* 347–361.

Eisen, S. V., & Culhane, M. A. (1999). Behavior and Symptom Identification Scale. In M. E. Maruish (Ed.), *The use of psychological testing for treatment planning and outcomes assessment* (2nd ed., pp. 759–790). Mahwah, NJ: Lawrence Erlbaum Associates.

Eisen, S. V., Dill, D. L., & Grob, M. C. (1994). Reliability and validity of a brief patient-report instrument for psychiatric outcome evaluation. *Hospital and Community Psychiatry, 45,* 242–247.

Eisen, S. V., Grob, M. C., & Klein, A. A. (1986). BASIS: The development of a self-report measure for psychiatric inpatient evaluation. *The Psychiatric Hospital, 17,* 165–171.

Eisen, S. V., Leff, H. S., & Schaefer, E. (1999). Implementing outcomes systems: Lessons from a test of the BASIS-32 and the SF-36. *Journal of Behavioral Health Services & Research, 26,* 18–27.

Eisen, S. V., Wilcox, M., Leff, H. S., Schaefer, E., & Culhane, M. A. (1999). Assessing behavioral health outcomes in outpatient programs: Reliability and validity of the BASIS-32. *Journal of Behavioral Health Services & Research, 26,* 5–17.

Eisen, S. V., Wilcox, M., Schaefer, E., Culhane, M. A., & Leff, H. S. (1997). *Use of BASIS-32 for outcome assessment of recipients of outpatient mental health services.* Report to Human Services Research Institute, Cambridge, MA.

Eisman, E. J., Dies, R. R., Finn, S. E., Eyde, L. D., Kay, G. G., Kubiszyn, T. W., Meyer, G. J., & Moreland, K. L. (1998). *Problems and limitations in the use of psychological assessment in contemporary healthcare delivery: Report to the Board of Professional Affairs, Psychological Assessment Work Group, Part II.* Washington, DC: American Psychological Association.

Eisman, E. J., Dies, R. R., Finn, S. E., Eyde, L. D., Kay, G. G., Kubiszyn, T. W., Meyer, G. J., & Moreland, K. L. (2000). Problems and limitations in using of psychological assessment in contemporary healthcare delivery. *Professional Psychology: Research and Practice, 31,* 131–140.

Elwood, R. W. (1993). Psychological tests and clinical discriminations: Beginning to address the base rate problem. *Clinical Psychology Review, 13,* 409–419.

Erdberg, P. (1979). A systematic approach to providing feedback from the MMPI. In C. S. Newmark (Ed.), *MMPI clinical and research trends* (pp. 328–342). New York: Praeger.

Ewing, J. A. (1984). Detecting alcoholism: The CAGE questionnaire. *Journal of the American Medical Asociation, 252,* 1905–1907.

Ewing, J. A., & Rouse, B. A. (1970, February). *Identifying the hidden alcoholic.* Paper presented at the 29th International Congress on Alcohol and Drug Dependence, Sydney, Australia.

Faustman, W. O., & Overall, J. E. (1999). Brief Psychiatric Rating Scale. In M. E. Maruish (Ed.), *The use of psychological testing for treatment planning and outcomes assessment* (2nd ed., pp. 791–830). Mahwah, NJ: Lawrence Erlbaum Associates.

Fee, practice, and managed care survey. (1995, January). *Psychotherapy Finances, 21*(1), Issue 249.

Feightner, J. W., & Worrall, G. (1990). Early detection of depression by primary care physicians. *Canadian Medical Association Journal, 142,* 1215–1221.

Feldman, S. (1998). Behavioral health services: Carved out and managed. *The American Journal of Managed Care, 4* (Special Issue), SP59–SP67.

Ficken, J. (1995). New directions for psychological testing. *Behavioral Health Management, 20,* 12–14.

Finn, S. E. (1996a). Assessment feedback integrating MMPI-2 and Rorschach findings. *Journal of Personality Assessment, 67,* 543–557.

Finn, S. E. (1996b). *Manual for using the MMPI-2 as a therapeutic intervention.* Minneapolis, MN: University of Minnesota Press.

Finn, S. E., & Martin, H. (1997). Therapeutic assessment with the MMPI-2 in managed health care. In J. N. Butcher (Ed.), *Objective personality assessment in managed health care: A practitioner's guide* (pp. 131–152). Minneapolis, MN: University of Minnesota Press.

Finn, S. E., & Tonsager, M. E. (1992). Therapeutic effects of providing MMPI-2 test feedback to college students awaiting therapy. *Psychological Assessment, 4,* 278–287.

Finn, S. E., & Tonsager, M. E. (1997). Information-gathering and therapeutic models of assessment: Complementary paradigms. *Psychological Assessment, 9,* 374–385.

First, M. B., Spitzer, R. L., Gibbon, M., & Williams, J. B. W. (1995). *Structured Clinical Interview for DSM-IV Axis I Disorders – Non-patient Edition* (SCID – I/NP), Version 2.0. (Available from Biometrics Research Department, New York State Psychiatric Institute, 722 West 168th Street, New York, NY 10032).

Fischer, C. T. (1970). The testee as co-evaluator. *Journal of Counseling Psychology, 17,* 70–76.

Fischer, C. T. (1985). *Individualizing psychological assessment.* Monterey, CA: Brooks/Cole.

Fischer, J., & Corcoran, K. (1994a). *Measures for clinical practice: A sourcebook (2nd ed.). Volume 1. Couples, families, and children.* New York: Free Press.

Fischer, J., & Corcoran, K. (1994b). *Measures for clinical practice: A sourcebook (2nd ed.). Volume 2. Adults.* New York: Free Press.

Fisher, D., Beutler, L. E., & Williams, O. B. (1999). Making assessment relevant to treatment planning: The STS Clinician Rating Form. *Journal of Clinical Psychology, 55,* 825–842.

Fombonne, E. (1991). The use of questionnaires in child psychiatry research: Measuring their performance and choosing an optimal cutoff. *Journal of Child Psychology and Psychiatry, 32,* 677–693.

Ford, W. E. (2000). Medical necessity and psychiatric managed care. *The Psychiatric Clinics of North American, 23,* 309–317.

Frankish, C. J., Herbert, C., Milsum, J. H., & Peters, H. F. (1999). Measurements of positive health and well-being. In G. C. Hyner, K. W. Peterson, J. W Travis, J. E. Dewey, J. J. Foerster, & E. M. Framer (Eds.), *SPM handbook of health assessment tools* (pp. 41–48). Pittsburgh, PA: The Society of Prospective Medicine & The Institute for Health and Productivity Management.

Frasure-Smith, N., Lesperance, F., & Talajic, M. (1993). Depression following myocardial infarction: Impact on 6-month survival. *JAMA: Journal of the American Medical Association, 270,* 1819–1825.

Frasure-Smith, N., Lesperance, F., & Talajic, M. (1995a). Depression and 18-month prognosis after myocardial infarction. *Circulation, 91,* 999–1005.

Frasure-Smith, N., Lesperance, F., & Talajic, M. (1995b). The impact of negative emotions on prognosis following myocardial infarction: Is it more than depression? *Health Psychology, 14,* 388–398.

Friedman, R., Sobel, D., Myers, P., Caudill, M., & Benson, H. (1995). Behavioral medicine, clinical health psychology, and cost offset. *Health Psychology, 14,* 509–518.

Frisch, M. B. (1994a). *Manual and treatment guide for the Quality of Life Inventory.* Minneapolis, MN: National Computer Systems.

Frisch, M. B. (1994b). *Quality of Life Inventory.* Minneapolis, MN: National Computer Systems.

Frisch, M. B. (1999). Quality of life assessment/intervention and the Quality of Life Inventory (QOLI). In M. E. Maruish (Ed.), *Handbook of psychological testing in primary care settings* (pp. 1277–1331). Mahwah, NJ: Lawrence Erlbaum Associates.

Future targets behavioral health field's quest for survival. (1996, April 8). *Mental Health Weekly,* pp. 1–2.

Gellman, R., & Frawley, K. A. (1996). The need to know versus the right to privacy. In T. Trabin (Ed.), *The computerization of behavioral healthcare: How to enhance clinical practice, management, and communications* (pp. 191–212). San Francisco: Jossey-Bass.

Goldstein, L., Bershadsky, B., & Maruish, M. E. (2000). The INOVA primary behavioral health care pilot project. In M. E. Maruish (Ed.), *Handbook of psychological testing in primary care settings* (pp. 735–760). Mahwah, NJ: Lawrence Erlbaum Associates.

Graham, J. R. (2000a, August). Clinical assessment in the 21st century. In M. E. Maruish (Chair), *Clinical, school, industrial and organizational psychology, and educational assessment in the 21st century.* Symposium conducted at the annual meeting of the American Psychological Association, Washington, DC.

Graham, J. R. (2000b). *MMPI-2: Assessing personality and psychopathology (3rd ed.).* New York: Oxford University Press.

Gray, G. V. (1999, May). What's best for you—paper and pencil or IVR? *Outcomes and Accountability Alert, 4*(5), 1, 9–11.

Greene, R. L. (2000).*The MMPI-2: An interpretive manual (2nd ed.).* Boston, MA: Allyn & Bacon.

Greenfield, T. K. (1989). *Consumer satisfaction with the Delaware Drinking Driver Program in 1987–1988* (Report to the Delaware Drinking Driver Program). University of California, San Francisco, Department of Psychiatry.

Greenfield, T. K., & Attkisson, C. C. (1989). Steps toward a multifactorial service satisfaction scale for primary care and mental health services. *Evaluation and Program Planning, 12,* 271–278.

Greenfield, T. K., & Attkisson, C. C. (1999). The UCSF client satisfaction scales: II. The Service Satisfaction Scale-30. In M. E. Maruish (Ed.), *The use of psychological testing for treatment planning and outcomes assessment* (2nd ed., pp. 1347–1367). Mahwah, NJ: Lawrence Erlbaum Associates.

Greenfield, T. K., Attkisson, C. C., & Pascoe, G. C. (1995). *Services Evaluation (SSS-30 Practitioner Version).* San Francisco, CA: Authors.

Greenfield, T. K., & Stoneking, B. C. (1993). *Service satisfaction with case management: An experimental test of augmenting staff teams with mental health consumers.* Paper presented at the Fourth Annual national Conference on State Mental Health Agency Research and Program Evaluation (NASMHPD Research Institute), Annapolis, MD.

Grissom, G. R., & Howard, K. I. (2000). Directions and COMPASS-PC. In M. E. Maruish (Ed.), *The use of psychological testing for treatment planning and outcomes assessment* (2nd ed., pp. 255–275). Mahwah, NJ: Lawrence Erlbaum Associates.

Groth-Marnat, G. (1999a). Current status and future directions of psychological assessment: Introduction. *Journal of Clinical Psychology, 55,* 781–795.

Groth-Marnat, G. (1999b). Financial efficacy of clinical assessment: Rational guidelines and issues for future research. *Journal of Clinical Psychology, 55,* 813–824.

Groth-Marnat, G., & Edkins, G. (1996). Professional psychologists in general medical settings: A review of the financial efficacy of direct treatment interventions. *Professional Psychology: Research and Practice, 27,* 161–174.

Gurland, B. J., Kuriansky, J., Sharpe, L., Simon, R., Stiller, P., & Birkett, P. (1977). The comprehensive Assessment and Referral Evaluation (CARE): Rationale, development, and reliability. *Internation Journal of Ageing and Human Development, 8,* 9–42.

Gurnee, M. C., & Da Silva, R. V. (1999). Constructing disease management programs. In S. Heffner (Ed.), *Disease management sourcebook 2000: Resources and strategies for program design and implementation* (pp. 12–18). New York: Faulkner & Gray.

Haas, L. J., & Cummings, N. A. (1991). Managed outpatient mental health plans: Clinical, ethical, and practical guidelines for participation. *Professional Psychology: Research and Practice, 22,* 45–51.

Haas, L. J., & Malouf, J. L. (1995). *Keeping up the good work: A practitioner's guide to mental health ethics* (2nd ed.). Sarasota, FL: Professional Resource Exchange.

Haber, J. D., & Mitchell, G. E. (Eds.). (1997). *Primary care meets mental health: Tools for the 21st century.* Tiburon, CA: CentraLink Publications.

Hahn, S. R., Kroenke, K., Williams, J. B., & Spitzer, R. L. (1999). Primary Care Evaluation of Mental Disorders (PRIME-MD). In M. E. Maruish (Ed.), *The use of psychological testing for treatment planning and outcomes assessment* (2nd ed., pp. 871–920.) Mahwah, NJ: Lawrence Erlbaum Associates.

Haley, W. E., McDaniel, S. H., Bray, J. H., Frank, R. G., Heldring, M., Johnson, S. B., Lu, E. G., Reed, G. M., & Wiggins, J. G. (1998). Psychological practice in primary care settings: Practical tips for clinicians. *Professional Psychology: Research and Practice, 29,* 237–244.

Hamilton, M. (1960). A rating scale for depression. *Journal of Neurology, Neurosurgery, and Psychiatry, 12,* 56–62.

Hamilton, M. (1967). Development of a rating scale for primary depressive illness. *British Journal of Social and Clinical Psychology, 6,* 278–296.

Hankin, J., & Otkay, J. S. (1979). *Mental disorder and primary medical care: An analytical review of the literature.* No. 5. Washington, DC: National Institute of Mental Health.

Hanson, K. M., & Sheridan, K. (1997). Ethics and changing mental health care: Concerns and recommendations for practice. *Journal of Clinical Psychology in Medical Settings, 4,* 231–242.

Harber, J. R. (1981). Evaluating utility in diagnostic decision making. *The Journal of Special Education, 15,* 413–428.

Harwood, T. M., Beutler, L. E., Fisher, D., Sandowicz, M., Albanese, A. L., & Baker, M. (1997). Clinical decision making in managed health care. In J. N. Butcher (Ed.), *Personality assessment in managed health care* (pp. 13–41). New York: Oxford University Press.

Hathaway, S. R., & McKinley, J. C. (1951). *MMPI manual.* New York: The Psychological Corporation.

Hays, R. D., Davies, A. R., & Ware, J. E. (1987). *Scoring the Medical Outcomes Study Patients Satisfaction Questionnaire-III* (Unpublished MOS memorandum). Santa Monica, CA: RAND Corporation.

Health Care Financing Administration (HCFA). (1998). *Guidelines for implementing and monitoring compliance with interim QISMC standards. Domain 1: Quality assessment and performance improvement program* [On-line]. Available: http://www.hcfa.gov/quality/docs/qismc-1g.htm.

Health Care Financing Administration (HCFA). (1999a). *Quality Improvement System for Managed Care (QISMC)* [On-line]. Available: http://www.hcfa.gov/quality/3a.htm.

Health Care Financing Administration (HCFA). (1999b). *Quality Improvement System for Managed Care (QISMC). Introduction* [On-line]. Available: http://www.hcfa.gov/quality/docs/qismc%2Din.htm.

Health Outcomes Institute. (1996). *Twelve-item Health Status Questionnaire (HSQ-12) Version 2.0 user guide.* Bloomington, MN: Author.

Hedlund, J. L., & Viewig, B. W. (1980). The Brief Psychiatric Rating Scale: A comprehensive review. *Journal of Operational Psychology, 11,* 49–65.

Helzer, J. R., Robins, J. N., McEvoy, L. T., Spitznagel, R. L., Soltzman, R. K., Farmer, A., & Brockington, I. F. (1985). A comparison of clinical and Diagnostic Interview Schedule diagnoses: Physician reexamination of lay-interviewed cases in the general population. *Archives of General Psychiatry, 42,* 657–666.

Herrmann, N., Mittmann, N., Silver, I. L., Shulman, K. I., Busto, U. A., Shear, N. H., & Naranjo, C. A. (1996). A validation study of the Geriatric Depression Scale Short Form. *International Journal of Geriatric Psychiatry, 11*, 457–460.

Hersch, L. (1995). Adapting to health care reform and managed care: Three strategies for survival and growth. *Professional Psychology: Research and Practice, 26*, 16–26.

Higgins, E. S. (1994). A review of unrecognized mental illness in primary care. *Archives of Family Medicine, 3*, 908–917.

Hodges, K. (1994). *Child and adolescent functional assessment scale.* Ypsilanti, MI: Eastern Michigan University.

Hoffman, F. L., Capelli, K., & Mastrianni, X. (1997). Measuring treatment outcome for adults and adolescents: Reliability and validity of BASIS-32. *Journal of Mental Health Administration, 24*, 316–331.

Hoge, M. A., Thakur, N. M., & Jacobs, S. (2000). Understanding managed behavioral health care. *The Psychiatric Clinics of North American, 23*, 241–253.

Hopkins, W. G. (1997). *A new view of statistics: A scale of magnitudes for effect statistics.* [On-line]. Available: http://www.sportsci.org/resource/stats/effectmag.html.

Horowitz, L. M., Rosenberg, S. E., Baer, B. A., Ureno, G., & Villasenor, V. S. (1988). Inventory of Interpersonal Problems: Psychometric properties and clinical applications. *Journal of Consulting and Clinical Psychology, 56*, 885–892.

Howard, K. I., Brill, P. L., Lueger, R. J., O'Mahoney, M. T., & Grissom, G. R. (1993). *Integra outpatient tracking assessment.* Philadelphia: Compass Information Services.

Howard, K. I., Kopta, S. M., Krause, M. S., & Orlinsky, D. E. (1986). The dose-effect relationship in psychotherapy. *American Psychologist, 41*, 159–154.

Howard, K. I., Lueger, R. J., Maling, M. S., & Martinovich, Z. (1993). A phase model of psychotherapy outcome: Causal mediation of change. *Journal of Consulting and Clinical Psychology, 61*, 678–685.

Howard, K. I., Moras, K., Brill, P. B., Martinovich, Z., & Lutz, W. (1996). Evaluation of psychotherapy: Efficacy, effectiveness, and patient progress. *American Psychologist, 51*, 1059–1064.

Hsiao, J. K., Bartko, J. J., & Potter, W. Z. (1989). Diagnosing diagnoses: Receiver operating characteristic methods and psychiatry. *Archives of General Psychiatry, 46*, 664–667.

Hsu, L. M. (1996). On the identification of clinically significant client changes: Reinterpretation of Jacobson's cut scores. *Journal of Psychopathology and Behavioral Assessment, 18*, 371–385.

Hsu, L. M. (1999). Caveats concerning comparisons of change rates obtained with five models of identifying significant client changes: Comment on Speer and Greenbaum (1995). *Journal of Consulting and Clinical Psychology, 67*, 594–598.

Hyner, G. C., Peterson, K. W., Travis, J. W., Dewey, J. E., Foerster, J. J., & Framer, E. M. (Eds.). (1999). *SPM handbook of health assessment tools.* Pittsburgh, PA: The Society of Prospective Medicine & the Institute for Health and Productivity Management.

Impara, J. C., & Plake, B. S. (Eds.). (1998). *The thirteenth mental measurement yearbook.* Lincoln, NE: The Buros Institute of Mental Measurements.

Ingram, F. (1996). The short Geriatric Depression Scale: A comparison with the standard form in independent older adults. *Clinical Gerontologist, 16*, 49–56.

Institute for International Research. (1997). [Announcement for the Integrating Behavioral Health Primary Care conference.]

Institute of Medicine: Committee on Quality Assurance and Accreditation Guidelines for Managed Behavioral Health Care. (1997). *Managing managed care: Quality improvement in behavioral health.* Washington, DC: National Academy Press.

InterStudy. (1991). Preface. *The InterStudy Quality Edge, 1*, 1–3.

Jacobson, N. S., Follette, W. C., & Revenstorf, D. (1984). Psychotherapy outcome research: Methods for reporting variability and evaluating clinical significance. *Behavior Therapy, 15*, 336–352.

Jacobson, N. S., Follette, W. C., & Revenstorf, D. (1986). Toward a standard definition of clinically significant change [Letter to the editor]. *Behavior Therapy, 17*, 309–311.

Jacobson, N. S., Roberts, L. J., Berns, S. B., & McGlinchey, J. B. (1999). Methods for defining and determining the clinical significance of treatment effects: Description, application, and alternatives. *Journal of Consulting and Clinical Psychology, 67*, 300–307.

Jacobson, N. S., & Truax, P. (1991). Clinical significance: A statistical approach defining meaningful change in psychotherapy research. *Journal of Consulting and Clinical Psychology, 59*, 12–19.

Jahoda, M. (1958). *Current concepts of mental health.* New York: Basic Books.

Jenkins, R. (1997). Lifting the global burden of mental disorders: Services policy and planning using epidemiology and disability measurement. *Behavioral Healthcare Tomorrow, 6*, 26–31, 94–96.

Jerome, L. W., DeLeon, P. H., James, L. C., Folen, R., Earles, J., & Gedney, J. J. (2000). The coming of age in telecommunications in psychological research and practice. *American Psychologist, 55,* 407–421.

Johnson, J. G., Spitzer, R. L., Williams, J. B., Kroenke, K., Linzer, M., Brody, D., deGruy, F., & Hahn, S. (1995). Psychiatric comorbidity, health status, and functional impairment associated with alcohol abuse and dependence in primary care patients: Findings of the PRIME MD–1000 study. *Journal of Consulting and Clinical Psychology, 63,* 133–140.

Joint Commission on Accreditation of Healthcare Organizations (JCAHO). (1997). *Comprehensive accreditation manual for managed behavioral health care.* Oak Brook Terrace, IL: Author.

Joint Commission on Accreditation of Healthcare Organizations (JCAHO). (1999). *Managed behavioral health care* [On-line]. Available: http://www.jcaho.org/trkhco_frm.html.

Judd, L. L., Akiskal, H. S., Maser, J. D., Zeller, P. J., Endicott, J., Coryell, W., Paulus, M. P., Kunovac, J. L., Leon, A. C., Mueller, T. I., Rice, J. A., & Keller, M. B. (1998). A prospective 12-year study of subsyndromal and syndromal depressive symptoms in unipolar major depressive disorders. *Archives of General Psychiatry, 55,* 694–700.

Kadera, S. W., Lambert, M. J., & Andrews, A. A. (1996). How much therapy is really enough? A session-by session analysis of the psychotherapy dose–effect relationship. *The Journal of Psychotherapy Practice and Research, 5,* 132–151.

Kanapaux, W. J. (1998). The mind and body connected: Integrating behavioral and primary care. *Behavioral Healthcare Tomorrow, 7,* 19–24.

Katon, W. (1999). Collaborative care models for the treatment of depression. *American Journal of Managed Care, 5*(13), S794–S810.

Katon, W., & Roy-Byrne, P. P. (1989). Panic disorder in the medically ill. *Journal of Clinical Psychiatry, 50,* 299–302.

Katon, W., & Schulberg, H. (1992). Epidemiology of depression in primary care. *General Hospital Psychiatry, 14,* 237–247.

Katon, W. J., & Walker, E. A. (1998). Medically unexplained symptoms in primary care. *Journal of Clinical Psychiatry, 59*(Supp. 20), 15–21.

Katz, M. M., & Lyerly, S. B. (1963). Methods for measuring adjustment and social behavior in the community: I. Rationale, description, discriminative validity and scale development. *Psychological Reports, 13,* 503–535.

Katz, M. M., & Warren, W. L. (1997). *Katz Adjustment Scales Relative Report Form (KAS-R) manual.* Los Angeles: Western Psychological Services.

Katzelnick, D. J., Kobak, K. A., Greist, J. H., Jefferson, J. W., & Henk, H. J. (1997). Effect of primary care treatment of depression on service use by patients with high medical expenditures. *Psychiatric Services, 48,* 59–64.

Kazdin, A. E. (1999). The meanings and measurement of clinical significance. *Journal of Consulting and Clinical Psychology, 67,* 332–339.

Kazis, L. E., Anderson, J. J., & Meenan, R. F. (1989). Effect sizes for interpreting changes in health status. *Medical Care, 27,* S178–S189.

Keller, S. D., & Ware, J. E. (1996). Questions and answers about SF-36 and SF-12. *Medical Outcomes Trust Bulletin, 4,* 3.

Kent, A. J., & Hersen, M. (2000). An overview of managed mental health care: Past, present, and future. In A. J. Kent & M. Hersen (Eds.), *A psychologist's proactive guide to managed mental health care* (pp. 3–19). Mahwah, NJ: Lawrence Erlbaum Associates.

Kessler, L. G., Burns, B. J., Shapiro, S., Tischler, G. L., George, L. K., Hough, R. L., Bodison, D., & Miller, R. H. (1987). Psychiatric diagnoses of medical service users: Evidence from the Epidemiologic Catchment Area program. *American Journal of Public Health, 77,* 18–24.

Kessler, L. G., McGonagle, K. M., Zhao, S., Nelson, C. B., Hughes, M., Eshelman, S., Wittchen, H. U., & Kendler, K. S. (1994). Lifetime and 12-month prevalence of DSM-III-R disorders in the U.S.: Results form the National Comorbidity Study. *Archives of General Psychiatry, 51,* 8–20.

Kiesler, C. A. (2000). The next wave of change for psychology and mental health services in the health care revolution. *American Psychologist, 55,* 481–487.

Kiesler, C. A., & Morton, T. L. (1988). Psychology and public policy in the "health care revolution." *American Psychologist, 43,* 993–1003.

Klinkman, M. S. (1999). Strategies for effective management of depression in primary care. *American Journal of Managed Care, 5*(13), S783–S793.

Knight, R. G., Williams, S., McGee, R., & Olaman, S. (1997). Psychometric properties of the Center for Epidemioloigc Studies Depression Scale (CES-D) in a sample of women in middle life. *Behaviour Research and Therapy, 35,* 373–380.

Kobak, K. A., Greist, J. H., Jefferson, J. W., & Katzelnick, D. J. (1996). Decision support for patient care: Computerized rating scales. *Behavioral Healthcare Tomorrow, 5,* 25–29.

Kobak, K. A., Mundt, J. C., Greist, J. H., Katzelnick, D. J., & Jefferson, J. W. (2000). Computer assessment of depression: Automating the Hamilton Depression Rating Scale. *Drug Information Journal, 34,* 145–156.

Kobak, K. A., Reynolds, W. M., Rosenfeld, R., & Greist, J. H. (1990). Development and validation of a computer-administered version of the Hamilton Depression Rating Scale. *Journal of Consulting and Clinical Psychology, 50,* 56–63.

Kobak, K. A., Taylor, L. V., Dottl, S. L., Greist, J. H., Jefferson, J. W., Burroughs, D., Katzelnick, D. J., & Mandell, J. M. (1997). Computerized screening for psychiatric disorders in an outpatient community mental health clinic. *Psychiatric Services, 48,* 1048–1057.

Kobak, K. A., Taylor, L. V., Dottl, S. L., Greist, J. H., Jefferson, J. W., Burroughs, D., Mantle, J. M., Katzelnick, D. J., Norton, R., Henk, H. J., & Serlin, R. C. (1997). A computer-administered telephone interview to identify mental disorders. *Journal of the American Medical Association, 278,* 905–910.

Koenig, H. G., Meador, K. G., Cohen, H. J., & Blazer, D. G. (1988). Depression in elderly hospitalized patients with medical illness. *Archives of Internal Medicine, 148,* 1929–1936.

Kopta, S. M., Howard, K. I., Lowry, J. L., & Beutler, L. E. (1994). Patterns of symtomatic recovery in psychotherapy. *Journal of Consulting and Clinical Psychology, 62,* 1009–1016.

Kramer, T. L., & Smith, G. R. (2000). Tools to improve the detection and treatment of depression in primary care. In M. E. Maruish (Ed.), *Handbook of psychological testing in primary care settings* (pp. 463–490). Mahwah, NJ: Lawrence Erlbaum Associates.

Kraus, D. R., & Horan, F. P. (1998). *Outcomes roadblocks; Problems and solutions. One company explains why — and how — to upgrade the practicality of outcomes measurement.* [On-line]. Available: http://www.consultnews.com/Magazines/BHMsept_oct/kraus.html.

Kubiszyn, T. W., Meyer, G. J., Finn, S. E., Eyde, L. D., Kay, G. G., Moreland, K. L., Dies, R. R., & Eisman, E. J. (2000). Empirical support for psychological assessment in clinical health care settings. *Professional Psychology: Research and Practice, 31,* 119–130.

Lachar, D., Bailley, S. E., Rhoades, H. M., & Varner, R. V. (1999). Use of BPRS—A percent change scores to identify significant clinical improvement: Accuracy of treatment response classification in acute psychiatric inpatients. *Psychiatry Research, 89,* 259–268.

Lambert, M. J. (1998, August). *Patterns of patient improvement: Implications of research for treatment planning and responsible social policy.* Paper presented at the Seventeenth World Congress of Psychotherapy, Warsaw, Poland.

Lambert. M. J., & Finch, A. E. (1999). The Outcome Questionnaire. In M. E. Maruish (Ed.), *The use of psychological testing for treatment planning and outcomes assessment* (2nd ed., pp. 831–869). Mahwah, NJ: Lawrence Erlbaum Associates.

Lambert, M. J., Finch, A. E., Okiishi, J., Burlingame, G. M., McKelvey, C., & Reisinger, C. W. (1997). *Administration and scoring manual for the OQS-10.0 Outcome Questionnaire Short Form.* Stevenson, MD: American Professional Credentialing Services.

Lambert, M. J., Hansen, N. B., Umphress, V., Lunnen, K., Okiishi, J., Burlingame, G., Huefner, J. C., & Reisinger, C. W. (1996). *Administration and scoring manual for the Outcome Questionnaire (OQ 45.2).* Wilmington, DE: American Professional Credentialing Services.

Lambert, M. J., & Lambert, J. M. (1999). Use of psychological tests for assessing treatment outcome. In M. E. Maruish (Ed.), *The use of psychological testing for treatment planning and outcomes assessment* (2nd ed., pp. 115–151). Mahwah, NJ: Lawrence Erlbaum Associates.

Lambert, M. J., Whipple, J. L., Smart, D. W., Vermeesch, D. A., Nielsen, S. L., & Hawkins, E. J. (2001). The effects of providing therapists with feedback on patient progress during psychotherapy: Are outcomes enhanced? *Psychotherapy Research, 11,* 49–68.

Larsen, D. L. (1979). Enhancing client utilization of community mental health services. (Doctoral dissertation, University of Kansas, 1978). *Dissertation Abstracts International, 39,* 4041B. (University Microfilms No. 7904220)

Larsen, D. L., Attkisson, C. C., Hargreaves, W. A., & Nguyen, T. D. (1979). Assessment client/patient satisfaction: Development of a general scale. *Evaluation and Program Planning, 2,* 197–207.

Lazarus, J. A., & Sharfstein, S. S. (2000). Ethics in managed care. *The Psychiatric Clinics of North America, 23,* 269–284.

Lecrubier, Y., Sheehan, D. V., Weiller, E., Amorim, P., Bonora, I., Sheehan, K. H., Janavs, J., & Dunbar, G. C. (1997). The validity of the Mini-International Neuropsychiatric Interview (M.I.N.I.): A short diagnostic structured interview: Reliability and validity according to the CIDI. *European Psychiatry, 12,* 224–231.

Lejoyeux, M., Feuche, N., Loi, S., Solomon, J., & Ades, J. (1999). Study of impulse-control disorders among alcohol-dependent patients. *Journal of Clinical Psychiatry, 60,* 302–305.

Lejoyeux, M., Haberman, N., Solomon, J., & Ades, J. (1999). Comparison of buying behavior in depressed patients presenting with or without compulsive buying. *Comprehensive Psychiatry, 40,* 51–56.

Leon, S. C., Kopta, S. M., Howard, K. I., & Lutz, W. (1999). Predicting patients' responses to psychotherapy: Are some more predictable than others? *Journal of Consulting and Clinical Psychology, 67,* 698–704.

Lesher, E. L., & Berryhill, J. S. (1994). Validation of the Geriatric Depression Scale-Short Form among impatients. *Journal of Clinical Psychology, 50,* 256–260.

Lesperance, F., Frasure-Smith, N., & Talajic, M. (1996). Major depression before and after myocardial infarction: Its nature and consequences. *Psychosomatic Medicine, 58,* 99–110.

Leung, K. K., Lue, B. H., Lee, M. B., & Tang, L. Y. (1998). Screening of depression in patients with chronic medical diseases in a primary care setting. *Family Practice, 15,* 67–75.

LeVois, M., Nguyen, T. D., & Attkisson, C. C. (1981). Artifact in client satisfaction assessment: Experience in community mental health settings. *Evaluation and Program Planning, 4,* 139–150.

Lewandowski, D., & Graham, J. R. (1972). Empirical correlates of frequently occurring two-point MMPI code types: A replicated study. *Journal of Consulting and Clinical Psychology, 39,* 467–472.

Lipkin, M. (1996). Dialogue: How should primary care address the problem of psychiatric disorders? Can primary care physicians deliver quality mental healthcare? *Behavioral Healthcare Tomorrow, 5,* 49, 52–53.

Lipsitt, D. R. (1997). From fragmentation to integration: A history of comprehensive patient care. In J. D. Haber & G. E. Mitchell (Eds.), *Primary care meets mental health: Tools for the 21st century* (pp. 3–12). Tiburon, CA: CentraLink Publications.

LoCastro, J., Mori, D., Grace, M., & Costello, T. (1996, August). *Psychological screening in primary care.* Paper present at the 104th Annual Convention of the American Psychological Association, Toronto, Ontario, Canada.

Locke, S. E. (1997). Treating somatization: An update. *Behavioral Health Management, 17,* 22–23.

Locke, S. E., & Larsson, K. M. (1997). Clinical presentation, screening, and treatment of somatization in primary care. In J. D. Haber & G. E. Mitchell (Eds.), *Primary care meets mental health: Tools for the 21st century* (pp. 179–191). Tiburon, CA: CentraLink Publications.

Lovelace, patients reap rewards primary care intervention in depression. (1997, September). *Behavioral Disease Management Report, 1,* 1–2.

Lyons, J. S., Howard, K. I., O'Mahoney, M. T., & Lish, J. D. (1997). *The measurement and management of clinical outcomes in mental health.* New York: Wiley.

Manocchia, M., Bayliss, M. S., Connor, J., Keller, S. D., Shiely, J. C., Tsai, C., Voris, R. A., & Ware, J. E. (1997). *SF-36 Health Survey annotated bibliography: Second edition (1988–1996).* Boston, MA: Health Assessment Lab, New England Medical Center.

Marsh, E., & Cochran, M. (2000, August). Behavioral health spending grows 6.8% annually over decade. *Open Minds, 12*(5), 8.

Maruish, M. E. (1999a). Symptom Assessment-45 Questionnaire (SA-45). In M. E. Maruish (Ed.), *The use of psychological testing for treatment planning and outcomes assessment* (2nd ed., pp. 725–757). Mahwah, NJ: Lawrence Erlbaum Associates.

Maruish, M. E. (Ed.). (1999b). *The use of psychological testing for treatment planning and outcomes assessment* (2nd ed.). Mahwah, NJ: Lawrence Erlbaum Associates.

Maruish, M. E. (2000a). Applications of the Symptom Assessment-45 Questionnaire (SA-45) in primary care settings. In M. E. Maruish (Ed.), *Handbook of psychological testing in primary care settings* (pp. 335–372). Mahwah, NJ: Lawrence Erlbaum Associates.

Maruish, M. E. (Ed.). (2000b). *Handbook of psychological testing in primary care settings.* Mahwah, NJ: Lawrence Erlbaum Associates.

Maruish, M. E., Bershadsky, B., & Goldstein, L. (1998). Reliability and validity of the SA-45: Further evidence from a primary care setting. *Assessment, 4,* 407–420.

Mayfield, D., McLeod, G., & Hall, P. (1974). The CAGE questionnaire: Validation of a new alcoholism screening instrument. *American Journal of Psychiatry, 131,* 1121–1123.

McGovern, M. P., & Morrison, D. H. (1992). The Chemical Use, Abuse, and Dependence Scale (CUAD): Rationale, reliability and validity. *Journal of Substance Abuse Treatment, 9,* 27–38.

McHorney, C. A., Kosinski, M., & Ware, J. E. (1994). Comparisons of costs and quality of norms for the SF-36 Health Survey collected by mail versus telephone interview: Results from a national survey. *Medical Care, 32,* 551–567.

McHorney, C. A., & Tarlov, A. R. (1995). Individual-patient monitoring in clinical practice: Are available health status surveys adequate? *Quality of Life Research, 4,* 293–307.

McLellan, A. T., & Durell, J. (1996). Outcomes evaluation in psychiatric and substance abuse treatments: Concepts, rationale, and methods. In L. I. Sederer & B. Dickey (Eds.), *Outcomes assessment in clinical practice* (pp. 34–44). Baltimore, MD: Williams & Wilkins.

McLellan, A. T., Luborsky, L., Woody, G. E., & O'Brien, C. P. (1980). An improved diagnostic evaluation instrument for substance abuse patients: The Addiction Severity Index. *Journal of Nervous and Mental Diseases, 168,* 26–33.

Melek, S. P. (1996). Behavioral healthcare risk-sharing and medical cost offset. *Behavioral Healthcare Tomorrow, 5,* 39–46.

Mental Health Net (June 21, 2000). *Assessment* [On-line]. Available: http://mentalhelp.net/guide/pro01.htm.

Mental Health Statistics Improvement Program Task Force (MHSIP). (1996, April). *Consumer-oriented Mental Health Report Card: The final report of the Mental Health Statistics Improvement Program Task Force on a consumer-oriented mental health report card.* Cambridge, MA: The Evaluation Center at Human Services Research Institute.

Metz, C. E. (1978). Basic principles of ROC analysis. *Seminars in Nuclear Medicine, 8,* 283–298.

Meyer, G. J., Finn, S. E., Eyde, L. D., Kay, G. G., Kubiszyn, T. W., Moreland, K. L., Eisman, E. J., & Dies, R. R. (1998). *Benefits and costs of psychological assessment in healthcare delivery: Report of the Board of Professional Affairs Psychological Assessment Work Group, Part I.* Washington, DC: American Psychological Association.

Midanik, L. T., Zahnd, E. G., & Klein, D. (1998). Alcohol and drug CAGE screeners for pregnant, low-income women: The California perinatal needs assessment. *Alcoholism: Clinical and Experimental Research, 22,* 121–125.

Migdail, K. J., Youngo, M. T., & Bengen-Seltzer, B. (Eds.). (1995). *The 1995 behavioral outcomes & guidelines sourcebook.* New York: Faulkner & Gray.

Millard, R. W., & Carver, J. R. (1999). Cross-sectional comparison of live and interactive voice recognition administration of the SF-12 Health Status Survey. *American Journal of Managed Care, 5,* 153–159.

Miller, I. J. (1996). Managed care is harmful to outpatient mental health services: A call for accountability. *Professional Psychology: Research and Practice, 27,* 349–363.

Miller, I. (1998). *Eleven unethical managed care practices every patient should know about* [On-line]. Available: http://www.nomanagedcare.org/eleven.html.

Millon, T. (1987). *Manual for the MCMI-II.* Minneapolis, MN: National Computer Systems.

Millon, T. (1993). *MACI manual.* Minneapolis: National Computer Systems.

Millon, T. (1994). *MCMI-III manual.* Minneapolis: National Computer Systems.

Mitchell, G. E., & Haber, J. D. (1997). The future of primary care/behavioral health integration: Questions . . . and some answers? In J. D. Haber & G. E. Mitchell (Eds.), *Primary care meets mental health: Tools for the 21st century* (pp. 238–245). Tiburon, CA: CentraLink Publications.

Monthly change in average health insurance premiums (2000, July 17). *Managed Care Week, 10*(25), p. 4.

Moran, P. W. (1999). Psychological interventions and medical cost offset: Implications for integrative health care. *Clinical Psychology: Science and Practice, 6,* 242–244.

Moreland, K. L. (1996). How psychological testing can reinstate its value in an era of cost containment. *Behavioral Healthcare Tomorrow, 5,* 59–61.

Morey, L. C. (1991). *The Personality Assessment Inventory professional manual.* Odessa, FL: Psychological Assessment Resources.

Morey, L. C. (1999). Personality Assessment Inventory. In M. E. Maruish (Ed.), *The use of psychological testing for treatment planning and outcomes assessment* (2nd ed., pp. 1083–1121). Mahwah, NJ: Lawrence Erlbaum Associates.

Mori, D. L., LoCastro, J. S., Grace, M., & Costello, T. (1999). Implementing the direct contact model to increase referrals for psychological services in primary care settings. *Professional Psychology: Research and Practice, 30,* 143–146.

Mori, D. L., LoCastro, J. S., Grace, M., Costello, T., & Gibeau, A. (1997, April). *Promoting behavioral medicine within primary care: A patient self-referral questionnaire.* Paper presented at the Society of Behavioral Medicine Annual Scientific Sessions, San Francisco, CA.

Mossman, D., & Somoza, E. (1991a). Neuropsychiatric decision making: The role of disorder prevalence in diagnostic testing. *The Journal of Neuropsychiatry and Clinical Neurosciences, 3,* 84–88.

Mossman, D., & Somoza, E. (1991b). ROC curves, test accuracy, and the description of diagnostic tests. *The Journal of Neuropsychiatry and Clinical Neurosciences, 3,* 330–333.

Mueller, R. M., Lambert, M. J., & Burlingame, G. M. (1998). Construct validity of the Outcome Questionnaire: A confirmatory factor analysis. *Journal of Personality Assessment, 70,* 248–262.

Murphy, L. L., Impara, J. C., & Plake, B. S. (Eds.). (1999). *Tests in print V.* Lincoln, NE: The Buros Institute of Mental Measurements.

Murphy, M. J. (1998). Evolution of practice and values of professional psychology. In R. F. Small & L. R. Barnhill (Eds.), *Practicing in the new mental health marketplace: Ethical, legal, and moral issues* (pp. 37–52). Washington, DC: American Psychological Association.

Murphy, M. J., DeBernardo, C. R., & Shoemaker, W. E. (1998). Impact of managed care on independent practice and professional ethics: A survey of independent practitioners. *Professional Psychology: Research and Practice, 29,* 43–51.

Nagy, T. F. (1998). Managed health care and the ethics of clinical practice in behavioral medicine. In R. F. Small & L. R. Barnhill (Eds.), *Practicing in the new mental health marketplace: Ethical, legal, and moral issues* (pp. 153–168). Washington, DC: American Psychological Association.

National Committee for Quality Assurance (1999). NCQA's managed behavioral health accreditation program: An overview [On-line]. Available: http://www.ncqa.org/pages/policy/accreditation/mbho/mbhoexec.html.

National Committee for Quality Assurance (2000a). *HEDIS 2001. Technical update #2.* [Online]. Available: http://www.ncqa.org/pages/programs/HEDIS/hedis2001.htm.

National Committee for Quality Assurance (2000b). *2001 standards and surveyor guidelines for the accreditation of MBHOs.* Washington, DC: Author.

Nearly 40 percent of older suicide victims visit doctor during week before killing themselves. (July 30, 1997). *InfoConsultNews.*

Nelson, E. A., Maruish, M. E., & Axler, J. L. (2000). Effects of discharge planning and compliance with outpatient appointments on readmission rates. *Psychiatric Services, 51,* 885–889.

Nerenz, D. R., Repasky, D. P., Whitehouse, F. W., & Kahkonen, D. M. (1992). Ongoing assessment of health status in patients with diabetes mellitus. *Medical Care, 30,* MS112–MS124.

Newman, F. L. (1991, Summer). Using assessment data to relate patient progress to reimbursement criteria. *Assessment Applications,* 4–5.

Newman, F. L., Ciarlo, J. A., & Carpenter, D. (1999). Guidelines for selecting psychological instruments for treatment planning and outcome assessment. In M. E. Maruish (Ed.), *The use of psychological testing for treatment planning and outcomes assessment* (2nd ed., pp. 153–170). Mahwah, NJ: Lawrence Erlbaum Associates.

Newman, F. L., & Dakof, G. A. (1999). Progress and outcomes assessment of individual patient data: Selecting single-subject design and statistical procedures. In M. E. Maruish (Ed.), *The use of psychological testing for treatment planning and outcomes assessment (2nd ed.,* pp. 211–223). Mahwah, NJ: Lawrence Erlbaum Associates.

Newman, F. L., & Tejeda, M. J. (1999). Selecting statistical procedures for progress and outcome assessment: The analysis of group data. In M. E. Maruish (Ed.), *The use of psychological testing for treatment planning and outcomes assessment (2nd ed.,* pp. 225–266). Mahwah, NJ: Lawrence Erlbaum Associates.

Newman, M. L., & Greenway, P. (1997). Therapeutic effects of providing MMPI-2 test feedback to clients at a university counseling service: A collaborative approach. *Psychological Assessment, 9,* 122–131.

Newman, R. (1999). Comment on Chiles et al. *Clinical Psychology: Science and Practice, 6,* 225–227.

Newman, R., & Bricklin, P. M. (1991). Parameters of managed mental health care: Legal, ethical, and professional guidelines. *Professional Psychology: Research and Practice, 22,* 26–35.

NIMH official cites high cost of schizophrenia. (1996, May 20). *Mental Health Weekly, 6,* 7.

Nguyen, T. D., Attkisson, C. C., & Stegner, B. L. (1983). Assessment of patient satisfaction: Development and refinement of a service evaluation questionnaire. *Evaluation and Program Planning, 6,* 299–313.

O'Brien, W. H. (2000). The economics of managed care in behavioral health: Basic concepts and incentives. *The Psychiatric Clinics of North America, 23,* 255–267.

Ofstead, C. L., Gobran, D. S., & Lum, D. L. (2000). Integrating behavioral health assessment with primary care services. In M. E. Maruish (Ed.), *Handbook of psychological testing in primary care settings* (pp. 153–187). Mahwah, NJ: Lawrence Erlbaum Associates.

O'Neill, G. W. (1998). Confidentiality in the age of managed care: From the MCO perspective. *The Clinical Psychologist, 51,* 34–35.

Oss, M. E., & Sloves, H. (2000, February). Customer-defined "quality" in behavioral health & social services: Marketing tools to respond to a new "customer-focused" era. *Open Minds,* 4–6.

Otto, M. W. (1999). Psychological interventions in the age of managed care: A commentary on medical cost offsets. *Clinical Psychology: Science and Practice, 6,* 239–241.

Outcomes indicators less prevalent atop Summit list. (1999, March 29). *Mental Health Weekly,* pp. 4–5.

Overall, J. E., & Gorham, D. R. (1962). The Brief Psychiatric Rating Scale. *Psychological Reports, 10,* 799–812.

Overall, J. E., & Gorham, D. R. (1988). The Brief Psychiatric Rating Scale: Recent developments in ascertainment and scaling. *Psychopharmacology Bulletin, 24,* 97–99.

Overall, J. E., & Klett, C. J. (1972). *Applied multivariate analysis.* New York: McGraw-Hill.

Pallak, M. S. (1994). National outcomes management survey: Summary report. *Behavioral Healthcare Tomorrow, 3,* 63–69.

Parkerson, G. R. (1999). *User's guide for the Duke health measures: Duke Health Profile (DUKE), Duke Severity of Illness Checklist (DUSOI), Duke Case-Mix System (DUMIX), Duke Social Support and Stress Scale (DUSOCS).* Durham, NC: Department of Community and Family Medicine, Duke University Medical Center.

Parkerson, G. R., & Broadhead, W. E. (1997). Screening for anxiety and depression in primary care with the Duke Anxiety-Depression Scale. *Family Medicine, 29,* 177–181.

Parkerson, G. R., Broadhead, W. E., & Tse, C. J. (1990). The Duke Health Profile: A 17-item measure of health and dysfunction. *Medical Care, 28,* 1056–1069.

Parkerson, G. R., Broadhead, W. E., & Tse, C. J. (1991). Development of the Duke Health Profile. *Family Practice, 8,* 396–401.

Parkerson, G. R., Broadhead, W. E., & Tse, C. J. (1996). Anxiety and depression symptom identification using the he Duke Health Profile. *Journal of Clinical Epidemiology, 49,* 85–93.

Peek, C. J. (1997, May). Integrating medical and behavioral care: Clinical, cultural, operational and financial roadmaps (syllabus materials). Workshop presented in the *How to design and implement your primary care behavioral health integration program* conference, San Francisco, CA.

Peek, C. J., & Heinrich, R. L. (1995). Building a collaborative healthcare organization: From idea to invention to innovation. *Family Systems Medicine, 13,* 327–342.

Perez-Stable, E., Miranda, J., Munoz, R., & Ying, Y. (1990). Depression in medical outpatients: Underrecognition and misdiagnosis. *Archives of Internal Medicine, 150,* 1083–1088.

Petrila, J. (1998). *Managed care technical assistance series. Vol. 5. Ethical issues for behavioral health care practitioners and organizations in a managed care environment* [Online]. Available: http://www.samhsa.gov/mc/Managed%2...tracting/MCRPT/volume5/volume5.html.

Phelps, R., Eisman, E. J., & Kohut, J. (1998). Psychological practice and managed care: Results of the CAPP practitioner survey. *Professional Psychology: Research and Practice, 29,* 31–36.

Pingitore, D. P. (1999). Postdoctoral training in primary care health psychology: Duties, observations, and recommendations. *Professional Psychology: Research and Practice, 30,* 283–290.

Piotrowski, C. (1999). Assessment practices in the era of managed care: Current status and future directions. *Journal of Clinical Psychology, 55,* 787–796.

Piotrowski, C., Belter, R. W., & Keller, J. W. (1998). The impact of "managed care" on the practice of psychological testing: Preliminary findings. *Journal of Personality Assessment, 70,* 441–447.

Plake, B. S., & Impara, J. C. (Eds.). (1999). *Supplement to the thirteenth mental measurement yearbook.* Lincoln, NE: The Buros Institute of Mental Measurements.

Pollack, E. (1998). Which master's voice? Ethical dilemmas for managed care reviewers. In R. F. Small & L. R. Barnhill (Eds.), *Practicing in the new mental health marketplace: Ethical, legal, and moral issues* (pp. 139–151). Washington, DC: American Psychological Association.

Pratt, S., Berman, W. H., & Hurt, S. W. (1998). Ethics and outcomes in managed behavioral health care: "Trust me, I'm a psychologist." In R. F. Small & L. R. Barnhill (Eds.), *Practicing in the new mental health marketplace: Ethical, legal, and moral issues* (pp. 121–137). Washington, DC: American Psychological Association.

Pruitt, S. D., Klapow, J. C., Epping-Jordan, J. E., & Dresselhaus, T. R. (1998). Moving behavioral medicine to the front line: A model for the integration of behavioral and medical sciences in primary care. *Professional Psychology: Research and Practice, 29,* 230–236.

Quirk, M. P., Strosahl, K., Krielkamp, T., & Erdberg, P. (1995). Personality feedback consultation in a managed mental health care practice. *Professional Psychology: Research and Practice, 26,* 27–32.

Radloff, L. S. (1977). The CES-D scale: A self-report depression scale for research in the general population. *Applied Psychological Measurement, 1,* 385–401.

Radosevich, D. M., McPherson, C. A., & Werni, T. L. (1994). The implementation process: A working guide. In M. Huber (Ed.), *Measuring medicine: An introduction to health status assessment and a framework for application* (pp. 51–73). Washington, DC: Faulkner & Gray.

Radosevich, D., & Pruitt, M. (1996). *Twelve-item Health Status Questionnaire (HSQ-12) Version 2.0 user's guide.* Bloomington, MN: Health Outcomes Institute.

Radosevich, D. M., Werni, T. L., & Cords, J. (1994). *Assessment of visit-specific satisfaction.* Bloomington, MN: Health Outcomes Institute.

Radosevich, D. M., Wetzler, H., & Wilson, S. M. (1994). *Health Status Questionnaire (HSQ) 2.0: Scoring comparisons and reference data.* Bloomington, MN: Health Outcomes Institute.

RAND Corporation. (1992). *RAND-36 Health Survey 1.0 RAND Health Science Program.* Santa Monica, CA: Author.

Regier, D. A., Myers, J. K., Kramer, M., et al. (1984). The NIMH Epidemiologic Catchment Area Program: Historical context, major objectives and study population characteristics. *Archives of General Psychiatry, 41*, 934–941.

Regier, D. A., Narrow, W. E., Rae, D. S., Manderscheid, R. W., Locke, B., & Goodwin, F. K. (1993). The de facto US mental and addictive disorders service system: Epidemiologic Catchment Area prospective 1-year prevalence rates of disorders and services. *Archives of General Psychiatry, 50*, 85–94.

Reynolds, W. M. (1991). *Adult Suicidal Ideation Questionnaire manual*. Odessa, FL: Psychological Assessment Resources.

Rice, D. P., & Miller, L. S. (1996, August). *Health economics and cost implications of anxiety and other disorders in the United States*. Paper presented at Satellite Symposium X: World Congress of Psychiatry, Madrid, Spain.

Richards, E., & Rathbun, K. (1983). *Medical risk management*. Rockville, MD: Aspen Systems.

Richardson, J. T. (1972). Nonparametric indexes of sensitivity and response bias. *Psychological Bulletin, 78*, 429–432.

Roberts, R. E., Attkisson, C. C., & Mendias, R. M. (1984). Assessing the Client Satisfaction Questionnaire in English and Spanish. *Hispanic Journal of the Behavioral Sciences, 6*, 385–396.

Roberts, R. E., Lewinsohn, P. M., & Seeley, J. R. (1991). Screening for adolescent depression: A comparison of depression scales. *Journal of the Academy of Child and Adolescent Psychiatry, 30*, 58–66.

Robins, L. N., Helzer, J. E., Croughan, J., & Ratcliff, K. S. (1981). National Institute of Mental Health Diagnostic Interview Schedule: Its history, characteristics, and validity. *Archives of General Psychiatry, 38*, 381–389.

Rosen, L. D., & Weil, M. M. (1996). Easing the transition from paper to computer-based systems. In T. Trabin (Ed.), *The computerization of behavioral healthcare: How to enhance clinical practice, management, and communications* (pp. 87–107). San Francisco: Jossey-Bass.

Rosenblatt, A., & Attkisson, C. C. (1993). Assessing outcomes for sufferers of severe mental disorder: A conceptual framework and review. *Evaluation and Program Planning, 16*, 347–363.

Rost, K., Burnam M. A., & Smith, G. R. (1993). Development of screeners for depressive disorders and substance disorder history. *Medical Care, 31*, 189–200.

Rost, K., Smith, G. R., Burnam, M. A., & Burns, B. J. (1992). Measuring the outcomes of care for mental health problems: The case of depressive disorders. *Medical Care, 30*, MS266–MS273.

Roth, L., Meisel, A., & Lidz, C. (1977). Tests of competency to consent to treatment. *American Journal of Psychiatry, 134*, 279.

Rothbaum, P. A., Bernstein, D. M., Haller, O., Phelps, R., & Kohout, J. (1998). New Jersey psychologists' report on managed mental health care. *Professional Psychology: Research and Practice, 29*, 37–42.

Rouse, B. A. (Ed.). (1995). *Substance abuse and mental health statistics sourcebook*. DHHS Publication No. (SMA) 95-3064. Washington, DC: Superintendent of Documents, U.S. Government Printing Office.

Rubin, H. R., Gandek, B., Rogers, W. H., Kosinski, M., McHorney, C. A., & Ware, J. E. (1993). Patients' ratings of outpatient visits in different practice settings. *Journal of the American Medical Association, 270*, 835–840.

Ruggeri, M., & Dall'Agnola, R. (1993). The development and use of the Verona Expectations for Care Scales (VECS) and the Verona Service Satisfaction Scale (VSSS) for measuring expectations and satisfaction with community-based psychiatric services in patients, relatives and professionals. *Psychological Medicine, 23*, 511–523.

Russo, J., Roy-Byrne, P., Jaffe, C., Ries, R., Dagadakis, C., Dwyer-O'Connor, E., & Reeder, D. (1997). The relationship of patient-administered outcome assessments to quality of life and physician ratings: Validity of the BASIS-32. *Journal of Mental Health Administration, 24*, 200–214.

Satcher, D. (2000). Mental health: A report of the Surgeon General—Executive summary. *Professional Psychology: Research and Practice, 31*, 5–13.

Sato, T., & Takeichi, M. (1993). Lifetime prevalence of specific psychiatric disorders in a general medicine clinic. *General Hospital Psychiatry, 15*, 224–233.

Saunders, S. M., Howard, H. I., & Newman, F. L. (1988). Evaluating the clinical significance of treatment effects: Norms and normality. *Behavioral Assessment, 10*, 207–218.

Sayetta, R. B., & Johnson, D. P. (1980). Basic data on depressive symptomatology, United States 1974–75. *Vital and Health Statistics* (Ser. 11, No. 216, DHEW Publication No. 80-1666). Washington, DC: U.S. Government Printing Office.

Schaefer, M., Murphy, R., Westerveld, M., & Gewirtz, A. (2000, August). *Psychological assessment and managed care: Guidelines for practice with children and adolescents*. Continuing education workshop presented at the annual meeting of the American Psychological Association, Washington, DC.

Schappert, S. M. (1992). National Ambulatory Medical Care Survey: 1989 Summary. *Vital Health Statistics, 13*(110).

Schlosser, B. (1995). The ecology of assessment: A "patient-centric" perspective. *Behavioral Healthcare Tomorrow, 4,* 66–68.

Schlosser, B. (1996). New perspectives on outcomes assessment: The philosophy and application of the subjective health process model. *Psychotherapy, 33,* 284–304.

Schreter, R. K. (1997). Essential skills for managed behavioral health care. *Psychiatric Services, 48,* 653–658.

Schulberg, H. C., & Burns, B. J. (1988). Mental disorders in primary care: Epidemiologic, diagnostic, and treatment research directions. *General Hospital Psychiatry, 10,* 79–87.

Schwenzfeier, E., Anderson, N. S., Hill, R. D., Rigdon, M. A., & Seelert, K. R. (2000). *Psychological well-being as a predictor of medication use in primary care outpatients.* Manuscript submitted for publication.

Science Directorate of the American Psychological Association (1995). *Finding information about psychological tests: A guide for locating and using both published and unpublished tests.* Washington, DC: Author.

Scogin, F., Rohen, N., & Bailey, E. (2000). Geriatric Depression Scale. In M. E. Maruish (Ed.), *Handbook of psychological assessment in primary care settings* (pp. 491–508). Mahwah, NJ: Lawrence Erlbaum Associates.

Sears, S. F., Danda, C. E., & Evans, G. D. (1999). PRIME-MD and rural primary care: Detecting depression in a low-income rural population. *Professional Psychology: Research and Practice, 30,* 357–360.

Sederer, L. I., & Dickey, B (Eds.). (1996). *Outcomes assessment in clinical practice.* Baltimore, MD: Williams & Wilkins.

Sederer, L. I., Dickey, B., & Hermann, R. C. (1996). The imperative of outcomes assessment in psychiatry. In L. I. Sederer & B. Dickey (Eds.), *Outcomes assessment in clinical practice* (pp. 1–7). Baltimore, MD: Williams & Wilkins.

Seelert, K. R., Hill, R. D., Rigdon, M. A., & Schwenzfeler, E. (1999). Measuring patient distress in primary care. *Family Medicine, 31,* 483–487.

Selden, D. R. (1997). Integration of primary care and behavioral health: The driving forces. In J. D. Haber & G. E. Mitchell (Eds.), *Primary care meets mental health: Tools for the 21st century* (pp. 13–25). Tiburon, CA: CentraLink Publications.

Senra, C. (1995). Measures of treatment outcome of depression: An effect-size comparison. *Psychological Reports, 76,* 187–192.

Shah, A., Phongsathorn, V., Bielawska, C., & Katona, C. (1996). Screening among geriatric inpatients with short versions of the Geriatric Depression Scale. *International Journal of Geriatric Psychiatry, 11,* 915–918.

Shedler, J. (2000). The Shedler QPD Panel (Quick PsychoDiagnostic Panel): A psychiatric "lab test" for primary care. In M. E. Maruish (Ed.), *Handbook of psychological testing in primary care settings* (pp. 277–296). Mahwah, NJ: Lawrence Erlbaum Associates.

Sheehan, D. V., Lecrubier, Y., Sheehan, K. H., Janavs, J., Weiller, E., Keskiner, A., Schinka, J., Knapp, E., Sheehan, M. F., & Dunbar, G. C. (1997). The validity of the Mini-International Neuropsychiatric Interview (M.I.N.I.) according to the SCID-P and its reliability. *European Psychiatry, 12,* 232–241.

Sheehan, D. V., Lecrubier, Y., Sheehan, K. H., Amorim, P., Janavs, J., Weiller, E., Thierry, H., Baker, R., & Dunbar, G. C. (1998). The Mini-International Neuropsychiatric Interview (M.I.N.I.): The development and validation of a structured diagnostic interview for DSM-IV and ICD-10. *Journal of Clinical Psychiatry, 59 (Suppl. 20),* 22–33.

Sheikh, J. I., & Yesavage, J. A. (1986). Geriatric Depression Scale (GDS): Recent evidence and development of a shorter version. *Clinical Gerontologist, 5,* 165–173.

Shore, K. (1998). Managed care and managed competition: A question of morality. In R. F. Small & L. R. Barnhill (Eds.), *Practicing in the new mental health marketplace: Ethical, legal, and moral issues* (pp. 67–102). Washington, DC: American Psychological Association.

Shueman, S. A. (1997). Confronting health care realities: A reply to Sank (1997). *Professional Psychology: Research and Practice, 28,* 555–558.

Silverstone, P. H. (1987). Depression and outcomes in acute myocardial infarction. *British Medical Journal, 294,* 219–220.

Skinner, H. (1982). The Drug Abuse Screening Test. *Addiction Behavior, 7,* 363–371.

Skinner, H. (1990). Spectrum of drinkers and intervention opportunities. *Canadian Medical Association Journal, 143,* 1054–1059.

Slade, M., Thornicroft, G., & Glover, G. (1999). The feasibility of routine outcome measures in mental health. *Social Psychiatry and Psychiatric Epidemiology, 34,* 243–249.

Smith, Jr., R. G. (1994). The course of somatization and its effects on utilization of health care resources. *Psychosomatics, 35,* 263–267.

Smith, G. R., Burnam, A., Burns, B., Cleary, P., & Rost, K. M. (1994). *Major Depression Outcomes Module user's manual.* Little Rock, AR: University of Arkansas for Medical Sciences.

Smith, Jr., R. G., Rost, K. M., & Kashner, M. T. (1995). A trial of the effect of a standardized psychiatric consultation on health outcomes and costs in somaticizing patients. *Archives of General Psychiatry, 52,* 238.

Somoza, E., & Mossman, D. (1990). Introduction to neuropsychiatric decision making: Binary diagnostic tests. *The Journal of Neuropsychiatry and Clinical Neurosciences, 2,* 297–300.

Somoza, E., & Mossman, D. (1991). Introduction to neuropsychiatric decision making: Designing nonbinary diagnostic tests. *The Journal of Neuropsychiatry and Clinical Neurosciences, 3,* 197–200.

Speer, D. C. (1992). Clinically significant change: Jacobson and Truax (1991) revisited. *Journal of Consulting and Clinical Psychology, 60,* 402–408.

Speer, D. C., & Greenbaum, P. E. (1995). Five methods for computing signficant individual client change and improvement rates: Support for an individual growth curve approach. *Journal of Consulting and Clinical Psychology, 63,* 1044–1048.

Sperry, L., & Brill, P. (1997). Computerized technology: Integrative treatment outcome technology in primary care practice. In J. D. Haber & G. E. Mitchell (Eds.), *Primary care meets mental health: Tools for the 21st century* (pp. 229–235). Tiburon, CA: CentraLink Publications.

Sperry, L., Brill, P. L., Howard, K. I., & Grissom, G. R. (1996). *Treatment outcomes in psychotherapy and psychiatric interventions.* New York: Brunner/Mazel.

Spielberger, C. D. (1983). *Manual for the State–Trait Anxiety Inventory (Form Y).* Palo Alto, CA: Consulting Psychologists Press.

Spierings, E. L., & van Hoof, M. J. (1996). Anxiety and depression in chronic headache sufferers. *Headache Quarterly, Current Treatment and Research, 7,* 235–238.

Spitzer, R. L., Kroenke, K., Linzer, M., Hahn, S. R., Williams, J. B., deGruy, F. V., Brody, D., & Davies, M. (1995). Health-related quality of life in primary care patients with mental disorders: Results from the PRIME–MD 1000 study. *Journal of the American Medical Association, 274,* 1511–1517.

Spitzer, R. L., Kroenke, K., Williams, J. B., & the Patient Health Questionnaire Primary Care Study Group (1999). Validation and utility of a self-report version of PRIME-MD: The PHQ Primary Care Study. *Journal of the American Medical Association, 282,* 1737–1744.

Spitzer, R. L., Williams, J. B., Gibbon, M., & First, M. B. (1990). *Structured Clinical Interview for DSM-III-R.* Washington, DC: American Psychiatric Press.

Spitzer, R. L., Williams, J. B., & Kroenke, K. (1997). *Quick guide to the Patient Problem Questionnaire.* NY: Biometrics Research, New York State Psychiatric Institute. Available from R. L. Spitzer.

Spitzer, R. L., Williams, J. B., Kroenke, K., Linzer, M., deGruy, F. V., Hahn, S. R., Brody, D., & Johnson, J. G. (1994). Utility of a new procedure for diagnosing mental disorders in primary care: The PRIME–MD 1000 study. *Journal of the American Medical Association, 272,* 1749–1756.

Staton, D. (1991). Psychiatry's future: Facing reality. *Psychiatric Quarterly, 62,* 165–176.

Steer, R. A., Cavalieri, D. O., Leonard, D. M., & Beck, A. T. (1999). Use of the Beck Depression Inventory for Primary Care to screen for major depression disorders. *General Hospital Psychiatry, 21,* 106–111.

Steere, J. (1984). *Ethics in clinical psychology.* Cape Town, South Africa: Oxford University Press.

Steiner, A., Raube, K., Stuck, A. E., Aronow, H. U., Draper, D., Rubenstein, L. Z., & Beck, J. C. (1996). Measuring psychosocial aspects of well-being in older community residents: Performance of four short scales. *Gerontologist, 36,* 54–62.

Stewart, A. S., Hays, R. D., & Ware, J. E. (1988). The MOS short-form General Health Survey: Reliability and validity in a patient population. *Medical Care, 26,* 724–732.

Stewart, A. L., & Ware, J. E., Jr. (1992). *Measuring functioning and well-being.* Durham, NC: Duke University Press.

Stoudemire, A., Frank, R., Hedemark, N., Kamlet, M., & Blazer, D. (1986). The economic burden of depression. *General Hospital Psychiatry, 8,* 387–394.

Stout, C. E. (1997). *Psychological assessment in managed care.* New York: John Wiley & Sons.

Stout, C. E., & Cook, L. P. (1999). New areas for psychological assessment in general health care settings: What to do today to prepare for tomorrow. *Journal of Clinical Psychology, 55,* 797–812.

Strategic Advantage, Inc. (1998). *Symptom Assessment – 45 Questionnaire (SA-45) technical manual.* North Tonawanda, NY: Multi-Health Systems.

Strosahl, K. (1996). Mind and body primary mental health care: New model for integrated services. *Behavioral Healthcare Tomorrow, 5,* 93–96.

Strupp, H. H. (1996). The tripartite model and the *Consumer Reports* study. *American Psychologist, 51,* 1017–1024.

Strupp, H. H., & Hadley, S. W. (1977). A tripartite model of mental health and treatment outcomes. *American Psychologist, 32,* 187–196.

Sturm, R., & Wells, K. B. (1996). Health policy implications of the RAND Medical Outcomes Study: Improving the value of depression treatment. *Behavioral Healthcare Tomorrow, 5*, 63–66.

Sweeney, T. E., Stutman, M. J., & Martin, R. H. (1998). Practitioner legal liability: When utilization review says no. In R. F. Small & L. R. Barnhill (Eds.), *Practicing in the new mental health marketplace: Ethical, legal, and moral issues* (pp. 187–203). Washington, DC: American Psychological Association.

Taylor, J. (1953). A personality scale of manifest anxiety. *Journal of Abnormal and Social Psychology, 48*, 285–290.

Tiemens, B. G., Ormel, J., & Simon, G. E. (1996). Occurrence, recognition, and outcome of psychological disorders in primary care. *American Journal of Psychiatry, 153*, 636–644.

Todd, W. E. (1999). Introduction: Fulfilling the promise of disease management: Where are we today? Where are we headed? In S. Heffner (Ed.), *Disease management sourcebook 2000: Resources and strategies for program design and implementation* (pp. xi–xxiii). New York: Faulkner & Gray.

Tsacoumis, S. (2000, August). Industrial and organizational assessment in the 21st century. In M. E. Maruish (Chair), *Clinical, school, industrial and organizational psychology, and educational assessment in the 21st century.* Symposium conducted at the annual meeting of the American Psychological Association, Washington, DC.

Umphress, V. J., Lambert, M. J., Smart, D. W., Barlow, S. H., & Clouse, G. (1997). Concurrent and construct validity of the Outcome Questionnaire. *Journal of Psychoeducational Assessment, 15*, 40–55.

United Behavioral Health. (2000). *United Behavioral Health level of care guidelines.* Minneapolis, MN: Author.

United HealthCare. (1994). *A glossary of terms: The language of managed care and organized health care systems.* Minnetonka, MN: Author.

Vendrig, A. A., Derksen, J. J., & de Mey, H. R. (1999). Utility of selected MMPI-2 scales in the outcome prediction for patients with chronic back pain. *Psychological Assessment, 11*, 381–385.

Vermeersch, D. A., Lambert, M. J., & Burlingame, G. M. (2000). Outcome questionnaire: Item sensitivity to change. *Journal of Personality Assessment, 74*, 242–261.

Vermillion, J., & Pfeiffer, S. (1993). Treatment outcome and continuous quality improvement: Two aspects of program evaluation. *Psychiatric Hospital, 24*, 9–14.

Volk, R. J., Pace, T. M., & Parchman, M. L. (1993). Screening for depression in primary care patients: Dimensionality of the short form of the Beck Depression Inventory. *Psychological Assessment, 5*, 173–181.

Von Korff, M., Shapiro, S., Burke, J. D., Teitelbaum, M., Skinner, E. A., German, P., Turner, R. W., Klein, L., & Burns, B. (1987). Anxiety and depression in a primary care clinic: Comparison of Diagnostic Interview Schedule, General Health Questionnaire, and practitioner assessments. *Archives of General Psychiatry, 44*, 152–156.

Wampold, B. E., & Jenson, W. R. (1986). Clinical significance revisited [Letter to the editor]. *Behavior Therapy, 17*, 302–305.

Ward, J. H. (1963). Hierarchical grouping to optimize objective function. *Journal of the American Statistical Association, 58*, 236–244.

Ward, L. C., & Dillon, E. A. (1990). Psychiatric symptom correlates of the Minnesota Multiphasic Personality Inventory (MMPI) Masculinity–Femininity scale. *Psychological Assessment: A Journal of Consulting and Clinical Psychology, 2*, 286–288.

Ware, J. E. (1999a). Future directions in health status assessment. *Journal of Clinical Outcomes Management, 6*, 34–37.

Ware, J. E. (1999b). SF-36 Health Survey. In M. E. Maruish (Ed.), *The use of psychological testing for treatment planning and outcomes assessment* (2nd ed., pp. 1227–1246). Mahwah, NJ: Lawrence Erlbaum Associates.

Ware, J. E., & Hays, R. D. (1988). Methods for measuring patient satisfaction with specific medical encounters. *Medical Care, 26*, 393–402.

Ware, J. E., Kosinski, M., & Keller, S. D. (1994). *SF-36 physical and mental summary scales: A user's manual.* Boston, MA: The Health Institute.

Ware, J. E., Kosinski, M., & Keller, S. D. (1995). *SF-12: How to score the SF-12 physical and mental summary scales* (2nd ed.). Boston, MA: New England Medical Center, The Health Institute.

Ware, J. E., & Sherbourne, C. D. (1992). The MOS 36-Item Short Form Health Survey (SF-36). I. Conceptual framework and item selection. *Medical Care, 30*, 473–483.

Ware, J. E., Snow, K. K., Kosinski, M., & Gandek, B. (1993). *SF-36 Health Survey manual and interpretation guide.* Boston: New England Medical Center, The Health Institute.

Watkins, C. E., Campbell, V. L., Nieberding, R., & Hallmark, R. (1995). Contemporary practice of psychological assessment by clinical psychologists. *Professional Psychology: Research and Practice, 26*, 54–60.

Waxman, H. M. (1996). Using outcomes assessment for quality improvement. In L. I. Sederer & B. Dickey (Eds.), *Outcomes assessment in clinical practice* (pp. 25–33). Baltimore, MD: Williams & Wilkins.

Weissman, M. M., & Bothwell, S. (1976). Assessment of social adjustment by patient self-report. *Archives of General Psychiatry, 33,* 1111–1115.

Wells, K. B., Golding, J. M., & Burnam, M. A. (1988). Psychiatric disorder in a sample of the general population with and without chronic medical conditions. *American Journal of Psychiatry, 145,* 976–981.

Wells, K. B., Sherbourne, C., Schoenbaum, M., Duan, N., Meredith, L., Unutzer, J., Miranda, J., Carney, M. F., & Rubenstein, L. V. (2000). Impact of disseminating quality improvement programs in depression in managed primary care. *Journal of the American Medical Association, 283,* 212–220.

Werthman, M. J. (1995). A managed care approach to psychological testing. *Behavioral Health Management, 15,* 15–17.

Wetzler, H. P. (1994). Evaluating an organization's readiness for outcomes management. In M. Huber (Ed.), *Measuring medicine: An introduction to health status assessment and a framework for application* (pp. 33–41). Washington, DC: Faulkner & Gray.

Wetzler, H. P., Lum, D. L., & Bush, D. M. (2000). Using the SF-36 Health Survey in primary care. In M. E. Maruish (Ed.), *Handbook of psychological testing in primary care settings* (pp. 583–621). Mahwah, NJ: Lawrence Erlbaum Associates.

Whooley, M. A., Avins, A. L., Miranda, J., & Browner, W. S. (1997). Case-finding instruments for depression: Two questions are as good as many. *Journal of General Internal Medicine, 12,* 439–445.

Winter, L. B., Steer, R. A., Jones-Hicks, L., & Beck, A. T. (1999). Screening for major depression disorders in adolescent medical outpatients with the Beck Depression Inventory for Primary Care. *Journal of Adolescent Health, 24,* 389–394.

Wong, Y-L. I. (2000). Measurement properties of the Center for Epidemiologic Studies-Depression Scale in an homeless population. *Psychological Assessment, 12,* 69–76.

World Health Organization (1992). *International Classification of Diseases, Tenth Revision.* Geneva, Switzerland: Author.

Yesavage, J. A., Brink, T. L., Rose, T. L., Lum, O., Huang, V., Adey, M., & Leirer, V. O. (1983). Development and validation of a geriatric depression screening scale: A preliminary report. *Journal of Psychiatric Research, 17,* 37–49.

Zich, J. M., Attkisson, C. C., & Greenfield, T. K. (1990). Screening for depression in primary care clinics: The CES-D and the BDI. *International Journal of Psychiatry in Medicine, 20,* 259–277.

Zimmerman, M., Coryell, W., Corenthal, C., & Wilson, S. (1986). A self-report scale to diagnose major depressive disorder. *Archives of General Psychiatry, 43,* 365–368.

Zimmerman, M., Lish, J. D., Farber, N. J., Hartung, J., Lush, D., Kuzma, M. A., & Plescia, G. (1994). Screening for depression in medical patients: Is the focus too narrow? *General Hospital Psychiatry, 16,* 388–394.

Zung, W. K. (1965). A self-rating depression scale. *Archives of General Psychiatry, 12,* 63–70.

Zung, W. K. (1971a). A rating instrument for anxiety disorders. *Psychosomatics, 12,* 371–379.

Zung, W. K. (1971b). The differentiation of anxiety and depression: A biometric approach. *Psychosomatics, 12,* 380–384.

Zung, W. K. (1972). The Depression Status Inventory: An adjunct to the Self-Rating Depression Scale. *Journal of Clinical Psychology, 28,* 539–543.

Zung, W. K. (1973a). From art to science: The diagnosis and treatment of depression. *Archives of General Psychiatry, 29,* 328–337.

Zung, W. K. (1973b). The differentiation of anxiety and depressive disorders: A psychopharmacological approach. *Psychosomatics, 14,* 363–366.

Zung, W. K. (1995). *The measurement of depression.* Indianapolis, IN: Eli Lilly and Company.

Zung, W. K., Broadhead, W. E., & Roth, M. E. (1993). Prevalence of depressive symptoms in primary care. *The Journal of Family Practice, 37,* 337–344.

Zung, W. K., Magruder-Habib, K., Velez, R., & Alling, W. (1990). The comorbidity of anxiety and depression in general medical patients: A longitudinal study. *Journal of Clinical Psychiatry, 51,* 77–80.

Zwick, R. J. (1982). The effect of pre-therapy orientation on client knowledge about therapy, improvement in therapy, attendance patterns, and satisfaction with services. (Masters thesis, University of California, Berkeley, 1981). *Masters Abstracts, 20,* 307. (University Microfilms No. 13-18082)

Author's Note

Portions of this book are adapted from the following sources:

M. E. Maruish, "Therapeutic Assessment: Linking Assessment and Treatment," in M. Hersen & A. Bellack (Series Eds.) and C. R. Reynolds (Vol. Ed.), *Comprehensive Clinical Psychology, Volume 4. Assessment* (1999), with permission of Elsevier Science LTD., The Boulevard, Langford Lane, Kidlington OX5 1GB, UK.

M. E. Maruish, "Introduction," in M. E. Maruish (Ed.), *The Use of Psychological Testing for Treatment Planning and Outcomes Assessment* (2nd ed.) (1999), with permission of Lawrence Erlbaum Associates, Mahwah, NJ.

M. E. Maruish, "Symptom Assessment-45 Questionnaire (SA-45)," in M. E. Maruish (Ed.), *The Use of Psychological Testing for Treatment Planning and Outcomes Assessment* (2nd ed.) (1999), with permission of Lawrence Erlbaum Associates, Mahwah, NJ.

M. E. Maruish, "Introduction," in M. E. Maruish (Ed.), *Handbook of Psychological Assessment in Primary Care Settings* (2000), with permission of Lawrence Erlbaum Associates, Mahwah, NJ.

L. Goldstein, B. Bershadsky, & M. E. Maruish, "The INOVA Primary Behavioral Health Care Project," in M. E. Maruish (Ed.), *Handbook of Psychological Assessment in Primary Care Settings* (2000), with permission of Lawrence Erlbaum Associates, Mahwah, NJ.

Author Index

C

Q

R

S

Subject Index

A

Abbreviated multidimensional measures, *see* Multidimensional measures

Acceptability, 103, *see* Outcomes assessment

Access, 94–95, 107, 111–112

Accountability, 7, 181

Accreditation
  groups, 18
  requirements
    meeting and psychological testing, 53–56
    outcomes assessments initiatives, 180–181

Accuracy, 140, 141, *see also* CAGE-AID

Actionable information, 104, 192

Administration data, *see* Data

Administrative challenges, 9, 10

Administrative errors, *see* Errors

Administrative services only (ASOs) programs, 5

Adolescents, 133, 266

Adult Suicidal Ideation Questionnaire (ASIQ), 51

Advocacy groups, 18

Affirmative response criterion, *see* Criteria

Affordability, 111

Alcohol abuse, 263, 267, 270

Alpha coefficient
  Behavior and Symptom Identification Scale, 123, 124
  Center for Epidemiologic Studies Depression Scale, 149
  Depression Arkansas Scale, 145
  Duke Anxiety–Depression Scale, 272
  Geriatric Depression Scale, 153
  Outcome Questionnaire Short Form, 273

SA-45, 131

Service Satisfaction Scale, 168

SF-16, 155

Zung Self-Rating Depression Scale, 134

Alternative test forms, 100, *see also* Test forms

American Psychological Association (APA), 1, 281–282

Analysis, 216

Analysis capacity, 209, 210

Antidepressants, 136

Anxiety disorders, 89, 271–273, 275

Anxiolytic agents, 136, 138

APA, *see* American Psychological Association

Applicability, 102–103

Area under the curve (AUC), 29, 272–273

ASIQ, *see* Adult Suicidal Ideation Questionnaire

ASOs, *see* Administrative services only programs

Assessment intervention session, 40

Attitude, MBHOs, 69–70

AUC, *see* Area under the curve

Audience, 203

Authority, irrational, 279, *see also* Ethics

Authorization
  psychological testing
    determination of medical necessity, 73–75
    improving chances of obtaining, 75–79, 80–81
    maximizing chances, 79, 82–84
    process, 72–73
    reimbursement, 75
  rigidity and conflicts with MBHOs, 299
  treatment requests and testing applications, 47–48

Availability, 94–95, 111